ADVANCED TORTS

IN A NUTSHELL®

PETER B KUTNER
Hugh Roff Professor of Law Emeritus
The University of Oklahoma

WEST ACADEMIC PUBLISHING

444 Cedar Street, Suite 700
St. Paul, MN 55101
1-877-888-1330

Printed in the United States of America

ISBN: 978-1-64242-779-0

PREFACE

Advanced Torts in a Nutshell is a compact text on major areas of tort law not typically covered in the required first-year Torts course of most law schools. It includes defamation, invasion of privacy torts, malicious prosecution, wrongful death, actions for injuries to family relationships, and most of the numerous and increasingly important economic torts. These are among the subjects included in Advanced Torts casebooks now in use.

This book is a successor to Wex Malone's *Torts in a Nutshell: Injuries to Family, Social and Trade Relations*, which was published in 1979. As in that Nutshell, the torts included are within the "injuries to relations" concept advanced by the prominent Torts scholar Leon Green. Although out of date in certain respects, Professor Malone's Nutshell is still a valuable resource for the subjects of tort law he addressed. *Advanced Torts in a Nutshell* is, however, a new work, not an update of the *Injuries to Relations* Nutshell.

The experience of research for and writing several editions of an Advanced Torts casebook—*Advanced Torts Cases and Materials* (Carolina Academic Press)—was exceptionally helpful in planning and writing the Nutshell. My renewed thanks to those who contributed to production of that book, including my former co-author Osborne (Mac) Reynolds. Special thanks to Leslee Roybal of the University of

Oklahoma College of Law Faculty Support Office for her work on the manuscript of this book.

Excerpts from the Restatements of Torts, Torts (Second), Torts (Third): Liability for Economic Harm, and Unfair Competition are Copyright by The American Law Institute and included with the permission of the ALI. Excerpts from the Uniform Trade Secrets Act are Copyright by the National Conference of Commissioners on Uniform State Laws and included with the permission of NCCUSL.

PETER B KUTNER

June 1, 2020

OUTLINE

PART VI. LEGAL PROCESS

TABLE OF CASES

References are to Pages

ADVANCED TORTS
IN A NUTSHELL®

PART I

INTRODUCTION

CHAPTER 1

RELATIONAL INTERESTS

Most of the torts included in a first-year Torts course are causes of action for physical interference with a person or tangible property. The damages recoverable are primarily compensation for injury, damage or loss resulting from such physical interference. There are, however, numerous torts in which liability arises from interference with an intangible interest, such as a person's interest in reputation or deriving revenue from a business. These torts protect intangible interests from certain types of interference and provide remedies when loss results or will result from the interference, even though the plaintiff has suffered no physical harm. Most, but not all, of these torts are discussed within this Advanced Torts Nutshell.

The torts included in the book come within the concept of "injuries to relational interests." The book's predecessor—Wex Malone's *Torts in a Nutshell: Injuries to Family, Social and Trade Relations* (1979)—was based on the injuries to relations concept. The prominent Torts scholar Leon Green advanced the proposition that tort law provides actions for injuries to relational interests as well as injuries to person or property. Green identified four categories of relations in which tort liability operates: family relations, trade relations (including commercial and employment relations), political and professional relations, and general social relations. The injury to the plaintiff's interests could stem from the defendant's causing physical harm to someone in a family or economic relationship with the plaintiff (as by severely injuring a member of the plaintiff's family or key employee, or converting or destroying property the plaintiff expected to acquire); preventing formation or continuance of an economic relationship (as by hindering the plaintiff's employment of workers or acquisition of materials); taking from the plaintiff the benefits of a relationship (as by diverting trade from the plaintiff to the defendant, or causing the plaintiff's spouse to leave the plaintiff and live with the defendant); or by impairing relationships (as by making false statements about the plaintiff that cause others to avoid business or social interaction with the plaintiff). A fundamental characteristic of injury to a relational interest is that it involves an existing or potential relationship between two parties and interference with the relationship by a third party. It is always a "three-party situation." See Green, Basic Concepts: Persons, Property, Relations, 24 A.B.A.J. 65 (1938).

This is easily found in the torts of interference with a family relationship, in most of the torts of interference with commercial or employment relations, and in defamation (libel and slander). A defendant who caused the plaintiff's spouse or child to leave the family home has interfered with the family relationship and caused the plaintiff to lose its benefits. A defendant who injured the plaintiff's spouse, causing the plaintiff to lose the companionship of the spouse and services the spouse performed within the household, has caused loss to the plaintiff on account of the plaintiff's relationship with the injured spouse. A defendant who persuaded someone not to perform the obligations of a contract made with the plaintiff, or otherwise caused the contract not to be performed, typically has caused loss to the plaintiff by interference with the plaintiff's relationship with the other contracting party. A defendant who has interfered with the plaintiff's ability to obtain employment, hire workers or make sales to customers or buyers of property has interfered with anticipated contractual or business relationships and thereby caused economic loss. A defendant who damaged the plaintiff's reputation by publishing defamatory statements about the plaintiff has interfered with the plaintiff's social or business relations with other people. Whether other torts, such as abuse of process or intrusion upon seclusion (a category of invasion of privacy), should be categorized as torts of interference with a relational interest is a debatable point, but they clearly belong in the group of torts that have at least an association with injuries to relations.

Within the injuries to relations torts there is much variety in the elements of liability. Each has a set of elements that is usually unique to that particular tort. Some of the torts require an intent to interfere with the relevant relationship. In other torts, it is sufficient that the defendant's conduct did cause interference and resulting loss to the plaintiff. For most of the torts, negligence is not a basis of liability. However, negligence plays an important role in liability arising from physical injury to a family member, and to a limited extent it can be the basis of liability for economic loss.

Part II of this book (Chapters 2 to 5) addresses torts of injuries to family relations. Part III (Chapters 6 to 14) addresses torts of injuries to economic relations. Parts IV and V (Chapters 15 to 23) address invasion of privacy and defamation, which injure social relations. Part VI (Chapters 24 to 26) addresses malicious prosecution and abuse of process, which might be regarded as interference with civil rights that causes injury to economic and social interests. The torts of deceit and negligent misrepresentation are economic torts but not within the subject-matter of the book, as they do not involve interference with a relational interest. They are included in Kionka, *Torts in a Nutshell* (6th ed. 2015).

PART II

FAMILY RELATIONS

CHAPTER 2

INJURIES TO FAMILY MEMBERS

A. INTRODUCTION

Serious personal injury usually has adverse consequences for the injured person's immediate family members, even when the injured person recovers fully from the injury. Typical consequences include the costs of treatment and care of the injured person, when borne by other family members; loss of benefits coming from the injured person's earnings, when family members were or would be supported by the earnings; and loss of the injured person's services in the household, including maintenance of the family home, supervision and care of children, obtaining and preparing food, and (historically) agricultural labor. Family members may incur the burden of caring for the injured person and even give up paid employment in order to do this. Additionally, depending upon the relationship between the injured person and the family member, the latter will suffer an impairment of the relationship that includes loss of society and companionship, inability to engage in enjoyable or fulfilling activities, and (for spouses and other intimate partners) loss or impairment of sexual relations.

For centuries the common law has provided a limited tort remedy for family members in instances of personal injury. The limitations prevailing until modern times are as significant as the existence of the remedy. A husband had an action when his wife was injured, but a wife had no action when her husband was injured. There was no action of this type unless a marriage existed at the time of the injury. When a child was injured, an action by its parent required allegation and proof that the parent lost the services of the child as a result of the injury, and the action could only be brought by the child's father—not its mother—unless the father had died or abandoned the child. A child had no action for injury to a parent. The injury had to be non-fatal: there was no common law remedy for fatal injury. As will be seen, some of the limitations no longer apply, including denial of liability to a wife whose husband was injured. But others remain, albeit with some modifications. Liability for fatal injury now arises under wrongful death and survival legislation, discussed in Chapter 3.

B. SPOUSES

The foundations of both the husband's action for the consequences of injury to his wife and the parent's action for the consequences of injury to a child are in the centuries-old action of a master for loss of the services of a servant: the action *per quod servitium amisit*. This action arose when someone entitled to the services of a servant lost them on account of an injury to the servant or other legally wrongful conduct. This included inducing a servant to leave the service of the plaintiff, or to not return to it, as well as causing a personal injury for which the defendant was or would be liable.

In the early seventeenth century, English courts accepted that a husband whose wife had been injured, or persuaded to leave the home shared with her husband, would have a cause of action on analogy to the master's action. Like a master, the husband was entitled to the services of his wife and had lost them, at least for a time, by the wrongful conduct of the defendant. The husband's action was not a master's action *per quod servitium amisit* as such. His right to sue was based on the spousal relationship and entitlement to his wife's services, not a master-servant relationship with the wife. He could sue for loss of the wife's "company" as well as loss of services. The husband's action was for loss of "*servitium*" and "*consortium*." It was distinct from any action to recover damages for the wife's injuries, which at the time would be brought by her husband rather than by the wife personally. *Guy v. Livesey*, (1618) Cro. Jac. 501, 79 Eng. Rep. 428 (K.B.).

A married woman had no such action when her husband was injured or persuaded to leave the marital home. The law recognized no legal right of a wife to the services or consortium of her husband, so there was no action when a wife lost her husband's services or company. According to Blackstone, such a legal right belonged only to the superior party of the relevant relationship. A wife was the inferior party in the relationship with her husband, as a servant was in the relationship with his master and a child in its relationship with the parent. "[T]he loss of the inferior by such injuries is totally unregarded. . . .[T]he inferior hath no kind of property in the company, care, or assistance of the superior, as the superior is held to have in those of the inferior; and therefore the inferior can suffer no loss or injury." 3 Blackstone, *Commentaries on the Laws of England* 142–143 (1768).

After many centuries of legal inferiority and limited ability to control and transfer property, make contracts and initiate legal proceedings independently of her husband, married women acquired (almost) full legal capacity by enactment of "Married Women's Acts" or "Married Women's Property Acts." This legislation, adopted primarily in the latter half of the nineteenth century, also established that what a wife earned by work outside the home was her own property. The proceeds of her labor no longer belonged to her husband. This suggested to some that the legal foundation of the husband's action for injury to his wife no longer existed. A husband no longer had the property interest in or other entitlement to the services of his wife recognized in the common law, and therefore an action for loss of spousal services was no longer maintainable. Some courts so held. But most courts decided that husbands still had a legally protected interest in spousal services within the family home and spousal consortium, and they could continue to claim damages for loss of services and consortium from defendants liable for causing injury to the plaintiff's wife. See Annot., 21 A.L.R. 1517.

The transformation of the legal status and capacity of married women by the Married Women's Acts and other legislation did not lead courts to conclude that a married woman now had an action for loss of services and consortium when her husband was injured. This began to change in 1950. In *Hitaffer v.*

Argonne Co., 87 U.S. App. D.C. 57, 183 F.2d 811 (1950), the court held that a wife had a cause of action for loss of consortium due to her husband's being injured by negligence. It rejected arguments to the contrary based on precedent and the wife having no right as such to her husband's services. In actions by husbands whose wives had been injured, the predominant factor in assessing compensation was now loss of consortium in the sense of "companionship, love, felicity, and sexual relations" rather than loss of material services. A wife's right to the consortium of her husband was equal to a husband's right to the consortium of his wife. A wife's loss of consortium was no more "indirect" or "remote" from the defendant's wrong than in an action by a husband whose wife had been injured. In the court's opinion there was no justification for denying a wife protection of an interest that was exactly the same as a husband's.

Whether a wife would be allowed an action for loss of consortium when her husband was injured was a question addressed by a number of courts in the years after *Hitaffer*. Some courts continued to limit the action to husbands. They were not oblivious to the argument that wives were entitled to equality with husbands in this respect, but this was countered by the weight of precedent, a belief that altering the law should be a decision for the state legislature rather than a court, and concern that damages awarded for loss of consortium and services would duplicate damages awarded in the action for personal injury. See *Nickel v. Hardware Mutual Casualty Co.*, 269 Wis. 647, 70 N.W.2d 205 (1955). In addition, some judges, as in *Neuberg v. Bobowicz*, 401 Pa. 146, 162 A.2d 662 (1960), believed that the husband's action was anomalous, in allowing an action on account of injury to another person, based on the former lowly status of a married woman as "property" of her husband. It was "a fossil from an earlier era" that should be not be extended further.

Eventually, though, the position that wives did have an action for loss of consortium prevailed. There was general acceptance that married women should have the right to sue on the same terms as married men. See Annot., 36 A.L.R.3d 900. To deny equality in this regard would be unjust and could be challenged as a violation of the Fourteenth Amendment right to equal protection of the laws and state constitutional rights. See *Karczewski v. Baltimore and Ohio Railroad Co.*, 274 F. Supp. 169 (N.D. Ill. 1967). Equality could be achieved by abolishing the husband's action rather than extending it to wives, but this rarely happened. Even the Pennsylvania Supreme Court, so critical of the husband's cause of action in *Neuberg v. Bobowicz*, decided to allow wives to sue rather than abolish the husband's action. *Hopkins v. Blanco*, 457 Pa. 90, 320 A.2d 139 (1974). Today it would be untenable to deny an action for loss of consortium or services caused by physical injury to a husband while allowing a similar action for loss caused by physical injury to a wife. It also would be untenable to deny an action for loss of consortium to spouses in legally valid same-sex marriages.

Rodriguez v. Bethlehem Steel Corp., 12 Cal. 3d 382, 525 P.2d 669 (1974), is one of the most important modern cases on tort liability for injury to a spouse. While in his early twenties, Mr. Rodriguez was in an accident that damaged his spinal cord and left him totally paralyzed below the mid-point of his chest. Mrs. Rodriguez gave up her job and undertook the arduous task of caring for her husband on a twenty-four-hour basis. Among the many consequences of Mr. Rodriguez's injuries was that Mrs. Rodriguez would never again have sexual intercourse with her husband or have children by him. California law had previously allowed only a limited recovery by a husband for loss of services and medical expenses caused by an injury to his wife. In *Rodriguez*, the court decided that both husbands and wives could recover damages for loss of consortium. Consortium was broadly defined to include spousal companionship, affection, comfort, support and sexual relations.

The court discussed and rejected rationales for denying liability for loss of consortium, including that it was only an indirect consequence of the defendant's wrong to the injured spouse, the impossibility of measuring loss of companionship and society, and the danger of double recovery for impairment of the injured spouse's ability to have a normal married life. Negligence law's duty of care depended upon foreseeability, and one who negligently caused a severely disabling injury could reasonably expect this would adversely affect the injured person's spouse. Loss of consortium was principally a form of mental suffering, which often was an element of compensation in tort cases. There would be no double recovery in compensating a wife for her loss, which was distinct from her husband's although caused by the same personal injury. Double recovery would be avoided by ensuring that each element of damages in the litigation was distinct from the others, and by not permitting a spouse to recover for what the injured spouse was primarily entitled to be compensated for.

Rodriguez indicates the limits as well as the extent of the spouse's action. A spouse was not to recover damages for loss of financial support due to injuries sustained by the other spouse. That would be covered by the injured person's claim to be compensated for loss of earnings and earning capacity. Mrs. Rodriguez was not permitted to recover for the value of the nursing care she was providing to her husband. That would duplicate his entitlement to claim damages for the cost of home nursing his injuries required. She was also denied recovery for loss of earnings due to quitting her job to care for her husband.

Liability to a spouse for loss of consortium and medical and care expenses stems from the tort committed upon the other spouse, which has caused the plaintiff to lose spousal consortium and incur expenses. In almost all instances, a party liable for loss of consortium is liable for physical injuries to the other spouse. However, there are cases in which a defendant was held liable for loss of consortium because the defendant was liable for a tort causing emotional distress to the other spouse, which resulted in loss of consortium. If defamation causes disabling emotional distress, a defendant might be held liable to the defamed person's spouse. See Annot., 16 A.L.R.4th 537.

C. PARENTS AND CHILDREN

Contemporary tort law allows parents to claim damages from defendants liable for injuries suffered by a minor child. Under English common law, a parent could maintain an action only as a master's action for loss of services. This severely limited the action. The action could not be maintained without pleading and proving some actual loss of services due to the child's injuries. This was not possible if the injured child was too young to provide services or if other circumstances excluded actual loss of services, as when the child had already left the family home or had been incapable of providing household services. See *Hall v. Hollander*, (1825) 4 B. & C. 660, 107 Eng. Rep. 1206 (K.B.). Only the "master" of the injured child could sue. The father was considered the master of the child in most instances, so mothers usually had no action unless the father had died or abandoned the household before the child was injured. Damages were limited to the value of the services the child could not perform because of the injuries.

English law eventually allowed parents to recover the medical expenses they would incur, but otherwise it never recognized any action based on the plaintiff being a parent. In the United States, however, loss of services became more of a technicality than a requirement of liability. It became sufficient to allege an entitlement to the child's services rather than an actual loss of services. A mother with sole custody of the child could sue. Eventually it was accepted that both fathers and mothers of injured children had a cause of action, at least when they were custodial parents. But damages other than the cost of the child's treatment and care were still limited to loss of services due to the injuries while the child was a minor, including loss of earnings. In modern-day American families, this could be minimal.

This is still the position in numerous jurisdictions. But since the 1970s a growing number of American courts have held that parents can recover for loss of the "consortium" of a minor child—the society, companionship and affection they would have enjoyed had the child not been injured. A few decisions even allow parents a claim when the child was an adult. See Annot., 54 A.L.R.4th 112. There is an obvious analogy between a parent's loss of the society and companionship of a child and a spouse's loss of society and companionship when a marital partner is injured, even though impairment of sexual relations is not involved. When serious injury to a minor is a foreseeable result of negligence, the economic consequences for the parent and loss of the child's companionship are also foreseeable. The child's companionship and affection might be treated as "services" the parent has lost. In jurisdictions where damages in wrongful death actions include loss of the companionship of a deceased child, denying damages for loss of a child's companionship in cases of severe but non-fatal injury may seem arbitrary. On the other hand, judges may regard the spousal relationship as unique, and they may be unwilling to accept a major change in the law that would increase the costs of personal injury liability and related insurance costs. It might also have an adverse effect upon the injured child's recovery of damages, when the defendant's liability insurance and available assets are insufficient to fully satisfy both the judgment for the injured child and the judgment for the parent.

There have also been actions brought on behalf of children when a parent has suffered a disabling injury. There is no common law basis for holding a tortfeasor liable to an injured person's child. But it is difficult to deny the likelihood and magnitude of loss of support, care, affection, guidance and the like when a parent of a minor child is severely injured, and an action might possibly be sustained by analogy to actions for loss of spousal or filial consortium. Beginning with *Berger v. Weber*, 82 Mich. App. 199, 267 N.W.2d 124 (1978), aff'd, 411 Mich. 1, 303 N.W.2d 424 (1981), a number of courts have allowed actions for a minor's loss of parental consortium when brought against defendants responsible for the parent's injury. A few have even allowed recovery by an adult child, at least when the child was disabled and dependent upon the parent. The majority view is that the child has no cause of action. See Annot., 4 A.L.R.7th Art. 1.

The Supreme Court of California, which had accepted expansive liability for loss of spousal consortium in *Rodriguez v. Bethlehem Steel Corp.* (see pp. 15–16), rejected liability in negligence actions for both loss of parental consortium and loss of a child's consortium. *Borer v. American Airlines*,

Inc., 19 Cal. 3d 441, 563 P.2d 858 (1977); *Baxter v. Superior Court of Los Angeles County*, 19 Cal. 3d 461, 563 P.2d 871 (1977). Reasons that in *Rodriguez* had been thought insufficient to deny liability for loss of consortium, such as the multiplication of actions arising from a personal injury, the difficulty of quantifying damages, and the prospect of double recovery for the same loss, were thought sufficient in the different contexts of parent-child relationships. In *Borer*, the court observed that awarding damages to the children would only "establish a fund so that upon reaching adulthood, when plaintiffs will be less in need of maternal guidance, they will be unusually wealthy men and women." Probably the most weighty reason for denial of liability was the great cost to the public, including increases in insurance premiums, of liability to parents and children and litigation of their claims. Almost any serious injury to a parent or child would engender a claim. That parents already had a common law cause of action for loss of services was not for the court a sufficient reason to allow parents to claim damages for loss of a child's consortium.

D. OTHER RELATIONSHIPS

To this point, the discussion of liability for loss of spousal, filial or parental consortium has assumed that the person seeking damages was legally the spouse, parent or child of the injured person at the time of the injury. What if a couple had a relationship like that of spouses, without having been legally married at the time of the injury? What if an adult had assumed the responsibility of supporting, caring for and protecting a child when either the child or the adult was injured, but the adult had not legally adopted the child?

Most cases require a valid marriage at the time of the injury in order for there to be liability for loss of spousal consortium. It is insufficient that the parties had a long-term spouse-like relationship as unmarried cohabitants, or that they were engaged and subsequently married. See Annot., 5 A.L.R.4th 300; Annot., 40 A.L.R.4th 553. This position rests upon precedent, perceived public and legal policies favoring marriage as a privileged status, and the difficulty of deciding what would be required for a loss of consortium action if marriage was not necessary. Also, judges might suspect that couples who could have married but did not lacked the mutual and supposedly life-long commitment that marriage involves. See *Hendrix v. General Motors Corp.*, 146 Cal. App. 3d 296, 193 Cal. Rptr. 922 (1983). Compare *Mueller v. Tepler*, 312 Conn. 631, 95 A.3d 1011 (2014) (same-sex partner who would have married injured partner if law allowed could bring action for loss of consortium). Legislation in some states permitting couples to enter a "civil union" or "domestic partnership" allows them to have a legally recognized relationship with most of the legal rights of spouses, including damages for loss of consortium.

There is less precedent on whether there is liability if there was a *de facto* but not *de jure* parent-child relationship. The old master's action for loss of services suggests that there is an action when an injured child was in the sole charge of the plaintiff.

See *Anderson v. Aupperle*, 51 Or. 556, 95 P. 330 (1908). But it seems that a legal relationship is now required. See *Ford Motor Co. v. Miles*, 967 S.W.2d 377 (Tex. 1998) (action by stepparent). Uniquely, New Mexico extends loss of consortium actions to grandparents who assumed a parental role, *Fernandez v. Walgreen Hastings Co.*, 126 N.M. 263, 968 P.2d 774 (1998), and cohabitants in an "intimate family relationship," *Lozoya v. Sanchez*, 133 N.M. 579, 66 P.3d 948 (2003).

E. DEFENSES

Liability to an injured person's spouse or parent is often thought of as a consequence of liability to an injured person. To a large extent this is a realistic view, but it is a generalization that does not apply in all cases. In some circumstances, such as seduction of a child (see pp. 61–63), the common law protected a parent's interests even if the child had no cause of action against the defendant. When a minor had entered dangerous employment with the defendant without parental consent, parents have been able to recover damages even when the child could not. See Annot., 94 A.L.R. 1211; Rest. 2d Torts § 707.

With these qualifications, a defendant is liable to an injured person's spouse or parent (or other relation, if possible) only when the injured person has a cause of action against the defendant for the injuries. If, for example, it is claimed that the defendant is liable because of negligence, the requirements of negligence liability, including a duty of care to the injured person and proximate cause of injury, must be satisfied. But there is a division of authority on whether the defendant must actually be liable to the injured person. Under some decisions, a defendant can be liable to the injured person's spouse or parent even though the defendant had a defense against liability to the injured person.

The prevailing view in the United States is that liability to the spouse or parent is "derivative." It derives from liability to the injured person. Consequently, a defendant is not liable to an injured person's spouse or parent when not liable to the injured person because of a defense. This applies principally to contributory negligence. See Rest. 2d Torts § 494. Parties who have a contributory negligence defense to the personal injury claim have the same defense to a spousal or parental claim. See Annot., 21 A.L.R.3d 469; Annot., 25 A.L.R.4th 118. It also applies to assumption of risk, pre-injury release of liability by the injured person, and other substantive defenses against liability.

A significant minority of courts have adopted the position that the action of the spouse or parent is "independent" of the injured person's action rather than "derivative." It is not defeated by defenses applicable to the injured person's action, at least contributory negligence. *E.g.*, *Lantis v. Condon*, 95 Cal. App. 3d 152, 157 Cal. Rptr. 22 (1979); *Feltch v. General Rental Co.*, 383 Mass. 603, 421 N.E.2d 67 (1981). There are some decisions that the injured person's release of liability, prior to the injury, does not bar the family member's claim. *E.g.*, *Bowen v. Kil-Kare*, 63 Ohio St. 3d 84, 585 N.E.2d 384 (1992). This position is supported by arguments that an otherwise valid claim should not be defeated on account of another person's negligence or agreement, and the negligence or contract of a family member is not a defense to personal injury or property damage claims generally (absent vicarious responsibility for the family member's conduct because of an employment or agency relationship). See *Handeland v. Brown*, 216 N.W.2d 574 (Iowa 1974).

The principal decisions on the effect of contributory negligence preceded the widespread adoption of comparative negligence. Under comparative negligence, the injured person's contributory negligence would reduce the damages to be paid for the injury by the person's percentage of fault, not bar the action entirely (unless barred by "modified" comparative negligence). Therefore, under the majority view concerning defenses, a defendant can be held liable to the injured person's spouse or parent when the injured person was contributorily negligent. But the contributory negligence defense operates to reduce the award to the spouse or parent by the injured person's percentage of fault. Under the minority view, there is no such reduction. See Annot., 25 A.L.R.4th 118. However, if a defendant's liability is limited by state law to that defendant's percentage at fault, the injured person's fault is likely to be taken into account.

If the injured person is found to be negligent, the injured person will not be liable to a spouse or parent for expenses incurred because of the injury or loss of consortium or services. Spouses and parents have actions only against third parties who are legally responsible for causing the injury. See *Clark v. Estate of Rice*, 653 N.W.2d 166 (Iowa 2002); *Plain v. Plain*, 307 Minn. 399, 240 N.W.2d 330 (1976).

If the defendant is liable to the injured person, the defendant may nevertheless avoid liability to a spouse or parent because of a defense applying to the spouse or parent. Applicable defenses include consent or assumption of risk, release of liability (pre- or post-injury), and the statute of limitations. (The limitation period for a claim by a parent may have expired prior to the end of the limitation period for the child's action.) Another important defense is contributory negligence, when negligent conduct by the spouse or parent is found to be a cause of the injury sustained by the other spouse or child. This may be found when the injured person was a passenger in a car driven by the spouse or parent and the car collided with a vehicle driven by the defendant. A parent considered to have been negligent in failing to protect a child from injury may be treated as contributorily negligent for purposes of the parent's action against the defendant even if the parent would not be liable to the child. An example is *Wright v. Standard Oil Co., Inc.*, 470 F.2d 1280 (5th Cir. 1972), in which a father left his five-year-old son at a small store and crossed the highway in front of the store. A few minutes later, the child attempted to cross the highway and was struck by the defendant's truck. Under the common law contributory negligence rule, the plaintiff's contributory negligence was a complete defense against the spouse or parent, assuming it was a defense to the type of tort the defendant committed against the injured person. Rest. 2d Torts § 704A. Under comparative negligence, the damages awarded to the negligent spouse or parent will be reduced by the party's percentage of fault.

In this scenario, it would be to the advantage of the injured person, and also the spouse or parent, if damages for the costs of treatment and care could be recovered in the injured person's action. State law is divided on whether medical and care costs during a child's minority can be recovered in the child's personal injury action rather than in an action by the child's parent. When a child with two parents was injured, some decisions held that the negligence of one parent applied to the claims of both parents. But the prevailing position today is that the negligence of one parent, or consent given by one parent, is not a defense to the other parent's claims unless one was the agent of the other. See *Wright v. Standard Oil Co., Inc., supra*; Annot., 26 A.L.R.4th 396. This suggests that a negligent spouse or parent should avoid paying or agreeing to pay for medical and care costs, to the extent possible, so they can be claimed as damages in the action of the injured person or (when a child is injured) the other parent.

CHAPTER 3
WRONGFUL DEATH

A. INTRODUCTION

For tort law, there are two fundamental issues or problems pertaining to death. One is what should be the consequence of the death of a person who could have maintained a tort action as a plaintiff or been held liable as a defendant. The person may actually have been a plaintiff or defendant at the time of death. For the most part, this is unrelated to the subject of tort liability for interference with family relations. But a connection exists when a tort results in death.

The other fundamental issue or problem is how should tort law respond to the harm or loss caused to others by a person's death. Typically, the death of a person whose work provided income to a family, or who was supporting family members by earnings or accumulated wealth, causes family members to lose income or support. Expected receipt of property by inheritance or gift may be lost on account of a premature death. Family members lose the unremunerated services the deceased person would have provided within the household. Businesses lose the value of an employee's services when an employee dies. There are also losses of a non-economic nature, depending on the relationship between the deceased and the survivor, which correspond to the "consortium" whose loss can be compensated in non-fatal injury cases: loss of the deceased's society, companionship, affection, personal attention, care, etc.

The losses of family members and other survivors because of a person's death are conceptually distinct from any loss to the person's estate, incurred because the deceased no longer earned income and could not inherit anything or successfully litigate a pending claim. However, the two are related because the economic losses of family members are primarily what they would have received from the income and assets of the deceased, but for the death.

The common law's response to the first issue was the rule *actio personalis moritur cum persona*: a personal action dies with the person. A cause of action died with the death of the plaintiff or defendant, or potential plaintiff or defendant. It could not be maintained by or against a person's estate or surviving family members. Under ancient English statutes, a claim for loss, damage or conversion of personal property could be maintained by a representative of a deceased person, but otherwise the *actio personalis* rule barred tort claims after the death of a party. The rule did not generally apply to actions for breach of contract, but it did apply to claims for personal injury even if founded on contract rather than tort.

For the second issue, the common law's response was that no action could be maintained for loss resulting from a person's death. In *Baker v. Bolton*, (1808) 1 Camp. 493, 170 Eng. Rep. 1033 (K.B.), Lord Ellenborough declared: "In a civil Court, the death of a human being could not be complained of as an injury."

The combination of the *actio personalis* rule and the absence of a remedy for the consequences of death meant that there was no civil liability at all for causing death by legally wrongful conduct. Why this was tolerated for so many centuries is unclear. The principal historical explanation is that homicide, including negligent homicide, was a felony and this required that the legal consequence be criminal prosecution rather than a civil action (the "felony-merger doctrine"). See *Moragne v. States Marine Lines, Inc.*, 398 U.S. 375, 382–383 (1970). It may have been thought that the criminal law and moral considerations provided an adequate deterrent and that awards of damages for causing death might be excessive. Also, it was rational to distinguish between situations in which liability would serve to compensate a person who had suffered personal injury and a situation in which liability would compensate or enrich persons who had themselves suffered no personal injury. What was less rational was allowing actions for loss of services and consortium when the injury was not fatal (as discussed in Chapter 2) but denying actions for the same type of loss to the same parties when the injury was fatal.

In the nineteenth century, the growing numbers of deaths in industrial, railway and road accidents required reform of the law. The reform adopted by the British Parliament in 1846 was legislation formally titled the Fatal Accidents Act but often called Lord Campbell's Act. This statute created a new cause of action to compensate immediate family members of the deceased for losses they sustained on account of the death, when death was caused wrongfully. Statutes modelled on Lord Campbell's Act were soon enacted not only in the British Empire but also much of the United States.

Later, legislation altering the *actio personalis* rule was enacted. "Survival acts" allow causes of action arising before a person's death to "survive" the death and be brought, or continued, by or against the executor, administrator or other representative of the deceased. Unlike the proceeds of a successful action under Lord Campbell's Act, the proceeds of a successful "survival action" by an executor or administrator go into the estate and then, after discharge of debt and tax obligations, to the heirs of the estate. When there is a judgment against an executor or administrator of an estate, the judgment is enforceable against the assets of the estate, reducing what will be inherited by the heirs. All states have some form of survival legislation. The statutes either set forth a list of actions that survive or provide for survival generally with specified exceptions. They differ on what types of tort actions survive. In many jurisdictions, defamation actions do not survive death. Actions for injuries to other intangible interests, such as invasion of privacy and malicious prosecution, may also be excepted from survival. Certain types of damages, such as pain and suffering and punitive damages, may be excluded from actions that survive. Unless otherwise provided in the survival legislation, the elements of liability and defenses in an action that survives are the same as they would have been had no death occurred.

The main type of legislation on liability for "wrongful death" consists of the statutes based on Lord Campbell's Act, with subsequent amendments. What is discussed in the remaining sections of this chapter is the cause of action arising from death that is created by Lord Campbell's Act-type wrongful death statutes. Some states provide instead for recovery in a survival action of loss to the decedent's estate, or for an action that combines elements of survival and compensation of family members' losses. The statutes provide the exclusive legal remedy for death and its consequences. With isolated exceptions, including federal maritime law, the enactment of wrongful death and survival legislation foreclosed the possibility that courts would allow some claims by judicial decision. This is the one major area of tort law in which liability originates in legislation rather than judicial innovation. Persons who suffer loss as a consequence of death but have no statutory entitlement to damages have no remedy.

B. LIABILITY UNDER WRONGFUL DEATH STATUTES (LORD CAMPBELL'S ACT)

Lord Campbell's Act, in its original language, provided:

> That whensoever the Death of a Person shall be caused by wrongful Act, Neglect, or Default, and the Act, Neglect, or Default is such as would (if Death had not ensued) have entitled the Party injured to maintain an Action and recover

> Damages in respect thereof, then and in every such Case the Person who would have been liable if Death had not ensued shall be liable to an Action for Damages, notwithstanding the Death of the Person injured. . . .

The act also provided that "One Action shall lie for and in respect of the same Subject Matter of Complaint," it would be brought by the executor or administrator of the deceased for the benefit of specified relatives of the deceased (wife, husband, parent and child, but extending the meaning of "parent" and "child" to include grandparents, grandchildren, stepparents and stepchildren), and damages would be awarded "proportioned to the Injury resulting from such Death to the Parties respectively for whom and for whose Benefit such Action shall be brought."

Instead of providing detailed rules on when there would or would not be liability, Lord Campbell's Act adopted a general rule of liability when "the Act, Neglect, or Default is such as would (if Death had not ensued) have entitled the Party injured to maintain an Action and recover Damages in respect thereof." In other words, if a defendant would have been liable to the victim had the injury not been fatal, the defendant will be liable to the statutory action when the injury is fatal and the defendant's "Act, Neglect, or Default" is a cause of the death. The rules of liability and causation in non-fatal injury cases apply to the actions for death.

Types of liability within the statute. In most instances in which there is liability, the underlining cause of action (*i.e.*, the action for which the defendant would have been liable if the injury had not been fatal) is a physical injury tort such as negligence, battery, or strict liability for harm caused by a dangerous activity or product defect. However, a defendant might be held liable for wrongful death if there would have been liability to the deceased person for injury on grounds of nuisance or infliction of emotional distress. Arguably liability for any tort qualifies, if it is found to be a proximate cause of the death. See *State ex rel. Richardson v. Edgeworth*, 214 So. 2d 579 (Miss. 1968) (abuse of process allegedly causing suicide); *Cauverien v. De Metz*, 20 Misc. 2d 144, 188 N.Y.S.2d 627 (Sup. Ct. 1959) (conversion of diamond that allegedly caused diamond broker's suicide). (On the limited circumstances in which there can be liability for suicide, see Annot., 77 A.L.R.3d 311.)

Lord Campbell's Act did not specify that the underlining cause of action must be for a tort. However, in some cases it has been decided that there is no action under the wrongful death statute if the defendant's liability for the deceased person's injury would have been for breach of contract. *E.g.*, *Whiteley v. Webb's City*, 55 So. 2d 730 (Fla. 1951). In other cases, actions based on breach of contract have been permitted. *E.g.*, *Greco v. S.S. Kresge Co.*, 277 N.Y. 26, 12 N.E.2d 557 (1938). See Annot., 86 A.L.R.2d 316. When death was allegedly caused by a defective product, some cases have treated breach of warranty as a wrongful act or default that is a basis of liability under Lord Campbell's Act, even if breach of contract was not. *E.g.*, *Torres v. Northwest Engineering Co.*,

86 Haw. 383, 949 P.2d 1004 (Ct. App. 1997). *Contra*, *DiBelardino v. Lemmon Pharmacal Co.*, 416 Pa. 580, 208 A.2d 283 (1965). There is no liability outside the wrongful death statute for breach of a contract with the plaintiff that resulted in the death of a family member. *Zostautas v. St. Anthony de Padua Hospital*, 23 Ill. 2d 326, 178 N.E.2d 303 (1961) (contract to perform surgery on plaintiff's son); *Bloss v. Dr. C.R. Woodson Sanitarium Co.*, 319 Mo. 1061, 5 S.W.2d 367 (1928) (contract to protect plaintiff's husband from suicide).

When tortfeasor dies first. In accidents caused by negligence, such as negligent operation of a vehicle, it is not unusual for the negligent party to die in or after the accident. This may affect a potential claim for the death of another person in the accident. If the victim died before the tortfeasor, the tortfeasor would have been liable for wrongful death once the death occurred. Consequently, there was a wrongful death action against the tortfeasor that could survive the tortfeasor's death and be brought against his executor or administrator, if allowed by state law. Older cases tended to hold that wrongful death actions did not come within statutes providing for survival of actions. Through interpretation or amendment of survival or wrongful death statutes, the general rule now is that wrongful death actions survive the death of a defendant or potential defendant.

There is greater difficulty when the tortfeasor died before the victim. If the tortfeasor was liable on an action for personal injury, that action would survive, under survival statutes, regardless of the order of death. But if the victim was still alive when the tortfeasor died, the tortfeasor was never liable for wrongful death, so there was no wrongful death action to survive the tortfeasor's death. It was held in a number of cases that a wrongful death could not be maintained in this situation against the tortfeasor's executor or administrator. *E.g.*, *Martinelli v. Burke*, 298 Mass. 390, 10 N.E.2d 113 (1937). There are contrary decisions. *E.g.*, *Fish v. Liley*, 120 Colo. 156, 208 P.2d 930 (1949). And in a number of states, it is now expressly provided that a wrongful death action can be maintained when the party liable for the injury died before the victim, or at the same time. It is doubtful that this extends to cases in which there is no injury before the tortfeasor's death. This might occur when negligence in the construction of a building or sale of product causes a fatality some years later.

Unborn child. One of the important issues of wrongful death law is whether an action can be maintained in cases of pre-natal injury—that is, when a child was injured before it was born. Until well into the twentieth century, there was no liability for pre-natal injury when the child was born alive. Although suffering from the injury after birth, the child had no action in which damages could be awarded. And there was no wrongful death action if the child died because of the injury. This was because a defendant could be liable for wrongful death only if the defendant would have been liable for the injury if death had not occurred.

Beginning with *Bonbrest v. Kotz*, 65 F. Supp. 138 (D.D.C. 1946), the law changed on liability for pre-natal injury when the child was born alive. It is now universally accepted that there can be liability when negligence or other tortious conduct causes injury before birth resulting in disability or other suffering after birth. If the child died after birth because of the injury a wrongful death action can be brought, provided the defendant would have been liable to a personal injury action.

What is controversial at present is whether there can be liability in a wrongful death action when an unborn child (fetus) dies. Even with acceptance of liability for pre-natal injury when the child survives birth, there are a number of grounds for concluding that there is no wrongful death action for fetal death. These include construction of the wrongful death statute. A fetus was not a legal person, as legal personality was achieved only upon live birth, so there was no death of a "person." A fetus had no cause of action for personal injury, so the essential liability requirement of the wrongful death statute could not be satisfied. Also, there was no liability for pre-natal injury when the statute was enacted, so liability for the death of a fetus because of negligence or other tortious conduct could not have been intended. A supporting policy consideration is that any assessment of damages for loss of the child's services and (where permitted) society would be speculative. There are also concerns about whether there would be sufficient proof of a causal link between the defendant's conduct and the death.

A number of major decisions reject liability for the death of an unborn child for such reasons. *E.g.*, *Giardina v. Bennett*, 111 N.J. 412, 545 A.2d 139 (1988) (death allegedly due to negligence of obstetrician); *Endresz v. Friedberg*, 24 N.Y.2d 478, 248 N.E.2d 901 (1969) (death in traffic accident). However, a considerable majority of the more recent cases allow actions to be brought for the death of an unborn child, at least when the child was "viable" at the time of death. See Annot., 84 A.L.R.3d 411. Viability has been significant because a viable fetus is capable of independent life outside the mother's womb, and that has been considered a basis for treating the fetus as a "person" for whose death an action can be brought. In some cases, there was support in other provisions of state law for legal recognition of a fetus as a person or object of legal protection. Underlying considerations include the gravity of the loss to the child's parents, if loss of the child's society and affection is taken into account; the lack of deterrence if there is no liability; and the arbitrariness of denying a wrongful death action when a child dies shortly before birth but allowing an action when a child dies shortly after birth. *E.g.*, *Todd v. Sandidge Construction Co.*, 341 F.2d 75 (4th Cir. 1964) (death when car plunged into unguarded opening in highway).

C. DEFENSES TO LIABILITY

Defendants not liable for injury. Defenses that apply to personal injury actions apply also to wrongful death actions. Lord Campbell's Act provides an action for death when the defendant's "Act,

Neglect, or Default" would have entitled the party injured to maintain an action and recover damages. The defendant must actually have been liable for the injury. Accordingly, if the defendant would have had a complete defense to liability in a personal injury action, the defendant is not liable for wrongful death. Relevant defenses include assumption of risk, consent, contributory negligence, and defenses to intentional torts such as self-defense and defense of property. While it may seem unfair that the contributory fault of the deceased person should bar innocent surviving family members from obtaining damages from a negligent defendant, contributory negligence has operated as a defense in many wrongful death actions. Under comparative negligence, a defendant can now be liable for wrongful death, when the defendant would have been liable in a personal injury action. But the damages awarded in the wrongful death action are usually reduced by the percentage of the deceased's fault, as they would have been in a personal injury action.

The one defense that may have defeated a personal injury action but may not, in a substantial number of states, defeat a wrongful death action is family immunity (spousal or parent-child). There are a number of decisions to the effect that a family immunity that would have barred a personal injury action does not bar a wrongful death action. One reason is that the rationale for the immunity applied only to the spousal or parent-child relationship between the defendant and the injury victim, which ended with the death. See Annot., 92 A.L.R.3d 901; Annot., 6 A.L.R.4th 1066.

Defenses against beneficiaries. Family members who can receive damages in wrongful death actions are the beneficiaries of the action, but generally they are not plaintiffs except in a representative capacity. There is a single action brought for their benefit, usually by someone appointed as executor or administrator. Lord Campbell's Act had no provision for defenses against the claims of individual beneficiaries. The statute could be interpreted to exclude such a defense and occasionally has been. But it is now widely accepted that such defenses as contributory negligence and assumption of risk can in effect be defenses to what is awarded for individual beneficiaries, without being applicable to the entire wrongful death action (unless there is only one beneficiary). Under the common law contributory negligence rule, the beneficiary's contributory negligence would be a complete defense to the claim of that beneficiary in the wrongful death action, if contributory negligence is a defense to the type of tort the defendant committed. Under comparative negligence, the damages awarded to the negligent beneficiary would be reduced by the percentage of the beneficiary's fault in causing the death. But damages awarded to innocent beneficiaries would not be barred or reduced because of the fault of another beneficiary (as distinct from the fault of the deceased person). Assumption of risk or consent by a beneficiary would have similar effects. A typical contributory negligence example is when a passenger is killed in a traffic accident while riding in a vehicle driven by a spouse or parent, the driver is a beneficiary in an action for the death of the passenger, and the defendant claims that negligent conduct by the driver was a cause of the accident.

Defendants not liable at time of death. In some circumstances, a defendant might have been held liable for the deceased's injury, if sued at some time, but is not liable to a personal injury action at the time of death. This may occur because the injured person released the defendant from liability as part of a settlement, because the injured person sued the defendant and judgment was entered in the action, or because the time period for a personal injury action in the applicable statute of limitations expired prior to the death.

Primarily in the context of judgments and settlements during the injured person's lifetime, numerous cases have adopted the rule that a defendant is liable to a wrongful death action only if liable to the injured person at the date of death. This protects defendants against "double recovery," but it leaves surviving relatives unprotected when a settlement does not compensate their losses or they do not inherit much of what the defendant paid. A strong minority view allows a wrongful death action when there was a release of the personal injury claim or a judgment for the personal injury while the injured person was alive. See Annot., 26 A.L.R.4th 1264. A prior judgment for the defendant in the personal injury action might preclude a wrongful death action even if a judgment for the plaintiff does not.

There is considerable division in the cases concerning the statute of limitations. In some of the cases, the defendant has been held not liable to a wrongful death action because not liable to a personal injury action at the date of death, due to the statute of limitations. The wrongful death statute is interpreted to require liability to the injured person at the date of death. *E.g.*, *Kelliher v. New York Central & Hudson River Railroad Co.*, 212 N.Y. 207, 105 N.E. 824 (1914). Other cases are to the contrary. *E.g.*, *Miller v. Estate of Sperling*, 166 N.J. 370, 766 A.2d 738 (2001) (death two decades after allegedly improper medication). One reason is that wrongful death actions have their own limitation period under the statute of limitations. This begins to run at the date of death, which is when an action for wrongful death arises. Also, as there was no personal injury action, there is no danger of "double recovery." Note that a defendant can be liable to both a wrongful death action and a personal injury action when the defendant is liable for personal injury at the date of death and the deceased person's action can be litigated after the death under a "survival" statute.

D. ELIGIBILITY FOR COMPENSATION

Lord Campbell's Act was intended to provide compensation to immediate family members who lost economic support or vital household services because of the death. The family members who could receive damages were limited to the wife, husband, parent and child of the deceased person, but with a proviso expanding the meaning of "parent" and "child" to include grandparents, grandchildren, stepparents and stepchildren. There is now considerable variation in state wrongful death statutes as to which relatives are to be compensated for what they have lost due to the death. For example, in some but not many states, a surviving brother and sister can receive damages. Grandchildren and grandparents may not be eligible. Numerous statutes have a provision for damages to go to the deceased's "next of kin." The statute may provide that damages are to be awarded to certain other relatives, or the deceased's next of kin, when the deceased was not survived by specific immediate family members such as a spouse or child. If one of the family members entitled to compensation subsequently dies, the claim might (or might not) survive to his estate. The legislation of each state must be examined for details. When the deceased was not survived by a family member eligible for compensation, the defendant can avoid liability.

The provisions for damages to go to surviving relatives require the legal relationship of spouse, parent, child, next of kin, etc., at the time of death. The survivor in an unmarried couple relationship does not qualify. (Parties to a "civil union" or "domestic partnership" do qualify, under the legislation in some jurisdictions that allows couples to formally establish this relationship.) Stepparents and stepchildren probably do not qualify without a specific provision for them in the applicable wrongful death statute, as in the original English statute. In the absence of legal adoption, the death of an adult who was acting "*in loco parentis*" is not equated with the death of a legal parent. The effect of adoption is not uniform, but it is likely to allow wrongful death damages to go to an adopting parent or adopted child and preclude a claim by the natural parent whose rights were terminated by the adoption. When a child is born outside marriage, there is now a legal parent-child relationship with the father as well as the mother. Any remaining discrimination in wrongful death law on grounds of illegitimacy is likely to be held unconstitutional, as a denial of equal protection, except conditioning an ex-nuptial child's claim to damages for the death of a father, or a father's claim for the death of a child, on some prior judicial determination of paternity or parent-child status. See Annot., 78 A.L.R.3d 1230. Under some statutes and a few judicial decisions, a parent's abandonment of the child or failure to provide support disqualifies the parent from receiving damages for the death of a child. See Annot., 53 A.L.R.3d 566.

Family members and others who lost income or support because of the death have no claim to compensation if they are not among the statutory beneficiaries—the categories of relatives specified in the wrongful death statute. Although there is historic basis for an action by a "master" when a "servant" is injured (see Chapter 10(B)), employers who suffer loss because of the death of an employee have no cause of action. See *Trump Taj Mahal Associates v. Costruzioni Aeronautiche Giovanni Agusta, S.p.A.*, 761 F. Supp. 1143 (D.N.J. 1991), aff'd, 958 F.2d 365 (3d Cir. 1992).

E. ASSESSMENT OF DAMAGES

Lord Campbell's Act provided that damages would be awarded for "the Injury resulting from such

Death" of each beneficiary. That would determine the distribution among the beneficiaries of what was recovered from the defendant. The statute provided no other guidance on the assessment of damages in wrongful death actions. Courts were required to decide what types of injury or loss were to be compensated and what was relevant to the assessment of damages. It soon became established in the case law that damages were to be given for losses of a "pecuniary" nature and not for loss of deceased's society, mental anguish, or other non-economic consequences of death. *Blake v. Midland Railway Co.*, (1852) 18 Q.B. 93, 118 Eng. Rep. 35; *Michigan Central Railroad Co. v. Vreeland*, 227 U.S. 59 (1913).

"Pecuniary loss" was not restricted to monetary losses. It meant losses of an economic nature. These included not only loss of the maintenance and gifts the deceased would have provided to the beneficiaries, but also loss of services within the household. Services that someone might be employed to provide, including child care, meal preparation, maintenance of the home and education of children, had an economic value, as did work in the family trade or farm. Loss of what the beneficiaries would have received from the deceased's earnings, other income and property also was and is an important element of damages. Much of this might consist of housing, food, clothing, payments for personal needs and wants, and education. It might include loss of a future inheritance.

The "pecuniary loss" rule came under pressure in the twentieth century, particularly when the deceased was a minor child. When wrongful death statutes were enacted in the nineteenth century, many children provided income for their families through work for employers or on the family farm, and children also did considerable work within their family households. Consequently, the death of a child might result in substantial "pecuniary loss." With the later decline of child labor and greatly increased costs of raising children, the death of a child was now unlikely to result in real economic loss for the child's parents, except when the child would have supported the parents to a large extent when they were elderly.

Troubled by the prospect that a restrictive pecuniary loss rule would result in minimal damages when a minor child was killed, some courts have reinterpreted wrongful death law to include loss of a child's society and companionship in the losses for which the child's parents could be compensated. *E.g.*, *Selders v. Armentrout*, 190 Neb. 275, 207 N.W.2d 686 (1973); *Green v. Bittner*, 85 N.J. 1, 424 A.2d 210 (1980). Society, companionship and affection might be considered services lost on account of the death. Excluding damages for loss of society, companionship and affection from awards for the death of a spouse has also been challenged and, in some cases, rejected. *E.g.*, *Flagtwet v. Smith*, 367 N.W.2d 188 (S.D. 1985). Statutes in numerous jurisdictions now specifically permit recovery for such losses by surviving spouses, parents or children, or at least surviving spouses. Awards of damages for this are likely to be high.

Without expansion of damages to include non-economic losses, awards for the death of someone who would not have engaged in paid work outside the home, such as a "non-working spouse" or retired person, can be quite low unless their household services are highly valued. A high value might be placed upon parental care, attention, guidance and training.

The standard rule has been that damages are not awarded for mental anguish or grief. This is not an economic loss or loss of something the deceased would have provided to other family members. In some states, the rule has been altered by statute or judicial decision.

In assessing damages, determination of what the deceased's life expectancy, earning capacity and income other than earnings would have been, but for the death, is important. The educational and career prospects of a young death victim might be inferred from the educational and career attainments of other family members. The type and degree of support or maintenance the deceased had provided to family members is highly relevant. Much else might be relevant to an assessment of damages for economic and (when allowed) non-economic losses, including evidence about the deceased's character traits and the relationship between the deceased and other family members. But some such evidence may be excluded as irrelevant or unduly prejudicial. *E.g.*, *Crenshaw v. McMinds*, 456 N.E.2d 433 (Ind. App. 1983) (twenty-year-old felony conviction); *Empire Metal Corp. v. Wohlwender*, 445 S.W.2d 685 (Ky.

1969) (deceased living in adultery); *Johnson v. Dobrosky*, 187 N.J. 594, 902 A.2d 238 (2006) (welfare fraud conviction, when no claim for loss of future financial contributions).

Support from unlawfully gained income. Occasionally there is evidence that the deceased's support of family members came from money obtained through unlawful activity. The deceased's earnings or income might have come from criminal activities. Another possibility is that the deceased's employment or business was unlawful because unlicensed or conducted in a prohibited location. An increasing number of cases involve people whose employment was illegal because of their immigration status. If the unlawful conduct was not so closely connected to the injury as to be a complete defense to liability, the defendant can be liable to a wrongful death action even if the deceased was engaged in unlawful employment or present illegally in the country at the time of the injury.

Beneficiaries of the action will probably not receive damages for loss of what would have come to them from unlawfully gained income. However, it is not assumed that because the deceased's income prior to death was from unlawful activity, future income used to support the deceased's family would also be unlawful. Damages could be awarded on the basis that the deceased person would have earned money legally in the future. Some cases indicate that the illegality of a foreign citizen's presence or employment in the United States is less important to the assessment of damages than the probability that the deceased would have been deported. See *Collins v. New York City Health and Hospitals Corp.*, 201 A.D.2d 447, 607 N.Y.S.2d 387 (1994); *Republic Waste Services, Ltd. v. Martinez*, 335 S.W.3d 401 (Tex. App. 2011).

Offsetting gains. Immediate family members may receive payment, property or support that to some extent offsets the economic loss resulting from the death. In principle the beneficiaries should receive compensation for their actual loss, but most of what they have received or will receive as a consequence of the death is not taken into account. Under the "collateral source rule," payments from life and accidental death insurance policies and other death benefits are not considered in assessment of the beneficiaries' losses. Receipt of an inheritance is, apparently, also disregarded, and in any event the "gain" may only be earlier receipt of what would have been inherited in the future.

Death of a married adult is often followed by remarriage of the surviving spouse. The survivor will then receive personal services, companionship and often considerable material support from the second husband or wife. The predominant rule in the United States (although not in other countries with similar wrongful death statutes) is that remarriage is not to be taken account in the assessment of damages for a surviving spouse. See Annot., 87 A.L.R.2d 252. This is based in part on the collateral source rule, but more on the proposition that damages should be based on conditions at the time of death, rather than subsequent events, and on policy considerations.

Remarriage would be deterred or postponed if it reduced damages. And courts do not want assessment of a surviving spouse's chances of remarriage.

If the deceased person was a parent as well as a spouse, the children of the marriage will acquire a stepparent when the surviving spouse remarries. In some instances they are legally adopted by the stepparent. It appears that support and services received from the stepparent will be disregarded in the assessment of damages for the children. See *Hardware State Bank v. Cotner*, 55 Ill. 2d 240, 302 N.E.2d 257 (1973).

Allocation and duplication of damages. Litigation of fatal injury claims is likely to involve a personal injury action that survives to the deceased person's estate as well as a wrongful death action. As discussed earlier (p. 40), a personal injury action may be precluded by a judgment or release of liability during the deceased person's lifetime, or by the statute of limitations. (State law differs on this.) But if the death occurred not long after the injury that caused it, the executor or administrator of the deceased person's estate will probably sue any defendants on both an action for the injury and an action under the wrongful death statute.

Some damages are clearly allocable to the wrongful death action. These include loss of the deceased person's services, loss of support and property benefits that would have come from sources other than the deceased's earnings, and (when allowed by state law) loss of the deceased's society, companionship, affection and the like. The amount recovered will go to the relatives eligible to receive damages under the wrongful death statute, according to their individual losses. Other damages are clearly allocable to the personal injury action. These include the costs of medical and other care, loss of earnings between the injury and the date of death, and the injured person's pain and suffering. The amount recovered in the personal injury action will go to the estate and be distributed to the heirs of the estate, after deductions for taxes, debts and expenses.

What is not clearly allocable to one of the two actions, and might lead to overlapping recovery of damages, is loss of earning capacity due to curtailment of the injured person's life and its consequences for the surviving family members. In personal injury actions litigated during the injured person's lifetime, when it is found that there will be a loss of potential earnings due to premature death caused by the injury, damages for this loss will usually be awarded. If damages for loss of earnings during the "lost years" are awarded in the personal injury action that survives to an injured person's estate and damages in the wrongful action include family members' loss of the support that would have come to them from the deceased person's earnings, the defendant is in effect made to pay twice for causing the loss of earning capacity.

There are a number of different positions on this problem that can be found in jurisdictions with wrongful death statutes. One, which does leave defendants exposed to "double recovery," is to allow both a claim for loss of earnings during the "lost years" in the personal injury action and claims for loss of support in the wrongful death action, including support that would have come from lost earnings, with a possible deduction from damages awarded in wrongful death actions for what the beneficiaries receive from the personal injury action damages as heirs of the estate. Another, which prioritizes compensation for loss of support over recovery by the deceased person's estate, is to award damages for loss of support from the deceased's earnings in the wrongful death action and deduct this from damages for loss of earning capacity in the personal injury action. Still another, which is effective to solve the "double recovery" problem but leaves some losses uncompensated, is to deny survival of a personal injury action when there is a cause of action for wrongful death. Numerically the main "solution" of the problem in the United States is to allow damages for loss of support from the deceased's earnings in the wrongful death action and limit damages for loss of earnings in the "survival" action to the loss preceding the date of the death. See Annot., 76 A.L.R.3d 125.

Recovery of funeral and burial expenses is another head of damages that is not clearly allocable to one of the two actions. Funeral and burial expenses are consequences of death, not injury to a living person, so they seem to be outside what can be recovered in a personal injury action, even one litigated as a "survival" action. As a consequence of death, funeral and burial expenses seem to fit within a claim for wrongful death. However, they are not a loss of benefits family members would have received from the deceased, which is the core concept of damages for wrongful death, and funeral expenses are often borne by the deceased's estate rather than by family members personally. Also, funeral and burial expenses may be viewed as inevitable rather than caused by death at a particular time (though perhaps different when the deceased was young). State law differs on whether funeral and burial expenses can be recovered in a wrongful death action, survival action or either, depending on who paid the expenses. In some states this is now specified by legislation. The prevailing position is to allow recovery in the wrongful death action.

CHAPTER 4

INTERFERENCE WITH FAMILY RELATIONSHIPS

A. INTRODUCTION

Family relationships may be impaired by conduct that causes estrangement or physical separation of spouses or parents and children. The common law developed a number of specific tort actions that could arise from interference with spousal or parent-child relationships. The ancestry of most is in the husband's action for loss of his wife's services and consortium and the master's action for loss of services of a servant, which could be used by a parent. These torts are often grouped under the title "intentional interference with family relationships." To be liable, the defendant must have acted intentionally in some way. There is no liability for failure to act or mere carelessness. However, a defendant can be liable for some of the torts without any intent to interfere with the plaintiff's family relationship.

Usually, the defendant is liable to the plaintiff without having committed a tort to the other family member. (The major exception is when the defendant is liable for battery or false imprisonment.) Damages include compensation for the plaintiff's emotional distress as well as for loss of services and consortium. In the past century there has been a strong movement toward abolition of these torts. However, it is far from complete, and a new tort of interference with child custody has emerged in recent years.

B. INTERFERENCE WITH SPOUSAL RELATIONSHIPS

1. ENTICEMENT AND HARBORING

The ancient action of a master for loss of the services of a servant (action *per quod servitium amisit*) was first recognized when a defendant had wrongfully persuaded a servant to leave the plaintiff's service or caused a servant not to return to the plaintiff's service. (See p. 95.) The action could also be brought when the defendant caused an injury to a servant that resulted in a loss of services. (See p. 151.) In the early seventeenth century, by analogy to the master's action, it was accepted that a husband could sue for loss of services and consortium when caused by the defendant's persuading the wife to leave the marital home, as well as for loss caused by injuring the plaintiff's wife. *Guy v. Livesey*, (1618) Cro. Jac. 501, 79 Eng. Rep. 428 (K.B.).

In the eighteenth century, two distinct wrongs were identified: "enticement" and "harboring." Enticement was to persuade or induce the plaintiff's wife to leave the home she had shared with the plaintiff. Harboring was to provide the plaintiff's wife with shelter and other necessities, so that she could remain apart from her husband. Liability required knowledge of the marriage and thus notice that a husband could be deprived of services and consortium as a consequence of the enticement or harboring. A defendant would also be subject to liability if he abducted the plaintiff's wife or detained her against her will. See *Place v. Searle*, [1932] 2 K.B. 497 (C.A.).

The defendant was not liable without some loss of spousal services or consortium. There might be no such loss in a harboring action if the wife would not have returned to her husband in any event. If misconduct by the plaintiff was one of the reasons why his wife left or did not return, this was not a defense to liability, although possibly relevant to the assessment of damages.

The torts of enticement and harboring became part of American tort law as well as English tort law. *E.g.*, *Hutcheson v. Peck*, 5 Johns. 196 (N.Y. Sup. Ct. 1809). However, they are scarcely known today. Harboring seems to have disappeared from American law. A contemporary American court surely would not find liability for harboring a spouse, even with knowledge that the other spouse objects. However, there could still be liability for inducing one spouse not to return to the other with a purpose of disrupting the marital relationship. Enticement has long been overshadowed by alienation of affections (see below). It is still a tort, but probably limited to defendants acting with a purpose to disrupt the marital relationship. Thus there would not be liability (absent such a purpose) for inducing the plaintiff's spouse to accept employment or prolonged medical treatment in a place distant from the place where the spouses had cohabitated. See Rest. 2d Torts § 684.

2. ALIENATION OF AFFECTIONS

Alienation of affections originally was a damages claim within enticement and harboring actions, but it emerged as a separate tort in nineteenth century U.S. cases. See *Heermance v. James,* 47 Barb. 120 (N.Y. Sup. Ct. 1866). (It was never a tort in English common law.) It has largely replaced enticement as a litigated tort. Departure of the plaintiff's spouse from the marital home is not required. The action is maintainable even if cohabitation continued, provided the spouse was "alienated" from the plaintiff because of the defendant's conduct. The focus is on the spouse's loss of affection for the plaintiff and how this deprived the plaintiff of spousal services and consortium that otherwise would have been enjoyed. When liability is established, much of the damages can be compensation for the plaintiff's emotional distress and embarrassment.

A defendant cannot be liable for only failing to prevent spousal alienation or causing it inadvertently. But whether alienation is strictly an intentional tort is debatable. Rest. 2d Torts § 683 would require a purpose to diminish or divert the spouse's affections for the plaintiff. However, it may be sufficient that the defendant knew of the marriage and acted in a wrongful manner calculated (in the sense of likely) to interfere with the marital relationship. See *Gibson v. Frowein*, 400 S.W.2d 418 (Mo. 1966). Thus, liability could be found when the defendant had an affair with the plaintiff's spouse and did not want or expect the plaintiff to notice a change in the marital relationship. See *Swearingen v. Vik*, 51 Wash. 2d 843, 322 P.2d 876 (1958). The defendant's conduct does not have to be the sole or principal cause of the alienation. Often there are other factors, including the plaintiff's conduct. It is sufficient that the defendant's conduct was one of the substantial causes. A defendant can be liable when there was already some alienation, including when the spouses had ceased cohabitation. *E.g.*, *McNelis v. Bruce*, 90 Ariz. 261, 367 P.2d 625 (1961). When the defendant's intervention prevented a reconciliation that otherwise would have occurred, or led to a total breakdown of the marriage, there is cause for liability. The spouses' divorce after the alienation does not bar liability.

One tends to think of defendants in alienation actions as people who wanted to take the plaintiff's place as a spouse or lover. However, many of the defendants sued for alienation of affections have been the plaintiff's in-laws, members of religious groups, and other persons who were in no sense romantic rivals of the plaintiff. Liability does not require that the defendant have the motive of taking the plaintiff's place. Persuasion of the spouse with an object of diminishing the spouse's affections for the plaintiff is sufficient.

Privilege. There has been much reluctance to find a spouse's parents liable for encouraging or assisting the spouse to leave the plaintiff when the parents believed this was in the best interests of the spouse. *E.g.*, *Oakman v. Belden*, 94 Me. 280, 47 A. 553 (1900). There is also a reluctance to find religious officials liable because of statements advancing their religious doctrine, even when it is a cause of spousal alienation. *E.g.*, *Bradesku v. Antion*, 21 Ohio App. 2d 67, 255 N.E.2d 265 (1969). Opinions in alienation actions against the spouse's parents, other immediate family members and religious officials recognize a privilege against liability when their advice to or persuasion of the spouse was due to a reasonable, or at least good faith, belief that this was in the spouse's best interests. (Conduct actuated primarily by hostility toward the plaintiff or the marriage would not be privileged, and the privilege would not include fraudulent statements.) Presumably, professional advisors such as attorneys and physicians would also be privileged as to advice given on reasonable grounds. Other persons might have a privilege when it is reasonable to provide advice because of the defendant's relationship with the spouse or the spouse's request for advice or assistance. See Rest. 2d Torts § 686.

3. CRIMINAL CONVERSATION

Criminal conversation is very different from other torts discussed in this chapter. The cause of action arises from the defendant's having sexual intercourse with the plaintiff's spouse. ("Criminal conversation" is a euphemism for this.) Liability requires no loss of spousal services, consortium or affection. Historically the action came into the common law from ecclesiastical law, in which intercourse with another man's wife was unlawful. Only the person who had sex with the plaintiff's spouse is liable. The erring spouse is not liable. *Cf.*

Cluck v. Cluck, 712 S.W.2d 599 (Tex. App. 1986) (spouse not liable for alienation of affections).

Obviously the tort includes an intentional act by the defendant, but in significant respects criminal conversation is a strict liability tort. There is no requirement that the defendant know or have reason to know that his sexual partner was married. A defendant can be liable even if the partner misled him about her marital status. No persuasion or inducement by the defendant is required. There can be liability if the spouse seduced the defendant. The spouse's alienation or separation from the plaintiff because of the plaintiff's misconduct is no defense. See *Bearbower v. Merry*, 266 N.W.2d 128 (Iowa 1978). The only substantive defense is the plaintiff's having consented to the spouse's adultery with the defendant. (Unlikely but not unheard of. See *Kaye v. Newhall*, 356 Mass. 300, 249 N.E.2d 583 (1969).)

A claim of criminal conversation has often been joined to an action for alienation of affections. In both, substantial damages can be obtained for the plaintiff's emotional distress and embarrassment, as well as for loss of consortium and household services. Punitive damages can also be awarded.

4. ACTIONS BY WIVES

As discussed earlier (pp. 11–12), under English common law a wife had no cause of action for loss of consortium when her husband was physically injured. The rule was the same when a wife suffered loss of consortium or impairment of a marital relationship because of enticement or harboring of her husband or "criminal conversation": there was no cause of action. While this was originally the rule in the United States, a considerable number of American cases extended to wives the right to sue for these torts or alienation of affections. This occurred earlier than extension to wives of the right to sue when a husband was injured. Today it is clear that wives have the same entitlements to the actions as husbands. *E.g.*, *Emerson v. Fleming*, 127 Ga. App. 296, 193 S.E.2d 249 (1972).

5. INJUNCTIVE RELIEF

In principle, if an award of damages would be an inadequate remedy, a court can grant an injunction in order to prevent harm. There have been a number of reported cases in which the plaintiff sought an injunction against the defendant's continuing an association with the plaintiff's spouse, or more specifically against conduct that included alienation of affection or adultery. *E.g.*, *Witte v. Bauderer*, 255 S.W. 1016 (Tex. App. 1923). The wisdom and practicality of such an injunction have long been doubted. See *Snedaker v. King*, 111 Ohio St. 225, 145 N.E. 15 (1924). Injunctive relief in cases of alienation of affections, criminal conversation or other interference with a spousal relationship is unlikely but not impossible, even in jurisdictions that have abolished damages claims for these torts. See *Henley v. Rockett*, 243 Ala. 172, 8 So. 2d 852 (1942).

C. INTERFERENCE WITH PARENT-CHILD RELATIONSHIPS

1. INTRODUCTION; ACTIONS FOR LOSS OF SERVICES

Under English common law, the relationship of husband and wife entitled a husband to sue for damages when the defendant's wrongful conduct caused the husband to lose the services and consortium of his wife. The relationship of parent and child gave the parent no similar entitlement to sue when the defendant's conduct interfered with the relationship. However, an aggrieved parent could use the master's action for loss of services, alleging that the child was the parent's servant and the parent had lost performance of services. This could be used not only when the child was physically injured as a result of a tort (see p. 17), but also when other wrongful conduct involving the child caused some loss of services. Four distinct wrongs were identified: abduction, enticement, harboring and seduction.

As in cases of injuries to children, that the parent's action had to fit the requirements of a master's action *per quod servitium amisit* limited potential liability. The child's father was considered the child's master, so the action was generally not available to mothers unless the father had died or abandoned the child. The action could not be maintained if the child was too young to provide services or if other circumstances indicated that there was no loss of services, as when the child had already left the family home or was incapable of providing household services. On the other hand, fathers of adult daughters were allowed to maintain seduction actions on proof of some actual loss of services to the father.

In the United States, over time the requirement of pleading and proving loss of services became a technicality. It was sufficient to allege an entitlement to the child's services. In some cases, notably *Pickle v. Page*, 252 N.Y. 474, 169 N.E. 650 (1930) (an action for abduction), it was decided that no loss of services need be proved or alleged. It became possible for mothers who had, or were entitled to have, custody to bring suit. In contrast to actions arising from a child's physical injury, when liability was established damages were awarded primarily for the plaintiff's distress and sense of outrage, loss of the child's society, and injury to family honor rather than for loss of services rendered by the child.

2. SEDUCTION

Until recently, seduction was the most frequently litigated of this group of torts. Although in form often an action for loss of services, it was in substance an action utilized to punish the defendant for sexual relations with the plaintiff's unmarried daughter and assuage the outrage and injury to reputation of her family. The loss of services was often trivial. An action for seduction shared some of the characteristics of actions brought by parents when a child was injured. The action arose because the defendant's conduct affected the child physically—in this instance, by causing pregnancy or illness—and caused the plaintiff loss of the child's services for a time. The defendant did not have to intend any loss of services or society to the parent. A plaintiff could recover medical expenses incurred because of the child's condition. However, an action based on injury to a child required that the defendant commit an actionable tort to the child, whereas a seduction action would lie when there was no tort because of the daughter's consent. (It would also lie when there was no valid consent.) In principle, an action could be brought for seduction of a son, if it caused an illness or injury that resulted in some loss of services to a parent; but there seems to be no reported case.

Despite the name of the tort, there was no requirement that the defendant engage in seduction in its popular meaning. It did not matter why the intercourse occurred. Culpable conduct by the plaintiff's daughter was no defense. The only substantive defense was the plaintiff's consent, which was not likely to be proved. The daughter's consent barred her bringing suit, unless it was legally ineffective because of her age, the defendant's deceit or other reason. However, over a dozen states enacted laws permitting actions by a seduced female, at least when under the age of majority.

3. ABDUCTION, ENTICEMENT, HARBORING

The common law action for loss of services could also be brought when the defendant intentionally caused physical separation of the child from a parent entitled to the custody of a child. Three different types of wrongful conduct became grounds for an action: abduction, enticement and harboring. Abduction was to take away the child (not necessarily against the will of the child). Enticement was to persuade or induce the child to leave the parental home. Harboring was to provide the child with shelter or other necessities so that the child could remain away from the plaintiff's household.

These have been considered intentional torts because in principle the defendant would not be liable without knowledge that his conduct would cause separation of a child from a parent who did not consent to this. However, the child's age and the absence of parental consent might be sufficient notice. See *Caughey v. Smith*, 47 N.Y. 244 (1872). Rest. 2d Torts § 700 would limit liability to those who actually knew the child's parent did not consent. § 700 also rejects liability for simply harboring a child, in the sense of providing "shelter and sustenance" to a child known to have left home without the parent's permission. Liability is limited to defendants who have in some other way induced the child not to return to the parent.

Abduction, enticement and harboring were, for some time, scarcely visible in American tort law. Occasionally there was a reported case involving an intra-family conflict, or a defendant who allegedly induced a teenager to enter employment in a distant locale without parental consent—as in *Tavlinksy v. Ringling Bros. Circus Co.*, 113 Neb. 632, 204 N.W. 388 (1925), in which a fifteen-year-old left home to work for a circus. But in the later part of the twentieth century the torts acquired a higher profile, primarily because of parental claims that the child's other parent, or members of the other parent's family, committed a tort in taking the child away from the plaintiff or denying access to the child. *E.g.*, *Rosefield v. Rosefield*, 221 Cal. App. 2d 431, 34 Cal. Rptr. 479 (1963). There were also some prominent actions brought against religious groups for what in substance was abduction, enticement or harboring of a child, such as *Murphy v. I.S.K.Con. of New England, Inc.*, 409 Mass. 842, 571 N.E.2d 340 (1991). Pleading and proving that the plaintiff had lost the services of the child was no longer required, at least beyond pleading that the plaintiff was entitled to the child's services. While the actions were used primarily to obtain a judgment for damages, injunctive relief requiring the defendant to refrain from causing the child not to return to the plaintiff was sometimes granted.

Particularly in the cases in which one parent sued the other parent, or relatives assisting the other parent in taking away the child, it was necessary for courts to decide what right to custody was necessary to maintain the action and whether a parent could be liable for taking or keeping the parent's own child. It could no longer be held that any right of action was in the child's father rather than the child's mother. The position that emerged was that one parent could maintain an action against other parent, or those acting on behalf of the parent, if the plaintiff had the sole legal right of custody by court order or otherwise. If the right to custody of the child was shared between the plaintiff and the defendant, an action would not lie. See Annot., 49 A.L.R.4th 7; Rest. 2d Torts § 700, comment *c*.

Defendants sued for abduction, enticement or harboring a child tend to justify their actions by contending that they acted in the best interests of the child. A belief that it would be better for the child if the child did not remain with or return to the plaintiff is not in itself a defense, even if the belief is reasonable. Greater justification is needed for interference with a parent's right to possession of a minor child. What is a valid defense to liability is the defendant having reasonable grounds to believe that there would be a high risk of imminent harm to the child if the child remained with or returned to the plaintiff. See Rest. 2d Torts § 700, comment *e*.

4. INTERFERENCE WITH CHILD CUSTODY AND VISITATION

Intentional interference with child custody (or custody rights) is now recognized in the United States as a distinct tort in itself. To a large extent, this is an outgrowth of modern cases involving abduction, enticement or harboring in which what was required for liability was the plaintiff's having a right to custody of the child and the defendant's intentionally depriving the plaintiff of physical custody by taking, keeping or hiding the child. See *Wyatt v. McDermott*, 283 Va. 685, 725 S.E.2d 555 (2012); Annot., 103 A.L.R.6th 461. Under Rest. 2d Torts § 700, there is liability when a defendant, with knowledge that the parent does not consent, "abducts or otherwise compels or induces a minor child to leave a parent legally entitled to its custody or not to return to the parent." Damages can include compensation for loss of the child's companionship, the plaintiff's mental anguish, and costs incurred in recovering possession of the child, as well as for any loss of services. They are not subject to the limitations of other remedies for violations of judicial custody orders.

As in the prior generation of cases involving abduction, enticement or harboring, the plaintiff's right to custody of the child vis-à-vis the defendant is a critical limitation of liability for interference with child custody. Parents who have a joint right of custody can bring an action against a third party. See *Anonymous v. Anonymous*, 672 So. 2d 787 (Ala. 1995). But under most authority, when one parent sues the other parent, or those who assisted the other parent in taking or keeping the child, the plaintiff must have had the sole right to custody by court order, agreement or otherwise. A parent who had custodial rights at the time would not be liable and a non-custodial parent would have no cause of action for a defendant's intentionally depriving the plaintiff of visitation or other contact with the child, even over a long period of time. See *Cosner v. Ridinger*, 882 P.2d 1243 (Wyo. 1994). However, in *Khalifa v. Shannon*, 404 Md. 107, 945 A.2d 1244 (2008), the court allowed an action for "substantial" interference with parental visitation rights—in this instance, taking the children to Egypt and thereby preventing the plaintiff from seeing them for years.

In *Larson v. Dunn*, 460 N.W.2d 39 (Minn. 1990), a majority of the court refused to accept intentional interference with custodial rights as a tort cause of action. The majority believed that such an action would intensify intrafamily conflict—it would be a "new weapon" in "intrafamily warfare"—and detrimentally affect the children involved by placing them in the middle of a vigorous and "probably vicious" lawsuit. Tort liability would not deter abductions, especially when a parent or grandparent believed the child was in danger of harm. Although followed in *Zaharias v. Gammill*, 844 P.2d 137 (Okla. 1992), the decision in *Larson v. Dunn* has not gained much support in other states.

When an action for interference with custody is not available because the plaintiff did not have the necessary right to custody, or because the action is not recognized under state law, an action for infliction of severe emotional distress might lie for taking or withholding the plaintiff's child if the conduct is egregious. See *Pankratz v. Willis*, 155 Ariz. 8, 744 P.2d 1182 (Ct. App. 1987).

5. ALIENATION OF CHILD'S AFFECTIONS

When a defendant is liable for intentionally causing a child to leave or remain separated from a parent, the damages can include compensation for alienation of the child's affection for the parent. Recognition of alienation of affections as a separate tort, rather than only a head of damages, when the defendant caused one spouse to be alienated from the other, naturally suggests that alienation of affections of a child is, likewise, a tort in itself. However, the prevailing position has long been and still remains that a parent has no cause of action for the alienation of a child's affections. See Annot., 60 A.L.R.3d 931; Rest. 2d Torts § 699. In part this was because the common law basis for a parent's action for interference with parent-child relations was the plaintiff's entitlement to the child's services and, later, entitlement to custody of the child. It was not loss of consortium, as in an action for interference with spousal relations. See *Pyle v. Waechter*, 202 Iowa 695, 210 N.W. 926 (1926).

An action for alienation of affections of a child has been permitted in a few cases. *Strode v. Gleason*, 9 Wash. App. 13, 510 P.2d 250 (1973), recognized an action for "malicious" alienation of a minor's affection ("malice" being equated to unjustified interference with the parent-child relationship). In *Hershey v. Hershey*, 467 N.W.2d 484 (S.D. 1991), an alienation action was allowed to a man whose former wife, after being awarded custody of the child, concealed the child's whereabouts for fourteen years. However, in most jurisdictions there is no recognized action for alienation of a child's affections. With the widespread abolition of actions for alienation of a spouse's affections (see pp. 71–74) and concern about potential use of a child alienation action as a "strategic tool" when a marriage has broken down, courts are unlikely to be persuaded to entertain such an action. See *Bock v. Lindquist*, 278 N.W.2d 326 (Minn. 1979).

6. ENTICEMENT OF PARENT AND ALIENATION OF PARENTAL AFFECTIONS

With enticement of a spouse or child, *i.e.*, inducing the spouse or child to leave the family home, being recognized torts, it is not surprising that there would be attempts to establish liability for causing a child's parent to depart from the family home and leave the child without parental support, guidance, protection and affection. However, the common law never accepted that a child had an interest protected by tort law in a parent's presence, services or companionship. The orthodox position is that there is no action for enticement of a parent. See *Morrow v. Yannantuono*, 152 Misc. 134, 273 N.Y.S. 912 (Sup. Ct. 1934); *Kane v. Quigley*, 1 Ohio St. 2d 1, 203 N.E.2d 338 (1964). In the 1940s, there were some significant cases upholding such an action. The opinions reasoned that a minor child's relationship with a parent should be protected from wrongful interference and that the absence of precedent for the action was not reason to deny its existence. *Russick v. Hicks*, 85 F. Supp. 281 (W.D. Mich. 1949); *Miller v. Monsen*, 228 Minn. 400, 37 N.W.2d 543 (1949). But the decisions in these cases have not been followed in recent times.

There have also been attempts to establish liability for alienation of a parent's affections for a child. These have been largely unsuccessful. See Annot., 60 A.L.R.3d 931; *Brent v. Mathis*, 154 So. 3d 842 (Miss. 2014). In addition to the absence of precedent for the action, courts have found reasons of policy for rejecting it, including how the action would be used by the child's other parent (bringing suit on behalf of the child) and how it might control a parent's personal associations. The widespread abolition of actions for alienation of a spouse's affections has also been an influence. See *Zarrella v. Robinson*, 492 A.2d 833 (R.I. 1985); *Scholberg v. Itnyre*, 264 Wis. 211, 58 N.W.2d 698 (1953).

It is probable in such cases that the defendant's object was to have a relationship with the child's parent, not to alienate the parent from the child or harm the child's interest in having the care and affection of a parent. And arguably if anyone is to be liable to the child it should be the parent who left the child, given the parent's primary responsibility for the welfare and emotional support of the child. However, for all the possible tort actions involving interference with family relationships, any action can only be brought against a third party, not the person in a family relationship with the plaintiff. See *Hobbs v. Christenson*, 198 Cal. App. 3d 189, 243 Cal. Rptr. 633 (1988).

D. ABOLITION OF ACTIONS

1. HEART BALM STATUTES

In the 1930s there was a concerted effort to have state legislatures enact statutes abolishing actions for alienation of affections, criminal conversation, seduction and breach of promise of marriage. The actions were well-known to the public because of newspaper reportage of lawsuits. Liability for the torts and breach of promise was strongly criticized—

primarily on the grounds that suits were brought for mercenary or vindictive motives; they caused embarrassment to innocent persons, including family members of the parties; damages were excessive; some claims were feigned; and the existence of the actions provided opportunities for extortionate settlements and blackmail. When suits were threatened, targets would pay substantial sums to avoid being sued because of the harm to reputation that would result.

Lawsuits seeking damages for alienation, criminal conversation, seduction and breach of promise were derisively called "heart balm" suits. Accordingly, legislation to abolish liability became known as "heart balm statutes" (or sometimes "anti-heart balm statutes"). During the 1930s such legislation was enacted in a number of states, including New York and Pennsylvania. Numerous other states enacted similar legislation in later years, especially in conjunction with the movement away from fault-based divorce and legal sanctions for morally disapproved behavior. Heart balm statutes have now been enacted in the great majority of states. Most, but not all, abolish both alienation of affections and criminal conversation. Many also abolish or limit liability for seduction.

2. JUDICIAL ABOLITION

In recent decades, some defendants have contended in appellate courts that liability for alienation of affections and criminal conversation should be abolished by judicial decision. While some courts decided that abolition of the torts was a decision to be made by the state legislature rather than the court, courts in a number of states engaged the merits of abolishing or retaining liability. In about a dozen, criminal conversation was abolished as a tort by judicial decision. Reasons found persuasive included the perception that the criminal conversation action was founded upon antiquated notions of a wife's body being the property of her husband; the unfairness of the action in allowing no defenses and holding the defendant (but not the spouse committing adultery) liable regardless of whether the defendant knew the person with whom (s)he had sexual relations was married, whether the plaintiff's own conduct was a cause of the adultery, and whether harm to the marital relationship actually resulted; the lack of deterrent effect; and the reasons discussed above for enactment of "heart balm statutes," including the potential use of the action for vindictive purposes or to extract payment by threatening a lawsuit. See *Saunders v. Alford*, 607 So. 2d 1214 (Miss. 1992).

There has been more division among and within courts about abolition of liability for alienation of spousal affections. For some judges, the tort was justifiable as a remedy for, and possible deterrent of, intentional interference with a marital relationship that resulted in marital breakdown. When a defendant's wrongful conduct was one of the causes of marital breakdown, liability was warranted even though there were other causes. Estranged spouses should have an opportunity to reconcile without interference by a third party. Alienation of affections liability lacked the unfairness of criminal conversation, as a defendant could not be liable without knowledge of the marriage and the risk of injuring it. That an alienation action might be brought for vindictive purposes or threatened as a form of blackmail, had embarrassing effects and lacked a definite standard for measuring damages was not sufficient reason for abolition. These were attributes of a number of other legal claims. See *Nelson v. Jacobsen*, 669 P.2d 1207 (Utah 1983).

In a larger number of cases, arguments for abolition prevailed. These included: potential liability does not actually have deterrent effects or preserve marital harmony; the alienation action is based on the false premise that third parties break up otherwise viable marriages; it is usually brought for vindictive reasons after a marriage has broken down; it is embarrassing not only to the parties but also other family members, including children, and infringes their dignity; damage awards have few standards and are influenced by disapproval of the defendant's conduct and sympathy for the plaintiff; and the action suggests that a spouse's affections can be sold for a monetary payment. See *O'Neil v. Schukardt*, 112 Idaho 472, 733 P.2d 693 (1986).

Through enactment of heart balm statutes or judicial decision, criminal conversation and alienation of affections are no longer litigated in most states. (The main exception is North Carolina.)

3. ACTIONS BARRED BY STATUTORY OR JUDICIAL ABOLITION

If a state statute or court decision has abolished or excluded liability for alienation of affections, criminal conversation or seduction, then clearly it bans an action explicitly brought as a claim for alienation, criminal conversation or seduction. Such a statute or decision is also likely to bar a claim under another tort, such as infliction of emotional distress, if the alleged facts are in substance what would be the basis of a claim for alienation, criminal conversation or seduction. See *McDermott v. Reynolds*, 260 Va. 98, 530 S.E.2d 902 (2000). If a professional providing marriage counselling is sued on allegations that the defendant began an affair with the plaintiff's spouse and damaged the marriage, this is likely to be treated as an action barred by the heart balm statute when only the plaintiff's spouse was counselled. But it could be considered a negligence or malpractice action that is not barred if the defendant counselled the plaintiff as well as the spouse. See *Weaver v. Union Carbide Corp.*, 180 W. Va. 556, 378 S.E.2d 105 (1989). A court might decide that the statute abolished by implication a tort not named in it. This could happen if the plaintiff sued for enticement of a spouse. See *Haskins v. Bias*, 2 Ohio App. 3d 297, 441 N.E.2d 842 (1981). In *State ex rel. Golden v. Kaufman*, 236 W. Va. 635, 760 S.E.2d 883 (2014), the court decided that the statutory abolition of alienation of affections actions also abolished actions for criminal conversation, even though the statute's omission of criminal conversation must have been deliberate. *Contra, Di Blasio v. Kolodner*, 233 Md. 512, 197 A.2d 245 (1964).

For the statutes that do explicitly bar alienation of affections actions, there is the question of whether this applies only to alienation of spouse's affections or extends to alienation of a child or parent. As the legislature probably did not contemplate possible actions for child or parent alienation (or enticement) when it enacted the heart balm statute, and they may be less objectionable than actions arising from sexual rivalry or misconduct, there is an argument that such actions were not abolished by the statute. It has been held that the statute does abolish actions for alienation of a child or parent. *Rudley v. Tobias*, 84 Cal. App. 2d 454, 190 P.2d 984 (1948); *Bouchard v. Sundberg*, 80 Conn. App. 180, 834 A.2d 744 (2003). But this is not an unanimous view. The court in *Russick v. Hicks*, 85 F. Supp. 281 (W.D. Mich. 1949), decided that the state heart balm statute did not bar an action for causing the plaintiffs' mother to desert them and leave the family home. The state legislature responded by amending the statute to specify abolition of actions for "alienation of the affections of any person, animal, or thing capable of feeling affection, whatsoever." Mich. Comp. Laws § 600.2901(1).

CHAPTER 5
WRONGFUL BIRTH

A. INTRODUCTION

"Wrongful death" is wrongfully causing a human being to die. "Wrongful birth" is wrongfully causing a human being to be born. It is a problematic concept. How can the birth of a baby be an injury to either the baby or its parents? And if it is an injury, who could have caused it other than the baby's biological parents? The standard answer to the second question is that in tort law, a person's conduct can be considered a cause of an event if the event would not otherwise have occurred. Consequently, the conduct of someone other than the baby's parents can be considered a cause of a birth if the birth probably would not have occurred without that conduct. The first question is not so readily answered, and in any event identifying an injury and some causal connection does not necessarily mean that there should be liability.

Wrongful birth actions are suits by parents of a child born alive, alleging that they did not want the birth to occur and that it occurred because of negligence or other tortious conduct on the part of the defendant. (If the result of an unwanted pregnancy was a miscarriage, stillbirth or termination of the pregnancy, the action would be for personal injury to the mother.) Sometimes the term "wrongful pregnancy" or "wrongful conception" is applied to claims involving unwanted pregnancies resulting in the birth of healthy children, as distinct from claims involving the birth of disabled children. The term "wrongful life" is used for an action that is or could be brought by the child that was born.

Whether wrongful birth involves interference with family relationships is debatable. It is sometimes considered an interference with the personal, and now constitutionally protected, right to make decisions about procreation and continuance of a pregnancy. Wrongful birth claims could be viewed as an extension of personal injury law, with defendants subject to liability because negligence or other conduct that is a basis of liability resulted in personal injury to the mother—the pregnancy and childbirth. However, the main question today is not whether a defendant can be liable to the mother for causing pregnancy and birth, but whether there is liability for the non-physical consequences of birth, especially the costs and burdens of raising the child. These consequences do affect family relationships. Wrongful birth also has an association with negligence liability for economic loss (see Chapter 10), as the costs of bringing up the child do not stem from pregnancy's physical effects on the mother.

B. BIRTH OF HEALTHY CHILD

The most typical wrongful birth action involving the birth of a healthy child alleges that a medical procedure intended to prevent pregnancy, such as a sterilization operation, was performed negligently. Providers of birth control products and pharmaceuticals might be sued for causing a pregnancy on allegations of negligence, or that the product was defective. Health care professionals, and other persons responsible for conducting or interpreting medical tests, might be sued on allegations that negligence resulted in a patient being inaccurately informed about the patient's fertility. An action could also be brought on a claim that there was a negligent failure to inform a patient or test client that she was pregnant. In this instance it would be necessary for the plaintiff to allege that she would have had an abortion procedure had she known of the pregnancy in time. The question of liability for the costs of raising a child might arise if the defendant was liable for a failure to protect the plaintiff from sexual assault and pregnancy resulted from the assault.

In judicial decisions on the question, the prevailing view has always been that a defendant is not liable for the costs and other burdens of raising the child. See Annot., 89 A.L.R.4th 632. The rationales of older cases were that the birth of a normal child cannot be regarded as an injury and that liability would be contrary to public policy. See *Terrell v. Garcia*, 496 S.W.2d 124 (Tex. Civ. App. 1973). Additional rationales are prominent in later cases. These include that an assessment of damages would be speculative, especially if benefits the parents derived from their relationship with the child were taken into account; a belief that the benefits, including emotional rewards, of having a child always outweigh the costs; and concern that it would be emotionally harmful to the child to learn of the litigation and that the child was unwanted. Also, while it is clear that failure to terminate the pregnancy or put the child up for adoption is not regarded as a failure to mitigate damages, the fact that the parents could have avoided the damages claimed from the defendants has been of some influence, in part because it arguably implies that the parents thought that the benefits of raising the child outweighed the burdens. Probably what has had the most influence, even if not articulated in the court's opinion, is the belief that to hold defendants liable for the costs of raising a child to maturity, and relieve the plaintiffs of costs that parents normally bear, would be disproportionate to the defendants' fault and unfair. See *Boone v. Mullendore*, 416 So. 2d 718 (Ala. 1982); *McKernan v. Aasheim*, 102 Wash. 2d 411, 687 P.2d 850 (1984).

Opposed to this are a number of decisions in state appellate courts allowing recovery of the costs of raising the child. In the most prominent decision, *Sherlock v. Stillwater Clinic*, 260 N.W.2d 169, 174 (Minn. 1977), the court stated:

> Pretermitting moral and theological considerations, we are not persuaded that public policy considerations can properly be used to deny recovery to parents of an unplanned, healthy child of all damages proximately caused by a negligently performed sterilization operation. Analytically, such an action is indistinguishable from an ordinary medical negligence action where a plaintiff alleges that a physician has breached a duty of care owed to him with resulting injurious consequences. Where the purpose of the physician's actions is to prevent conception or birth, elementary

> justice requires that he be held legally responsible for the consequences which have in fact occurred.

Liability for the cost of raising the child to the age of maturity would serve the useful purpose of deterring the negligent performance of sterilization operations. The court thought it "myopic" to declare that the benefits of having a child outweighed the costs as a matter of law, given that millions of Americans used various methods of birth control, including sterilization, in order to prevent a birth. And it implied that liability for birth resulting from negligence in performance of a birth control or abortion procedure cannot be contrary to public policy because the "right to limit procreation" is a constitutional right under *Griswold v. Connecticut*, 381 U.S. 479 (1965), and *Roe v. Wade*, 410 U.S. 113 (1973).

A conspicuous feature of some of the cases allowing damages for the costs of raising the child is the court's decision to allow an offset for the benefits to the parents of having the child: the affection, joy, companionship and assistance the parents would receive. See, in addition to *Sherlock*, *University of Arizona Health Sciences Center v. Superior Court*, 136 Ariz. 579, 667 P.2d 1294 (1983). *Contra*, *Marciniak v. Lundborg*, 153 Wis. 2d 59, 450 N.W.2d 243 (1990). Such an emphasis on offsetting the benefits of the "injury" against its costs, and allowing an offset for non-economic benefits against the economic costs resulting from an injury, is unusual in tort cases. It seems to be a pragmatic attempt to limit the damages awarded for wrongful birth to moderate amounts.

While many people wish to avoid pregnancy and birth because of the burden and expense of raising a child, or adverse social consequences (as when the parents are not married to each other), in other instances the reason is that pregnancy would or might be damaging to the mother's health. If this is the case, the costs of raising the child may not be considered a legal injury to the parent. See *Hartke v. McKelway*, 228 U.S. App. D.C. 139, 707 F.2d 1544 (1983). The same reasoning could apply if the plaintiffs wanted to avoid childbirth because of the risk that the child would be disabled but the child was not disabled.

C. BIRTH OF DISABLED CHILD

Distinct from the cases discussed in the previous section are cases in which the parents' reason to avoid the birth of a child was the risk, or known certainty, that the child would be disabled because of a genetic condition or illness or injury during pregnancy, and a disabled child was born. When the parents were aware of the risk prior the child's conception, the basis of the claim against the defendant usually would be similar to the basis of liability in a case arising from the birth of a healthy child—for example, negligent performance of a procedure intended to prevent pregnancy, or failure to correctly advise a patient about fertility or sterilization. But it could be an alleged failure to correctly advise the parents of the high probability that a future child would be disabled. When the parents were not aware of the risk prior to conception, the allegation against the defendant is likely to be that because of the defendant's negligence, the plaintiff was not informed of the child's defective condition, or its probability, and had the plaintiff been informed in time the pregnancy would have been terminated. The alleged negligence would be some failure to correctly perform or report to the parent a test or diagnostic procedure that would indicate that the child had (or was likely to have) a serious defect or injury. As in healthy child cases, the birth of a child might also result from a failure to correctly inform the mother that she was pregnant or negligent performance of an abortion.

Speck v. Finegold, 497 Pa. 77, 439 A.2d 110 (1981), is an egregious example of multiple failures. Mr. and Mrs. Speck wanted to prevent additional pregnancies because their two daughters suffered from neurofibromatosis, a crippling and disfiguring hereditary disease. For this purpose, Mr. Speck had a vasectomy. He was assured that it was effective, but it was not. Mrs. Speck became pregnant. To prevent birth, she had an abortion. The surgeon advised her that the operation was successful and the pregnancy had been terminated. But it was not. Mrs. Speck gave birth to another daughter affected with neurofibromatosis.

While the majority position is that there is no liability for the costs of raising a healthy child, most of the relevant decisions have allowed recovery of at least the extraordinary costs of raising the child when parents wanted to avoid the birth of a disabled child and a disabled child was born. *E.g.*, *Keel v. Banach*, 624 So. 2d 1022 (Ala. 1993); *Smith v. Cote*, 128 N.M. 231, 513 A.2d 341 (1986). The primary reason for these decisions is clearly to enable parents to obtain compensation for the major expenses they would incur for the treatment, care, education and assistance of a seriously disabled child. The cases are divided on whether the parents are to receive damages for emotional distress due to child's condition and "normal" costs—those that would have been incurred in raising a child who was not disabled. There is also disagreement on recovery for costs to be incurred after the child is no longer a minor. In some cases, such as *Blake v. Cruz*, 108 Idaho 253, 698 P.2d 315 (1984), the court has directed the type of offset for the emotional benefits of raising the child seen in actions for the birth of a healthy child. *Contra, Arche v. United States Department of Army*, 247 Kan. 276, 798 P.2d 477 (1990).

There is no specific rule concerning how serious the child's disability must be. The plaintiff in each action must establish that the anticipated disability, considered with the probability of its occurrence, was sufficiently serious that the plaintiff would have terminated the pregnancy or prevented conception. It is usually assumed that both parents can maintain the action when they are a married couple who are both raising the child. But it might be decided that the defendant owed no duty to the father when the father was not the defendant's patient or test client. In *Plowman v. Fort Madison Community Hospital*, 896 N.W.2d 393 (Iowa 2017), the court held that there was a duty to the father, even though there was no physician-patient relationship and it was the mother who would have made the ultimate decision to terminate the pregnancy if informed of the child's abnormalities.

Excepting decisions subsequently overruled, only a few state supreme courts have decided that damages would not be awarded for at least expenses due to the disabled child's condition. The leading case so deciding is *Azzolino v. Dingfelder*, 315 N.C. 103, 337 S.E.2d 528 (1985). The court was "unwilling to say that life, even life with severe defects, may ever amount to a legal injury." It believed that wrongful birth claims did not fit within traditional tort concepts of causation, injury and measure of damages. The child's genetic defect was not caused by the defendants. The court did not want to have doctors held liable because of a parental decision that the child would have been aborted if the defect had been known. See also *Atlanta Obstetrics & Gynecology Group v. Abelson*, 260 Ga. 711, 398 S.E.2d 557 (1990). There were several dissents in both cases.

Legislative restrictions. A number of states have statutes barring or limiting claims for wrongful birth or wrongful life (discussed in the next section). *E.g.*, Ariz. Rev. Stat. 12–719; Kan. Stat. Ann. § 60–1906, Mich. Comp. Laws § 600.2971. The enactment of the statutes is due primarily to the association of wrongful birth and wrongful life actions with abortion. Depending on the terms and interpretation of the particular statute, it may bar claims in which it is alleged that the pregnancy would have been terminated if the parents had known of the pregnancy or the child's disability, but not claims of negligence preceding the child's conception. See *Molloy v. Meier*, 679 N.W.2d 711 (Minn. 2004).

D. WRONGFUL LIFE

An action for "wrongful life" is one that was or might be brought by the child that was born. In most reported cases, the child was born with a serious disability. Damages were sought for the expenses of meeting the child's needs (treatment, care, special education, equipment, etc.) for the duration of the child's life, loss of earning capacity due to the child's condition, and physical and emotional pain and suffering. In other cases, the child had no physical defect. The action was to claim damages for other disadvantages the child would suffer from as a result of being born.

Disabled child. In most of the cases where a wrongful life action was brought on behalf of a disabled child, the court has decided that there is no liability. *E.g., Siemieniec v. Lutheran General Hospital*, 117 Ill. 2d 230, 512 N.E.2d 691 (1987); *Kassama v. Magat*, 368 Md. 113, 792 A.2d 1102 (2002). The principal reasons given in the opinions are that being born alive, even with a serious defect, cannot be regarded legally as an injury; to entertain the action would require a court or jury to decide whether being born with the condition is worse than never being born, a question which cannot be resolved in a judicial process; and it would not be possible to compute damages because it would require a comparison between the child's condition and nonexistence. See *Willis v. Wu*, 362 S.C. 146, 607 S.E.2d 63 (2004).

The supreme courts of three states—California, New Jersey and Washington—decided that a wrongful life action could be brought on behalf of the child, but it would be limited to recovery of expenses to be incurred because of the child's condition. See *Procanik v. Cillo*, 97 N.J. 339, 478 A.2d 755 (1984). These expenses were a measurable basis for awarding damages, unlike general damages for being born and life with the disability. To allow recovery would address the financial impact of medical care and other "extraordinary" expenses required by the child, including after the child reached the age of majority. It would not, in the courts' view, require a comparison between the child's impaired life and nonexistence. While parents could recover damages for such expenses in a wrongful birth action, recognition of a wrongful life action would enable the child to obtain damages for expenses when the parents had not obtained or could not obtain them.

Disadvantaged child. A distinct type of wrongful life action is one in which damages are sought because the child is disadvantaged. In the reported cases, the primary disadvantage for which damages were sought was being born out of wedlock or being born to a mother who was incapable of caring for the child because of mental disability. In some, the alleged negligence causing the child's birth was failure to protect a female prison inmate or patient in a mental health institution from sexual assault. The courts in every case rejected the wrongful life claim. This is primarily because the court would not accept any action for wrongful life. But even the courts accepting wrongful life actions would not allow a healthy child to recover damages for the disadvantaged circumstances of its life, as damages have been limited to expenses for the treatment and other needs of a disabled child. See *Daniels v. Delaware*, 120 F. Supp. 2d 411 (D. Del. 2000); *Foy v. Greenblott*, 141 Cal. App. 3d 1, 190 Cal. Rptr. 84 (1983).

E. ACTION AGAINST PARENT

In addition to actions against medical professionals and other parties outside the child's family, there is also the possibility of an action against one of the child's parents, alleging that wrongful conduct by the parent resulted in the birth of a child that was disabled or disadvantaged. In *Curlender v. Bio-Science Laboratories*, 106 Cal. App. 3d 811, 165 Cal. Rptr. 477 (1980), the court suggested that a parent who knew that a seriously impaired child would be born and made a deliberate choice to proceed with the pregnancy could be liable to the child. This could be a tenable claim in the states that allow wrongful life actions for disabled children. But the few reported cases in which a child brought a wrongful life action against a parent have involved children suing their fathers for causing them to be born illegitimate. In each case the court decided that such an action could not be maintained. See *Pinkney v. Pinkney*, 198 So. 2d 52 (Fla. App. 1967); *Zepeda v. Zepeda*, 41 Ill. App. 2d 240, 190 N.E.2d 849 (1963).

In a somewhat larger number of cases the plaintiff was the other parent, suing on allegations that the defendant's tort caused an unwanted child to be conceived. In most it was claimed that the defendant induced the plaintiff to have intercourse by representing that he or she was sterile, or using birth control, and that the defendant was liable on the basis of deceit, negligence or battery for damages that included the costs of raising the child and emotional distress. See Annot., 2 A.L.R.5th 301. If the defendant's false representation was made negligently, this would seem to provide the same foundation for a wrongful birth action as a negligent misrepresentation by a medical professional. If the plaintiff had intercourse with the defendant because of reliance on a fraudulent representation that conception could not occur, the plaintiff would seem to have a valid action for either deceit or battery (with the plaintiff's consent being invalid because of the fraud) that would enable the plaintiff to recover damages for the physical, financial and possibly the emotional consequences of the pregnancy and birth. However, in most of the reported cases, including all in which the plaintiff was male, the court decided that such an action could not be maintained.

The principal reasons given for these decisions are that allowing the action would create an unacceptable invasion of sexual privacy and recovery for the costs of supporting the child would conflict with the plaintiff's obligation to pay for the child's support. See *C.A.M. v. R.A.W.*, 237 N.J. Super. 532, 568 A.2d 556 (App. Div. 1990); *Wallis v. Smith*, 130 N.M. 214, 22 P.3d 682 (Ct. App. 2001). A few cases allow a woman to sue for injuries caused by a pregnancy when she alleged that intercourse was due to the defendant's fraudulent or negligent misrepresentation. *Barbara A. v. John G.*, 145 Cal. App. 3d 369, 193 Cal. Rptr. 422 (1983); *Alice D. v. William M.*, 113 Misc. 2d 940, 450 N.Y.S.2d 350 (N.Y. City Civ. Ct. 1982).

PART III

ECONOMIC RELATIONS

CHAPTER 6

INTRODUCTION: ECONOMIC TORTS

The term "economic torts" groups together a large number of specific torts. What they have in common is that the interest protected by the tort is economic, and the injury which gives rise to liability is economic or pecuniary loss. This distinguishes economic torts from other torts that provide compensation for economic loss that is a consequence of another type of injury, such as personal injury, property damage or loss, injury to reputation, misuse of legal process, or injury to a family member. Anyone who conducts a business, engages in employment or is offering something for sale (or expects to do so) has an economic interest that might be interfered with in a way that provides grounds for a tort claim. Some non-business interests or expectations, such as the expectation of receiving an inheritance or damages in a lawsuit, might also be the basis of a tort action. If successful, a tort action would provide damages for the economic loss the plaintiff suffered or injunctive relief to protect the plaintiff against economic loss. Going beyond these generalizations, one finds considerable diversity in the economic torts' elements of liability and the specific problems they address.

Most of the economic torts come within the concept of injury to relational interests discussed in Chapter 1. There is an interference by the defendant with an existing or potential economic relationship between the plaintiff and one or more third persons, such as customers and other purchasers, sellers, employers, employees, investors, and providers of supplies and services. These are the torts discussed in Part III of this book. Some economic torts pertain to a relationship between the plaintiff and defendant and do not fit the concept of injury to relational interests. The most important of these are the torts of deceit (fraudulent misrepresentation) and negligent misrepresentation. They are covered in Kionka, *Torts in a Nutshell* (6th ed. 2015), Chapter 15.

Many federal and state statutes now regulate economic activities and relationships that can potentially generate economic torts claims. These include antitrust, labor, securities, copyright, patent, trademark, trade practices (unfair trade) and trade secrets laws. For the most part, the operation of the statutes and the remedies they provide are outside the law of torts. However, for economic torts it is necessary to consider whether federal statutes have the effect of preempting tort claims under state common law. This primarily involves the federal copyright and patent statutes and labor legislation. Also, if the defendant's conduct is made illegal by statute, this can furnish the element of unlawful conduct in some torts. Liability under the Uniform Trade Secrets Act is discussed in the chapter on trade secrets (Chapter 13), as this statute has superseded common law trade secret liability in most states but is based on common law principles.

CHAPTER 7

INTERFERENCE WITH CONTRACT

A. ORIGINS AND DEVELOPMENT

The foundation of the tort of interference with contract is the ancient common law action of a master for loss of the services of a servant: the action *per quod servitium amisit*. This was a legal consequence of the great loss of life due to the "Black Death" plague of the mid-fourteenth century. Surviving laborers were able to demand high wages for their services, and they were leaving their masters when better pay and conditions could be obtained elsewhere. To counteract this, Parliament enacted the Statute of Labourers. The Statute of Labourers required able-bodied persons who were not already in service or self-employed to enter service, on customary (pre-plague) wages, and made it a punishable offense for a servant or laborer to depart from service before the term agreed to. It also made it an offense to receive or retain in service someone who had illegally departed from service for another person. Because of the statute, courts allowed an action for damages when the plaintiff lost the services of a servant because the defendant had unlawfully persuaded the servant to leave the plaintiff's service or retained the servant with knowledge of the servant's obligation to serve the plaintiff.

This was long before a servant's relationship with a master was considered a contractual relationship. The master's action for loss of services became a basis of liability for interference with contract in *Lumley v. Gye*, (1853) 2 El. & Bl. 216, 118 Eng. Rep. 749 (Q.B.), one of the most famous of all economic torts cases. The person induced to leave the "service" of the plaintiff was not an ordinary servant or employee. She was Johanna Wagner, a star opera performer who had agreed to sing in operas presented by Lumley for a three-month period. The agreement provided that Wagner was not to perform elsewhere during that period without Lumley's written authorization. Knowing that Wagner was unhappy about her agreement with Lumley, Gye, a rival opera manager, induced Wagner to sing for his company instead during the period she had committed to perform for Lumley. (Gye offered her much more money than she was to get from Lumley.)

Lumley could have sought damages from Wagner for breach of contract, but he claimed damages from Gye, who was not liable under contract law. Allowing Lumley's action, a majority of the court extended the action *per quod servitium amisit* to loss of services of someone who was an independent professional "artiste" rather than an ordinary employed servant, and to someone who had not yet actually entered service with the plaintiff but had made a binding contract with the plaintiff to perform services. There would thus be an action for persuading someone to break a contractual commitment to provide personal services (exclusively) for the plaintiff for a period of time.

The greater importance of the case is language in the opinions supporting an action for procuring a breach of the plaintiff's contract with a third person, causing the plaintiff loss, even when it was not a contract to perform personal services for the plaintiff. These opinions rejected arguments that the act causing loss to the plaintiff was that of the party breaking the contract, not the person who induced the breach, and that an action against the contracting party would provide a sufficient remedy. Damages for breach of contract might not extend to consequential losses.

In subsequent decades it was accepted that there was a tort action against a defendant who induced or procured a breach of the plaintiff's contract with a third person. The action was not limited to personal services contracts. The rationale of this liability was that there was liability for knowingly violating a person's legal rights, unless there was justification for it, and it was a violation of a person's legal rights to interfere with rights under a contract. Injunctive relief against interference with contract could be obtained, as well as judgments for damages. Knowingly procuring the breach of the plaintiff's contract was sufficient for liability. There was no requirement that the defendant act maliciously or with the object of causing loss to the plaintiff. See *Glamorgan Coal Co., Ltd. v. South Wales Miners' Federation*, [1903] 2 K.B. 545 (C.A.), aff'd, [1905] A.C. 239 (H.L.).

Liability for intentional interference with contract expanded beyond inducing breach of contract by a party to the contract. It extended to two other types of interference: preventing a contracting party from performing the contract and causing the termination of a contract that otherwise would have continued to operate. Liability for this was necessarily limited to instances in which the defendant's conduct was wrongful for a reason other than the defendant's knowing that the plaintiff's contractual expectation would be interfered with. A defendant would not be liable only because the defendant in some way knowingly interfered with the performance of a contract or procured the termination of an at-will contract, as by persuading an employee of the plaintiff to work for the defendant instead, or persuading someone who purchased or supplied products under an exclusive contract with the plaintiff to end the arrangement and do business with the defendant.

Interference with contract has never been a stable area of tort law, or one in which there was a broad consensus concerning the limits of liability. The first two Restatements of Torts reformulated rather than restated the law. Both stated a general "black letter" principle that was to apply not only to liability for interference with contract, but also liability for interference with existing and prospective business relations.

In the first Restatement, liability arose from purposely causing a third person not to perform a contract with the plaintiff or not to continue or enter into a business relationship with the plaintiff. Rest. Torts § 766. This was qualified by privileges to act without liability that were elaborated at length. Under the Restatement (Second), liability is to arise from "intentional and improper" interference with an existing contract or prospective contractual relations. Rest. 2d Torts §§ 766, 766A, 766B. Whether interference is improper can depend upon whether it causes breach of contract or only loss of prospective contractual relations. See Rest. 2d Torts § 767, comment *e*. "Intentional" interference includes knowing that the interference will result (or is substantially certain to result) as well as having the purpose or desire to cause it. Rest. 2d Torts § 766, comment *j*; Rest. 2d Torts § 766B, comment *d*.

The recently published Restatement (Third) of Torts: Liability for Economic Harm separates interference with existing contracts from interference with economic expectations (interference with prospective advantage). However, it applies the rules of liability for interference with economic expectations to interference that causes the termination of an at-will contract rather than breach of contract. It also sets forth requirements of liability that are tighter than the Second Restatement's "improper interference" rule. Rest. 3d Torts—Economic Harm §§ 17–18. This has support in some but not most of the case law.

B. INDUCING BREACH OF CONTRACT

1. TRADITIONAL LAW

The traditional view of the *Lumley v. Gye* tort of inducing breach of contract is that its elements of liability are the intentional inducement or procurement of breach of a contract between the plaintiff and another person, causing breach of the contract and resulting damage (pecuniary loss) to the plaintiff. A defense of justification or privilege is allowed in some circumstances.

Intent and knowledge. Interference with contract in all its forms has always been an intentional tort. A defendant can be liable for causing a breach of the plaintiff's contract intentionally, but not for causing breach unintentionally. This requires that the defendant know of the contract and have sufficient knowledge of its terms to know that what the defendant is inducing or causing the contracting party to do is a breach of contract. However, it is arguable that a defendant who knew of a contract is liable even if the defendant believed (incorrectly) that it would not be violated or that the contract was unenforceable. See Rest. 2d Torts § 766, comment *i*. In *American Cyanamid Co. v. Elizabeth Arden Sales Corp.*, 331 F. Supp. 597 (S.D.N.Y. 1971), a defendant who knew of the plaintiff's agreement for purchase of a corporation avoided liability for inducing breach of contract on a finding that it was reasonable to believe the agreement was not binding. But in *Robey v. Sun Record Co.*, 242 F.2d 684 (5th Cir. 1957), the defendant was held liable despite its alleged belief that the contract was invalid. In *State of Minnesota by Burlington Northern Railroad Co. v. Big Stone-Grant Industrial Development and Transportation, L.L.C.*, 990 F. Supp. 731 (D. Minn. 1997), aff'd, 131 F.3d 144 (8th Cir. 1997), the defendant was held liable even though the party induced to break the contract obtained a legal opinion stating there would not be a breach.

Active procurement. The tort of inducing breach of contract requires some active inducement or persuasion to break the contract. *Wolf v. Perry*, 65 N.M. 457, 339 P.2d 679 (1959). The main significance of this is that a defendant is not liable if it can only be proved that the defendant made an agreement with a contracting party with knowledge that the party would break a contract with the plaintiff. See Rest. 2d Torts § 766, comment *n*; *Lamport v. 4175 Broadway, Inc.*, 6 F. Supp. 923 (S.D.N.Y. 1934). Or that the defendant knew that the defendant's refusal to transact business with the plaintiff or a third party would result in a contracting party's decision to break a contract with the plaintiff. See Rest. 2d Torts § 766, comment *l*.

There can be liability when the defendant offered the contracting party benefits to be received if the contract with the plaintiff was not performed, such as employment, sales, investment or better terms for a transaction; or when the defendant threatened negative consequences for the contracting party if the contract was performed, such as loss of a transaction or business relations with the defendant. There can also be liability for inducing breach of contract by simply persuading the contracting party that the contract should not be performed or continued. See Rest. 2d Torts § 766, comments *k–m*. Typical examples include inducing breach of a covenant not to compete with the plaintiff by offering employment in a competing business. *Kallok v. Medtronic, Inc.*, 573 N.W.2d 356 (Minn. 1998). A competing business' inducing breach of the plaintiff's contract with a customer to be the exclusive provider of goods or services. *White Plains Coat & Apron Co., Inc. v. Cintas Corp.*, 8 N.Y.3d 422, 867 N.E.2d 381 (2007). Or exclusive sales agent. *Bergman v. Gitelson & Neff Associates, Inc.*, 267 A.2d 360 (D.C. 1970). A defendant's inducing the plaintiff's tenant to break the lease and move to the defendant's property. *Daugherty v. Kessler*, 264 Md. 281, 286 A.2d 95 (1972). A defendant's causing a third party to break a contract with the plaintiff by threatening withdrawal of labor or cutting off the supply of products if the contract was not broken. *Temperton v. Russell*, [1893] 1 Q.B. 715 (C.A.); *Knickerbocker Ice Co. of Baltimore City v. Gardiner Dairy Co. of Baltimore City*, 107 Md. 556, 69 A. 405 (1908). And a defendant's persuading the plaintiff's client to break an exclusive management contract. *Lee v. Silver*, 262 App. Div. 149, 28 N.Y.S.2d 333 (1941), aff'd, 287 N.Y. 575, 38 N.E.2d 233 (1941).

Causation. To obtain damages, the plaintiff is required to prove that the defendant's conduct was a cause of the breach of contract and this resulted in loss to the plaintiff. A claim will fail if the contracting party would have broken the contract without the defendant's involvement. See *Tri-Continental Leasing Co. v. Neidhardt*, 540 S.W.2d 210 (Mo. App. 1976).

Invalid and unenforceable contracts. When a contract is invalid, there is no liability for interfering with it by inducing a party to violate the contract. See Rest. 2d Torts § 774, comment *b*. This includes contracts that are invalid because they violated state law, as in *Carruthers v. Flaum*, 365 F. Supp. 2d 448

(S.D.N.Y. 2005) (contracts for development of illegal gambling facilities), and *Gunnels v. Atlanta Bar Association*, 191 Ga. 366, 12 S.E.2d 602 (1940) (loan contracts with usurious interest). Contracts invalid because they violated public policy by restraining trade or competition, as in *AMX International, Inc. v. Battelle Energy Alliance, LLC*, 744 F. Supp. 2d 1087 (D. Idaho 2010) (invalid employee covenant not to compete). And contracts whose terms were too indefinite or uncertain to be valid, as in *Silicon International Ore, LLC v. Monsanto Co.*, 155 Idaho 538, 314 P.3d 593 (2013) (verbal sales agreement that did not specify price, quantity or duration).

The position is different when the contract is unenforceable but not invalid. Most authority allows an action for interference with a contract that was unenforceable under the Statute of Frauds or other laws establishing formal requirements for contracts. Some decisions permit an action when the contract was unenforceable due to lack of mutuality or consideration. See Annot., 96 A.L.R.3d 1294. Rest. 2d Torts § 766, comment *f*, endorsed in broad terms liability for intentional interference with unenforceable contracts. However, some cases indicate that a claim for interference with an unenforceable contract should be an action for interference with prospective advantage. *PMC, Inc. v. Saban Entertainment, Inc.*, 45 Cal. App. 4th 579, 52 Cal. Rptr. 2d 877 (1996); *Guard-Life Corp. v. S. Parker Hardware Manufacturing Corp.*, 50 N.Y.2d 183, 406 N.E.2d 445 (1980).

Justification and privilege. Since the late nineteenth century, it has been recognized that an action for interference with contract may be defended on grounds of justification or privilege. (The two terms are interchangeable.) What is justification for inducing breach of contract has never been clear, despite (or perhaps because of) the many cases in which justification has been discussed. However, it has been generally accepted that advancement of the defendant's economic interests is not itself justification for inducing breach of another's contract. Thus, a defendant would be liable for inducing someone who had agreed to sell land to the plaintiff to break the contract so the defendant could obtain the land for business purposes. *Blum v. William Goldman Theatres*, 69 F. Supp. 468 (E.D. Pa. 1946), modified, 164 F.2d 192 (3d Cir. 1947). Or inducing a tenant of the plaintiff to break a lease and move to the defendant's property. *Daugherty v. Kessler*, 264 Md. 281, 286 A.2d 95 (1972). A defendant's interest in increasing its sales would not be justification for procuring a breach of another company's exclusive sales contract. *White Plains Coat & Apron Co., Inc. v. Cintas Corp.*, 8 N.Y.3d 422, 867 N.E.2d 381 (2007). Or inducing a former employee or business partner of the plaintiff to breach a valid covenant not to compete. *Imperial Ice Co. v. Rossier*, 18 Cal. 2d 33, 112 P.2d 631 (1941). Business competition with the plaintiff is not justification. See Rest. Torts § 768(2).

Justification for procuring breach has, however, been found when the defendant's conduct was regarded as defense or protection of an existing economic interest. The strongest justification has been protection of the defendant's own contractual or property rights. See Rest. Torts § 773, comment *a*; *Quinlivan v. Brown Oil Co.*, 96 Mont. 147, 29 P.2d 374 (1934) (protection of contractual price maintenance rights); *Wartensleben v. Willey*, 415 P.2d 613 (Wyo. 1966) (protection of land from nuisance). Justification has also been found when a lender procured a breach of the plaintiff's contract in order to improve the prospects of repayment of the loan, as in *Nitzberg v. Zalesky*, 370 So. 2d 389 (Fla. App. 1979).

A number of cases go further in recognizing protection of an investment as justification for inducing breach of contract. The best-known example, because of its distinct facts, is *Knapp v. Penfield*, 143 Misc. 132, 256 N.Y.S. 41 (Sup. Ct. 1932). Investors in a musical demanded that the plaintiff be discharged and replaced as the lead actress because they thought she lacked the ability to sing and dance the role required. A parent corporation's economic interest in its subsidiaries has been justification for causing breach of a subsidiary's contract. *Felsen v. Sol Cafe Manufacturing Co.*, 24 N.Y.2d 682, 249 N.E.2d 459 (1969). (When the subsidiary was wholly owned, an action against its parent might fail on the ground that there was no interference with the contract by a third party. See *Schoellkopf v. Pledger*, 778 S.W.2d 897 (Tex. App. 1989).)

Protection of the public or community interest has occasionally been a justification for interference with contract. It could involve such matters as prevention of environmental damage, protecting public morality, or preventing discriminatory practices. See Rest. 2d Torts § 767, comment *f*. In *Middlesex Concrete Products and Excavating Corp. v. Carteret Industrial Association*, 37 N.J. 507, 181 A.2d 774 (1962), the justification was municipal taxpayers' interest in preventing an unwarranted settlement payment by the municipality to the plaintiffs.

A more widely recognized ground of justification or privilege is that the defendant acted as a business advisor to the contracting party or as a professional responsible for the party's interests. An advisor or professional is not liable for procuring a breach of contract if this was done in the good faith belief that breaking the contract would be in the contracting party's best interests. The privilege does not protect a consultant or professional who acted primarily for his or her own benefit rather than for the benefit of the client, but a motivation to earn fees by work as a consultant or professional does not take the defendant outside the privilege. See *J.D. Edwards Co. v. Podany*, 168 F.3d 1020 (7th Cir. 1999) (consultant); *Brown Mackie College v. Graham*, 768 F. Supp. 1457 (D. Kan. 1991) (attorney); Rest. Law Governing Lawyers § 57, comment *g*. There is a similar privilege for a person who has a responsibility for the welfare of a party to a contract and interferes with performance of the contract to protect the party's welfare. See Rest. 2d Torts § 770. A spouse or parent of the contracting party may have an absolute privilege against liability when persuading the party not to perform the contact, regardless of the motive for doing so. See *Joel v. Weber*, 153 Misc. 2d 549, 581 N.Y.S.2d 579 (Sup. Ct. 1992).

Breach of contract by a business is often advised or otherwise caused by an officer, director or employee of the business. This is necessarily the case when the business is a corporation. The officer, director or employee is not liable for interference with contract if acting within the scope of his or her authority or employment in the interest of the business. See *Gruhlke v. Sioux Empire Federal Credit Union, Inc.*, 756 N.W.2d 399 (S.D. 2008); Annot., 72 A.L.R.4th 492. Plaintiffs have attempted to overcome this by allegations that the defendant acted with malice or to advance the defendant's own career or business interests, but a court may require evidence that personal gain was the sole or predominant motivation for causing breach of the plaintiff's contract. See *Los Angeles Airways, Inc. v. Davis*, 687 F.2d 321 (9th Cir. 1982); Rest. 3d Torts—Economic Harm § 17, comment *o*.

2. SECOND AND THIRD RESTATEMENTS

The rules of liability for inducing breach of contract under the Restatement (Second) of Torts are quite different from those of the prior case law and the first Restatement. The basic rule is that "One who intentionally and improperly interferes with the performance of a contract. . .between another and a third person by inducing. . .the third person not to perform the contract, is subject to liability. . . ." Rest. 2d Torts § 766. Improper interference is an element of the plaintiff's cause of action. To some extent, interference that is "improper" corresponds to what had been regarded as intentional interference without justification or privilege, but the emphasis is on identifying interference as improper rather than absence of justification or privilege. This suggests, but does not necessarily require, that the plaintiff has the burden of establishing that the defendant's interference with the contract was improper. See Rest. 2d Torts § 767, comment *k*.

The Second Restatement rules of liability for "tortious interference" have been adopted or quoted in many cases, but they have not greatly altered the ambit of liability for inducing breach of contract. As the Restatement contemplates, the interest in protection of existing contractual expectations may be sufficient to make intentional procurement of breach improper in the absence of justification. See Rest. 2d Torts § 767, comment *e*. However, the Restatement does provide some opportunity for defendants to prevail when they would have been liable under traditional law. A plaintiff may lose an action for failure to establish that the interference with the plaintiff's contract was improper as well as intentional. As in cases of interference with prospective advantage (see pp. 125–126), improper interference may be equated with use of improper means or acting with improper motives. A defendant who did not employ improper means and whose only motive was financial benefit may avoid liability. See *United Truck Leasing Corp. v. Geltman*, 406 Mass. 811, 551 N.E.2d 20 (1990).

The Restatement (Third) of Torts: Liability for Economic Harm provisions on interference with contract contain rules of liability that are more precise and narrow than those of the Second Restatement but are not intended to cause substantial change in the results that would be reached. See Rest. 3d Torts—Economic Harm § 17, comment *a*. A defendant is to be liable for intentionally causing breach of the plaintiff's contract if the defendant's conduct was "wrongful" because (a) "the defendant acted for the purpose of appropriating the benefits of the plaintiff's contract," (b) "the defendant's conduct constituted an independent and intentional legal wrong," or (c) "the defendant engaged in the conduct for the sole purpose of injuring the plaintiff." Rest. 3d Torts—Economic Harm § 17(2). The category of defendants who "acted for the purpose of appropriating the benefits of the plaintiff's contract" includes many of those who would be liable if the basis of liability were intentional inducement or procurement of breach without justification.

C. INTERFERENCE WITH PERFORMANCE OF CONTRACT

Interference with the performance of a contract began to emerge as a basis of liability some decades after *Lumley v. Gye*. It was recognized that there could be intentional prevention or hindrance of a party's performance of a contract by means other than inducing breach. In some circumstances, the party prevented from performing would not be liable for breach of contract, so there would be no remedy other than a tort action for interference with contract. See *National Phonograph Co., Ltd. v. Edison-Bell Consolidated Phonograph Co., Ltd.*, [1908] 1 Ch. 335 (C.A.). But it was also recognized that one could engage in lawful conduct, including the refusal to provide goods or services, in the knowledge that this would result in another's breaching a contractual obligation, without incurring liability. This, in turn, was often subject to the qualification that there could be liability if the defendant's conduct was actuated by a purpose to cause harm or other improper objectives. Liability for intentional interference with performance of a contract is included in the Second Restatement's general rule of liability for intentional and improper interference with contracts. Rest. 2d Torts § 766. Whether interference is to be found improper depends upon a number of factors, including the type of conduct and the defendant's motivation. Rest. 2d Torts § 767.

There are some modern cases of liability based on improper motives or conduct rather than conduct that was unlawful. *E.g., Nesler v. Fisher and Co., Inc.*, 452 N.W.2d 191 (Iowa 1990). However, in contemporary law the principal basis of liability for intentionally preventing performance of a contract is that the defendant employed unlawful means. Unlawful means include intentional wrongs that can be grounds for civil liability, as well as conduct that is criminal or unlawful under legislation. There can thus be liability when a defendant intentionally prevents performance of a contract by fraudulent misrepresentation. *Glover v. Lee, Higginson Corp.*, 95

F. Supp. 504 (D. Mass. 1950). Trespass to land. *Piedmont Cotton Mills, Inc. v. H.W. Ivey Construction Co., Inc.*, 109 Ga. App. 876, 137 S.E.2d 528 (1964). Conversion of property. *Hickman Construction, Inc. v. South Umpqua Bank*, 109 Or. App. 527, 820 P.2d 838 (1991). Bribery. *Angle v. Chicago, St. Paul, Minneapolis and Omaha Railway Co.*, 151 U.S. 1 (1894). Or battery. *Keene Lumber Co. v. Leventhal*, 165 F.2d 815 (1st Cir. 1948) (hypothetically). Under the Third Restatement, conduct that is an "independent and intentional legal wrong" is a basis of liability for intentional interference with contract. Conduct engaged in for the sole purpose of injuring the plaintiff, or to appropriate the benefits of the plaintiff's contract, is also a basis of liability. Rest. 3d Torts—Economic Harm § 17(2).

The Second Restatement and Third Restatement extend liability to cases in which the plaintiff was a party to the contract interfered with and the defendant intentionally prevented or disrupted the plaintiff's performance of the contract. Rest. 2d Torts § 766A; Rest. 3d Torts—Economic Harm § 17, comment *i*. This is accepted in some cases, but *Price v. Sorrell*, 784 P.2d 614 (Wyo. 1989), rejected liability for making the plaintiff's performance more expensive or burdensome.

To be liable, the defendant must have had an intent to interfere with the plaintiff's contract, at least to the extent of knowing that the contract would be interfered with. See *Keene Lumber Co. v. Leventhal*, *supra*. It is not enough that the defendant intended to commit the wrong that interfered with the contract's performance.

D. INDUCING TERMINATION OF CONTRACT

Many contracts, including the employment contracts of much of the American workforce, can be terminated "at will" or on short notice. Liability for causing the termination of the plaintiff's contract with a third person is necessarily different from liability on a claim of inducing breach of a contract or preventing its performance. As there is no breach of contract, causing a contracting party to commit a legal wrong cannot be the basis of liability. Usually there is nothing improper about persuading someone who had been making purchases from the plaintiff, or providing services or supplies to the plaintiff, to end the operation of the contract and do business with another. It is part of normal business competition. Any liability rationally must be based upon the defendant's conduct being improper because of its objectives or the means used, or a need to protect the plaintiff's contractual interests from interference and resulting loss.

The generally accepted requirements of liability for inducing or procuring termination of a contract parallel those of liability for inducing breach of a contract. The defendant must have had an intent to cause termination (or breach) of the contract, actively have procured it, and thereby caused damage (pecuniary loss) to the plaintiff. Damage could be caused only if the contract would have continued but for the defendant's actions. Beyond this there has never been consensus on the elements of liability.

One approach, adapted from liability for inducing breach and some authority on interference with prospective advantage, was to find a cause of action in the intentional procurement of the contract's termination and damage to the plaintiff and limit liability on grounds of justification or privilege, with economic competition being the principal ground of justification. This was adopted in the first Restatement of Torts, although with the requirement that the defendant have a purpose to cause termination of the contractual relationship. Rest. Torts §§ 766–774. Another approach focused on the nature of the defendant's conduct and its objectives, distinguishing between lawful and unlawful or legally improper conduct and between lawful and unlawful or legally improper objectives. Acting with a primary purpose to cause harm to the plaintiff was a ground of liability. There was, however, sharp dispute on whether lawful conduct could be actionable because of improper motives.

There was also sharp dispute about whether certain objectives, such as the objective of labor unions and their members to deter businesses from employing non-union labor, were lawful or provided justification for causing termination of employment or business contracts. A worker's interest in the continuance of employment and a business proprietor's interest in being able to continue in business could receive more protection from interference than other contractual interests or expectations. In both labor and business disputes, "coercion" causing termination of the plaintiff's contract was distinguished from procuring voluntary termination by the contracting party.

The rules of the Second Restatement on liability for causing loss by procuring the termination of a contract are different from those of the first Restatement. The starting point is the general rule that the Second Restatement applies to all actions for interference with contract: liability arises from "intentionally and improperly" interfering with performance of the contract. Rest. 2d Torts § 766. Whether interference is "improper" is to be determined by reference to a number of factors set forth in Rest. 2d Torts § 767: "(a) the nature of the actor's conduct, (b) the actor's motive, (c) the interests of the other with which the actor's conduct interferes, (d) the interests sought to be advanced by the actor, (e) the social interests in protecting the freedom of the actor and the contractual interests of the other, (f) the proximity or remoteness of the actor's conduct to the interference and (g) the relations between the parties." The same factors apply to other types of "tortious interference" actions, but it is clear from the comments to § 767 that their application is to be different in an action for causing termination than in an action for causing breach or preventing performance of a contract. In practice liability for causing termination of a contract is more dependent upon a court's application of the various factors than liability for inducing breach or intentionally preventing performance of a contract.

One of the prominent cases of liability under the Second Restatement is *Adler, Barish, Daniels, Levin and Creskoff v. Epstein*, 482 Pa. 416, 393 A.2d 1175 (1978). Four salaried associates of the Adler Barish law firm left to form their own partnership. They immediately informed Adler Barish clients on whose cases they had worked that the clients could transfer their legal affairs to the former associates (or any other attorney). One client who indicated a desire to do so was sent a form letter with which the client could discharge Adler Barish and direct it to hand over the client's file to one of the former associates. Adler Barish obtained an injunction which permanently restrained the former associates from communicating with clients represented by the firm in active legal matters. The Supreme Court of Pennsylvania upheld the injunction.

The court concluded that the departing associates had improperly interfered with the Adler Barish firm's client contracts. It emphasized that the defendants had violated a provision of the state Code of Professional Responsibility prohibiting self-recommendation (lawyers were prohibited from recommending themselves or their firms to a non-lawyer who had not sought advice on employment of a lawyer) and that they had taken advantage of confidential information and the clients' trust in them, acquired while working for Adler Barish, and "unduly suggested a course of action" for the clients, to the prejudice of the firm.

In *Ronald M. Sharrow, Chartered v. State Farm Mutual Automobile Insurance Co.*, 306 Md. 754, 511

A.2d 492 (1986), the court held that an attorney representing a client under a contingent fee contract stated a cause of action against an insurance company for inducing the client to discharge the attorney and accept a settlement payment offered by the insurance company. The element of improper interference was found in the insurer's alleged purpose to induce the client to discharge the attorney and settle the claim with the insurer directly and conduct calculated to bring this about.

As in cases of intentionally preventing performance of a contract (see pp. 110–111), the most solid ground for finding "improper" interference with an at-will contract is that the defendant's conduct was unlawful. This includes commission of intentional wrongs that are the basis of civil liability. *E.g.*, *Reeves v. Hanlon*, 33 Cal. 4th 1140, 95 P.3d 513 (2004) (unlawful destruction of client files and misappropriation of confidential information); *Kraemer v. Harding*, 159 Or. App. 90, 976 P.2d 1160 (1999) (defamation). In the *Adler, Barish* case, the defendants' conduct was unlawful because it violated the Code of Professional Responsibility. Under the Restatement (Third) of Torts: Liability of Economic Harm, liability for causing termination of a contract without breach is the same as liability for "interference with economic expectation" (interference with prospective advantage), and commission of "an independent and intentional legal wrong" is required. Rest. 3d Torts—Economic Harm § 18.

CHAPTER 8

INTERFERENCE WITH PROSPECTIVE ECONOMIC ADVANTAGE—COMMERCIAL EXPECTATIONS

A. OVERVIEW AND HISTORY

The tort discussed in this chapter is known by several different names. Here, as in Prosser's influential treatise on tort law, it will be referred to as interference with prospective advantage. Other names for the tort include interference with prospective economic advantage, interference with trade, interference with business relations, interference with prospective contractual relations (its name in the Restatement (Second) of Torts) and interference with economic expectation (its name in the Restatement (Third) of Torts: Liability for Economic Harm). Its central concept is wrongful conduct that interferes with the plaintiff's ability to receive income expected from business, employment or other sources, or valuable property, resulting in loss of the expected income or property. It has always been an intentional tort; but whether the intent required for liability is a purpose or object to interfere with the plaintiff's expectation, knowledge that the interference would result, or knowledge in combination with another element of wrongful or improper conduct has never been an agreed point.

The terms interference with prospective advantage and interference with prospective economic advantage can be applied to depriving a plaintiff of expected income or property from a non-commercial source, such as a gift or inheritance. That will be discussed in the next chapter. This chapter addresses interference with the prospect of income or property that would be received in a commercial or contractual transaction. A liable defendant has interfered with the plaintiff's ability to make transactions with parties other than the defendant, such as customers, suppliers or providers of services, or enter into economic relationships with them, such as employment. Loss of income or property expected under an existing contract—one in effect at the time of the defendant's interference—comes under the tort of interference with contract, discussed in Chapter 7. Under some authority, including the Third Restatement, the principles of liability for interference with prospective advantage apply to claims that the defendant caused termination of a contract without a breach, as when the contract was terminable at will. Rest. 3d Torts—Economic Harm § 18, comment *f*.

The oldest cases of what now would be recognized as tortious interference with prospective advantage involved intentional physical interference with the plaintiff's trade or livelihood. The principal cases of this nature were *Garret v. Taylor*, (1620) Cro. Jac. 567, 79 Eng. Rep. 485 (K.B.), in which the defendant verbally threatened workmen with violence if they if they worked for the plaintiff at his stone pit and threatened other persons with violence if they bought from the plaintiff; *Tarleton v. M'Gawley*, (1793) Peake 270, 170 Eng. Rep. 153 (K.B.), in which the defendant fired at natives on the coast of Africa to prevent them from trading with the plaintiffs' ship; and *Keeble v. Hickeringill*, (1706) 11 East 574, 103 Eng. Rep. 1127 (Q.B.), in which the defendant prevented the plaintiff catching wild ducks at his decoy pond by firing guns laden with gunpowder, frightening and driving away the ducks. In *St. Johnsbury & Lake Champlain Railroad Co. v. Hunt*, 55 Vt. 570 (1882), the defendant allegedly delayed a train, causing loss to the railroad, by having the engineer arrested on an invalid charge.

Knowingly interfering with the plaintiff's business revenue through physical interference continues to be a basis of liability, even if the interference is not violent, threatening or trespassory. See *Morra v. Hill*, 103 N.H. 492, 175 A.2d 824 (1961) (trailer park owner denying entry to oil dealer selling to occupants of trailers); *Italverde Trading, Inc. v. Four Bills of Lading*, 485 F. Supp. 2d 187 (E.D.N.Y. 2007) (freight forwarder converting shipment of products en route to plaintiff to satisfy debt claim against manufacturer).

It was in the last half of the nineteenth century that liability for intentional interference with prospective advantage expanded beyond physical interference and became a major field of tort law. With the great increase of commercial activity, including large-scale industrial enterprise, and the increasing membership and militancy of labor unions, many disputes among businesses and between business proprietors and unions or their members resulted in actions for what in substance was interference with prospective advantage. Injunctions as well as damages were often sought. In some cases, liability for interference with prospective advantage developed as an extension of liability for interference with contract, with what were regarded as appropriate modifications. In others, it proceeded from general propositions, such as the actionability of economic loss caused intentionally without justification or intentionally and maliciously, or by an unlawful conspiracy. Usually there was no liability for loss caused by defendants who acted lawfully in the course of business competition or pursuit of their own economic interests. But in numerous instances whether a defendant would be held liable and the basis on which a court would decide the question of liability were not readily predictable.

In some cases, courts and individual judges adopted a *laissez-faire* approach to liability for business and labor practices that caused financial harm to others, absent conduct unlawful in itself such as fraud, physical obstruction or intimidation, or intentional procurement of a legal wrong such as breach of contract. A leading case adopting this approach is *Mogul Steamship Co., Ltd. v. McGregor, Gow, & Co.*, (1889) 23 Q.B.D. 598 (C.A.), aff'd, [1892] A.C. 25 (H.L.), in which owners of ships carrying tea from China to Europe organized a conference that acted for the purpose of driving competitors from the trade. Their tactics included offering shippers below-cost freight rates and a rebate if they would not deal with the plaintiff (a competing shipowner), pressuring agents to ship tea only on the defendants' vessels, and sending special ships to a Chinese port to deprive the plaintiff of profitable freight. Another, although primarily a case of inducing termination of contract, is *Allen v. Flood*, [1898] A.C. 1 (H.L.), in which a union leader caused the plaintiffs to lose their employment by telling their employer that union members would stop work if the plaintiffs were not discharged.

In other cases, judges were more interventionist, protecting plaintiffs against conduct intended to cause them to lose employment, put them out of business, or coerce them on who they could employ or conduct business with. One is *Martell v. White*, 185 Mass. 255, 69 N.E. 1085 (1904), in which an association of granite quarriers, manufacturers and polishers deprived a non-member manufacturer of customers, ruining his business, by imposing heavy fines on members who purchased granite from a non-member. The court concluded that "as against the plaintiff, the defendants failed to show that the coercion or intimidation of the plaintiff's customers by means of a fine is justified by the law of competition." The *Mogul Steamship* case was distinguished because the defendants in that case had not employed coercion to cause customers not to deal with the plaintiff. They had held out positive inducements to customers, including discounted rates. In *Auburn Draying Co. v. Wardell*, 227 N.Y. 1, 124 N.E. 97 (1919), the plaintiff operated a trucking business that employed mostly non-union labor. It was the target of an effort by local unions to compel the business to employ only workers who were members of a union. To this end, the unions withdrew or threatened to withdraw union labor from the plaintiff's customers. The plaintiff lost many customers as a consequence. The court held the unions' conduct to be unlawful and sustained a judgment awarding damages and a permanent injunction.

A distinct rule found liability if the defendant intentionally damaged the plaintiff's business with what Justice Holmes called "disinterested malevolence"—acting with the sole (or at least primary) purpose of causing harm to the plaintiff rather than economic advantage for the defendant. *American Bank & Trust Co. v. Federal Reserve Bank of Atlanta, Georgia*, 256 U.S. 350, 358 (1921). The leading case of this nature is *Tuttle v. Buck*, 107 Minn. 145, 119 N.W. 946 (1909). The plaintiff, a barber who had a profitable barber shop in a Minnesota village, alleged that a local banker, endeavoring to destroy the plaintiff's business and compel the plaintiff to abandon it, furnished a barber shop in the village and hired two barbers to operate it, at a salary exceeding the income from the shop, to draw customers away from the plaintiff. The banker also personally induced the plaintiff's customers not to patronize his shop. The court held that the barber had a good cause of action, stating:

> To divert to one's self the customers of a business rival by the offer of goods at lower prices is in general a legitimate mode of serving one's own interest, and justifiable as fair competition. But when a man starts an opposition place of business, not for the sake of profit to himself, but

> regardless of loss to himself, and for the sole purpose of driving his competitor out of business, and with the intention of himself retiring upon the accomplishment of his malevolent purpose, he is guilty of a wanton wrong and an actionable tort. . . .To call such conduct competition is a perversion of terms.

Id., 105 Minn. 145, 151, 119 N.W. 946, 948.

Business proprietors are unlikely to damage other businesses out of "disinterested malevolence," but occasionally a defendant has been held liable, or potentially liable, on allegations that the defendant acted with the purpose of driving the plaintiff out of business. This occurred in *Dunshee v. Standard Oil Co.*, 152 Iowa 618, 132 N.W. 371 (1911), where a wholesale oil dealer hired and equipped people to make retail sales of oil in order to take customers away from the plaintiff, an oil retailer, and drive the plaintiff out of business. When this object was accomplished, the defendant "retired" from the retail trade. The defendant's motive was the plaintiff's refusal to purchase all its supplies from the defendant.

B. CONTEMPORARY LAW

Much of the conduct at issue in the older cases is now regulated or prohibited by antitrust, trade practices and labor legislation. The relevant legislation typically allows a party harmed by prohibited conduct to obtain damages or an injunction. There may also be an action for interference with prospective advantage when the defendant's conduct is unlawful as well as intentional. (See pp. 126–129.) For conduct that is not unlawful by statute, the contemporary law of interference with prospective advantage in the United States proceeds primarily from the Restatement (Second) of Torts and themes emerging in the case law since publication of the Restatement.

In the Second Restatement, the general rule of liability for interference with prospective advantage is: "One who intentionally and improperly interferes with another's prospective contractual relation. . .is subject to liability to the other for the pecuniary harm resulting from loss of the benefits of the relation. . . ." Rest. 2d Torts § 766B. The interference is considered intentional if the actor desires to bring it about or knows that it is substantially certain to result from the actor's conduct. Rest. 2d Torts § 766B, comment *d*. Whether interference is "improper" is to be determined by consideration of the factors set forth in § 767: "(a) the nature of the actor's conduct, (b) the actor's motive, (c) the interests of the other with which the actor's conduct interferes, (d) the interests sought to be advanced by the actor, (e) the social interests in protecting the freedom of action of the actor and the contractual interests of the other, (f) the proximity or remoteness of the actor's conduct to the interference and (g) the relations between the parties."

This is the same in substance as the Second Restatement's rules of liability for interference with contract. However, it is clear from the comments and the case law that what is "improper" interference with the prospects of revenue from future business or contractual transactions is quite different from what is "improper" when performance of existing contracts is interfered with. "[G]reater protection is accorded an interest in an existing contract (as to which respect for contract rights outweighs the public benefit to be derived from unfettered competition) than to the less substantive, more speculative interests in a prospective relationship (as to which liability will be imposed only on proof of more culpable conduct on the part of the interferer)." *Guard-Life Corp. v. S. Parker Hardware Manufacturing Corp.*, 50 N.Y.2d 183, 191, 406 N.E.2d 445, 449 (1980). Intentional (in the sense of knowing) interference with another's prospects of receiving income is extremely common in normal business, property and employment transactions. It is not to result in liability unless there is impropriety in the defendant's conduct.

The Restatement directs courts to give "consideration" to the seven factors in § 767 when deciding whether interference with prospective advantage was improper and therefore grounds for liability. However, in the case law the major grounds for finding improper interference have become improper motives or improper means. See *Top Service Body Shop, Inc. v. Allstate Insurance Co.*, 283 Or. 201, 582 P.2d 1365 (1978); *Leigh Furniture and Carpet Co. v. Isom*, 657 P.2d 293 (Utah 1982). Under the opinion in *Top Service Body Shop*, means of interference may be wrongful "by reason of a statute or other regulation, or a recognized rule of common law, or perhaps an established standard of a trade or profession." Under the *Leigh Furniture* opinion, an improper purpose must have been predominant to be sufficient for motive-based liability. Improper motives include a purpose to inflict injury. Improper (or wrongful) motives and improper (or wrongful) means are alternatives bases of liability, but a defendant's conduct may be found improper because of a combination of improper motives and improper means, as in *Pleas v. City of Seattle*, 112 Wash. 2d 794, 774 P.2d 1158 (1989).

The proposition that liability could arise from improper motives, without conduct that is unlawful or improper in itself, has come under criticism. It invites claims based upon alleged improper motives, although actual liability by reason of motive alone appears to be rare. Findings about a defendant's motive may not be accurate, and the public can benefit from business competition commenced with a bad motive. See Rest. Unfair Competition § 1, comment *c*. A number of major cases require "independently unlawful" acts and reject liability based on improper purpose or motive alone. These include *Korea Supply Co. v. Lockheed Martin Corp.*, 29 Cal. 4th 1134, 63 P.3d 937 (2003), and *Wal-Mart Stores, Inc. v. Sturges*, 52 S.W.3d 711 (Tex. 2001). In *Eldridge v. Johndrow*, 345 P.3d 553 (Utah 2015), the court overruled *Leigh Furniture* to the extent it allowed liability to be based on improper purpose. Plaintiffs in tortious interference actions were required to prove improper means.

Improper or wrongful means. The Second Restatement adopted a wide view of what could be improper means of interference with prospective advantage. It included not only conduct that was unlawful under legislation or rules of common law, but also threats of unlawful action, violation of ethical codes and established business customs, and economic pressure applied to someone who would otherwise transact business with the plaintiff. Rest. 2d Torts § 767, comment *c*. This is accepted in some cases, such as *Yoakum v. Hartford Fire Insurance Co.*, 129 Idaho 171, 923 P.2d 416 (1996). *Cf. Duggin v. Adams*, 234 Va. 221, 360 S.E.2d 832 (1987) (interference with at-will contract; "sharp dealing," "overreaching" and "unfair competition" included in description of improper interference). In *Volt Services Group v. Adecco Employment Services, Inc.*, 178 Or. App. 121, 35 P.3d 329 (2001), the court held that violation of an industry association's code of ethics was a basis for finding the defendant's conduct improper. However, there has been an accelerating trend to require that the defendant's conduct be unlawful under legislation or rules of common law (an "independent legal wrong"). See *Trade 'N Post, L.L.C. v. World Duty Free Americas, Inc.*, 628 N.W.2d 707 (N.D. 2001); *Wal-Mart Stores, Inc. v. Sturges*, 52 S.W.3d 711 (Tex. 2001). This is the position of the Third Restatement. Rest. 3d Torts—Economic Harm § 18. The unlawful conduct can be a tort to or directed at a third party rather than the plaintiff.

The Second Restatement specifies that interference with a plaintiff's prospective contractual relations by a competitor is not improper if the competitor does not employ "wrongful means." Rest. 2d Torts § 768. "Wrongful means" apparently signifies conduct that is unlawful, threats of unlawful conduct, and unlawful restraint of trade. On this basis, proof of legally wrongful means may be required in an action against a competitor of the plaintiff, while continuing to apply the requirement of "improper means" in an action against a non-competitor. See *Brokerage Concepts, Inc. v. U.S. Healthcare, Inc.*, 140 F.3d 494 (3d Cir. 1998).

Despite broad statements that there can be liability when the interference is by means that are unlawful, it is clear that not every act that is unlawful under legislation or common law rules is a basis of liability. Conduct that violates a statute may not qualify as a basis for tortious interference liability when the statute did not have the purpose of protecting the interest of a party such as the plaintiff. An example is *Klinger v. Morrow County Grain Growers, Inc.*, 102 Or. App. 375, 794 P.2d 811 (1990), in which the operator of a retail gasoline station sued a competitor that allegedly caused the plaintiff to lose business by violation of the state's prohibition of self-service pumping. The law had a purpose of protecting safety, not business interests or competition. Participants in an illegal strike by public employees usually have not been liable to businesses predictably harmed by the strike. *E.g.*, *Burns Jackson Miller Summit & Spitzer v. Lindner*, 59 N.Y.2d 314, 451 N.E.2d 459 (1983). There is a line of cases, not limited to actions for tortious interference as such, refusing to allow actions for damages or an injunction by plaintiffs claiming to have suffered economic harm because of the illegal conduct of a competitor, unless the defendant violated a franchise granted to the plaintiff. See Annot., 90 A.L.R.2d 7; *Clark v. Crown Drug Co.*, 348 Mo. 91, 152 S.W.2d 145 (1941).

It is also clear that only some types of conduct that are grounds for civil liability qualify as legally wrongful conduct for purposes of liability for interference with prospective advantage. Intentional torts, deceit, breach of fiduciary duty, defamation, injurious falsehood and other torts involving a similar level of culpability qualify, but not negligence and conduct that is the basis of strict liability. See Rest. 3d Torts—Economic Harm § 18, comment *b*. A question of considerable practical importance is whether the "independent wrong" requirement is satisfied when the defendant committed a breach of contract that resulted in interference with the plaintiff's economic expectations. It is fairly clear that a defendant will not be held liable for interference with prospective advantage when it can only be shown that the defendant acted in breach of a contractual obligation and knew this would result in the plaintiff incurring a loss of income from transactions with others, such as the plaintiff's customers. This is especially the case when the contract was between the defendant and the plaintiff, as an action for breach of contract would be the appropriate claim. However, an action for interference with prospective advantage may lie if breach of contract was committed with the purpose of interfering with the plaintiff's prospective business relations and caused loss beyond that recoverable in a breach of contract action. See *Pizza Management, Inc. v. Pizza Hut, Inc.*, 737 F. Supp. 1154 (D. Kan. 1990); *K & K Management, Inc. v. Lee*, 316 Md. 137,

557 A.2d 965 (1989). Rest. 3d Torts—Economic Harm § 18, comment *b*, would exclude breach of contract as a basis of liability.

Strength of expectation; causation. The plaintiff's claim is to obtain a judicial remedy for loss of expected income or receipt of property. The plaintiff's expectation must be greater than a mere hope or possibility, but it need not be a near certainty. According to Rest. 3d Torts—Economic Harm § 18, comment *d*, a "reasonable probability" that the economic benefit would be received is required. The plaintiff "need not show an expectation that was more likely than not to bear fruit." The plaintiff must also establish that the defendant intended to interfere with the plaintiff's expectation and that the interference caused its loss. When the interference was with the prospect of multiple transactions, as with customers, the loss does not have to be quantified with precision.

Duplication and overlap with other torts. Actions for interference with prospective advantage are sometimes brought alleging conduct that comes within other torts—for example, making false statements concerning the plaintiff or the plaintiff's business, which comes within defamation and injurious falsehood; unmeritorious litigation, for which the specific tort remedy is an action for malicious prosecution or abuse of process; trade secret misappropriation; conversion; and slander of title. Plaintiffs have usually been permitted to do this. This has raised concerns that plaintiffs may avoid limitations of liability in the applicable torts by bringing actions for tortious interference.

This concern applies especially to actions alleging economic loss caused by false statements. When the alleged wrongful conduct by the defendant was a defamatory statement about the plaintiff, courts have applied the First Amendment limitations on defamation liability, which are discussed in Chapter 23. See *Jefferson County School District No. R-1 v. Moody's Investor's Services, Inc.*, 175 F.3d 848 (10th Cir. 1999) (statement must contain factual assertion capable of being proved false); *Medical Laboratory Management Consultants v. American Broadcasting Companies, Inc.*, 306 F.3d 806 (9th Cir. 2002) (plaintiff must demonstrate statements' falsity and defendants' fault); *Lakeshore Community Hospital, Inc. v. Perry*, 212 Mich. App. 396, 538 N.W.2d 24 (1995) (when plaintiff is public figure, must prove that defendant made factual statement with knowledge or reckless disregard of falsity). A court may also apply the qualified privileges of the common law of defamation. *A & B-Abell Elevator Co., Inc. v. Columbus/Central Ohio Building & Construction Trades Council*, 73 Ohio St. 3d 1, 651 N.E.2d 1283 (1995).

On a similar basis, a court may apply the limitations of liability for injurious falsehood to an action for interference with prospective advantage based on allegations of false statements resulting in economic loss, as in *Blatty v. New York Times Co.*, 42 Cal. 3d 1033, 728 P.2d 1177 (1986). Or apply the limitations of liability for malicious prosecution to an action based on the alleged initiation or use of groundless litigation. See *JPMorgan Chase Bank, N.A. v. KB Home*, 740 F. Supp. 2d 1192 (D. Nev. 2010). An action for tortious interference is appropriate when loss is caused by wrongful threats of litigation. An example is *Voorhees v. Guyan Machinery Co.*, 191 W. Va. 450, 446 S.E.2d 672 (1994), in which the plaintiff lost his job because a former employer threatened to enforce a noncompetition agreement that was not valid.

There is no defamation liability for a communication whose defamatory meaning is true (See Chapter 22.) The prevailing view is that there is no liability for interference with prospective advantage, or interference with contract, caused by the communication of true information. See Rest. 2d Torts § 772(a); Rest. 3d Torts—Economic Harm § 20(a). Consequently, a defendant sued for causing the plaintiff to lose current or potential employment by communication of information about the plaintiff will not be liable when the information is found to be true. See *Moore v. Hoff*, 821 N.W.2d 591 (Minn. App. 2012). An alternative view is that the truthfulness of the defendant's statements is to be considered in the determination of whether the interference was improper, but not conclusive. See *Kachmar v. SunGard Data Systems, Inc.*, 109 F.3d 173 (3d Cir. 1997).

C. CONSPIRACY; PRIMA FACIE TORT

Concerted action. Many actions for interference with prospective advantage and interference with contract have alleged that the defendants, or the defendants and others, acted in concert to deprive the plaintiff of employment or to prevent the plaintiff from conducting business in a certain way (or at all). Allegations and proof of concerted action, as distinct from individual action, may bear on liability in a number of ways. First, if one or more of the defendants is liable for a tort, those acting in concert with the liable defendant(s) are also liable as joint tortfeasors. Rest. 2d Torts § 876. Second, while numerous opinions have endorsed the position that actions which could be taken without liability by an individual could be taken without liability by a group, others have found in concerted action an element of coercion, oppression, intimidation or object of harming the plaintiff sufficient for tortious interference liability. Third, the plaintiff may claim that there is liability on the basis of conspiracy, either on its own or as the wrongful means element of liability for tortious interference.

The conventional view of liability on the ground of conspiracy is that it requires participation in a combination or agreement to accomplish an unlawful purpose, or to accomplish a lawful purpose by unlawful means, resulting in harm to the plaintiff. *E.g.*, *Fenestra Inc. v. Gulf American Land Corp.*, 377 Mich. 565, 141 N.W.2d 36 (1966); *Morgan v. Union County Board of Chosen Freeholders*, 268 N.J. Super. 337, 633 A.2d 985 (App. Div. 1993). A purpose to harm the plaintiff may be the unlawful purpose.

This overlaps liability for interference with prospective advantage and interference with contract. It is questionable whether finding a defendant liable on grounds of civil conspiracy adds to the liability that would exist otherwise. Some cases specify that there is no cause of action for conspiracy without tort liability on an independent basis. *Larobina v. McDonald*, 274 Conn. 394, 876 A.2d 522 (2005); *Dunlap v. Cottman Transmission Systems, LLC*, 287 Va. 207, 754 S.E.2d 313 (2014). If conspiracy makes a difference to liability, it is probably only for defendants who agreed to the commission of the tort but did not do enough to otherwise be liable as a joint tortfeasor. See Rest. 3d Torts—Economic Harm § 27, comment *a*.

Civil conspiracy now has less importance than previously. Liability for tortious interference depends primarily on the Second Restatement's factors for determination of whether the interference was improper, which do not depend upon whether defendants acted in concert, or findings of wrongful purpose or wrongful means. (See pp. 124–128.) Much of the concerted action by businesses and unions that once resulted in tort actions now is prohibited or regulated by antitrust, trade practices and labor relations statutes. However, there remain many instances in which an action for interference with prospective advantage or conspiracy remains the only ground (absent other torts) for suit over concerted action that deprived the plaintiff of opportunities to operate a business or engage in gainful employment—for example, denying a physician hospital privileges. See Annot., 7 A.L.R.4th 572.

Prima facie tort. "Prima facie tort" is another possible alternative to an action explicitly brought as an action for interference with prospective advantage. However, it has only limited acceptance and application. Its existence stems from the statement of Lord Justice Bowen in the *Mogul Steamship* case that "intentionally to do that which is calculated in the ordinary course of events to damage, and which does, in fact, damage another in that person's property or trade, is actionable if done without just cause or excuse." *Mogul Steamship Co., Ltd. v. McGregor, Gow, & Co.*, (1889) 23 Q.B.D. 598, 613 (C.A.). In *Aikens v. Wisconsin*, 195 U.S. 194, 204 (1904), Justice Holmes interpreted this to mean that "*prima facie*, the intentional infliction of temporal damage is a cause of action, which. . .requires a justification if the defendant is to escape." He went on to say that justification may depend upon the defendant's motives or the end for which the act was done.

These propositions were applied primarily to determine liability for interference with prospective advantage or interference with contract. However, in a few jurisdictions they led to recognition of a distinct "prima facie tort" action based on allegations that the defendant intentionally inflicted harm upon the plaintiff. The plaintiff's cause of action would be established by proof that the defendant intentionally caused harm to the plaintiff, and the defendant would be liable unless the defendant established justification for causing the harm.

Although seemingly a powerful theory of liability, prima facie tort has not had much effect on liability for causing economic harm. It has been accepted as a viable tort action in only a small number of states—primarily Missouri, New Mexico and New York. In those, liability has been limited by rules that conduct falling within specific tort categories is not actionable as prima facie tort and that liability requires that the defendant act with malice, or a purpose to cause harm. See Annot., 16 A.L.R.3d 1191. To apply it broadly to what in substance is interference with prospective advantage or interference with contract would conflict with the modern liability rules of those torts.

CHAPTER 9

INTERFERENCE WITH PROSPECTIVE ECONOMIC ADVANTAGE—NON-COMMERCIAL EXPECTATIONS

A. INTRODUCTION

Most actions for interference with prospective advantage claim loss of income or property from anticipated commercial or contractual transactions, such as sales of goods, supply of services or employment. By analogy, liability for interference with prospective advantage might attach to intentional interference with the plaintiff's prospects of obtaining something of economic value from sources other than contractual transactions—for example, interference with the receipt of an expected inheritance or with the plaintiff's ability to harvest natural resources. See Rest. 2d Torts § 774B, Special Note.

Reported cases on intentional interference with non-commercial expectations concern interference with prospects of receiving an inheritance or gift; interference with prospects of winning a competition or contest and receiving a prize; and interference with prospects of obtaining money in a lawsuit. These will be discussed in turn.

B. INTERFERENCE WITH INHERITANCE OR GIFT

There is now a body of case law recognizing intentional interference with inheritance and intentional interference with a gift as valid tort actions. They are included in the "black letter" provisions of both the Second Restatement and the Third Restatement. Rest. 2d Torts § 774B; Rest. 3d Torts—Economic Harm § 19. The case law is, however, somewhat divided. See Annot., 22 A.L.R.4th 1229. In some jurisdictions, courts have either rejected the action for interference with inheritance or greatly restricted it by excluding liability when a remedy could be sought in a probate action or when the plaintiff cannot prove with some certainty that the plaintiff would have received the inheritance, but for the defendant's tortious interference. This can apply to actions for loss of what is technically a gift rather than an inheritance, such as payments from a trust or life insurance policy, when litigated after the donor's death (as it typically is). There is particular difficulty in proving loss of an expectancy when there is no document by the donor expressing an intent to leave property or money to the plaintiff.

After a thorough review of the decisions of other courts, the Supreme Court of South Dakota decided in 2019 not to accept a tort action for intentional interference with inheritance. *Re Matter of Certification of Question of Law*, 931 N.W.2d 510 (S.D. 2019). Its principal reasons were the extensive statutory regulation of wills and trusts and the remedies for wrongful conduct in probate and trust law, including constructive trust. The opinion distinguished actions for interference with prospective contractual relations because "the pursuit of a contractual or business relationship. . .often involves upfront economic costs that could never be recouped" without such an action. More elaborate reasons are given in the majority opinion of *Archer v. Anderson*, 556 S.W.3d 228 (Tex. 2018).

Harmon v. Harmon, 404 A.2d 1020 (Me. 1979), is a representative of cases accepting actions for interference with an inheritance or gift, but in this instance allowing an action for interference with an anticipated inheritance prior to the death of the testator. The court reasoned that "If the law protects a person from interference with an opportunity to receive a benefit by entering into contractual relations in the future, the same protection should be accorded to a person's opportunity to receive a benefit as a prospective legatee. The uncertainty attendant upon the expectancy is equivalent. Neither the [prospective] employee nor the prospective legatee has any enforceable right to his likely benefit." *Id.*, 1023.

A generally agreed point is that for liability, the defendant's interference must be by means that are tortious in themselves or include the use of duress or undue influence. Tortious means include fraud, breach of fiduciary duty, intentional destruction of the property which the plaintiff would receive and destruction, alteration or concealment of documents providing for the inheritance or gift. The alleged interference may be persuading someone to give property or money to the defendant instead of the plaintiff, or otherwise not to grant it to the plaintiff. See Rest. 2d Torts § 774B, comment *c*; Rest. 3d Torts—Economic Harm § 19, comment *b*.

C. INTERFERENCE WITH COMPETITION FOR PRIZE

Another possible claim for interference with prospective advantage is for intentional interference with the plaintiff's prospects of winning a monetary prize in a competition or contest. It may be alleged that the defendant deprived the plaintiff of a winning place in the competition by fraud or physical obstruction.

The Second Restatement is supportive of such claims if it can be proved that the plaintiff had "a substantial certainty" of winning the competition, but for the defendant's tortious interference, or at least "a high probability of success." Rest. 2d Torts § 774B, Special Note. However, in the reported cases plaintiffs have been unsuccessful. The principal reasons have been (a) the lack of any certainty that the plaintiff would have won the competition without the interference and (b) the conclusion that participants in a competition are bound by the decisions of those who conduct or regulate the competition concerning who has won and remedies for violation of the rules. See *White v. Turfway Racing Association, Inc.*, 909 F.2d 941 (6th Cir. 1990) (action by bettor at race track against track management); *Harrison v. Jones*, 54 Ga. App. 852, 184 S.E. 889 (1936) (action by participant in newspaper subscription contest against another contestant); *Jones v. Duff*, 85 A.D.2d 713, 445 N.Y.S.2d 838 (1981) (action by professional boxer's manager and agent against promoters of match). *Cf. Smitha v. Gentry*, 20 Ky. L. Rptr. 171, 45 S.W. 515 (1898) (plaintiffs planned to capture murder suspect and obtain reward; defendant learned suspect's whereabouts by impersonating constable, arrested suspect and received reward).

Youst v. Longo, 43 Cal. 3d 64, 729 P.2d 728 (1987), is the leading modern case. The owner of a horse entered in a harness race sued the driver of another horse on allegations that the defendant drove his horse into the path of the plaintiff's horse and struck the horse with a whip. This allegedly caused the plaintiff's horse to break stride and finish the race in sixth place rather than in a better position. The plaintiff sought to recover the purse amount for the position in which his horse would have finished but for the defendant's action, less the purse the plaintiff received. The court affirmed dismissal of the action. It reasoned that a "threshold requirement" of liability for interference with prospective advantage was that it be reasonably probable the economic advantage would have been realized but for the interference. In most sporting events, including horse races, the probability that a competitor would have won the contest or a prize, but for the interference, was too speculative to be a basis of tort liability. The plaintiff's complaint therefore failed to meet the threshold requirement of probable advantage.

Furthermore, as a matter of public policy, it would be undesirable to entertain actions for prospective economic loss between competitors in a sporting contest. Supervision of horse racing and other sports by regulatory agencies was a relatively successful and generally accepted method of dealing with competitors' misconduct. The prospect of tort liability and intensive litigation scrutiny of participants' conduct could, the court feared, seriously harm competitive sports.

When there was a contract between the disappointed contestant and the provider of the contest, the contestant's claim might be framed as one for interference with contract. However, the inability to show a probability that the plaintiff would have won the competition, but for the interference, may defeat the claim. See Rest. 2d Torts § 912, comments *d*, *f*. And there may have been no actual interference with performance of the contract. There may be a successful action for deceit if the plaintiff was induced by the defendant's fraud to place losing bets on sports events or in card games. See Annot., 85 A.L.R.4th 1048.

D. INTERFERENCE WITH RECOVERY OF DAMAGES

1. SPOLIATION OF EVIDENCE

A financial expectation or hope that can amount to many millions of dollars is obtaining money through a lawsuit seeking damages. That expectation may be defeated by destruction or loss of evidence that would have supported the plaintiff's claims concerning liability and the magnitude of injury. In the 1980s, courts began to accept that there was a tort action for intentional spoliation of evidence. Spoliation of evidence was already a well-known concept, but when found its usual consequences were sanctions within the litigation in which the evidence was to be used and possible criminal prosecution.

Tort actions for intentional spoliation have usually involved allegations that the defendant destroyed evidence that would have been important for the plaintiff's litigation of a negligence or product liability action—for example, medical or business records which would support a claim that the plaintiff was injured by negligence, or the product or part that was the basis of a claim of injury by a defective product. However, the action in *Hazen v. Municipality of Anchorage*, 718 P.2d 456 (Alaska 1986), was based on allegations that a prosecutor intentionally altered a tape recording made when the plaintiff was arrested, removing exculpatory evidence. In *Elliott-Thomas v. Smith*, 154 Ohio St. 3d 11, 110 N.E.3d 1231 (2018), the plaintiff alleged destruction and concealment of evidence relevant to an action for wrongful termination from employment.

Judicial acceptance of the tort was based in part on the proposition that there is tort liability for intentionally causing economic loss by wrongful means and the analogy that could be drawn to intentional interference with prospective advantage in commercial transactions. Recognition of the tort would provide a financial remedy that otherwise would be unavailable, and it would deter wrongful conduct. Other remedies for spoliation were thought insufficient. See *Rizzuto v. Davidson Ladders, Inc.* 280 Conn. 225, 905 A.2d 1165 (2006). In *Smith v. Howard Johnson Co., Inc.*, 67 Ohio St. 3d 28, 615 N.E.2d 1037 (1993), the court specified that the elements of the cause of action were (1) pending or probable litigation involving the plaintiff, (2) the defendant's knowledge that litigation exists or is probable, (3) wilful destruction of evidence by the defendant, designed to disrupt the plaintiff's case, (4) disruption of the plaintiff's case, and (5) damages proximately caused by the defendant's acts. An action may be denied when the evidence has been concealed instead of destroyed. See *Elliott-Thomas v. Smith, supra.* Or when the plaintiff was aware of the spoliation before the trial of the case. See *rsc The Quality Measurement Co. v. IPSOS-ASI, Inc.*, 196 F. Supp. 2d 609 (S.D. Ohio 2002), aff'd, 56 Fed. Appx. 639 (6th Cir. 2003).

Intentional spoliation of evidence remains a recognized tort in a number of states, but the trend of the more recent state supreme court decisions is against its acceptance. See Annot., 70 A.L.R.4th 984. One of the main reasons for rejection of the tort is the availability of non-tort remedies for spoliation of evidence, especially sanctions against the party responsible for loss of the evidence and adverse evidentiary inferences. Another is the speculative nature of the damage that may have resulted—not only the amount of damage, but also whether any damage resulted. Without knowing the content and weight of the spoliated evidence, it could be impossible for a jury to assess what role the evidence would have played in the determination of the underlying action. There have also been concerns about the generation of spoliation actions and relitigation of issues when evidence was lost. See *Goff v. Harold Ives Trucking Co., Inc.*, 342 Ark. 143, 27 S.W.3d 387 (2000); *Cedars-Sinai Medical Center v. Superior Court*, 18 Cal. 4th 1, 954 P.2d 511 (1998).

Those cases rejected tort actions for "first party" spoliation—that is, spoliation by a party to the action in which the lost evidence would have been used. Arguably, there is a stronger reason for allowing a tort action for spoliation by a third party—someone who was not a party to the underlying action. Adverse inferences, litigation sanctions and similar alternatives to a tort action would have no application to a third party. Furthermore, viable claims of intentional spoliation by a non-litigant might not be so numerous as to engage concerns about burdening the legal system with additional lawsuits. See *Hibbits v. Sides*, 34 P.3d 327 (Alaska 2001); *Oliver v. Stimson Lumber Co.*, 297 Mont. 336, 993 P.2d 11 (1999). However, rejection of spoliation actions against first parties has been extended to actions against third parties. *Downen v. Redd*, 367 Ark. 551, 242 S.W.3d 273 (2006); *Temple Community Hospital v. Superior Court*, 20 Cal. 4th 464, 976 P.2d 223 (1999). *Contra, Raymond v. Idaho State Police*, 165 Idaho 682, 451 P.3d 17 (2019).

Opinions in cases allowing a tort action for intentional spoliation of evidence vary on what is required for proof of causation and damages. This is discussed in *Rizzuto v. Davidson Ladders, Inc., supra*. Some opinions indicate that the plaintiff must show that the plaintiff was unable to establish a *prima facie* case in the underlying litigation because of the spoliation of evidence. Others indicate that significant impairment of the plaintiff's prospects of success is sufficient. If the plaintiff meets these requirements, the plaintiff might be allowed recovery of all compensatory damages that would have been received if the prior action was successful.

2. INTERFERENCE WITH ENFORCEMENT OF JUDGMENT

Prospects of recovering money in a lawsuit may also be defeated by preventing enforcement of a judgment. There have been many cases on alleged wrongful transfer or concealment of assets that defeated recovery of money due under a judgment, but these have not been litigated as interference with prospective advantage actions. See Annot., 11 A.L.R.4th 345.

Outside this the reported case law is sparse. In the old case of *Yates v. Joyce*, 11 Johns. 136 (N.Y. Sup. Ct. 1814), the court held that the plaintiff had an action against the defendant for demolishing property to prevent its being taken in satisfaction of a judgment debt assigned to the plaintiff. In *Hoefler v. Hoefler*, 12 App. Div. 84, 42 N.Y.S. 1035 (1896), the court allowed an action against the defendant "for advising and procuring the [plaintiff's] husband to leave the state, and remain out of it," for the purpose of avoiding court-ordered payment of alimony.

Sharum v. Sharum, 101 Okla. 273, 225 P. 682 (1924), allowed a child to sue for alleged malicious interference by a third party with the child's receipt of court-ordered support from his father. However, in *Folmer & Associates LLP v. Holberg*, 776 So. 2d 112 (Ala. 2000), the court rejected a claim for intentionally depriving the plaintiff of amounts due under a divorce judgment, framed as a claim for interference with a contractual or business relationship. The judgment did not constitute a contractual or business relationship, and the court declined to extend the action for tortious interference to claims of interference with a judgment of divorce. There were other remedies when a judgment debtor failed to satisfy a judgment. *Cf. Coventry Group, Inc. v. Gottlieb*, 7 N.E.3d 611 (Ohio App. 2014), rejecting an action for "tortious interference with a business expectancy" by a judgment creditor against defendants who allegedly prevented collection of the judgment debt by causing the debtor to file for bankruptcy.

CHAPTER 10
NEGLIGENCE

A. INTRODUCTION

Negligence liability generally is outside the subject-matter of this book. However, there are some issues of negligence liability for economic loss that are related to subjects discussed in the book, such as injurious falsehood, defamation, malicious prosecution and loss resulting from physical injury to another person. An overview of four of these issues will be presented in this chapter: whether there is liability for loss caused by injury to an employee; whether an attorney is liable for negligence that causes loss to a non-client; whether there is liability for loss caused by negligent spoliation of evidence; and whether there is liability for loss caused by a negligently made false statement, other than in cases of a negligent misrepresentation relied upon by the plaintiff.

Essential background to the discussion is the general rule that there is no tort liability for "pure economic loss"—that is, economic loss which is not a consequence of personal injury or property damage to the plaintiff—on grounds of negligence, outside cases in which a professional's negligence causes loss to a client or the plaintiff has an action under the law of negligent misrepresentation. This is not an absolute rule operating in all cases. Some courts have decided that in some situations a negligence action for economic loss is maintainable. An example is *A.C. Excavating v. Yacht Club II Homeowners Association,*

Inc., 114 P.3d 862 (Colo. 2005), which allowed homeowners to bring negligence actions against subcontractors to recover losses caused by construction defects. Another is *J'Aire Corp. v. Gregory*, 24 Cal. 3d 799, 598 P.2d 60 (1979), which allowed the operator of a restaurant to sue for loss of business revenue caused by a contractor's delay in completion of a heating and air conditioning project in the building. Usually the decision to permit a negligence action has been based on considerations of the foreseeability of a person in the plaintiff's position suffering economic loss, the closeness of the connection between the negligence and the loss, the ability to identify a limited category of parties to whom the duty to prevent economic loss would be owed, and policy factors including deterrence of negligence and allocating the loss to the party better able to bear it. See *People Express Airlines, Inc. v. Consolidated Rail Corp.*, 100 N.J. 246, 495 A.2d 107 (1985). But it is still accurate to regard the absence of negligence liability for pure economic loss as the norm outside professional-client cases (with some extension to business services performed for the plaintiff's benefit) and liability for negligent misrepresentation. There will be no liability unless a court is persuaded that liability for economic loss should be possible in a particular type of case or fact pattern. This reinforces the intent requirements of liability for interference with contract and interference with business or prospective advantage.

B. INJURY TO EMPLOYEE

As discussed in the text on actions for injuries to family members (pp. 10, 54), English common law developed an action by which a master could claim damages for loss of a servant's services—the action *per quod servitium amisit.* The action could be brought when a servant was injured by wrongful conduct. It was by analogy to this action that an action for loss of a spouse's services and consortium was established, and for many years parental claims for loss caused by injury to a child were in form the action of a master for loss of the services of a servant. The action *per quod servitium amisit* could also be brought when a servant had been induced to leave the master's service. That was a foundation of the liability for intentional interference with a contract for service recognized in *Lumley v. Gye.* (See pp. 95–97.)

The master's action for loss of a servant's services would appear to provide a sufficient basis for an action by an employer for loss of the services of an employee, when the employee was injured by negligence or other tort. However, in the twentieth century American courts rejected such actions. There is thus no liability in modern American tort law for an employer's economic loss when an employee is injured and cannot work. A variety of reasons for this appear in the opinions, including that allowing an employer to sue as the master of a servant is out of keeping with modern employer-employee relationships, the loss of the employer is too indirect or remote from the defendant's negligence, it would be undesirable to add to the litigation brought when a person is injured, and it would be anomalous to allow an employer to recover damages when generally, outside the family relationship, there is no action for loss resulting from physical injury to another person. See *Morton v. Merrillville Toyota, Inc.*, 562 N.E.2d 781 (Ind. App. 1990); *Nemo Foundations, Inc. v. New River Co.*, 155 W. Va. 149, 181 S.E.2d 687 (1971); Annot., 4 A.L.R.4th 504.

In a few states, nineteenth century codifications of common law provide statutory authority for a master to claim damages on account of injury to a servant. Cal. Civil Code § 49; Mont. Code Ann. § 27–1–516; 76 Okla. Stat. § 8. The court in *I.J. Weinrot and Son, Inc. v. Jackson*, 40 Cal. 3d 327, 708 P.2d 682 (1985), decided that this allowed recovery only for injuries to servants who were members of a master's household. Earlier, the English Court of Appeal had decided that the common law action was maintainable only in cases of injuries to domestic or menial (household) servants. *Inland Revenue Commissioners v. Hambrook*, [1956] 2 Q.B. 641 (C.A.). These decisions bar potential employer claims for injuries to all but a small proportion of the employed workforce.

C. ATTORNEY LIABILITY TO NON-CLIENT

It was long the standard rule that in performing professional services, an attorney owed a duty of care only to clients and was not liable for negligence that resulted in economic losses to other persons. However, in the past half-century, a majority of courts presented with the issue have decided that a person deprived of an intended inheritance by an attorney's negligence in the drafting or execution of a will or trust can have a cause of action against the attorney. See *Heyer v. Flaig*, 70 Cal. 2d 223, 449 P.2d 161 (1969); *Hale v. Groce*, 304 Or. 281, 744 P.2d 1289 (1987). Unlike other services performed by attorneys, preparation of a will, or a trust providing for income or property to go to survivors of the client, is intended primarily to benefit persons other than the client. And if there is no legal duty to the intended beneficiaries, a negligent attorney will avoid liability to anyone except in the unlikely event that negligence is discovered by the client before the client's death.

In some jurisdictions the intent to leave property or money to the plaintiff must be expressed in the document and not provided by extrinsic evidence. See *Espinosa v. Sparber, Shevin, Shapo, Rosen and Heilbronner*, 612 So. 2d 1378 (Fla. 1993). *Contra*, *Simpson v. Calivas*, 139 N.H. 1, 650 A.2d 318 (1994). There remain a number of states in which an alleged intended beneficiary of a testamentary disposition has no cause of action against the deceased person's attorney. This is mainly because of precedent supporting the rule of no liability and the belief that owing a duty to intended beneficiaries would create conflicts of interest. See *Noble v. Bruce*, 349 Md. 730, 709 A.2d 1264 (1998); *Barcelo v. Elliott*, 923 S.W.2d 575 (Tex. 1996). This is sometimes expressed as the position that an attorney is subject to liability only when there was "privity of contract" between the attorney and the plaintiff.

Apart from this, an attorney may be liable to a non-client because of negligent misrepresentation, as when the attorney of the seller of property provides an erroneous approval of title for the buyer; or because the attorney was engaged by an intermediary to provide legal services for the plaintiff, as when the negligence of an attorney for a debt collection agency prevents recovery of a debt by a creditor. See *Metzger v. Slocum*, 272 Or. 313, 537 P.2d 74 (1975). That an attorney's work would benefit the plaintiff if performed properly does not mean that the attorney was engaged to provide services for the benefit of the plaintiff, even when the plaintiff was a member of the client's family. See *Pelham v. Griesheimer*, 92 Ill. 2d 13, 440 N.E.2d 96 (1982) (attorney for mother in divorce action not liable to children for failure to ensure enforcement of provision in divorce decree for children to be beneficiaries of father's life insurance); *Metzger v. Slocum, supra* (attorney for adoptive parent not liable to child for failure to perfect adoption, preventing child from claiming support); *Burger v. Pond*, 224 Cal. App. 3d 597, 273 Cal. Rptr. 709 (1990) (attorney for husband in divorce case not liable to woman husband intended to marry for negligence that caused divorce to be set aside and invalidity of her marriage to husband).

Attorneys owe no duty of care to opposing parties in their cases and are not held liable for harm to opposing parties caused by professional negligence. There is thus no negligence action against an attorney for harm caused by bringing a meritless action against the plaintiff. *Berlin v. Nathan*, 64 Ill.

App. 3d 940, 381 N.E.2d 1367 (1978); *Friedman v. Dozorc*, 412 Mich. 1, 312 N.W.2d 585 (1981). *Cf. Allied Financial Services, Inc. v. Easley*, 676 F.2d 422 (10th Cir. 1982) (no negligence action against attorney for invalid garnishment of plaintiff's funds). To allow such an action would undermine the limits of liability for use of legal process established in the law of malicious prosecution, and it would create a conflict between the attorney's duty to a client and the attorney's duty to the adversary. An attorney's violation of a statute or rule of court regulating the conduct of attorneys is not a basis of liability to an opponent. See *Baxt v. Liloia*, 155 N.J. 190, 714 A.2d 271 (1998); *Bob Godfrey Pontiac, Inc. v. Roloff*, 291 Or. 318, 630 P.2d 840 (1981).

D. SPOLIATION OF EVIDENCE

"Spoliation of evidence" has connotations of intentionally causing loss, destruction or alteration of evidence, but the term is also applied to causing loss, destruction or alteration of evidence unintentionally. As in instances of intentional spoliation (see Chapter 9), the unintentional spoliation of evidence may have the consequence that a party to litigation does not win a case, or does not pursue a claim, when otherwise the party would have recovered damages. Another possible consequence is that the party receives less in a court judgment or settlement than what the party would have recovered with the evidence. The lost evidence could, for example, be a defective component of a manufactured product, needed to prove that the product was defective when sold by the defendant or that the defendant was negligent in using the product. It could be a document supporting the plaintiff's allegations of negligence.

There is now a body of case law on whether there is liability for negligent spoliation of evidence by the defendant. In a number of cases courts have held that there is a cause of action for loss caused by negligent spoliation of evidence, at least when the defendant had voluntarily assumed a duty to preserve evidence. See *Smith v. Atkinson*, 771 So. 2d 429 (Ala. 2000); *Oliver v. Stimson Lumber Co.*, 297 Mont. 336, 993 P.2d 11 (1999). In a larger number of cases, such an action has been rejected. See *Fletcher v. Dorchester Mutual Insurance Co.*, 437 Mass. 544, 773 N.E.2d 420 (2002); *Ortega v. City of New York*, 9 N.Y.3d 69, 876 N.E.2d 1189 (2007); Annot., 101 A.L.R.5th 61.

The main reasons given for refusal to accept negligent spoliation actions are similar to those given for refusal to recognize intentional spoliation as a tort. (See pp. 144–145.) These include the existence of other remedies for spoliation, including sanctions against the party responsible for loss of the evidence and adverse inferences, and the speculative nature of the alleged pecuniary loss sustained by a plaintiff. (How can one know what difference the evidence would have made to the result of the plaintiff's earlier damages claim?) Additionally, there is generally no duty to act to protect another's interests, even when requested, and negligent spoliation claims are within the general rule of no negligence liability for pure economic loss. See *Lips v. Scottsdale Healthcare Corp.*, 224 Ariz. 266, 229 P.3d 1008 (2010). Even if an action lies against third parties for negligent spoliation, there may be no action against the party the evidence was to be used against, as such "first party spoliation" can be deterred or remedied by other means. See *Martino v. Wal-Mart Stores, Inc.*, 908 So. 2d 342 (Fla. 2005); *Hannah v. Heeter*, 213 W. Va. 704, 584 S.E.2d 560 (2003).

E. FALSE STATEMENTS

Liability for economic loss caused by a negligently made false statement must be distinguished from liability for economic loss caused by negligent misrepresentation. There is a large and complex body of case law regulating whether there is liability for loss caused by the plaintiff's reliance on a false statement or representation. This is discussed in Kionka, *Torts in a Nutshell* (6th ed. 2015), Chapter 15. There is much less case law on whether there is negligence liability for harm to a person's economic interests because of a false or misleading statement made to someone other than the plaintiff.

In the majority of cases, courts rejected the plaintiffs' negligence actions. These include an action against a consultant whose report allegedly caused a hospital to stop using the plaintiff's radiology services. *Rodriguez v. ECRI Shared Services*, 984 F. Supp. 1363 (D. Kan. 1997). An action against an accountant whose report of an audit of corporate records caused dismissal of the corporation's business manager. *Demetracopoulos v. Wilson*, 138 N.H. 371, 640 A.2d 279 (1994). An action against a bank for telling another bank that the plaintiff failed to repay a loan when due, causing the plaintiff to be refused a loan. *Graney Development Corp. v. Taksen*, 92 Misc. 2d 764, 400 N.Y.S.2d 717 (Sup. Ct. 1978), aff'd, 66 A.D.2d 1008, 411 N.Y.S.2d 756 (1978). And an action against the publisher of an encyclopedia of chemicals and drugs for misrepresenting the toxicity of a chemical utilized in the plaintiff's product, causing a loss of sales. *Demuth Development Corp. v. Merck & Co., Inc.*, 432 F. Supp. 990 (E.D.N.Y. 1977).

These decisions are due more to the reasoning that the plaintiff was owed no duty of care by the plaintiff, or that the actions were outside the scope of liability for negligent misrepresentation because the plaintiff did not rely on the false statement, than to the general rule of no negligence liability for economic loss. An additional factor in some cases is the court's perception that the plaintiff's negligence claim was an attempt to avoid the limitations of liability for defamation or injurious falsehood. See *Ross v. Gallant, Farrow & Co., P.C.*, 27 Ariz. App. 89, 551 P.2d 79 (1976) (accountants' audit report stated or implied that union business manager withdrew money from bank account without authorization); *Dairy Stores, Inc. v. Sentinel Publishing Co., Inc.*, 191 N.J. Super. 202, 465 A.2d 953 (Law Div. 1983), aff'd, 198 N.J. Super. 19, 486 A.2d 344 (App. Div. 1985), aff'd, 104 N.J. 125, 516 A.2d 220 (1986) (statements that bottled water sold by plaintiff was contaminated by chlorine); *Ramsay v. Mary Imogene Bassett Hospital*, 113 A.D.2d 149, 495 N.Y.S.2d 282 (1985) (derogatory statements by plaintiff's former employer to prospective new employers).

There are, however, some decisions supporting negligence liability for economic harm caused by a false or misleading statement. A number stem from cases in which the defendant conducted drug tests on an employee and reported a positive result to the employer, causing the employee's dismissal or suspension. In *Stinson v. Physicians Immediate Care, Ltd.*, 269 Ill. App. 3d 659, 646 N.E.2d 930 (1995), the court held that the laboratory conducting the test owed the tested employee a duty of care. It emphasized the defendant's knowledge that the plaintiff was likely to lose his job as a consequence of a report that he tested positive for drug use, the magnitude of the harm, and the laboratory's being in the best position to guard against the injury and bear the financial burden of the loss caused by a false positive report. See also *Sharpe v. St. Luke's Hospital*, 573 Pa. 90, 821 A.2d 1215 (2003); *Shaw v. Pyschemedics Corp.*, 426 S.C. 194, 826 S.E.2d 281 (2019). In *Landon v. Kroll Laboratory Specialists, Inc.*, 22 N.Y.3d 1, 999 N.E.2d 1121 (2013), the court held that a laboratory was under a duty of care to a person required to have random drug tests as a condition of probation. But in *Willis v. Roche Biomedical Laboratories, Inc.*, 61 F.3d 313 (5th Cir. 1995), it was held that a laboratory owed no duty to a person required to undergo drug tests as a condition of employment.

An analogous situation is that in which the plaintiff was discharged because the defendant reported that the plaintiff had failed a polygraph test. The court in *Lawson v. Howmet Aluminum Corp.*, 449 N.E.2d 1172 (Ind. App. 1983), held that the polygraph examiner, although hired by the employer, owed a duty of care to the employee. However, another court held there was no negligence liability in this situation. The court decided that the problem of harm caused by lie detector tests, whose validity was questionable, was more appropriately resolved by legislation than by the creation of a new tort action. *Hall v. United Parcel Service of America, Inc.*, 76 N.Y.2d 27, 555 N.E.2d 273 (1990).

A person may also be terminated from employment, or denied employment, because of a physician's report that the person is medically unfit for the position. Some cases hold that the physician owes no duty to the person examined. *Felton v. Schaeffer*, 229 Cal. App. 3d 299, 279 Cal. Rptr. 713 (1991); *Rand v. Miller*, 185 W. Va. 705, 408 S.E.2d 655 (1991). *Cf. Erpelding v. Lisek*, 71 P.3d 754 (Wyo. 2003) (assessment of employee by psychological counsellor). But the court in *Armstrong v. Morgan*, 545 S.W.2d 45 (Tex. Civ. App. 1976), declared that the physician owed the person being examined "a duty not to injure him physically or otherwise."

A different type of case is that in which the plaintiff claimed to have lost a deserved insurance payment or workers' compensation because a physician or claims investigator made an erroneous report. The courts appear to be unanimous in holding that a physician is not liable to a negligence action in this situation. See *Hafner v. Beck*, 185 Ariz. 389, 916 P.2d 1105 (Ct. App. 1995); *Martinez v. Lewis*, 969 P.2d 213 (Colo. 1998). But there is some support for a claims investigator or insurance adjuster having a duty to the insured. See *Morvay v. Hanover Insurance Companies*, 127 N.H. 723, 506 A.2d 333 (1986), *Contra, Sanchez v. Lindsey Morden Claims Services, Inc.*, 72 Cal. App. 4th 249, 84 Cal. Rptr. 2d 799 (1999); *Hamill v. Pawtucket Mutual Insurance Co.*, 179 Vt. 250, 892 A.2d 226 (2005).

A major argument against recognizing a duty to prevent economic loss by communication of a false statement, and liability if the misstatement was due to negligence, is that it would allow a plaintiff to have a negligence action for what in substance is defamation or injurious falsehood and avoid the substantive limitations and procedural requirements of those torts. This argument was central to the leading English case, *Spring v. Guardian Assurance Plc.*, [1995] 2 A.C. 296 (H.L.). The defendant had been sued because it furnished such a negative reference about the plaintiff, a former employee, to potential new employers that he was denied employment. One ground for the plaintiff's action was injurious falsehood. That claim failed because the persons responsible for the reference did not act with malice. As qualified privilege attached to giving employment references, the absence of malice would also defeat a defamation claim. The Court of Appeal, reasoning that liability for giving a damaging reference was governed by the rules of defamation and injurious falsehood, and that to recognize a duty of care would bypass the limits of liability established by those rules, held that a negligence action was not maintainable. The House of Lords disagreed and held that a former employer did owe a duty of care to a former employee in giving an employment reference.

A duty arose because of the employer-employee relationship, the dependence of employees on references furnished by former and present employers, the clear foreseeability of harm, and the benefits of providing a remedy and inducing greater accuracy in references. This was thought not to be in conflict with the torts of defamation and injurious falsehood, which did not have the concept of a duty of care.

The decision in this case has not, to date, been accepted or rejected by American courts. As indicated earlier (see p. 158), the perception that the plaintiff's negligence claim was an attempt to avoid the limitations of liability for defamation or injurious falsehood has been a factor in some opinions that rejected negligence actions. But in *Bulkin v. Western Kraft East, Inc.*, 422 F. Supp. 437 (E.D. Pa. 1976), the court allowed a negligence action to proceed on facts resembling those of *Spring v. Guardian Assurance Plc*. Arguably the First Amendment rules that limit liability for defamation (see Chapter 23) should apply to any negligence action for harm caused by a defamatory statement.

CHAPTER 11

INJURIOUS FALSEHOOD

A. INTRODUCTION

Injurious falsehood is a long-established tort with concrete rules of liability. Its function is to provide a remedy for false statements that cause harm to economic interests, especially a plaintiff's prospects of selling property, goods or services. While important, it is one of the less prominent torts. The main reason is that because of the stringent conditions for liability, most people who suffer economic loss because of a false statement could not win an action for injurious falsehood. Also, in many instances in which an injurious falsehood action could be successful, the plaintiff would instead sue for defamation (libel or slander), in which most of the main rules of liability are more favorable to plaintiffs. Corporations and other legal entities, as well as natural persons, can bring actions for defamation. (See pp. 345–346.)

Injurious falsehood resembles defamation and is sometimes confused with it. In both, plaintiffs sue for harm caused by the defendant's making a false statement about the plaintiff, or something connected with the plaintiff. For some of the less litigated parts of injurious falsehood law, such as privileges, it is assumed that rule for injurious falsehood is the same as the rule for defamation. Injurious falsehood and actions for slander both require pleading and proving "special damage" (unless the slander is "slander per se"). Labelling injurious falsehood actions as "slander of title," "slander of goods," or "trade libel" suggests, misleadingly, that injurious falsehood is libel or slander and that oral injurious falsehood and written injurious falsehood are different torts.

Despite the resemblances between injurious falsehood and defamation and the number of instances in which liability for both could be found, they are distinctly different in substance. Their elements of liability differ in critical respects, especially in injurious falsehood's requirements that the plaintiff plead and prove the statement's falsity, the defendant's malice in making it, and special damage. Injurious falsehood is an economic tort. It provides a remedy for statements harmful to reputation only when they are proved in a specific way to be harmful to an economic interest of the plaintiff. Defamation law provides a remedy for statements harmful to a person's reputation. It provides a remedy for economic loss only when caused by a statement harmful to the plaintiff's reputation. See Rest. 2d Torts § 623A, comment *g*. A statement that falsely describes the plaintiff may be harmful but not defamatory because not injurious to reputation. An example would be a false statement that a professional athlete or actor is suffering from terminal cancer. See *Chuy v. Philadelphia Eagles Football Club*, 595 F.2d 1265 (3d Cir. 1979).

For plaintiffs, the primary benefits of an action for injurious falsehood are (1) it can provide a remedy for statements that are economically harmful but not defamatory; (2) an injurious falsehood action is usually not subject to the statutory limitations and procedural requirements for defamation actions; (3) a plaintiff may obtain injunctive relief against repetition of a false statement; and (4) the action can survive the death of a party.

The origins of the tort are in actions on the case for causing damage by statements meaning that the plaintiff lacked good or complete title to land. Such a statement impaired the plaintiff's ability to sell or lease the land. The action acquired the name of "slander of title" although it did not necessarily involve any defamation. Gradually the scope of the action extended to aspersions on title to personal property, and eventually to aspersions on the conduct of a business or trade. The actions acquired labels such as "slander of goods," "trade libel" and "disparagement". These terms are still widely used. But whatever the label given to what in substance is an injurious falsehood action, and regardless of whether the defendant's statement was written or oral, the law applying to it is the same, with one important qualification: a court may treat slander of title as a tort distinct from the other types of injurious falsehood, and in some jurisdictions a defendant may have to justify the "slander" by showing that it was a *bona fide* (good faith) claim.

The essential requirements of liability for injurious falsehood are the defendant's publication of a false statement calculated to injure an economic interest of the plaintiff; the defendant made the statement with "malice"; and the statement caused "special damage." These requirements will be discussed in turn below. The plaintiff has the burden of pleading and proving facts that satisfy these requirements.

B. FALSE STATEMENT CALCULATED TO INJURE ECONOMIC INTEREST

The requirement of proof that the defendant published a false statement calculated to injure an economic interest combines three distinct elements: (1) the defendant's publication of the statement, (2) the statement's falsity, and (3) the capacity of the statement to harm an economic interest.

Publication. In injurious falsehood, "publication" has the same meaning as in defamation. It is the defendant's communication of the statement to some person other than the plaintiff, not publication to large numbers of persons. (See pp. 378–380.) Publication has not been a major legal issue in most injurious falsehood cases. The defendant has usually deliberately communicated the statement to one or more persons. In slander of title cases, publication has occurred if the defendant filed some claim to the plaintiff's property, including a security interest, in a public record. What might raise legal issues in an injurious falsehood action concerning publication is the defendant's responsibility for harm caused by repetition of the statement by others. The defendant's responsibility for Internet statements composed by other persons may also be an issue, as in defamation actions. It is usually assumed that the law on publication developed in defamation cases will apply to injurious falsehood actions. See Rest. 2d Torts §§ 630–632.

Falsity of statement. One of the clear differences between the law of injurious falsehood and the common law of defamation is the requirement that the plaintiff allege and prove the falsity of the defendant's statement. Whether the statement is provably false may be a major contested issue in an injurious falsehood case. Certain types of statements, such as expressions of opinion and assertions that another's product or service is superior to the plaintiff's, can be particularly difficult to prove false. There is no rule of non-liability for statements of opinion, but the plaintiff may have to prove the falsity of facts that are included in or implied by the statement. See Rest. 2d Torts § 634, comment *c*.

Capacity of statement to harm an economic interest. Although expressed in a number of different ways, it appears to be a requirement of liability that the statement be calculated to injure an economic interest, meaning that the statement have a likelihood or tendency to cause harm to a property, financial or other economic interest. (Rest. 2d Torts § 623A requires that the defendant recognized or should have recognized that the statement was likely to harm the plaintiff's pecuniary interests.) A statement that makes no adverse reflection on the plaintiff's business, but that could damage it, is actionable—for example a statement that the business has closed. When the plaintiff can prove than the statement caused "special damage" to an economic interest, it is probable that the statement had a likelihood or tendency to cause such damage. This is not always the case, but plaintiffs able to prove special damage do not seem to have lost injurious falsehood actions on the ground that it would not have been recognized in advance that the statement could cause the plaintiff economic loss.

While the statement must have been understood to convey some meaning about the plaintiff's business or what the plaintiff was trying to sell or market, the statement need not contain a direct reference to the plaintiff or the plaintiff's business, goods or title. The classic example is *Riding v. Smith*, (1876) 1 Ex. D. 91, in which the defendant had said that the plaintiff's wife, who assisted in the plaintiff's grocery business, committed adultery on the premises. (The premises included the marital residence.) The court thought it was a natural consequence of the statement that people would "cease to resort to the shop." Another example is when it was said that a competitor's business service was the only one of its kind. *Dale System, Inc. v. Time, Inc.*, 116 F. Supp. 527 (D. Conn. 1953). Slander of title is found when the defendant claims ownership of property that the plaintiff owns. See Rest. 2d Torts § 629, comment *c*.

A court may nevertheless decide there is no liability because there was not a sufficient reference to the plaintiff's property or business. See *Hartford Casualty Insurance Co. v. Swift Distribution, Inc.*, 59 Cal. 4th 277, 326 P.3d 253 (2014). In *Keith v. Laurel County Fiscal Court*, 254 S.W.3d 842 (Ky. App. 2008), it was held that a landowner had no action for loss resulting from false statements about adjacent property. *Blatty v. New York Times Co.*, 42 Cal. 3d 1033, 728 P.2d 1177 (1986), rejected an author's action against *The New York Times* for omission of his novel from the newspaper's "best seller" list. When the statement disparages a large group of business persons or companies, or their products, an injurious falsehood action will probably fail (as would a defamation action) because the statement did not refer to particular members of the group. This was a problem for the plaintiffs in *Auvil v. CBS "60 Minutes,"* 800 F. Supp. 928 (E.D. Wash. 1992), a class action disparagement claim by nearly five thousand Washington apple growers, litigated because of a broadcast on use in the apple industry of an alleged carcinogen.

The requirement that the statement be calculated to injure an economic interest, and the understanding that injurious falsehood is an economic tort, would deny liability when a false statement was calculated to cause and did cause harm to the plaintiff that was not economic—for example, physical attack or criminal prosecution. See *Neshewat v. Salem*, 173 F.3d 357 (6th Cir. 1999). Arguably there should be a remedy if the defendant knowingly made a false statement that was likely to cause and did cause particular harm, even if it was not economic. A few cases support this. One is *Al Raschid v. News Syndicate Co.*, 265 N.Y. 1, 191 N.E. 713 (1934), in which the defendant allegedly gave false information to immigration officials that caused the plaintiff to be arrested and deported. And it could be contended that there is an injurious falsehood action when a statement is calculated to cause and does cause identifiable financial loss, although the primary harm is non-economic—for example, a statement that causes the plaintiff to be prosecuted, or causes the plaintiff's fiancé to break off an engagement. See Rest. 2d Torts § 623A, comment *a*.

Comparisons. Numerous injurious falsehood actions have been brought for statements that unfavorably compared the plaintiff's product or service with a competitor's. The leading case is *White v. Mellin*, [1895] A.C. 154 (H.L.), in which the proprietor of a brand of prepared food for infants attached to the plaintiff's product a notice stating that the proprietor's product was far more nutritious and healthful than any other. A lower court's dismissal of the action was affirmed. The judges deciding the case gave a number of reasons why there would be no liability for statements that the defendant's product was superior or that the plaintiff's product was inferior to the defendant's. These included that mere "puffing" of one's own product was not actionable, even if it included representing the plaintiff's product as inferior, or inferior in particular qualities; the type of statement made by the defendant was not calculated to cause injury to the plaintiff because it would not be taken seriously and cause consumers to buy the defendant's product; and there should not be actions in which the court would have to decide which of two products was better. It previously had been made clear that when the defendant's statement consisted of a comparison between the defendant's product and the plaintiff's, the plaintiff had to plead and prove that special damage was caused by making a false representation about the plaintiff's product, as distinct from a false representation about the defendant's product. This could be difficult to prove. See *Young v. Macrae*, (1862) 3 B. & S. 264, 122 Eng. Rep. 100 (Q.B.).

Nevertheless, there have been some instances in which courts have sustained injurious falsehood actions for statements that unfavorably compared the plaintiff's product or service with a competitor's. In deciding which statements are actionable courts have used, either singly or in combination, the criteria of whether the defendant's statement made a specific allegation of defect or demerit in the plaintiff's product or service, rather than a more general allegation of inferiority; whether it was a statement of fact, whose truth or falsity could be ascertained, rather than opinion or "puffing"; and whether it was likely to be taken seriously and influence buying decisions. See *Testing Systems, Inc. v. Magnaflux Corp.*, 251 F. Supp. 286 (E.D. Pa. 1996). There can be liability if the defendant falsely stated that the plaintiff has fewer sales or a smaller audience than a competitor. See *Brunson Communications, Inc. v. Arbitron, Inc.*, 266 F. Supp. 2d 377 (E.D. Pa. 2003).

Comparisons of products or services are made by third parties as well as competitors. If the third party is a company or organization that purports to provide unbiased reports, its statements are likely to contain specific facts and be taken seriously. If its statements are false, an action for injurious falsehood is possible. But the malice requirement would bar liability for statements published in the good faith belief that they were true, and special damage may be difficult to prove. See *Brunson Communications, Inc. v.*

Arbitron, Inc., supra; *Bose Corp. v. Consumers Union of United States, Inc.*, 692 F.2d 189 (1st Cir. 1982), aff'd, 466 U.S. 485 (1984).

C. MALICE

Allegation and proof of the defendant's "malice" is a critical element of liability for injurious falsehood. "Malice" is a label for the state of mind required for liability. The malice requirement is the main reason why there is usually no tort liability for false statements that result in economic loss, unless there is liability for defamation or misrepresentation. In most instances malice cannot be proved.

As fundamental as malice is to the law of injurious falsehood, it is the element of liability about which there is the greatest uncertainty. One reason is that in older cases involving what is now recognized as injurious falsehood, especially cases involving slander of title claims, malice was not treated as an element of liability that the plaintiff was required to allege and prove. Instead, defendants were thought to have a privilege or defense when they acted in good faith, without malice, and plaintiffs could overcome this by showing that there was malice or an absence of good faith. However, the main reason for uncertainty now is that the authorities are not in complete agreement on what constitutes malice for purposes of an injurious falsehood action.

That said, and putting aside any restriction of liability to be derived from constitutional law (see below), it is fairly clear that a defendant will be regarded as having malice if any of the following is alleged and proved: (1) the defendant had a primary motive of ill will, spite or desire to do harm; (2) the defendant acted with the purpose of causing harm or loss to the plaintiff or damage to the plaintiff's interests, at least when there is no legal justification or privilege; or (3) the defendant had knowledge of the statement's falsity or reckless disregard for truth or falsity. See *Hurlbut v. Gulf Atlantic Life Insurance Co.*, 749 S.W.2d 762 (Tex. 1987); Rest. 2d Torts § 623A, comment *d*. Reckless disregard would be making a statement without believing it was true or caring whether it was true. It could also include making a statement while having serious doubts about its truth.

Mere carelessness in making a statement is not a basis of liability for injurious falsehood, no matter how damaging the result. When someone makes a statement believing it is true, without a motive of spite or purpose to do harm, there is no liability for this tort. *Balden v. Shorter*, [1933] Ch. 427.

D. CONSTITUTIONAL LAW LIMITATIONS

In a series of Supreme Court cases that will be discussed in Chapter 23, the First Amendment has been interpreted to require substantial limitations on recovery of damages for defamation. The primary limitation is that when a defamation action is brought by a public official or public figure, the plaintiff must prove that the defendant made the statement with knowledge of its falsity or reckless disregard for truth or falsity. *New York Times Co. v. Sullivan*, 376 U.S. 254 (1964); *Curtis Publishing Co.*

v. Butts, 388 U.S. 130 (1967). Also, the plaintiff must prove the defendant's knowledge of or reckless disregard for falsity in order to recover punitive or presumed damages, when the statement involved a matter of public concern. *Gertz v. Robert Welch, Inc.*, 418 U.S. 323 (1974), as interpreted in *Dun & Bradstreet, Inc. v. Greenmoss Builders, Inc.*, 472 U.S. 749 (1985). And the statement must have a factual connotation that is provably false. *Milkovich v. Lorain Journal Co.*, 497 U.S. 1 (1990).

It is arguable that the constitutional limitations on liability for defamation apply to injurious falsehood also. Both involve claims for harm allegedly caused by communication of a false statement. In an injurious falsehood case, the statement complained of may involve a matter of public concern and the plaintiff may be a public figure, such as a prominent business or business proprietor. It has been held in several cases that the First Amendment limitations of defamation liability apply to injurious falsehood actions. See *SCO Group, Inc. v. Novell, Inc.,* 692 F. Supp. 2d 1287 (D. Utah 2010); *Granada Biosciences, Inc. v. Forbes, Inc.*, 49 S.W.3d 610 (Tex. App. 2001), rev'd, 124 S.W.3d 67 (Tex. 2003). But some courts have decided that because "commercial speech" has received less First Amendment protection than non-commercial speech, the defamation law requirement that a public figure prove the defendant's knowledge of falsity, or reckless disregard for truth or falsity, does not apply to injurious falsehood actions arising from commercial speech. A statement is classified as commercial speech if the primary motivation for making it was economic. See *U.S. Healthcare, Inc. v.*

Blue Cross of Greater Philadelphia, 898 F.2d 914 (3d Cir. 1990); *Procter & Gamble Co. v. Amway Corp.*, 242 F.3d 539 (5th Cir. 2001).

It is generally accepted, on the basis of both common law and the First Amendment, that government departments and agencies cannot maintain actions for defamation. (See p. 346.) This rule may apply also to injurious falsehood actions. There is not much case law on this. A federal court has held that a state government agency which operated a college tuition savings program could not sue for injurious falsehood, despite its "proprietary" functions. *College Savings Bank v. Florida Prepaid Postsecondary Education Expense Board*, 919 F. Supp. 756 (D.N.J. 1996). But *cf. South Carolina State Ports Authority v. Booz-Allen & Hamilton, Inc.*, 676 F. Supp. 346 (D.D.C. 1987) (state port authority's negligence action against consulting firm, for loss allegedly caused by false statements in report prepared for competitor, not barred by First Amendment). The Supreme Court has not yet addressed the issue of First Amendment limitations on liability for injurious falsehood.

E. SPECIAL DAMAGE

Liability for injurious falsehood requires pleading and proof of "special damage." This reflects the action's historic origins as an action on the case for special damage (or particular damage) caused by slander of title or other falsehoods about land or goods. Without special damage the plaintiff has no cause of action, even if there is evidence that the defendant's statement did cause economic loss. The special damage requirement has been one of the main limitations of liability for injurious falsehood.

This element of liability requires the plaintiff to establish that specific pecuniary loss was directly caused by the defendant's false statement. Usually, this has required the plaintiff to allege loss of revenue from specific property or business transactions with identifiable persons, or expense to remove a cloud on title caused by the defendant. Proof of a general decline in revenue or price levels following publication of the falsehood would not suffice. In some jurisdictions, a third person's breach of a contract with the plaintiff will not satisfy the special damage requirement because the plaintiff can obtain damages for breach of contract, or specific performance. Special damage would thus be limited to pecuniary loss from loss of prospective contracts. *Burkett v. Griffith*, 90 Cal. 532, 27 P. 527 (1891); *Felt v. Germania Life Insurance Co.*, 149 App. Div. 14, 133 N.Y.S. 519 (1912). *Contra, Humble Oil & Refining Co. v. McLean*, 268 S.W. 179 (Tex. Civ. App. 1924), rev'd, 280 S.W. 557 (Tex. Comm. App. 1926); Rest. 2d Torts § 633, comment *c*.

At one time, when most businesses were small and had a local clientele, a business proprietor suing for injurious falsehood might well have been expected to specify loss of particular transactions with particular persons, in order to show special damage. But as businesses grew in size and increasingly sold to the ultimate consumer through intermediaries, and as faster means of transport and communications made it more likely that a business would have many buyers in distant locations, it became increasingly difficult to identify specifically who was induced not to make purchases from the plaintiff because of the defendant's false statement. In recognition of this, courts in a line of cases stemming primarily from *Ratcliffe v. Evans*, [1892] 2 Q.B. 554 (C.A.), have decided that when evidence of specific lost transactions is not practically obtainable, the special damage requirement can be satisfied by proof of a decline in the plaintiff's business revenue and sufficient evidence that this was due to the defendant's falsehood, not market conditions and other factors affecting revenue. See *Erick Bowman Remedy Co. v. Jensen Salsbery Laboratories*, 17 F.2d 255 (8th Cir. 1926); *Teilhaber Manufacturing Co. v. Unarco Materials Storage*, 791 P.2d 1164 (Colo. App. 1989). However, not all courts will allow this, and those that do in business disparagement cases may still require loss of particular transactions if the case is one of slander of title or disparagement of a single item—for example, the painting in *Kirby v. Wildenstein*, 784 F. Supp. 1112 (S.D.N.Y. 1992).

If the plaintiff does succeed in proving special damage, as well as the other elements of the cause of action for injurious falsehood, to some extent the plaintiff may obtain damages for other pecuniary losses as consequential damages. However, these appear to be restricted to losses directly caused by the falsehood. The plaintiff may not recover for more remote losses, such as loss of what the plaintiff could have made from investing the money that was not received because of the falsehood, or for non-economic losses such as emotional distress. See Rest. 2d Torts § 633, comments *i–j*.

F. PRIVILEGES (DEFENSES)

It is generally accepted that the privileges which apply to defamation actions also apply to actions for injurious falsehood. See Rest. 2d Torts §§ 635–650A. The privileges of importance for injurious falsehood are primarily the absolute privileges, especially the privilege for statements made within or in connection with judicial proceedings. An example is *Western Technologies, Inc. v. Sverdrup & Parcel, Inc.*, 154 Ariz. 1, 739 P.2d 1318 (Ct. App. 1986). A report that assigned blame to the plaintiff for cracks in a stadium was held to be absolutely privileged because it was commissioned in contemplation of litigation. See also *Conservative Club of Washington v. Finkelstein*, 738 F. Supp. 6 (D.D.C. 1990) (in slander of title action, absolute privilege applied to statements of attorney made in contemplation of litigation).

In principle, the qualified privileges of defamation law, as well as the absolute privileges, apply to injurious falsehood cases. However, the malice that a plaintiff must prove as part of the *prima facie* case would usually cause a defendant to lose a claim of qualified privilege. Qualified privilege could have significance if the court adhered to the older view that a plaintiff in a slander of title action did not have to allege and prove malice, except to rebut a defendant's claim to have spoken or acted in good faith. (See p. 172.) It could also have significance if the plaintiff alleged the defendant had malice because of a motive of ill will or purpose to damage the plaintiff but this would not in itself defeat a claim of qualified privilege under state law. Possibly, recognition that a claim to a property interest is privileged if the claimant genuinely believes there is a real chance the claim will be sustained (see Rest. 2d Torts § 647) will provide protection from liability when it is contended that the claimant had malice because the claimant had doubts about the validity of the claim. Otherwise, qualified privilege would have little effect upon liability for injurious falsehood. It is sometimes asserted that competitors for business or sales of property have a privilege to make favorable comparisons between what they are trying to sell and competing goods, property or services. See Rest. 2d Torts § 649. But this seems to extend no further than the limitation of liability for comparisons discussed earlier (pp. 170–172).

G. INJUNCTIONS

For most economic torts, injunctive relief may be granted in order to prevent harm to the plaintiff, when an award of damages would not be an adequate remedy. Given the difficulty of proving what revenue has been lost because of a false statement and recovering damages after the harm has been done, there can be a strong argument in an injurious falsehood case that an award of damages would not be an adequate remedy. However, cases are divided on whether a plaintiff who establishes a *prima facie* case of injurious falsehood can obtain an injunction against its repetition. The primary reason is that

American courts do not grant injunctions against repetition of defamatory statements, in part because of the First Amendment rule of "no prior restraint" of speech. (See pp. 446–447.) Injurious falsehood resembles defamation as a tort action for harm caused by communication of false statements, and in numerous instances the statements are defamatory. Therefore, it is arguable that the rule for injunctions in injurious falsehood cases should be the same as in defamation cases.

While some courts have denied injunctions for this reason, or historic restrictions on equitable remedies, other courts are willing to grant them, at least on a strong showing that the plaintiff will suffer irreparable harm if the injunction is not granted. As constitutional doctrine gives less protection to speech that is "commercial" or does not involve a matter of public concern, an injunction may be available in a slander of title case, or action for disparagement of a commercial competitor, but not in actions against citizens who are criticizing the plaintiff's business practices or products, or those who publish the criticism. That is noncommercial speech, and it may be on a matter of public concern. See *In re National Service Corp.*, 742 F.2d 859 (5th Cir. 1984); *Schmoldt v. Oakley*, 390 P.2d 882 (Okla. 1964).

The special damage requirement applies to injunctions as well as actions for damages. If the plaintiff cannot show special damage caused by the falsehood, the plaintiff has no cause of action. See *White v. Mellin*, [1895] A.C. 154 (H.L.); *Marlin*

Firearms Co. v. Shields, 171 N.Y. 384, 64 N.E. 163 (1902).

H. FALSE REPRESENTATIONS CONCERNING DEFENDANT (FALSE ADVERTISING)

An action for injurious falsehood is possible only when the statement is understood to convey a false meaning about the plaintiff, the plaintiff's business, or the plaintiff's property, goods or services. There is no injurious falsehood action for a statement that makes a false representation about the defendant or what the defendant is offering for sale. Neither is there an action for "unfair competition." There is thus no common law action for economic loss caused to a competitor by deliberate misrepresentations pertaining to the defendant's business, property, goods or services.

The leading cases are *American Washboard Co. v. Saginaw Manufacturing Co.*, 103 F. 281 (6th Cir. 1900), and *Mosler Safe Co. v. Ely-Norris Safe Co.*, 273 U.S. 132 (1927), rev'g 7 F.2d 603 (2d Cir. 1925). In *American Washboard*, the sole manufacturer of washboards with aluminum rubbing surfaces sought an injunction against the defendant's misrepresenting its zinc washboards as aluminum (aluminum being the superior product). The injunction was denied. The court believed that deception was actionable only when the defendant induced the public to purchase goods in the belief that they were the plaintiff's, *i.e.*, the "passing off" discussed in the next chapter. The court expressed concern over the "Pandora's box of litigation" that would ensue if other alleged falsehoods attaching names to goods gave rise to an action.

In the *Mosler Safe* case, the plaintiff sold safes containing a patented "explosion chamber" that protected against burglary. It claimed that the defendant was selling safes by false representations that they contained explosion chambers and sought an injunction against this. The Second Circuit (in an opinion by Judge Learned Hand) decided that the plaintiff had an action if it was shown that the plaintiff lost customers on account of the defendant's deceit. The Supreme Court held for the defendant on the ground that the plaintiff's allegations did not exclude the possibility that there were safes with explosion chambers other than the plaintiff's patented one. Therefore, "there is nothing to show that customers had they known the facts would have gone to the plaintiff rather than to other competitors in the market, or to lay a foundation for the claim for a loss of sales."

The Supreme Court did not endorse the position adopted in the *American Washboard* case. However, its opinion appears to foreclose an action, including a petition for injunctive relief, when a competitor sells goods by misrepresenting their qualities, unless the plaintiff's allegations and evidence exclude the possibility that a customer wanting goods with certain qualities could get them from a supplier other than the plaintiff. This would be a rarity, although possible if the defendant actually had a monopoly on a type of product because of a patent, or if the defendant misrepresented its product as a suitable replacement part for existing equipment and the plaintiff sold the only replacement part that fit or worked properly. See *Electronics Corp. of America v. Honeywell, Inc.*, 428 F.2d 191 (1st Cir. 1970).

A particular situation in which an action might be allowed, although the plaintiff is not the sole supplier of a product with specific qualities desired by buyers, is when the plaintiff is one of a number of sellers of a product that is regarded as distinct because it is produced in a certain geographic area. Some authority allows an action against a defendant who misrepresented its product as coming from that area, to take advantage of its reputation. See *Newman v. Alvord*, 51 N.Y. 189 (1872) (Akron cement); *Douglas v. Newark Cheese Co.*, 153 Misc. 85, 274 N.Y.S. 406 (Sup. Ct. 1934) (Roquefort cheese). *Contra*, *New York & Rosendale Cement Co. v. Coplay Cement Co.*, 44 F. 277 (C.C.E.D. Pa. 1890), reh'g denied, 45 F. 212 (C.C.E.D. Pa. 1891) (Rosendale cement).

Someone who purchased a product from the defendant because of a misrepresentation about the product would have an action against the defendant, but a purchaser is unlikely to sue when the price of the product, or loss from using it, is not large. So in practice the common law did little to deter false advertising or other false representations in the marketing of goods or services, other than "passing off." The subject of false and misleading advertising is now governed by an extensive body of federal and state legislation which provides for both administrative action and private remedies (though in some situations not an award of damages). This has addressed primarily defendants' false or misleading representations about their own products and services. However, 1988 amendments to section 43(a) of the federal Lanham Act, 15 U.S.C. § 1125(a), extended its coverage to misrepresentation about the goods, services or commercial activities of another person. It thus provides, to a substantial extent, a federal statutory remedy for injurious falsehoods in "commercial advertising or promotion." A business proprietor seeking damages for, or injunctive relief against, false or misleading statements made to the public by another business proprietor will now typically rely primarily on statutory remedies rather than a common law tort action.

CHAPTER 12

PASSING OFF (UNFAIR COMPETITION)

A. INTRODUCTION

Passing off is one of the principal economic torts. Like other important economic torts, such as interference with prospective advantage, it provides a remedy for businesses that claim to have lost anticipated revenue from sales of products or services because of the defendant's conduct. It shares with injurious falsehood an element of false representation. Beyond that there is not much resemblance between passing off and the other economic torts. Passing off is distinct because liability arises when the defendant's conduct in the marketplace creates a particular effect. That effect is to create the impression in the minds of potential buyers that the plaintiff is the source of goods or services, when that is untrue, and thereby cause some pecuniary harm to the plaintiff. There is no intent or fault requirement. Thus it need not be proved that the defendant intended to cause deception or acted with disregard for the probability that potential buyers would be deceived.

Passing off has a close association with the law of trademarks and trade names. The earliest cases of passing off involved business competitors who placed on their wares a mark that was identical to, or deceptively similar to, the plaintiff's and thereby caused potential buyers to think that what the defendant offered for sale had been made by the plaintiff. Many later cases involved defendants who sold goods with names and labels that were the same as, or confusingly similar to, those used by the plaintiff, or established a business with a name that might lead customers to think the plaintiff was the proprietor.

Statutory trademark law, both federal and state, now provides the principal remedy for such practices. Almost any case in which the plaintiff complains of the use of a trademark, trade name or "trade dress" will claim that the defendant is liable under federal trademark law, if interstate or international commerce is involved, or state trademark or trade practices legislation. (For details, see Janis, *Trademark and Unfair Competition in a Nutshell* (2d ed. 2017), and McManis & Friedman, *Intellectual Property and Unfair Competition in a Nutshell* (7th ed. 2013).) But it is typical for plaintiffs to add to this a claim of common law liability. Common law liability is more prominent when the dispute involves the name used for a small business rather than the names or products of larger businesses.

In many passing off cases, application of statutory and common law principles would produce the same result, depending on whether the defendant's use of certain names, designs, and the like was likely to cause potential customers to believe that the plaintiff was a seller or producer of what the defendant was offering for sale. However, the exclusive ownership of trademarks and trade names acquired under provisions of trademark legislation is not part of the common law of passing off. As far as tort law is concerned, the plaintiff does not have an action on the basis of owning a certain mark, name or design, even if the plaintiff was the first to use it. Others are free to use the same mark, name or design, so long as they do not by doing so create the false impression that the plaintiff is the seller or producer.

For some time, almost all actions in the United States for what in substance is passing off, under both common law and statute, have been labelled as actions for "unfair competition." However, actions for other economic torts have often been labelled as unfair competition claims, so the term does not necessarily signify that passing off is the basis of the plaintiff's lawsuit. The American Law Institute's Restatement of Unfair Competition, which melds statutory and common law liability, includes liability for false advertising, acquisition or use of trade secrets, misappropriation, and infringement of the right of publicity as well as passing off and violation of trademark rights. For clarity, the tort action under discussion in this chapter will be called passing off rather than unfair competition. Because liability under statutory trademark law now dominates the area, the discussion of the tort (non-statutory) liability in this chapter will be focused on its most important elements. These are also relevant to statutory liability.

B. GENERAL PRINCIPLES

Judge Learned Hand said in *Yale Electric Corp. v. Robertson*, 26 F.2d 972, 973 (2d Cir. 1928), "[T]he whole Law and the Prophets on the subject" is that "one merchant shall not divert customers from another by representing what he sells as emanating from the second." The essence of passing off is to market goods or services by a practice, or combination of practices, that is likely to create the false impression that the plaintiff is the source of the goods or services, or participant in their sale. The defendant is subject to liability if prospective purchasers are likely to be misled and if some harm to the plaintiff has or would ensue.

Usually, but not always, the false impression is created by the defendant's use of the same business or product name, design, identifying symbol or packaging that the plaintiff is known to use, or something quite similar. Therefore, most passing off cases involve names, titles, designs, symbols and the like that designate goods or services, or the business providing them. The false impression may, however, be created by other means, especially advertising. Thus, passing off may occur if the defendant markets goods or services by use of an advertising theme or slogan that the public identifies with the plaintiff, or a variant that is confusingly similar to the plaintiff's. See Annot., 2 A.L.R.3d 748. The effect must be to mislead potential purchasers into believing that the plaintiff is the source of what is being offered for sale, or that the plaintiff has participated in or authorized the sale. If potential purchasers are misled in other respects, such as the qualities of what is being offered for sale, it is not passing off. (A possible limited exception, discussed above at p. 183, is when purchasers regard products of a certain geographic area as distinct and the defendant "passes off" what it sells as such a product.)

It is not necessary to establish that most or even a majority of potential purchasers will be misled. It is sufficient for relief that a "significant" proportion of the potential purchasers is likely to be misled. See *President and Trustees of Colby College v. Colby College-New Hampshire*, 508 F.2d 804 (1st Cir. 1975); Rest. Unfair Competition § 4, comment *c*. There is no numerical standard. While discussions of passing off typically refer to sellers and buyers (as this discussion does), passing off also includes those who market products through rental or license arrangements, and their potential customers.

The plaintiff must demonstrate actual harm in order to receive damages, and in principle there must be a likelihood of harm in order to obtain an injunction—harm that would occur if the defendant was not enjoined. In practice, however, especially for preliminary injunctions, courts appear willing to grant injunctive relief when there really is not much likelihood of actual harm, once it has been found that there is a likelihood that people will be misled about the plaintiff's connection with what the defendant is selling. *E.g., Standard Brands v. Smidler*, 151 F.2d 34 (2d Cir. 1945) (action by seller of V-8 vegetable juice against seller of V-8 vitamin tablets); *Safeway Stores, Inc. v. Safeway Properties, Inc.*, 307 F.2d 495 (2d Cir. 1962) (action by proprietor of Safeway grocery chain against Safeway Properties real estate company). Surveys may be commissioned by the parties and introduced into evidence to support, or refute, the contention that the conduct objected to by the plaintiff causes the public to believe that the plaintiff is involved in the defendant's business or product.

As a tort, passing off serves to protect the public from being misled about the identity or source of businesses and products. A purchaser who is misled in this way could also sue, but the damage to the individual consumer is usually too small to warrant a lawsuit. The tort in some instances prevents competition that would be beneficial to the public. It can be difficult to compete effectively with well-known brands without use of names, labels, packaging or designs which signal that what the defendant offers for sale is similar to what is sold by a familiar brand. Those who sell or use products made by others are entitled to include the product's brand name or name of the manufacturer in labelling and advertising. But they risk liability if they do so in a way that implies some other business connection with the plaintiff. For example, in *Dodge Bros. v. East*, 8 F.2d 872 (E.D.N.Y. 1925), the defendant, a business specializing in sale of second-hand Dodge cars and repair of Dodges, was permitted to use the name Dodge; but it was not permitted to use the distinct typography used by the Dodge car company in its advertising for new cars, or the term "Dodge Dealer," as this was thought to deceive the public into thinking that the defendant had a business association with the Dodge company.

In deciding whether prospective purchasers are likely to be misled into believing that the plaintiff is a provider of the product or service, courts take into account the conditions in which the product or service is usually sold and typical consumer behavior. For consumer products that are usually purchased quickly, without much deliberation or inspection of the product, a likelihood of confusion can be found even though, on closer examination of its label or package, the purchaser would find that the product is not the plaintiff's. Even placement of the defendant's name on the package may not be sufficient to avoid liability. *E.g., Tas-T-Nut Co. v. Variety Nut & Date Co.*, 245 F.2d 3 (6th Cir. 1957) (retail sales of nut meats). When purchase is a more serious decision, or purchasers have a sophisticated knowledge of the products or services available from different sources, similar names, designs and the like may not be misleading to a significant number of potential buyers. *E.g., McGregor-Doniger Inc. v. Drizzle Inc.*, 599 F.2d 1126 (2d Cir. 1979) (sales of expensive coats).

Secondary meaning. "Secondary meaning" is a key concept in the law of passing off and trademarks. A name, term or "trade dress" acquires secondary meaning if the public (or much of the public) associates it with a single business or the products of a single business. A name or term that was not originally distinctive—usually a geographic designation or a term that served to describe a product or business or its qualities—can acquire secondary meaning if the public comes to regard it as designating the product or services of one business entity. Similarly, trade dress (the appearance of a product, including its packaging and labelling, or the appearance of business premises) acquires secondary meaning if the public comes to regard it as designating the product or services of one business entity, rather than a type of product or business. When the public has come to associate a name, term or trade dress with the plaintiff's product or business, the defendant's use of it may imply an association with the plaintiff and constitute passing off. See Rest. Unfair Competition § 13, comment *e*.

Courts do not readily find secondary meaning when the term used by the defendant is descriptive of the product or service it offers, or when the appearance of its product, though very similar to the plaintiff's, is part of the product's attractiveness to consumers. But findings are secondary meaning are not uncommon. *E.g., SK&F, Co. v. Premo Pharmaceutical Laboratories, Inc.*, 625 F.2d 1055 (3d Cir. 1980) (drug capsule's packaging and color combinations, imitated by generic equivalent); *Phenix Cheese Co. v. Kirp*, 176 App. Div. 735, 164 N.Y.S. 71 (1917) ("Philadelphia Cream Cheese"); *Zimmerman v. Holiday Inns of America, Inc.*, 438 Pa. 528, 266 A.2d 87 (1970) (in Harrisburg area, but not beyond, "Holiday" had secondary meaning as designation of plaintiff's motels). Compare *Kellogg Co. v. National Biscuit Co.*, 305 U.S. 111 (1938) (name and appearance of "shredded wheat" cereal did not acquire secondary meaning as product of plaintiff); *Quality Weaving Co. v. Regan*, 245 Pa. Super. 66, 369 A.2d 296 (1976) ("Quality" lacked secondary meaning in Philadelphia area as designation of plaintiff's label manufacturing business). A defendant may be required to add to its name or design something that more clearly distinguishes its product or business from the plaintiff's.

Fault. At one time, proof of the defendant's wrongful intent was required when the plaintiff sought damages for passing off. But the primary remedy for passing off has long been an injunction, and no proof of the defendant's intent to cause deception, or other fault, was necessary for this. After the merger of common law and equity, it became generally accepted that proof of fault was not necessary for recovery of damages, or an accounting of profits. Whether the defendant actually intended to create the false impression that the plaintiff was associated with the defendant's product or business can have some bearing on whether the court will grant an injunction or a nonmonetary remedy and its extent. If the defendant intended deception of consumers, a court may presume that deception was likely to occur if not enjoined. See Rest. Unfair Competition § 4, comment *d*.

Parties not competing for business in same market. If the plaintiff and defendant do not offer to the public the same type of product or service, in the same market, the defendant will not divert trade from the plaintiff to the defendant by creating the false impression that the plaintiff is the source of the defendant's product or service. No harm to the plaintiff may actually occur. Formerly, liability for passing off arose only when there was some competition for business between the plaintiff and the defendant. But in the past century liability has extended to non-competitors. The principal expansion has involved parties that did not sell the same type of product or business service. This is discussed below at pp. 206–211. There has also been some extension of liability to parties who had not competed with each other because their sales were in different geographic areas.

A passing off action might succeed if the plaintiff is sufficiently famous that it is well-known far from where it is currently doing business. An example is *Stork Restaurant v. Sahati*, 166 F.2d 348 (9th Cir. 1948). A plaintiff's interest in being able to expand its business into other states might be protected by enjoining defendants from using the plaintiff's names and designs there. See *Sweet Sixteen Co. v. Sweet "16" Shop*, 15 F.2d 920 (8th Cir. 1926); *Food Fair Stores, Inc. v. Lakeland Grocery Corp.*, 301 F.2d 156 (4th Cir. 1962). With contemporary methods of communication and advertising, and high rates of personal mobility and travel, it is increasingly likely that the plaintiff will not only be well-known far from its physical place of business but also will actually have a market that includes customers in distant locations. If so, the plaintiff will be in a position to maintain a passing off action if the defendant's use of a name or design there falsely implies a connection with the plaintiff.

Some cases involve the issue of whether there is liability for passing off when the plaintiff has ceased to use the name it is trying to protect, or to actively conduct business. The general rule is that if the name has been abandoned by the plaintiff, others are free to use it. Abandonment may be inferred from disuse of the name for a lengthy period. As abandonment can be considered a matter of intent, closure of the business is not necessarily abandonment of the name. If the name has not been abandoned, the plaintiff can maintain an action for passing off while the name continues to signify for the public the plaintiff or its products. See Rest. Unfair Competition § 30.

C. PRODUCTS

Claims that the defendant is passing off its products by selling them with names, labels, packaging or product designs similar to those of the plaintiff present some distinct issues beyond those discussed above. These include:

"Generic" use of product name. When there is one brand that dominates the market for a type of product and it is well-known to the general public, people may use the brand name in common speech when they refer to a type of product. For example, they may refer to tissues as "kleenex," gelatin desserts as "jello," cellophane tape as "Scotch tape," bandages as "band-aids," small plastic bags as "baggies," and photocopiers as "xerox machines." If consumers nevertheless continue to recognize these terms as one company's brand name, it would probably be actionable passing off (and almost certainly actionable trademark infringement) for a competitor to use the same name in labelling or advertising its product. But the public may no longer regard a name as the brand of one company if it is very widely used "generically" to mean a type of product. If so, other sellers can use the name to describe their products. The leading example is "aspirin," which originated as a brand name of the Bayer company and still is protected as such in other countries. Others include "cellophane," "escalator," "linoleum" and "thermos." See Rest. Unfair Competition § 15.

Product substitution. If a customer ordering a product uses a name that is understood by many customers to signify the product of one company, it is passing off to supply the product of another company without first making this clear. Thus it would be passing off to supply a different cola beverage to a restaurant patron who ordered "Coca-Cola." It would also be passing off to supply something other than a Coca-Cola product to a customer who ordered a "Coke," provided that numbers of customers would expect to receive a Coca-Cola rather than some cola beverage. In this situation, posting signs stating that the establishment does not serve Coca-Cola may not be enough to avoid liability. See *Coca-Cola Co. v. Dorris*, 311 F. Supp. 287 (E.D. Ark. 1970).

Products actually made or sold by plaintiff. If the products sold by the defendant were actually made or marketed by the plaintiff, there would seem to be little likelihood of liability for passing off the products. As discussed above (at p. 190), those who sell products made by others are entitled to include the product's brand name or name of the manufacturer in advertising or labelling the products, provide they do not represent themselves falsely as having some other business connection with the manufacturer or its distributors. However, there has sometimes been liability for marketing products when they were not in the condition that products supplied by the plaintiff or its authorized distributors would have. Thus a defendant could be liable for "passing off" products when they were used, altered or reconditioned, without making this clear at the point of sale, or when they deteriorated because the plaintiff's quality control requirements were not adhered to. See Rest. Unfair Competition § 24. Examples include *Champion Spark Plug Co. v. Sanders*, 331 U.S. 125 (1947), in which the defendants sold reconditioned spark plugs bearing the plaintiff's name, and *Adolph Coors Co. v. A. Genderson & Sons, Inc.*, 486 F. Supp. 131 (D. Colo. 1980), in which beer was distributed by the defendant after the expiry date set by the brewer. There is also a possibility of passing off liability when the defendant sells an imported product that was made or sold by the plaintiff, or an authorized licensee, but is materially different from the product the plaintiff sells in the United States. See *Societe Des Produits Nestle, S.A. v. Casa Helvetia, Inc.*, 982 F.2d 633 (1st Cir. 1992). Federal legislation provides the more important basis for restricting sales of so-called "parallel imports" or "grey market goods." See Rest. Unfair Competition § 24, comments *e–f*.

Titles of literary and dramatic works. Passing off might be alleged when the defendant is selling or distributing a book, magazine, film, play or broadcast program with a title similar to another that is already well-known to the public. If the author or proprietor of the well-known work brings suit, it will be claimed that the public (or a substantial portion of the public) will believe that the plaintiff was the author or producer of what the defendant was selling. But it is a legitimate practice to use a title that is descriptive or suggestive of what the work is about, even if it might be confused with someone else's. Most works would be unsaleable without such a title.

Courts usually do not find passing off on account of a work's title. *E.g.*, *Eirinberg v. CBS Inc.*, 521 F. Supp. 450 (N.D. Ill. 1981) (programs entitled *Your Dollar's Worth* and *Your Dollars*); *McGraw-Hill Book Co., Inc. v. Random House, Inc.*, 32 Misc. 2d 704, 225 N.Y.S.2d 646 (Sup. Ct. 1962) (books *PT 109: John F. Kennedy in World War II* and *John F. Kennedy and PT-109*); *Brown v. Lyle Stuart, Inc.*, 42 Misc. 2d 909, 249 N.Y.S.2d 370 (Sup. Ct. 1964) (books *Sex and the Single Girl* and *Sex and the Single Man*). There can, however, be liability if the title is not descriptive or suggestive of the work's content, or if there is a strong showing that the title has acquired "secondary meaning" as the work of the plaintiff. See *Jackson v. Universal International Pictures*, 36 Cal. 2d 116, 222 P.2d 433 (1950). There might also be liability if something other than the title was also copied, such as the typography on the cover of a book or magazine. See *Avon Periodicals, Inc. v. Ziff-Davis Publishing Co.*, 27 Misc. 2d 160, 113 N.Y.S.2d 737 (Sup. Ct. 1952), modified, 282 App. Div. 200, 122 N.Y.S.2d 92 (1953). The content of the defendant's work may make it unlikely that the public would confuse it with the plaintiff's. An example is *Litwin v. Maddux*, 7 Misc. 2d 750, 164 N.Y.S.2d 489 (Sup. Ct. 1957), in which *The Green Kingdom* was the title of both an adventure novel and a book of garden-inspired poetry and prose.

Federal law preemption. Most federal legislation on trademarks and trade practices does not preempt state law. Plaintiffs can bring actions under state common law and state statutes even though there is also applicable federal law. In many cases, plaintiffs make claims under both federal law and state law. But federal copyright and patent laws do preempt state law. For items within the scope of federal copyright and patent laws, state law cannot grant equivalent rights, including the right to control production and sale of copies.

For passing off, the most important decisions on federal preemption are in the companion cases of *Sears, Roebuck & Co. v. Stiffel Co.*, 376 U.S. 225 (1964), and *Compco Corp. v. Day-Brite Lighting, Inc.*, 376 U.S. 234 (1964). In both, the defendants had sold lighting products that were virtually identical to the plaintiffs'. The lower courts found that there was a likelihood that the defendants' products would be confused with the plaintiffs' and that such confusion had actually occurred. The defendants were held liable for damages and enjoined from selling products confusingly similar to the plaintiffs'. The Supreme Court reversed, holding that when an article is not patentable under federal law, state law cannot prohibit the copying of the article or award damages for copying. Unpatented articles, and articles produced under expired patents, were in the public domain and could be freely copied. The inability of the public to "tell two identical articles apart" did not permit an injunction against copying or damages for copying.

The opinions in *Sears* and *Compco* left room for state law to protect trademarks and distinctive package "dress" and require labelling of products, in order to prevent consumer confusion about the source of goods. Thus a defendant could be liable for passing off on the basis of causing consumers to think its products were the plaintiff's because of how the defendant labelled, or failed to label, its products or product containers. But it could not be liable for copying the product itself, even if purchasers would assume from the appearance of the defendant's product that it was made by the plaintiff. Under the opinion in *Compco*, a defendant cannot be liable under state law because it copied "nonfunctional" elements of the plaintiff's product design. However, it appears that a defendant can be liable if it has copied an element of the plaintiff's design that serves no function other than to identify the source of the product. Arguably there can be some further restraint of copying nonfunctional elements of a product that have "secondary meaning" and would cause potential buyers to think the defendant's product was the plaintiff's, but the extent of this is not clear. See Rest. Unfair Competition § 16, comment *c*.

D. BUSINESS NAMES AND OTHER IDENTIFIERS

Actual and potential passing off liability for use of a name, design or something else that identifies the plaintiff's business, or the services it provides, is for the most part governed by the general principles discussed earlier at pp. 187–195. Often it is not only the name, but how it is displayed, that identifies the business. If the public almost always sees the name in a distinct typography or color, passing off is likely to be found if the defendant used the same typography or color. There is also likely to be liability if the name itself is so distinct that the public would assume that any business using it is the plaintiff or affiliated with the plaintiff—for example "Kodak" or "Rolls-Royce." With less distinct names, especially names that indicate the service provided by the business or its geographic location, the plaintiff may have to show that for much of the purchasing public the name has "secondary meaning"—it means the plaintiff's business or what is provided by the plaintiff specifically. The public is less likely to be misled by the defendant's use of a name if what the defendant sells is not the same as, or related to, what the plaintiff sells.

Businesses can also be identified by the distinct appearance of their business premises, the appearance of their vehicles, their advertising themes, or even their telephone numbers. If potential customers understand these to signify a particular business, the use of something confusingly similar by another business can mislead potential customers about the identity of that business and constitute passing off. See *White Tower System v. White Castle System of Eating Houses Corp.*, 90 F.2d 67 (6th Cir. 1937) (imitation of hamburger chain's building design and slogan); *Yellow Cab Co. v. Creasman*, 185 N.C. 551, 117 S.E. 787 (1923) (taxicabs having same appearance, including colors, as plaintiff's); *Dial-a-Mattress Franchise Corp. v. Page*, 880 F.2d 675 (2d Cir. 1989) (plaintiff mattress dealer with advertising featuring local telephone number dialed as "MATTRESS"; defendant mattress seller acquiring and advertising number "800-MATTRESS").

The development and expansion of the Internet has given rise to numerous complaints about the use of domain names that include the complainant's name or something confusingly similar, web pages whose content suggests that the web site is the complainant's, and use of "key words" to display someone else's web site or advertising when the complainant's name is typed in a search engine such as Google. The purpose of this conduct is sometimes to communicate a message rather than to sell goods or services. A domain name that would be confused with the plaintiff's, or otherwise attract traffic, may have been registered in order to sell the name.

A passing off claim may succeed when the defendant has adopted a ".com" domain name that includes the plaintiff's well-known company or brand name, leading people to believe the plaintiff is responsible for the web site. A good example is a Canadian case, *Saskatoon Star Phoenix Group Inc. v. Noton*, (2001) 206 Sask. R. 106, [2001] 9 W.W.R. 63

(Q.B.). However, most users of the Internet know that similar domain names have different proprietors, and often it would be apparent from the web pages displayed that the web site is not the plaintiff's. If so, a passing off action is likely to fail. (The defendant might, however, be liable under statute for misleading use of the plaintiff's trademark or trade name, or domain name "cybersquatting.")

Personal names. A number of cases involve defendants who conducted business under a personal name or family name that was the same as the name used by the plaintiff. Courts have enjoined the use of corporate names that included the name of the founder when this was likely to cause confusion with the plaintiff's business. See Annot., 72 A.L.R.3d 8. Also, adopted personal names that were likely to be confused with the plaintiff's, as in *Cockrell v. Davis*, 198 Miss. 660, 23 So. 2d 256 (1945). But there was a widespread belief that the proprietor of a business had the right to honestly use the proprietor's own name or surname as a business name even if it caused confusion with an existing business. Today the prevailing view is that there is no such absolute right: use of one's own name as a business name can be enjoined when it is likely to cause confusion with the plaintiff's business or the belief that the defendant's business is affiliated with the plaintiff. Usually, the result is to attach conditions to the defendant's use of the name that will prevent such confusion rather than an absolute bar to use of the name. See Annot., 44 A.L.R.2d 1156.

When a family has achieved prominence in a certain line of business and both the defendant and the plaintiff (or their owners) are members of that family, the defendant may contend that the defendant as well as the plaintiff is entitled to use the family name and benefit from its reputation. But even in this situation the defendant's use of the family name may be prohibited or limited. See *Cunetto House of Pasta v. Tuma*, 689 S.W.2d 690 (Mo. App. 1985); *David B. Findlay, Inc. v. Findlay*, 18 N.Y.2d 12, 218 N.E.2d 531 (1966), amended, 18 N.Y.2d 676, 219 N.E.2d 872 (1966). A professional expected to practice under the professional's personal name, such as an attorney, would not be required to use a different name because of possible confusion with another person. But there could be liability for use of a firm name that may be confused with the plaintiff's practice, even though it consists of the partners' actual names. See *Suisman, Shapiro, Wool, Brennan, Gray & Greenberg P.C. v. Suisman*, 80 U.S.P.Q.2d 1072 (D. Conn. 2006).

Names of non-profit entities. Passing off actions can be maintained by non-profit organizations as well as proprietors of commercial businesses. See 37 A.L.R.3d 277. The Fourth Circuit has stated,

> [I]t is well established that a benevolent, fraternal, or social organization will be protected in the use of its name by injunction restraining another organization from using the same or another name so similar as to be misleading. . . ."The fact that a corporation is an

> eleemosynary or charitable one and has no goods to sell, and does not make money, does not take it out of the protection of the law of unfair competition. Distinct identity is just as important to such a company, oftentimes, as it is to a commercial company. Its financial credit—its ability to raise funds, its general reputation, the credit of those managing it and supporting it, are all at stake if its name is filched away by some other organization, and the two become confused in the minds of the public."

Grand Lodge of Improved, Benevolent and Protective Order of Elks of the World v. Grand Lodge, Improved, Benevolent and Protective Order of the Elks of the World, 50 F.2d 860, 862–863 (4th Cir. 1931), quoting Nims, *The Law of Unfair Competition and Trade-Marks* § 86 (3d ed. 1929).

Schisms in charitable, social and religious organizations have resulted in a considerable number of such cases. A long-established organization may prevail in an action against a body of secessionists, on the basis that the defendant's use of the name represents a connection with the plaintiff that does not now exist. Disputes involving the names of religious organizations are generally considered secular matters that can be resolved by courts rather than matters of religious doctrine. See *Purcell v. Summers*, 145 F.2d 979 (4th Cir. 1944). But a court may be reluctant to find that a religious term is understood as referring to the plaintiff specifically and prevent its use by others professing the same religion. See *Christian Science Board of Directors of*

First Church of Christ, Scientist v. Evans, 105 N.J. 297, 520 A.2d 1347 (1987). Preventing a political organization from using its chosen name also raises First Amendment concerns, but courts have granted injunctions in some cases where the name was found to convey a misleading connection with the plaintiff's party. *E.g., Tomei v. Finley*, 512 F. Supp. 695 (N.D. Ill. 1981).

E. PARTIES IN DIFFERENT LINES OF BUSINESS

A major issue in the law of passing off is whether there can be liability when the parties do not sell the same types of products or services. If, as Learned Hand said, "the whole Law and Prophets on the subject" is that "one merchant shall not divert customers from another by representing what he sells as emanating from the second" (see pp. 187–188), there can be no liability when the defendant causes no diversion of customers from the plaintiff because the plaintiff does not sell what the defendant does, or something close enough to be competitive. Nevertheless, during the past century there has been a strong trend toward finding liability for passing off (or "unfair competition") in cases where the parties sold different products or services.

The principal reason for this has been the courts' belief that the defendants' conduct was likely to harm the plaintiffs' economic interests even though it would not divert the plaintiffs' trade to the defendants. The opinion in *Philadelphia Storage Battery Co. v. Mindlin*, 163 Misc. 52, 54–55, 296

N.Y.S. 176, 178–179 (Sup. Ct. 1937), observed: "[D]iversion of trade is not the only injury which may be caused by the second use. The normal potential expansion of the plaintiff's business may be forestalled. His reputation may be tarnished by the use of his mark upon an inferior product. . . .A mark. . .serves as a 'silent salesman' to attract custom. The dilution of its selling powers and 'the whittling away of its uniqueness' by use on noncompeting products constitutes a real injury for which there should be redress." Learned Hand himself accepted that "a merchant may have a sufficient economic interest in the use of his mark outside the field of his own exploitation to justify interposition by a court. . .unless the borrower's use is so foreign to the owner's as to insure against any identification of the two." *Yale Electric Corp. v. Robertson*, 26 F.2d 972, 974 (2d Cir. 1928).

Proprietors of famous and distinct business names, brand names and trade symbols have usually been successful in actions seeking to prevent or limit use of the same names or symbols by others, despite the absence of competition. See Annot., 148 A.L.R. 12. Among the many examples are *Safeway Stores v. Safeway Construction Co.*, 74 F. Supp. 455 (S.D. Cal. 1947) (Safeway grocery stores vs. Safeway Construction Company); *Triangle Publications v. Rohrlich*, 167 F.2d 969 (2d Cir. 1948) (*Seventeen* magazine vs. Miss Seventeen girdles); *Tiffany & Co. v. Tiffany Productions*, 147 Misc. 679, 264 N.Y.S. 459 (Sup. Ct. 1932), aff'd, 237 App. Div. 801, 260 N.Y.S. 821 (1932), aff'd, 262 N.Y. 482, 188 N.E. 30 (1933) (famous Tiffany store in New York City vs. Tiffany motion picture production and distribution company); *Churchill Downs Distilling Co. v. Churchill Downs*, 262 Ky. 567, 90 S.W.2d 1041 (1936) (Churchill Downs race track vs. Churchill Downs bourbon whisky); and *Horlick's Malted Milk Corp. v. Horlick*, 143 F.2d 32 (7th Cir. 1944) (Horlick's malted milk vs. Horlick's dog food).

Courts tend to decide in such cases that members of the public are likely to believe that the defendant is part of, or affiliated with, the plaintiff's business or that the plaintiff authorized the defendant's business activities. This is necessary if the defendant is to be liable on the basis of passing off. While the decision may have been warranted by the evidence before the court, it seems implausible in some of the cases where the plaintiff prevailed. In those cases, it appears that the plaintiff gained an injunction in reality in order to protect it against dilution of the strength of its business or trade name if associated with the defendant as well as the plaintiff. *E.g., John Walker & Sons, Ltd. v. Bethea*, 305 F. Supp. 1302 (D.S.C. 1969) (action by seller of Johnny Walker whisky against operator of Johnny Walker Motel); *Caesars World, Inc. v. Caesar's Palace*, 490 F. Supp. 818 (D.N.J. 1980) (suit by owners of Nevada resort hotel Caesars Palace over small beauty salon in New Jersey with same name). Or against tarnishment by association with a lower-status business or something disreputable. *E.g., Schieffelin & Co. v. Jack Co. of Boca, Inc.*, 850 F. Supp. 232 (S.D.N.Y. 1994) ("Dom Popignon" popcorn sold in champagne bottles with labels resembling labels of Dom Pérignon champagne); *Chemical Corp of America v.*

Anheuser-Busch, Inc., 306 F.2d 433 (5th Cir. 1962) (action by seller of Budweiser beer, which had long used slogan "Where there's life. . .there's Bud," against company that advertised its insecticidal floor wax with slogan "Where there's life. . .there's bugs"). *Cf. Dallas Cowboys Cheerleaders, Inc. v. Pussycat Cinema, Ltd.*, 467 F. Supp. 366 (S.D.N.Y. 1979), aff'd, 604 F.2d 200 (2d Cir. 1979) (court concluding that public was likely to believe that pornographic film was sponsored by Dallas Cowboys Cheerleaders).

When the defendant sells clothing, toys or other merchandise that the public will buy because its association with a popular film or television program, a court may sustain an action by the producer of the film or program on the ground that the public is likely to believe that the merchandise is being sold by the plaintiff, or with a license from the plaintiff. See *Wyatt Earp Enterprises, Inc. v. Sackman, Inc.*, 157 F. Supp. 621 (S.D.N.Y. 1958); *Paramount Pictures Corp. v. Dorney Park Coaster Co.*, 698 F. Supp. 1274 (E.D. Pa. 1988). On a similar basis, a product manufacturer, sports club or individual celebrity may have an action if the defendant sells clothing, toys or other articles that the public is likely to believe were licensed by the plaintiff. *Cf. Anheuser-Busch, Inc. v. VIP Products, LLC*, 666 F. Supp. 2d 974 (E.D. Mo. 2008) (action by producer of Budweiser beer against seller of "Buttwiper" dog toy); *National Football League Properties, Inc. v. Wichita Falls Sportswear, Inc.*, 532 F. Supp. 651 (W.D. Wash. 1982) (action by National Football League licensing agent and member club against seller of replicas of NFL jerseys); *Hirsch v. S.C. Johnson & Son, Inc.*, 90 Wis.

2d 379, 280 N.W.2d 129 (1979) (action by football player nicknamed "Crazylegs" against seller of Crazylegs shaving gel for women).

This serves to protect the plaintiffs' interests in selling licenses to market such articles, as well as to protect plaintiffs against unwanted association with what the defendant is selling. There is no passing off if the public does not believe that the plaintiff produces or sponsors the product and purchases the product because of its appearance rather than an assumed association with the plaintiff. See *Bi-Rite Enterprises, Inc. v. Button Master*, 555 F. Supp. 1188 (S.D.N.Y. 1983) (sale of buttons bearing likenesses and logos of rock performers).

Non-profit organizations can maintain actions when businesses use their names in a way that is likely to cause members of the public to believe that the business is associated with the organization. See *Girl Scouts of United States of America v. Hollingsworth*, 188 F. Supp. 707 (E.D.N.Y. 1960) (action by Girl Scouts and Boy Scouts against seller of "Safety Scout" articles); *Cornell University v. Messing Bakeries,* 285 App. Div. 490, 138 N.Y.S.2d 280 (1955), aff'd, 309 N.Y. 722, 128 N.E.2d 421 (1955) (action by Cornell University against baker's sale of "Cornell Recipe Bread"); *Golden Slipper Square Club v. Golden Slipper Restaurant & Catering*, 371 Pa. 92, 88 A.2d 734 (1952) (action by charity Golden Slipper Square Club against use of Golden Slipper as name for defendant's restaurant and night club).

Dilution statutes. While claims of liability under common law continue to be made, when the parties are in different types of commercial activity the primary basis of liability is now statutory. Rights to the exclusive use of a trademark or trade name extend beyond the common law. The enactment of "dilution" (or "anti-dilution") statutes in over half the states and (in 1995) a federal dilution act expanded liability for use of very well-known marks and names in enterprises that do not compete with the plaintiff. Liability under a dilution statute requires no finding of source confusion, *i.e.*, that the public would believe that the plaintiff is the producer or seller of what the defendant is selling, or associated with the sale.

A defendant is subject to liability (primarily injunctive relief) when the defendant diminishes the value of a trademark or name by "diluting" or "blurring" its unique association with the plaintiff, or tarnishing it by a negative association with the defendant's product or service. There would be "blurring" if the defendant's use of a brand or business name that was the same as the plaintiff's caused the public to think of both businesses' products or services, not the plaintiff's alone, when the name was seen or heard. See *Mattel, Inc. v. MCA Records, Inc.*, 296 F.3d 894, 903 (9th Cir. 2002), for a crisp explanation of dilution. The federal statute is limited to "famous" marks—marks widely recognized by the American public as designations of the source of goods or services.

CHAPTER 13

TRADE SECRETS AND CONFIDENTIAL INFORMATION

A. INTRODUCTION

Trade secret liability emerged in cases of the nineteenth century, but its primary doctrinal development was in the twentieth century. The first Restatement of Torts, which addressed trade secrets in §§ 757–759, was influential in shaping the relevant case law. When the Restatement (Second) of Torts was being prepared, the American Law Institute decided to classify some economic torts, including trade secret liability, as parts of the law of "unfair competition and trade regulation" and exclude them from the Torts Restatement. In 1995, the ALI published a Restatement of Unfair Competition for these subjects, with trade secrets covered in §§ 39–45. Meanwhile, the National Conference of Commissioners on Uniform State Laws promulgated a statute codifying common law principles of liability for "misappropriation" of trade secrets: the Uniform Trade Secrets Act. This statute has now been adopted in almost all states. Furthermore, legislation enacted by Congress in 2016 (the "Defend Trade Secrets Act") provides a federal civil action for misappropriation of trade secrets related to interstate or international commerce.

The two Restatements, Uniform Act and federal statute share common principles but differ in some significant details. This Nutshell will focus on the main principles of trade secret liability as a tort. For full details of liability under the common law, Restatements, Uniform Act and federal legislation, see Sandeen & Rowe, *Trade Secret Law in a Nutshell* (2d ed. 2018). The Uniform Trade Secrets Act preempts any tort or "restitutionary" claim outside the Act for misappropriation of a trade secret, but not contract-based claims (§ 7).

Cases and literature on trade secrets contain many references to a trade secret as the "property" of its "owner" or "proprietor." However, the proprietor of a trade secret, unlike the proprietor of a patent or owner of tangible property, is not protected against any nonconsensual use of the "property." Tort law provides a remedy for acquisition or use of a trade secret, without the plaintiff's consent, only when (a) the acquisition or use is wrongful in itself, because the defendant used improper means to acquire the secret or was in breach of duty in using or disclosing the secret; or (b) the defendant was on notice that the defendant's knowledge of the secret resulted from another person's wrongful acquisition of the secret, breach of duty or (to some extent) mistake. There is no liability for using or disclosing a trade secret when the information was acquired by proper means, such as analysis of a product made with a secret formula, and without any breach of duty.

The main bases of liability are (1) liability because the defendant acquired the trade secret by improper means; (2) liability because the defendant's use or disclosure of the secret was or would be in breach of a duty of confidence owed to the plaintiff; (3) liability because the defendant had reason to know that the defendant acquired the secret because of another person's wrongful acquisition of it or breach of duty of confidence; and (4) liability because the defendant had reason to know that the information was a trade secret acquired as a result of mistake or accident. Use or disclosure of a trade secret in these circumstances is considered "misappropriation" of the secret. Rest. Unfair Competition § 40; Uniform Trade Secrets Act § 1. Plaintiffs commonly seek injunctions against use or disclosure of the information as well as monetary remedies. The protection of trade secrets by civil liability for misappropriation is thought to encourage invention and innovation, and valuable commercial uses of the results. See *Kewanee Oil Co. v. Bicron Corp.*, 416 U.S. 470 (1974).

Most actions for misappropriation of a trade secret are based on an alleged breach of a duty of confidence rather than only a wrongful means of acquiring the secret. In most instances, inventors and other proprietors of commercially valuable information cannot profit from it without disclosure to others. The proprietors of a secret formula for making a product will usually have to disclose it to some other persons in order for the product to be manufactured and distributed, or to sell the business. The proprietor of valuable secret marketing information will usually have to disclose it to some employees or business associates in order to use the information profitably. Tort law protects those who voluntarily disclose trade secrets when a duty to keep the information confidential and limit its use was assumed by the recipient. An action can be brought not only against the original recipient, when the recipient made an unauthorized use or disclosure of the information, but also others who eventually acquired the information with knowledge of the breach of duty. The duty of confidence may arise from a contract, an express promise, or the circumstances in which the trade secret was disclosed. See Rest. Unfair Competition § 41.

B. DEFINITIONS OF TRADE SECRET

A defendant can be held liable for misappropriation of a trade secret only if the information is found or admitted to be a trade secret. Whether information was a trade secret depends upon the type of information and its secrecy at the time of its alleged misappropriation. There is a great variety of information that may be a trade secret—not only manufacturing methods, formulae, technical elements of designs and computer programs, but also marketing and pricing techniques, the identities and details of customers, and compilations of information. See Rest. Unfair Competition § 39, comment *d*. The first Restatement of Torts contained an elaborate definition of "trade secret." Rest. Torts § 757, comment *b*. Although supplemented by comments, the definitions of trade secret in the Uniform Trade Secrets Act and Restatement of Unfair Competition are much less detailed. The Uniform Act states (in § 1(4)):

> "Trade secret" means information, including a formula, pattern, compilation, program, device, method, technique, or process that:
>
> (i) derives independent economic value, actual or potential, from not being generally known to, and not being readily ascertainable by proper means by, other persons who can obtain economic value from its disclosure or use, and
>
> (ii) is the subject of efforts that are reasonable under the circumstances to maintain its secrecy.

In the Restatement of Unfair Competition (§ 39), "A trade secret is any information that can be used in the operation of a business or other enterprise and that is sufficiently valuable and secret to afford an actual or potential economic advantage over others."

Under the first Restatement, a trade secret was a process or device for continuous use in the operation of a business. Information that had not been used, or was simply information pertaining to a single or ephemeral event in the conduct of a business, was not a trade secret. Rest. Torts § 757, comment *b*. However, under both the Restatement of Unfair Competition and the Uniform Trade Secrets Act, valuable information that had not been used, or that could be used for only a short time before it ceased to become a secret or valuable, can qualify as a trade secret. Rest. Unfair Competition § 39, comment *d*; Uniform Trade Secrets Act § 1(4). For the requirement of secrecy, the Restatement of Unfair

Competition adopts and elaborates the Uniform Act's position that information which is generally known or readily ascertainable through proper means is not a trade secret. This includes information that can be found in patents, published material, and what can readily be ascertained from examination of a product sold or displayed to the public. Presumably it also includes information in open public records. Information that could be discovered by proper means, but only with considerable difficulty, cost or consumption of time, can be a trade secret. Information can remain a secret when someone has actually discovered it independently, as well as when it has been disclosed under conditions of confidentiality. Precautions taken to maintain the secrecy of the information are "relevant" to whether the information is a trade secret but not, as in Uniform Act, a necessary condition. A combination of non-secret components may be a trade secret. Rest. Unfair Competition § 39, comments *f–g*. (See also the discussion of trade secrets and employees, below at pp. 224–226.)

C. LIABILITY WHEN TRADE SECRET ACQUIRED BY IMPROPER MEANS

A defendant can be held liable for acquisition, use or disclosure of a trade secret when the defendant acquired the secret by "improper means." A defendant can also be liable for use or disclosure of a trade secret when the defendant knew or had reason to know that the information was acquired from or through a third person who acquired it by improper means. Rest. Unfair Competition §§ 40, 43; Uniform

Trade Secrets Act § 1(1)–(2). This is similar to the liability rules of § 757 in the first Restatement.

"Improper means" include means that are illegal under criminal law or tortious in themselves. Uniform Trade Secrets Act § 1 specifies theft, bribery, misrepresentation, breach or inducement of breach of a duty to maintain secrecy, and espionage through electronic or other means. Rest. Unfair Competition § 43 contains a similar list. Inducing another person to disclose information with knowledge that by doing so the other person will be in violation of an obligation of confidence, a contractual obligation, or an employee's duty of loyalty is tortious in itself. (See the discussion of inducing breach of contract in Chapter 7.) It is therefore "improper means" of acquiring information and a basis of trade secret liability. However, it is clear from the text and comments of both the Uniform Act and the Restatement that some means of acquiring trade secrets can be held to be improper "under the circumstances of the case" even if not illegal or independently a legal wrong.

The leading case on "improper" but not illegal means of acquiring a trade secret is *E.I. duPont deNemours & Co., Inc. v. Christopher*, 431 F.2d 1012 (5th Cir. 1970). DuPont was constructing a facility for producing methanol at one of its plants in Texas. According to DuPont, the process to be used for providing methanol was highly secret and would give the company a competitive advantage over other producers. During the construction, portions of what was being built were not under cover. DuPont discovered that the defendants, who were photographers, had taken photographs of the facility from an airplane. They had done so for a client whose identity they would not disclose. The airplane was in public airspace at the time. DuPont alleged that a skilled person could deduce the secret process for making methanol by examination of the photographs. It claimed that taking the photographs and delivering them to the client was misappropriation of its trade secret. It sought damages and injunctions against further photography of its plants and circulation of photographs already taken.

The Court of Appeals rejected the defendants' argument that they committed no "actionable wrong" because their conduct was not illegal, fraudulent, trespassory, or in breach of confidence. Under Restatement of Torts § 757, there could be liability when a defendant had discovered a trade secret by improper means. In the Restatement, improper means were described as "means which fall below the generally accepted standards of commercial morality and reasonable conduct." Rest. Torts § 757, comment *f*. The "industrial espionage" in this case was held to be improper and grounds for DuPont to bring suit. Texas cases indicated that it was unfair and improper to obtain knowledge of a process, without spending the time and money to discover it by independent research or "reverse engineering," when the secret's holder was taking reasonable precautions to maintain its secrecy. DuPont was not required to put a roof over the plant during construction, at enormous expense, "to prevent another from doing that which he ought not do in the first place." The court believed that "Commercial privacy must be protected from espionage which could not have been reasonably anticipated or prevented."

Restatement of Unfair Competition § 43 specifies that "Independent discovery and analysis of publicly available products or information are not improper means of acquisition." But comments to both the Restatement and the Uniform Act indicate approval of the *DuPont* opinion. Rest. Unfair Competition § 43, comment *c*; Uniform Trade Secrets Act § 1, comment. While potentially an expansive basis of liability, it appears that there have not been many trade secret cases in which liability turned on improper means of acquiring a trade secret, apart from inducing someone to breach a duty of confidence or contractual obligation. In most cases, the basis of liability has been a breach of confidence by the defendant or by someone through whom the defendant received the information.

D. LIABILITY ON BASIS OF BREACH OF CONFIDENCE

Breach of confidence is the most important basis of trade secret liability. Under both Restatements and the Uniform Trade Secrets Act, there is liability for use or disclosure of a trade secret, without the plaintiff's consent, when the defendant acquired the information under circumstances creating a duty to maintain its secrecy. There is also liability for use or disclosure of a trade secret when the defendant had reason to know it was acquired through a person whose disclosure of the information was a breach of duty. Rest. Torts § 757(b), (d); Rest. Unfair Competition § 40(b); Uniform Trade Secrets Act § 1(2). Unlike cases in which it is alleged that information was acquired from the plaintiff by theft or "espionage," cases with claims of breach of duty involve proprietors of trade secrets who voluntarily disclosed the secret to some other persons, such as employees or business partners, but allegedly under conditions prohibiting or limiting further disclosure or use of the information.

Obligations to maintain the confidentiality of information and limit how it is used can, of course, be created by express provisions in a contract. This is the most effective means of acquiring legal protection against disclosures or uses of the information, or a remedy when an unauthorized disclosure or use is discovered—provided the "confidentiality clause" does extend to the information disclosed or used, which may not have been known to the parties when the contract was drafted. Fiduciary relationships such as attorney and client clearly involve obligations to maintain the confidentiality of information and limit its use. The more challenging cases are those in which it is claimed that an obligation of confidence arose by implication from a contract or from the relationship of the parties.

There is no precise rule on when the recipient of information that may be a trade secret is under an obligation not to disclose it, or to limit the disclosure or use of the information. In general it depends upon the nature of the information, the circumstances in which it is disclosed, the relationship of the parties, the transactions they have entered or have in contemplation, and sometimes customary practice in the business or industry. Courts frequently refer to business relationships in which there is an obligation of confidence as "confidential relationships." These include employer-employee and other ongoing business relationships such as licensor-licensee and business partners. They also can include prospective purchasers, licensees, investors or partners when disclosure to them of confidential information is necessary to permit them to evaluate the merits of the proposed transactions. *E.g.*, *Smith v. Dravo*, 203 F.2d 369 (7th Cir. 1953) (product design revealed to potential purchaser of plaintiff's manufacturing business); *Forest Laboratories, Inc. v. Formulations, Inc.*, 299 F. Supp. 202 (E.D. Wis. 1969), aff'd *sub nom. Forest Laboratories, Inc. v. Pillsbury Co.*, 452 F.2d 621 (7th Cir. 1971) (packaging process revealed to potential packager of plaintiff's tablets); *Mineral Deposits Ltd. v. Zigan*, 773 P.2d 606 (Colo. App. 1988) (product lent by plaintiff to potential purchaser for testing). See Rest. Unfair Competition § 41, comment *b*.

Not all information disclosed in a "confidential relationship" is disclosed "in confidence." The obligation of confidence arises only when the recipient of the information knows or has reason to know that the disclosure was intended to be subject to an obligation of confidence. The owner of a trade secret has an action when the person to whom the secret was disclosed has violated such an obligation of confidence. The owner also can bring an action for disclosure or use of the secret against a third party who knew or had reason to know it was acquired as a result of a breach of confidence. Rest. Unfair Competition §§ 40–41; Uniform Trade Secrets Act § 1(2)(ii).

Employees. Many claims of trade secret misappropriation have been brought against a former employee of the plaintiff or a former employee's new employer. The usual basis for the claim against the former employee is that the employee has disclosed or used the plaintiff's trade secret, or would do so if not enjoined. The usual basis of the claim against a subsequent employer is that it used (or would use, if not enjoined) information received from the employee with knowledge that it was the plaintiff's trade secret. It might also be alleged that the subsequent employer induced the employee to violate an obligation of confidentiality owed to the former employer or (if the employee was working for the former employer at the time of the disclosure) the employee's duty of loyalty to the employer.

Employees generally have an implied obligation to refrain from unauthorized disclosure or use of confidential information acquired through their employment. This obligation continues after the end of the employment. However, not all non-public information acquired during employment is a trade secret, and there will be liability only if the defendant knew or had reason to know that there was a duty of confidence with respect to the information. See Rest. Unfair Competition § 42, comments *b–c*.

Defendants may contend that the information used or disclosed was not the plaintiff's trade secret but rather part of the general knowledge, skill or experience acquired during the employment (or previously). This depends, of course, on the facts and circumstances of the case, including the employee's contribution to development of the information and whether skilled persons working elsewhere would also know the information or be able to acquire it. Courts have also taken into account the importance of permitting employees to change their employment, or establish their own businesses, and use their skills and experience there. This serves not only the employees' own interests but also the public interest in facilitating business competition. See Rest. Unfair Competition § 42, comments *b–e*; *Wexler v. Greenberg*, 399 Pa. 569, 160 A.2d 430 (1960) (chemist's knowledge of plaintiff's chemical formulas considered part of technical knowledge and skill acquired during employment, not as trade secrets).

Knowledge of the identities of the plaintiff's customers, or what they purchase, can qualify as a trade secret, even if the employee has memorized it. If so, disclosure or use of the information can be trade secret misappropriation. But customer identities and preferences are not trade secrets when they can be readily ascertained by people in the trade, or when knowledge of this provides no particular competitive advantage. See Rest. Unfair Competition § 42, comment *f*. Compare *Suburban Gas of Grand Junction, Inc. v. Bockelman*, 157 Colo. 78, 401 P.2d 268 (1965) (no liability where visible propane tanks indicated potential propane gas customers), and *Leo*

Silfen, Inc. v. Cream, 29 N.Y.2d 387, 278 N.E.2d 636 (1977) (no liability where potential industrial and commercial customers for building maintenance supplies were known in trade), with *American Credit Indemnity Co. v. Sacks*, 213 Cal. App. 3d 622, 262 Cal. Rptr. 92 (1989) (identity of policyholders for credit insurance, which relatively few businesses purchased, a trade secret); *Town & Country House & Home Service v. Newbery*, 3 N.Y.2d 554, 147 N.E.2d 724 (1958) (identity of customers for contract cleaning in homes a trade secret).

E. THIRD-PARTY RECIPIENTS OF SECRETS

One of the most important features of the law of trade secrets and confidential information is the potential liability of parties who themselves did not acquire the information by improper means or violate an obligation of confidence they had assumed. A party who for some reason has received the information can be held liable for using or disclosing it if the party was on notice that a source of the information had acquired it by improper means or disclosed it in breach of an obligation of confidence. Under the Uniform Trade Secrets Act, a party's use or disclosure of a trade secret is misappropriation if, at the time, the party knew or had reason to know that his knowledge of the secret was derived from a person who had used improper means to acquire it or owed the plaintiff a duty to maintain the secrecy of the information or limit its use. Uniform Trade Secrets Act § 1(2)(ii)(B). Restatement of Unfair Competition § 40(b) is somewhat narrower.

Disclosure or use of a trade secret is actionable when "the actor knows or has reason to know that the information is a trade secret that the actor acquired from or through a person who acquired it by means that are improper. . .or whose disclosure of the trade secret constituted a breach of a duty of confidence." It appears that there can be liability for use of a trade secret without the plaintiff's consent when it is known that the information had been disclosed under an obligation to limit its use. See *Forest Laboratories, Inc. v. Pillsbury Co.*, 452 F.2d 621 (7th Cir. 1971).

A common instance of third-party liability is in actions against defendants who have employed someone who formerly worked for the plaintiff. Apart from any vicarious liability for the employee's misappropriation of the secret, such defendants can be held liable for use of a trade secret acquired through the employee, if they had knowledge or reason to know of a breach of confidence or improper means of acquisition. They can be enjoined from further use of the secret. See *Cybertek Computer Products, Inc. v. Whitfield*, 203 U.S.P.Q. 1020 (Cal. Super. Ct. 1977); *Infinity Products, Inc. v. Quandt*, 810 N.E.2d 1028 (Ind. 2004). A letter from the plaintiff claiming rights in a trade secret and demanding that the defendant refrain from use of it can provide the requisite notice, as in *Cybertek*.

A controversial application of third-party liability for disclosure of trade secrets is to parties who have disclosed information through the Internet or other media with reason to know that it is a misappropriated trade secret. In *DVD Copy Control*

Association, Inc. v. Bunner, 31 Cal. 4th 864, 75 P.3d 1 (2003), an association representing the motion picture, computer and consumer electronic industries claimed as trade secrets the technology that encrypted DVDs and prevented users from making and distributing copies. The defendant posted on his web site a computer program that enabled users of DVDs containing films to decrypt them and make copies. He had downloaded the program from another web site. The program had been developed by one Johannsen (a resident of Norway), allegedly in violation of a "click license" agreement prohibiting reverse engineering of a DVD's software. Claiming that posting the decryption program on a web site was a misappropriation of the trade secrets in the encryption technology, the plaintiff sought an order that would enjoin the defendant from disclosing or distributing the decryption program and the encryption technology. The trial court, concluding that the defendant knew or should have known that Johannsen had acquired the plaintiff's trade secrets by improper means, granted a preliminary injunction. In an appeal which assumed that the plaintiff was liable to prevail on the merits of its action, the California Supreme Court held that the preliminary injunction was not a "prior restraint" that violated the First Amendment.

Mistaken release of trade secret. Under the Restatements and Unfair Trade Secrets Act, someone who acquires knowledge of a trade secret without improper means or breach of confidence is liable for disclosing or using the information if the party knew or had reason to know that it was a trade secret and that the party's knowledge of it was acquired because of a mistake or accident. Rest. Torts § 757(d); Rest. Unfair Competition § 40(b)(4); Uniform Trade Secrets Act § 1(2)(ii)(C). This is subject to the requirement of reasonable efforts to maintain the secrecy of the information, but a preventable mistake is not necessarily a failure to use reasonable efforts to maintain secrecy. Compare *Defiance Button Machine Co. v. C & C Metal Products Corp.*, 759 F.2d 1053 (2d Cir. 1985) (no trade secret liability for use of customer lists left in memory of computer plaintiff sold to defendant), with *B.C. Ziegler and Co. v. Ehren*, 141 Wis. 2d 19, 414 N.W.2d 48 (Ct. App. 1987). In the second case, paper containing a securities underwriter's confidential customer information, which was supposed to be shredded or burned after use, was instead delivered to a scrap paper dealer. One of the dealer's employees, who happened to be a former securities salesman, recognized the value of the information and sold it to a securities broker. The employee was enjoined from further use or disclosure of the information. In some cases, the mistake which led to the defendant's acquiring the information was not the plaintiff's. *E.g.*, *Myers v. Williams*, 819 F. Supp. 919 (D. Or. 1993), in which the Food and Drug Administration mistakenly released the plaintiff's drug formula in response to a Freedom of Information Act request.

When a court enjoins the use or disclosure of a trade secret communicated by mistake, or grants damages for its use, the plaintiff's economic interest in exploitation of the secret prevails over the defendant's interest in exploitation of information acquired without a breach of confidence or other wrongful conduct. (By contrast, when a defendant is found to have discovered the secret by "reverse engineering" of the plaintiff's product, or other "independent research" or development, the defendant's interest in exploitation of the information prevails over the plaintiff's interest. See Uniform Trade Secrets Act § 1, comment.)

F. BEYOND TRADE SECRETS: LIABILITY FOR BREACH OF CONFIDENCE

In the United States, tort liability for use or disclosure of information that the plaintiff wanted to keep secret for economic reasons is usually found in the law of trade secrets. However, there is a general theory of liability for "breach of confidence." It applies to revelation or use of confidential information to the detriment of the plaintiff, in violation of a legal obligation not to disclose or use the information. An example is *Djowharzadeh v. City National Bank and Trust Co. of Norman*, 646 P.2d 616 (Okla. App. 1982). Learning that a building could be purchased for much below its market value, the plaintiff applied to his bank for a loan of the down payment. The bank's loan officer rejected the loan and told the wives of the bank's president and senior vice president about the availability of the property. They purchased the property for themselves, depriving the plaintiff of the opportunity to buy it. The court held that the loan officer owed the plaintiff a duty to keep the contents of the loan application confidential.

An action for breach of confidence can be brought when disclosure or use of the information deprived the plaintiff of a prospective economic gain or business advantage. It might also be brought when disclosure of the information would result in economic loss for other reasons, as when disclosure would damage the plaintiff's relations with customers or employees, or compromise business security. The tort does not actually require that the damage resulting from the breach of confidence be financial. As will be seen in Chapter 18, an action for breach of confidence may be maintained for disclosures that are invasions of personal privacy or harmful to personal reputation. In Britain, actions for breach of confidence have been brought for disclosures of government secrets—most prominently, in litigation arising from publication of the memoirs of a senior officer of Britain's domestic intelligence service. See *Attorney-General v. Guardian Newspapers Ltd. (No. 2)*, [1990] 1 A.C. 109 (H.L.). In the United States, a CIA agent's publication of a book containing information about the agency has been held to be a breach of fiduciary duty. *Snepp v. United States*, 444 U.S. 507 (1980).

The tort is not well defined in American law, especially on what types of relationships involve an obligation of confidence. However, it is fairly clear that the fundamental requirements of liability are the secrecy of the information, the existence of a duty or obligation of confidentiality owed to the plaintiff, the breach of that obligation, and resulting harm to the plaintiff. As with trade secrets, a defendant can incur liability by acquiring the information by improper means, or by disclosing or using the information with reason to know that the defendant acquired it as a result of another's breach of confidence or use of wrongful means.

Preemption by Uniform Trade Secrets Act. § 7 of the Uniform Trade Secrets Act precludes actions for misappropriation of a trade secret outside the provisions of the act, other than actions for a contractual remedy. This clearly bars actions, other than breach of contract, for misappropriation of information that falls within the act's definition of trade secret. What is debatable is the extent to which the act bars actions for breach of confidence concerning information that does not fit the act's definition of trade secret. This is complicated by the different versions of § 7 the states have enacted. One possible interpretation is that § 7 precludes any non-contractual action outside the act for disclosure or use of confidential information that does not meet the requirements of a trade secret, other than information to be protected for personal rather than business reasons (*e.g.*, medical information). A more narrow interpretation is that the act provides the exclusive non-contractual remedy for use or disclosure of trade secrets, but not other information. See the discussion in *BlueEarth Biofuels, LLC v. Hawaiian Electric Co., Inc.*, 123 Haw. 314, 235 P.3d 310 (2010) (adopting the broader view of § 7's preemptive effect). A distinction might be made between "competitively significant secret information," which the Uniform Act addressed (see comment to § 7), and negative information that would be economically harmful if "leaked," or information that an organization wanted to keep confidential for non-economic reasons.

As contract remedies outside the act are not barred, a plaintiff might prevail on an action claiming that disclosure or use of information was violation of an express or implied term of a contract with the defendant. It has been held that there is a breach of implied contract when a bank divulges information about a depositor's account. *Milohnich v. First National Bank of Miami Springs*, 224 So. 2d 759 (Fla. App. 1969); *Peterson v. Idaho First National Bank*, 83 Idaho 578, 367 P.2d 284 (1961).

G. FEDERAL PREEMPTION OF STATE TRADE SECRET LAW

As discussed earlier in connection with "unfair competition" (see pp. 199–200), the Supreme Court decided in *Sears, Roebuck & Co. v. Stiffel Co.*, 376 U.S. 225 (1964), and *Compco Corp. v. Day-Brite Lighting, Inc.*, 376 U.S. 234 (1964), that when an article is not patentable under federal law, state law cannot prohibit the copying of the article or award damages for copying. Federal patent law preempts state law that would afford such a remedy. The state law remedy for misappropriation of a trade secret typically includes an injunction against use of the secret or a monetary remedy for the defendant's use of it. As this could in effect hold a defendant liable for producing articles or forbid production, the *Sears* and *Compco* decisions immediately put in doubt liability under state law for misappropriation of a trade secret, at least when the secret pertained to production of an article or creation to which federal patent or copyright law had some application.

In *Kewanee Oil Co. v. Bicron Corp.*, 416 U.S. 470 (1974), the Supreme Court decided that state trade secret law was not preempted by federal patent law. It did not interfere with the policies of the federal law. The court believed that state trade secret law did not discourage patent applications for patentable inventions, as a patent would exclude any unlicensed use of the invention for a period of years, and that it encouraged non-patentable innovations. Accordingly, as a general rule, a claim of trade secret misappropriation under the Uniform Trade Secrets Act or other state law is not preempted by federal patent law. However, federal law may preempt any liability for use of a trade secret after disclosure of it in a patent. See *Evans v. General Motors Corp.*, 51 Conn. Supp. 44, 976 A.2d 84 (Super. Ct. 2007).

There is also a question of preemption of state law trade secret claims by federal copyright law. Under older law, federal copyright protection did not extend to unpublished documents, but it does under the Copyright Act of 1976. If a trade secret misappropriation claim is based on unauthorized copying of such a document, there is an argument that the only remedy is under federal copyright law. Preemption depends upon whether the rights under state law are "equivalent to any of the exclusive rights within the general scope of copyright." 17 U.S.C. § 301. Copyright protection does not extend to any "idea, procedure, process, system, method of operation, concept, principle, or discovery." 17 U.S.C.

§ 102(b). The prevailing view is that trade secret law is not preempted, as it is based upon violation of obligations of confidence, not copying; the substance of the information, not the expression of it; and loss of the information's value as a secret, not infringement of the right to reproduce it. See *Balboa Insurance Co. v. Trans Global Equities*, 218 Cal. App. 3d 1327, 267 Cal. Rptr. 787 (1990); *M. Bryce & Associates, Inc. v. Gladstone*, 107 Wis. 2d 241, 319 N.W.2d 907 (Ct. App. 1982). But preemption has been found in some instances. See *Videotronics, Inc. v. Bend Electronics*, 564 F. Supp. 1471 (D. Nev. 1983) (claim for misappropriation of computer program).

First Amendment. The First Amendment rights of freedom of speech and freedom of press, made applicable to state law by the Fourteenth Amendment, potentially limit liability for communication of trade secrets and other confidential information. Arguably, it is a violation of the First Amendment to impose liability for or restrain publication of trade secrets, especially by issuance of a preliminary injunction. However, there is not much in the case law to support the argument. In *Ford Motor Co. v. Lane*, 67 F. Supp. 2d 745 (E.D. Mich. 1999), it was decided that an injunction against publication of the plaintiff's trade secrets on the defendant's web site would violate the First Amendment. But the Supreme Court of California decided the opposite in *DVD Copy Control Association, Inc. v. Bunner*, 31 Cal. 4th 864, 75 P.3d 1 (2003).

If the First Amendment does operate to limit liability or remedies for publication of secret information, this is more likely to benefit defendants who were third-party recipients of the information than defendants whose disclosure or use of the information was in breach of a contractual obligation of confidence or fiduciary duty. (This distinction is made in *Ford Motor Co. v. Lane*.) The First Amendment may also have more effect when the information is not a commercial trade secret. These distinctions are supported by some decisions of the Supreme Court. In *Bartnicki v. Vopper*, 532 U.S. 514 (2001), the court held that the First Amendment barred liability when the defendants had disclosed a matter of public concern, knowing or having reason to know that the information was obtained through another person's illegal interception and recording of a telephone conversation. But defendants who themselves violated an obligation of confidentiality they had agreed to were held liable, despite the newsworthiness of the information disclosed, in *Snepp v. United States*, 444 U.S. 507 (1980), involving a CIA officer who had agreed not to publish information about the agency without its permission, and *Cohen v. Cowles Media Co.*, 501 U.S. 663 (1991), in which reporters had promised the source of a news story that his identity would not be revealed.

H. REMEDIES

As in other economic torts, both monetary remedies and injunctions can be granted in trade secrets cases and other actions for wrongful disclosure or use of confidential information.

Monetary remedies. In tort cases generally, the amount awarded in the judgment is usually based on the loss caused to the plaintiff by the defendant's wrongful conduct. This may be what is awarded for misappropriation of a trade secret. However, there is a strong tradition in trade secret law to grant a monetary remedy based on principles of restitution or unjust enrichment and award an amount representing the defendant's profit (including cost savings) from wrongful use of the secret. Monetary awards may be based on both compensatory damages and unjust enrichment, provided there is no duplication. In some cases, the monetary award is for what would be a reasonable royalty to the plaintiff for the defendant's use of the information. See Rest. Unfair Competition § 45, comment *c*. The Uniform Trade Secrets Act is consistent with this. § 3(a) (as amended) provides that damages can include both the actual loss caused by misappropriation and unjust enrichment; in lieu of damages measured by any other method, damages may be measured by a reasonable royalty.

Injunctions. Injunctions, including preliminary injunctions, are often issued in trade secret cases. They are the only remedy that can preserve the secrecy of the information and prevent loss to the plaintiff from disclosure or use of the information. They are also warranted by the difficulty of measuring in monetary terms the plaintiff's loss or the defendant's gain from wrongful disclosure or use of the information. See Rest. Unfair Competition § 44, comments *b–c*. Injunctions to prevent actual or threatened misappropriation of trade secrets are authorized by Uniform Trade Secrets Act § 2. Parties may be ordered to take steps to protect a trade secret as well as prohibited from disclosing or using it.

An issue of prominence in the last several decades is whether injunctive relief can or should extend to prohibition of certain employment on grounds of "inevitable disclosure." In *PepsiCo, Inc. v. Redmond*, 54 F.3d 1262 (7th Cir. 1995), the court approved an order barring a competitor's employment of a former high-level employee of the plaintiff for a period of six months. A basis for the injunction was that the plaintiff's trade secrets would inevitably be disclosed by the employee to the competitor if he worked there. The "inevitable disclosure" theory or doctrine has been accepted, at least in principle, in quite a number of cases. It has even led to a former employee's being prohibited from operating a business in competition with the plaintiff, as he would inevitably use the plaintiff's trade secrets. *Christopher M's Hand Poured Fudge, Inc. v. Hennon*, 699 A.2d 1272 (Pa. Super. Ct. 1997). But the inevitable disclosure doctrine has been rejected in some jurisdictions—most notably California, whose law protects the freedom to compete with a former employer or work for a competitor of a former employer. *Whyte v. Schlage Lock Co.*, 101 Cal. App. 4th 1443, 125 Cal. Rptr. 2d 277 (2002). And courts have often refused to enjoin employment (as distinct from disclosure or use of trade secrets during employment) in specific cases. See Annot., 36 A.L.R.6th 537. The statute providing a federal civil action for misappropriation of a trade secret, which generally contemplates that state substantive law will be applied, contains a provision intended to withhold the grant of injunctions prohibiting a person from entering employment, 18 U.S.C. § 1836(b)(3).

Duration. Another issue of prominence, especially for injunctions, concerns the period for which the remedy is granted. One position was that the remedy was limited to the period in which the information was protectable as a trade secret. It did not extend to the period after the information was no longer secret or it would have been discovered by the defendant without misappropriation. Under *Conmar Products Corp. v. Universal Slide Fastener Co.*, 172 F.2d 150 (2d Cir. 1949), an injunction could not issue or continue after the information became public. An alternative position was that a defendant could be restrained from use of the information after it was no longer secret, or liable for a monetary remedy, to prevent the defendant from profiting from misappropriation of the trade secret. See *Shellmar Products Co. v. Allen-Qualley Co.*, 87 F.2d 104 (7th Cir. 1936). Under the Uniform Trade Secrets Act, the remedy is generally limited to the period in which the information is or was a trade secret, but an injunction may be continued for an additional period to eliminate commercial advantage that the defendant would otherwise derive from the misappropriation, and a monetary remedy may include the period in which the defendant had an advantage over competitors because of the misappropriation. Uniform Trade Secrets Act §§ 2(a), 3(a) (comments).

When secret used in good faith prior to notice. As discussed earlier (pp. 226–230), there can be liability for use or disclosure of a trade secret because the defendant knew, or had reason to know, that the defendant received the secret because of another person's misappropriation of it, or by mistake. Such a defendant may, prior to acquiring this knowledge, have made a considerable investment in the secret, as in amounts spent to acquire it or to develop a commercial process utilizing the secret. Restatement of Torts § 758 protected defendants from liability when they had, in good faith, "paid value for the secret" or had so changed their position that liability would be inequitable. Uniform Trade Secrets Act § 3(a) excludes liability for damages when "a material and prejudicial change of position prior to acquiring knowledge or reason to know of misappropriation renders a monetary recovery inequitable." An injunction may also be denied for this reason, but under § 2(b) a court may require payment of a reasonable royalty for future use of the information.

CHAPTER 14

LITERARY, ARTISTIC AND COMMERCIAL CREATIONS

A. INTRODUCTION

Outside what is discussed in Chapters 12 and 13, legal rights to prevent or seek damages for unauthorized use of literary, artistic and commercial creations generally arise only from statute—usually the federal copyright or patent laws—or from contract. However, in some instances courts have sustained actions for the unauthorized publication or use of literary or artistic creations, or commercial inventions, under what was understood to be the common law or law of equity. This chapter discusses in turn (1) liability for infringement of "common law copyright," (2) liability for "misappropriation," (3) liability for use of a character, and (4) liability for use of an idea.

B. COMMON LAW COPYRIGHT

1. COMMON LAW RIGHTS

Copyright statutes have long provided legal remedies for unauthorized copying or sales of copies of copyrighted works, although with limitations concerning the types of works that could be copyrighted, the requirements for obtaining copyright protection, such as registration, and the number of years before the protection expired. However, for about two centuries, the law has recognized a non-statutory right in the creator of a work to prevent copying or sale of copies without the creator's consent. This right, which acquired the title "common law copyright," is not subject to most of the limitations of statutory copyright. There is no registration or notice requirement, and there is no time limitation. Common law copyright can continue indefinitely. However, for at least most of the works that can be protected by common law copyright, the protection is lost when the work has been published with the creator's consent. Common law copyright is thus essentially a right to control publication of works that have not already been published. It can be used to control the conditions under which a work will initially be published as well as to prevent any publication.

Early cases recognizing common law copyright, in substance if not in name, included actions to enjoin publication of the contents of unpublished manuscripts and letters, and an action brought by Prince Albert to enjoin publication of etchings that he and Queen Victoria had made. *Prince Albert v. Strange*, (1849) 1 H. & Tw. 1, 47 Eng. Rep. 1302 (L.C.). In *Palmer v. De Witt*, 47 N.Y. 532 (1872), the plaintiff was successful in an action to restrain the defendant from publishing and selling copies of the script of a drama the plaintiff had presented in theatres. Common law copyright applies to speeches and lectures delivered orally, so an action can be brought to prevent publication of the contents, or obtain damages. *Public Affairs Associates, Inc. v. Rickover*, 268 F. Supp. 444 (D.D.C. 1967) (speeches of vice admiral of U.S. Navy not made as part of official duties); *Williams v. Weisser*, 273 Cal. App. 2d 726, 78

Cal. Rptr. 542 (1969) (university professor's class lectures). It can also apply to musical compositions. *McCarthy & Fisher v. White*, 259 F. 364 (S.D.N.Y. 1919). While the work must be an original creation rather than a copy itself, there is no requirement that it have literary or artistic merit. *Baker v. Libbie*, 210 Mass. 599, 97 N.E. 109 (1912).

Questions of whether there was sufficient copying to be infringement of a common law copyright are likely to be resolved by reference to cases on infringement of federal copyrights, as in *Golding v. R.K.O. Pictures*, 35 Cal. 2d 690, 221 P.2d 95 (1950). Whether "fair use" is a defense to copyright in unpublished works is debatable. See *Harper & Row Publishers, Inc. v. Nation Enterprises*, 471 U.S. 539 (1985).

As common law copyright has been considered a property right, it is transferable by assignment, or succession after death, and enforceable by the assignee, heir or executor of the work's creator. In *Palmer v. De Witt*, the drama's author had assigned to the plaintiff the exclusive right to publish and produce it in the United States. The right is distinct from property in the document containing the work. When A writes a letter and sends it to B, the letter usually becomes the property of B, but A retains common law copyright in the contents of the letter. See *Baker v. Libbie, supra*. When a work of art is sold or donated by the artist, there is, however, a strong argument that any right to control publication of copies goes to the buyer or donee. See *Pushman v. New York Graphic Society*, 287 N.Y. 302, 39 N.E.2d

249 (1942). When a photographer creates photographs for a customer, it appears that the right to control publication belongs to the customer, unless otherwise agreed. See *Lawrence v. Ylla*, 184 Misc. 807, 55 N.Y.2d 343 (Sup. Ct. 1945).

2. PUBLICATION

It is basic to the law of common law copyright that the right terminates upon publication of the work by the plaintiff or the plaintiff's predecessor in title. But courts made a distinction between a "general publication," which terminated common law copyright, and "limited publication," which did not. "General publication" was equated with "communication or dedication to the public." A "limited publication" was one which communicated the contents of the work, but "under conditions expressly or impliedly precluding its dedication to the public." *Werckmeister v. American Lithographic Co.*, 134 F. 321, 324 (2d Cir. 1904).

Whether there had been a "general" or "limited" publication has been a major issue in a number of cases. The difficulty of resolving it is well-illustrated by litigation over a film containing much of Dr. Martin Luther King, Jr.'s famous "I Have a Dream" speech. The district court judge, and one judge of the Court of Appeals, concluded that there had been general publication of the speech because of its widespread dissemination to very large live and broadcast audiences and encouragement of media coverage, with no express or implied limitation being placed on reproduction of the contents of the speech or use of film footage of it. A second judge of the Court of Appeals took the position that performance of a work without distribution of a tangible copy is not a general publication, regardless of the size of the audience or widespread dissemination of the work through the media. The third judge agreed that generally performance of a work without distribution of tangible copies was not a general publication and concluded that distribution of copies of Dr. King's speech to the media, in order to obtain press coverage, was only a limited publication, but thought there might be general publication if a work was exhibited or displayed in such a manner as to permit unrestricted copying by the general public. *Estate of Martin Luther King, Jr., Inc. v. CBS, Inc.*, 194 F.3d 1211 (11th Cir. 1999), rev'g 13 F. Supp. 2d 1347 (N.D. Ga. 1998).

When a speech, lecture, drama or work of art had been presented to audiences or viewers in places where admission was limited, the usual decision was there had been only a limited publication. *E.g., Ferris v. Frohman*, 223 U.S. 424 (1912) (play); *Werckmeister v. American Lithographic Co.*, 134 F. 321 (2d Cir. 1904) (art); *McCarthy & Fisher, Inc. v. White*, 259 F. 364 (S.D.N.Y. 1919) (music); *National Institute, Inc., for the Improvement of Memory v. Nutt*, 28 F.2d 132 (D. Conn. 1928), aff'd, 31 F.2d 236 (2d Cir. 1929) (lectures). But display of art in a public place could be a general publication. See *Letter Edged in Black Press, Inc. v. Public Building Commission of Chicago*, 320 F. Supp. 1303 (N.D. Ill. 1970).

Distribution of tangible copies of the work to the general public with the consent of the work's creator (or assignee) was the principle example of a "general" publication that would terminate common law copyright. However, while this was undoubtedly the rule for the verbal and pictorial works that could be protected from copying under the federal copyright law, it was held in some cases that selling a sound recording to the public did not terminate common law copyright in the recording—primarily because at the time of the sale sound recordings could not be copyrighted under the federal statute. (Now they can be.) See *Capital Records, Inc. v. Naxos of America, Inc.*, 4 N.Y.3d 540, 830 N.E.2d 250 (2005).

3. PREEMPTION BY FEDERAL LAW

The federal copyright statute has always provided the exclusive remedy for unauthorized copying of works that had been "published" with the consent of the work's creator and were of a type that could be copyrighted under the statute. But under the 1909 Copyright Act and its predecessors, common law copyright operated to protect works that had not been published. It could also operate for works of a type that could not at the time be copyrighted under the federal statute, such as musical recordings. See *Goldstein v. California*, 412 U.S. 546 (1973).

This fundamentally changed with enactment of the Copyright Act of 1976, 17 U.S.C. §§ 101 *et seq*. Under the 1976 act, federal copyright law applies when a work has been "fixed in a tangible medium of expression" with the authority of the author. It thus applies whenever a work has been "fixed" by being written down or recorded in some way. And numerous types of written, pictorial, dramatic, musical and choreographic works, and recordings of them, are now included. The Copyright Act preempts any copyright protection under state law for these works. 17 U.S.C. § 301. The effect of this is to limit the operation of common law copyright, as a doctrine of state law, to works that are not "fixed." These are primarily the contents of oral presentations, such as speeches and lectures, and live performances of drama, dance and music, assuming they were not simultaneously "fixed" (recorded) with the authority of the author.

How much literary, artistic or dramatic content is required for common law copyright is uncertain. Courts have denied the protection of common law copyright to brief performances of various types. *Glazer v. Hoffman*, 153 Fla. 836, 16 So. 2d 53 (1943) (magician's act); *Dane v. M. & H. Co.*, 136 U.S.P.Q. 426 (N.Y. Sup. Ct. 1963), aff'd, 21 A.D.2d 751, 251 N.Y.S.2d 901 (1964) (brief choreographic "number"); *Zacchini v. Scripps-Howard Broadcasting Co.*, 47 Ohio St. 2d 224, 351 N.E.2d 454 (1976), rev'd, 433 U.S. 562 (1977) (human cannonball act). But see *Columbia Broadcasting System, Inc. v. Documentaries Unlimited, Inc.*, 42 Misc. 2d 723, 248 N.Y.S.2d 809 (Sup. Ct. 1964) (noted broadcast announcer's announcement on national television of President Kennedy's assassination). Imitation of a performer's style is not an infringement. See *Murray v. Rose*, 30 N.Y.S.2d 6 (Sup. Ct. 1941) (dance performance); *Miller v. Universal Pictures Co.,* 11

A.D.2d 47, 201 N.Y.S.2d 632 (1960), modified, 13 A.D.2d 473, 214 N.Y.S.2d 645 (1961), aff'd, 10 N.Y.2d 972, 180 N.E.2d 248 (1961) (band leader's "sound"). Generally there is no common law copyright in material communicated orally to an interviewer or in conversation. But perhaps an interview or conversation with sufficient literary content, provided by a person who had "marked it off" as literary property, could be the subject of a common law copyright action. See *Estate of Hemingway v. Random House, Inc.*, 23 N.Y.2d 341, 244 N.E.2d 250 (1968).

The Copyright Act does not preempt state law to the extent it provides legal rights that are not equivalent to rights under copyright law, such as the right to make copies of a work or perform a work publicly. 17 U.S.C. § 301(b). Rights under state law to sue for violation of privacy, appropriation of a trade secret or passing off are not equivalent to rights under copyright law and therefore not preempted.

C. MISAPPROPRIATION

1. INTERNATIONAL NEWS SERVICE V. ASSOCIATED PRESS

Liability for misappropriation arises from and remains grounded in a decision of the Supreme Court of the United States: *International News Service v. Associated Press*, 248 U.S. 215 (1918). International News Service (INS) and Associated Press (AP) were competitors in providing news reports to newspapers. A few newspapers obtained news from both, but most subscribed to only one of the news services. INS engaged in the practice of taking news that AP member newspapers had published or posted on bulletin boards and transmitting the news to INS subscribing newspapers, which published it without crediting AP. When INS copied news from AP newspapers in eastern cities, it could be published in INS newspapers in the western United States as soon as, or even earlier, than in the western AP newspapers. A principal reason for its conduct was that the British and French governments had banned INS from transmitting news because of the anti-British and French coverage of World War I in the Hearst newspapers, which controlled INS. INS was therefore unable to supply much contemporaneous news of the war without use of information obtained by other news services. See Epstein, *International News v. Associated Press*: Custom and Law as Sources of Property Rights in News, 78 Va. L. Rev. 85, 91–92 (1992).

AP brought an action to restrain INS from copying news from AP newspapers and selling the news to INS's customers. AP's news reports were not copyrighted under federal law. According to AP, the large number of news dispatches made copyrighting them impractical. Also, news (as distinct from newspaper articles containing news) could not be copyrighted. Drawing on the law of common law copyright, INS contended that once news had been published in newspapers or bulletin boards with AP's consent, without a copyright under the federal act, AP lost any property right in the news and any use of the news by the public, including INS, was lawful.

Rejecting this argument, a majority of the Supreme Court affirmed the Court of Appeals' decision that INS be enjoined from taking or using AP's news "until its commercial value as news to the complainant and all of its members has passed away." A court of equity could protect AP against "unfair competition in business," which INS's conduct was found to be. INS's conduct was unfair competition because AP had acquired the news as a result of its organization and a large expenditure of money, skill and effort, and INS was interfering with AP's business "precisely at the point where the profit is to be reaped, in order to divert a material portion of the profit from those who have earned it to those who have not; with special advantage to defendant in the competition because of the fact that it is not burdened with any part of the expense of gathering the news." 248 U.S. 215, 240. Also, if "indiscriminate publication by anybody. . .for purposes of profit in competition with the news-gatherer" were allowed, the cost of gathering the news would be prohibitive in comparison with the reward and the service would end. AP was entitled to an equitable remedy for "misappropriation" of its "property" in the news it had gathered. Allowing publication of the news by AP newspapers, for the benefit of the readers, was a publication for limited purposes that was not abandonment by AP of its interest in the news for all purposes.

Justice Brandeis delivered an elaborate dissent. There was also a dissenting opinion by Justice Holmes. Both concluded that no legal right of AP had been violated other than (for Justice Holmes) a right in AP to be credited by INS for the news obtained from AP. The dissenters denied that news was "property." According to Justice Brandeis, "To appropriate and use for profit, knowledge and ideas produced by other men, without making compensation or even acknowledgment, may be inconsistent with a finer sense of propriety; but. . .the law has heretofore sanctioned the practice. . . . Such taking and gainful use of a product of another. . .does not become unlawful because the product happens to be taken from a rival and is used in competition with him." 248 U.S. 215, 257–258. Competition was not unfair in a legal sense because profits were unearned. Justice Brandeis argued that recognition of a property right in news should occur only through enactment of legislation. Recognition of a property right in the news would be a danger to the public interest without legislative limits on the right and the imposition upon newsgatherers of corresponding obligations.

2. LIABILITY FOR MISAPPROPRIATION

The question of when there can be liability for misappropriation, on the basis of the majority opinion in *International News Service v. Associated Press*, admits of no simple answer. It is complicated by the case's status as a pre-*Erie* decision that can be rejected by state courts, or by federal courts interpreting state law, as in *Triangle Publications v. New England Newspaper Publishing Co.*, 46 F. Supp. 198 (D. Mass. 1942). Liability based on misappropriation is disapproved by the Restatement of Unfair Competition. § 38, comments *b–c*. But it has been accepted in most of the relevant state court cases. *E.g., United States Sporting Products, Inc. v. Johnny Stewart Game Calls, Inc.*, 865 S.W.2d 214 (Tex. App. 1993).

One possible reading of the *INS* case is that it creates a potentially wide-ranging theory of liability, operating outside copyright and patent law, when a competitor or other business appropriates to itself what the plaintiff has created, avoiding most of the cost and effort borne by the plaintiff, and deprives the plaintiff of much of the profit that the plaintiff would otherwise earn. Another interpretation, which was advanced by Judge Learned Hand, is that the decision in *INS* applies only to cases with very similar facts, including the appropriation of news or other information valuable only when it is fresh. *RCA Manufacturing Co. v. Whiteman*, 114 F.2d 86 (2d Cir. 1940).

Arguably, even if misappropriation liability is not as limited as that, it arises only when there is competition between the defendant and the plaintiff, or at least the licensees of the plaintiff; when the defendant's conduct would injure the plaintiff commercially in its primary market; and when there is a risk that the plaintiff would not continue to provide its services in that market if not protected. See *United States Golf Association v. St. Andrews Systems, Data Max, Inc.*, 749 F.2d 1028 (3d Cir. 1984) (defendant marketing computer system that used USGA's formula for golf handicaps). But misappropriation has been found in some cases when the parties were not competitors and the plaintiff's primary market was not threatened. A notable example is *Board of Trade of City of Chicago v. Dow Jones & Co., Inc.*, 98 Ill. 2d 109, 456 N.E.2d 84 (1983), which held that the Chicago Board of Trade's offering stock index futures contracts utilizing the Dow Jones Industrial Average was a misappropriation of Dow Jones' index and averages. A court that might otherwise limit misappropriation liability to competitors might find liability when the defendant's conduct greatly impairs the value and marketability of what the plaintiff sells—for example, providing answers to problems in the plaintiff's educational text. *Addison-Wesley Publishing Co. v. Brown*, 207 F. Supp. 678 (E.D.N.Y. 1962). Or presenting a film that discloses how a magician's famous illusion is performed. *Goldin v. Clarion Photoplays,* 202 App. Div. 1, 195 N.Y.S. 455 (1922).

Perhaps the most accurate generalization is that to come within the misappropriation doctrine a case does not have to have facts similar to those of the *INS* case (although it helps), but the equitable reasons for finding liability in *INS*—including the plaintiff having made a substantial investment in expectation of profit and being deprived of much of the profit by the defendant's appropriation of what the plaintiff created, without much change—must strongly fit the case. Also, liability must not conflict with federal copyright or patent law, including preemption of state law claims. (See below at pp. 256–259.)

The cases with facts that most resemble those of *INS* are cases in which the defendant used the plaintiff's newspaper or radio broadcast to provide fresh news, including descriptions of sports events, and deprived the plaintiff of revenue. Plaintiffs have been successful in a number of cases of this type. See *Associated Press v. KVOS*, 80 F.2d 575 (9th Cir. 1935), rev'd (for want of jurisdiction), 299 U.S. 269 (1936); *Mutual Broadcasting System, Inc. v. Muzak Corp.*, 177 Misc. 489, 30 N.Y.S.2d 419 (Sup. Ct. 1941); *Pottstown Daily News Publishing Co. v. Pottstown Broadcasting Co.*, 411 Pa. 383, 192 A.2d 657 (1963). Proprietors of major sports events, who derive much revenue from licensing rights to broadcast the events, could also have an action when someone other than the licensee broadcasts contemporaneous details of the event. See *Pittsburgh Athletic Co. v. KQV Broadcasting Co.*, 24 F. Supp. 490 (W.D. Pa. 1938).

In the mid-twentieth century, the misappropriation doctrine was a successful theory for plaintiffs in actions complaining of record or tape "piracy." To produce and sell records or tapes by making copies of recordings authorized by the performers was held to be actionable misappropriation in a number of actions brought by major record companies. See Annot., 40 A.L.R.3d 566. The court in *Metropolitan Opera Association v. Wagner-Nichols Recorder Corp.*, 199 Misc. 786, 101 N.Y.S.2d 483 (Sup. Ct. 1950), aff'd, 279 App. Div. 632, 107 N.Y.S.2d 795 (1951), found misappropriation in the sale of records made by recording radio broadcasts of opera performances. Another variety of misappropriation was picking up and distributing signals of television or radio programs that the plaintiff was transmitting to paid subscribers. See

American Television and Communications Corp. v. Manning, 651 P.2d 440 (Colo. App. 1982). (These matters now come with the federal copyright act.)

In contrast, misappropriation did not succeed as a theory of liability when the plaintiff's complaint was essentially that the defendant had copied or imitated the plaintiff's product. *E.g.*, *Cheney Brothers v. Doris Silk Corp.*, 35 F.2d 279 (2d Cir. 1929) (silk patterns); *Harvey Hubbell, Inc. v. General Electric Co.*, 262 F. 155 (S.D.N.Y. 1919) (electrical parts designed to be interchangeable with plaintiff's); *Societe Comptoir De L'Industrie Cotonniere Etablissements Boussac v. Alexander's Department Stores, Inc.*, 299 F.2d 33 (2d Cir. 1962) (garments advertised as copies of plaintiff's designs). *Cf. Hartford Charga-Plate Associates v. Youth Centre-Cinderella Stores, Inc.*, 215 F.2d 668 (2d Cir. 1954) (retail store's use of address plates made for credit sales at department stores).

Reverse passing off. In the *INS* case, Justice Holmes would have granted limited relief to Associated Press on the ground that INS's copying of news gathered by AP denied AP credit for collecting the news and (when newspapers subscribing to INS published news earlier than AP newspapers in western states) created the impression that AP was copying news collected by INS. Lower courts have occasionally found a cause of action when the defendant created the false impression that the defendant was the source of something the plaintiff had created or accomplished, especially when it would be injurious for the plaintiff to be denied credit for this. *Capital Films Corp. v. Charles Fries Productions, Inc.*, 628 F.2d 387 (5th Cir. 1980) (production and television broadcast of film with same title and subject-matter as plaintiff's earlier film); *Bajpayee v. Rothermich*, 53 Ohio App. 2d 117, 372 N.E.2d 817 (1977) (defendant allegedly presenting biochemist's discoveries as his own at meeting of professional medical group). But such a claim would probably not succeed when the "reverse confusion" was caused by the defendant's lawful copying of the plaintiff's product or use of a product the plaintiff had made. See *Mastro Plastics Corp. v. Emenee Industries, Inc.*, 16 A.D.2d 420, 228 N.Y.S.2d 514 (1962), aff'd, 12 N.Y.2d 826, 187 N.E.2d 360 (1962) (plaintiff's products and photographs of them used by defendant as trade samples and for advertising). Reverse confusion or passing off that is a misrepresentation about the actual producer of goods or services might be actionable under the trademark laws. See *Dastar Corp. v. Twentieth Century Fox Film Corp.*, 539 U.S. 23 (2003).

3. PREEMPTION BY FEDERAL LAW

There has always been potential conflict between liability for misappropriation and rights to copy works that did not qualify for protection from copying under the federal patent or copyright statutes, or works with a patent or copyright that had expired. In the *INS* case, the Supreme Court upheld an injunction against copying uncopyrighted news reports that the Associated Press had published. This indicated that the misappropriation doctrine could prevent copying of published material when statutory and common law copyright did not. But Judge Learned Hand cautioned against reading *INS* as creating a "sort of common-law patent or copyright for reasons of justice." This would, in his view, flagrantly conflict with what Congress had devised in the patent and copyright statutes. *Cheney Brothers v. Doris Silk Corp.*, 35 F.2d 279, 280 (2d Cir. 1929).

In the *Sears* and *Compco* cases (see pp. 199–200), the Supreme Court decided that state law could not be applied to forbid, or create liability for, copying of articles that was permitted by the federal patent laws. This rather clearly excluded misappropriation liability for the copying of articles or designs for articles. For patented articles, federal patent law provided the remedy for unauthorized copying, and for unpatented articles there was a right to make copies without prohibition or liability for damages. Even misappropriation by direct use of the plaintiff's creation to manufacture duplicates would not be actionable. *Cf. Bonito Boats, Inc. v. Thunder Craft Boats, Inc.*, 489 U.S. 141 (1989) (preemption of state statute that prohibited duplication of boat hulls by direct molding from another person's hull and sale of hulls so duplicated).

It also appeared that the "*Sears-Compco* doctrine" excluded liability for copying of verbal, visual and musical works and recordings that were not protected from copying under the federal copyright statute. See *Columbia Broadcasting System, Inc. v. DeCosta*, 377 F.2d 315 (1st Cir. 1967). But this was not so clear, and in *Goldstein v. California*, 412 U.S. 546 (1973), the Supreme Court held that a state was free to protect subject-matter that Congress had left "unattended"—in this instance, music recordings—by not regulating it in the Copyright Act. So a misappropriation action for unauthorized duplication of sound recordings was not preempted. It seemed that a claim under state law would be preempted only if the federal statute expressed an intention to leave a work unprotected from copying or there was conflict with the scheme established in the federal legislation.

Under the 1976 Copyright Act, state law claims are preempted if they assert legal rights "equivalent to any of the exclusive rights within the general scope of copyright" "in works of authorship that are fixed in a tangible medium of expression and come within the subject matter of copyright." 17 U.S.C. § 301(a). Sound recordings are included, so misappropriation actions for unauthorized duplication of recordings and distribution of copies are now preempted. Broadcasts are also included when they are simultaneously "fixed" (recorded). (The act also regulates "secondary transmissions" of broadcasts.) But there is no preemption of actions for copying or distributing works "not fixed in any tangible medium of expression," including live performances. 17 U.S.C. § 301(b). The act now provides a federal remedy for unauthorized "bootleg" copies or communications of live musical performances, but liability under state law is not preempted. 17 U.S.C. § 1101.

For works of the type that are protected by copyright when they are "fixed," misappropriation claims under state common law are preempted to the extent they assert rights "equivalent to any of the exclusive rights within the general scope of copyright." These include the exclusive rights to reproduce the work, to distribute copies of it, to prepare derivative works, and to perform or display the work publicly. 17 U.S.C. § 106. It is questionable whether misappropriation can be distinguished from any of these rights. But copyright rights do not include an exclusive right to be the provider of information. See 17 U.S.C. § 102(b). In a major case that bore a resemblance to *INS*, as the defendant was providing fresh information gleaned from the plaintiff, the court concluded that a claim of misappropriation of "hot news" was not preempted when it contained "extra elements" that went beyond copyright infringements: (1) the factual information was highly time-sensitive; (2) the defendant's use of the information was "free-riding" on the plaintiff's costly efforts to generate or collect the information; and (3) the "free-riding" threatened the existence of the plaintiff's service or product. *National Basketball Association v. Motorola, Inc.*, 105 F.3d 841 (2d Cir. 1997).

D. CHARACTERS

Creators of a literary, dramatic or marketing character, and producers of works containing such a character, may claim that their legal rights are infringed when others use or imitate the character without their consent. There are numerous situations in which a character created by one person may be used or imitated by someone else. A character in a live performance or film may be performed or imitated in another performance. A novel, short story or drama may feature a character, such as a private detective or "super hero," created or originally publicized by someone else, or something similar. With the development of motion pictures, radio broadcasting, television and the Internet, as well as the expansion of print publication, it has become increasingly likely that a character originally found in one type of media will appear in another—for example, use of a character from a book in a film or broadcast drama, or a film character in a television program. There is now a large market for "character products"—products based on characters from popular films and television programs, products based on comic book characters, and even products based on advertising characters.

Copyright law may sometimes provide a remedy for detailed copying of a character and related story line in a copyrighted work. But most copying of characters is not copyright infringement (except copying of cartoons). See *Warner Bros. Pictures v. Columbia Broadcasting System*, 216 F.2d 945 (9th Cir. 1954) (additional stories featuring detective Sam Spade, who had been in *The Maltese Falcon*). The more viable claim, if any, is for "unfair competition" (passing off). A plaintiff may prevail on this basis if it is established that the public associates the character with the plaintiff and the defendant's use of the character created the false impression that the plaintiff was the author or sponsor of the defendant's work.

For example, the author of the novel *Stella Dallas* was held to have an unfair competition action when the defendant broadcast *Stella Dallas* radio programs based on the novel. *Prouty v. National Broadcasting Co.*, 26 F. Supp. 265 (D. Mass. 1939). The creator of the "Mutt" and "Jeff" cartoon characters obtained an injunction against publication of other cartoons using those names. *Fisher v. Star Co.*, 231 N.Y. 414, 132 N.E. 133 (1919). In *Lone Ranger, Inc. v. Cox*, 124 F.2d 650 (4th Cir. 1942), the court sustained an action by the company that produced the popular *Lone Ranger* radio program when a small circus advertised an appearance by "The Lone Ranger." The court concluded that this would mislead the public, especially children, to believe that he was the Lone Ranger in the radio program. A more doubtful example is *DC Comics Inc. v. Unlimited Monkey Business, Inc.*, 598 F. Supp. 110 (N.D. Ga. 1984), in which the publisher of "Superman" and "Wonder Woman" comic books was granted an injunction against companies in the business of delivering "singing telegrams." The telegrams were delivered by persons portraying characters that were "take-offs" of the plaintiff's—"Super Stud" and "Wonder Wench"—and had similar costumes and slogans.

Liability for "unfair competition" might also be found when the defendant has imitated the character performance of an actor or musician. In *Chaplin v. Amador*, 93 Cal. App. 358, 269 P. 544 (1928), the defendant used the name "Charles Aplin" and made a film in which he imitated the dress and mannerisms made famous on screen by Charlie

Chaplin. Chaplin was granted an injunction against an imitation likely to mislead the public about his being in the defendant's film. In *Estate of Presley v. Russen*, 513 F. Supp. 1339 (D.N.J. 1981), the defendant produced a stage show patterned on that of Elvis Presley, with a performer imitating Presley's appearance and singing style. The court found a likelihood of public confusion about the Presley estate's sponsorship or association with defendant's show and granted an injunction. Analogously, imitation of the distinct vocal style of an actor or musician for commercial purposes is actionable if it creates the false impression that the actor or musician is performing. *E.g., Lahr v. Adell Chemical Co.*, 300 F.2d 256 (1st Cir. 1962).

An unfair competition action will fail if no such false impression is created, even if the plaintiff's character or performing style is imitated. See *West v. Lind*, 186 Cal. App. 2d 563, 9 Cal. Rptr. 288 (1960) (defendant making stage appearances as "Diamond Lil," as Mae West had earlier); *Booth v. Colgate-Palmolive Co.*, 362 F. Supp. 343 (S.D.N.Y. 1973) (deliberate imitation of plaintiff's voice in commercial). In *DeCosta v. Columbia Broadcasting System, Inc.*, 520 F.2d 499 (1st Cir. 1975), the defendants were found to have copied a character invented by the plaintiff and used it as the basis of their television program. But the defendants did not pass off their character or program as creations of the plaintiff, who was unknown to the public. If a character is particularly associated in the public mind with an actor who has performed the character, commercial exploitation of the character for other performances or advertising might be an infringement of the actor's "right of publicity." (See the discussion of the right of publicity in Chapter 16.)

Concerning sales of "character products" or "character merchandise"—toys, clothing and other merchandise that the public will buy or use because of its association with characters in popular films, television programs and other media—there may be liability to the producer of the film or program on the ground that the public is likely to believe that the merchandise is being sold by the plaintiff, or with a license from the plaintiff. *E.g., Wyatt Earp Enterprises, Inc. v. Sackman, Inc.*, 157 F. Supp. 621 (S.D.N.Y. 1958). This is governed by the law of passing off or unfair competition discussed in Chapter 12. When the originator of a character will have an action for another's use of the character in media or merchandise without consent, the originator will be in a position to offer licenses for use of the character. The existence of many such licensing arrangements lends support to the argument that the public will believe that a defendant's use of a character was licensed by the character's originator or proprietor.

E. IDEAS

Litigation over ideas typically involves a claim that the plaintiff submitted a valuable idea to the defendant with the expectation that the plaintiff would be paid if the defendant used the idea, or that the defendant would not use the idea without having made an agreement with the plaintiff about the terms for use of the idea. The defendant's use or disclosure of the idea without the plaintiff's consent, or a payment reflecting the value of the idea, may be characterized as "misappropriation" of the idea.

The plaintiff's action may be based on an alleged express contractual agreement to pay for the use of the idea, or not to use it without a further agreement with the plaintiff. Alternatively, it may be based on a claim that the defendant impliedly agreed with the plaintiff to pay for the use of the idea, or not to use it without a further agreement. Using the idea without payment or the plaintiff's consent would be the breach of the express or implied contract. If there was an implied-in-fact agreement, it would be derived from the communications and conduct of the parties, including any solicitation of ideas by the defendant. Its existence might be supported by evidence that it is industry custom or understanding that use of an idea requires further agreement, or that compensation is to be paid for ideas that are used. However, a contract-based claim may fail for a number of reasons. Commercial recipients of ideas, especially unsolicited ideas, are unlikely to agree to any legal obligation concerning the use of an idea as a condition of receiving and evaluating an idea. Receiving and reading an idea is not necessarily assent to any conditions the plaintiff states in transmitting the idea. Also, liability for breach of contract requires consideration for the defendant's alleged promise. It is usually (but not universally) required that the idea be novel, or at least original. If the plaintiff's idea is something that is already general knowledge or readily deducible from general knowledge, the plaintiff has not provided something of value to the defendant and there is no consideration. See *Masline v. New York, New Haven & Hartford Railroad Co.*, 95 Conn. 702, 112 A. 639 (1921) (informing railroad that it could make much money by selling advertising space on stations, cars, rights of way and fences).

Another possible basis of liability is the law of trade secrets. The plaintiff's valuable idea might qualify as a trade secret, and the defendant might have violated an obligation of confidence in using or disclosing it without the plaintiff's agreement. However, an idea that is already within general knowledge or readily deducible from general knowledge is not a trade secret, and submission of even a novel idea usually does not itself place the recipient under an obligation of confidence. *Cf. J. Irizarry y Puente v. President and Fellows of Harvard College*, 248 F.2d 799 (1st Cir. 1957) (idea for foreign tax service).

Other possible bases of liability go under various labels, including quasi-contract, unjust enrichment, restitution, quantum meruit and misappropriation. In substance they amount to a claim that the defendant was under a non-contractual obligation to make payment to the plaintiff because of the circumstances in which the idea was submitted and the defendant's gains from using it. The underlying rationale is that the defendant would be unjustly enriched if the defendant was not required to make payment. The circumstances in which liability may arise cannot readily be delineated. Liability appears to depend upon the court's sense of equity as between the idea's originator and the defendant and the reasonable expectations of the parties. See *Materese v. Moore-McCormack Lines*, 158 F.2d 631 (2d Cir. 1946); *Schott v. Westinghouse Electric Corp.*, 436 Pa. 279, 259 A.2d 443 (1969).

In most instances, when the recipient of an idea is under no contractual duty or obligation of confidence concerning the use of the idea, there will be no liability for using or disclosing the idea or obligation to share profits with the idea's provider. And any possible liability is constrained by requirements that the idea be concrete ("not "abstract") and that it be novel, or at least original. A considerable number of actions involving ideas have failed because of these requirements. *E.g.*, *Bowen v. Yankee Network*, 46 F. Supp. 62 (D. Mass. 1942) (plan for radio program with musical broadcast from different city each week, using musicians from that city); *Women Golfer, Inc. v. Meredith Corp.*, 792 F. Supp. 211 (S.D.N.Y. 1992) (proposal to establish magazine for women golfers); *Smith v. Recrion Corp.*, 91 Nev. 666, 541 P.2d 663 (1975) (idea that hotel construct recreational vehicle park); *Thomas v. R.J. Reynolds Tobacco Co.*, 350 Pa. 262, 38 A.2d 61 (1944) (proposal to advertise plaintiff's testimonial that defendant's brand of cigarettes was best and burned longest). And a plaintiff may fail to establish that the defendant used the plaintiff's idea.

Preemption by federal law. In principle, claims under state law concerning ideas are not preempted by federal patent or copyright law, as the statutes do not protect ideas as such. § 102(b) of the 1976 Copyright Act specifies that "In no case does copyright protection for an original work of authorship extend to any idea, procedure, process, system, method of operation, concept, principle, or discovery. . . ." However, courts have decided that intangible uncopyrightable ideas embodied in writings and other copyrightable material are within the "subject matter of copyright." See *United States ex rel. Berge v. Board of Trustees of the University of Alabama*, 104 F.3d 1453 (4th Cir. 1997); *Wrench LLC v. Taco Bell Corp.*, 256 F.3d 446 (6th Cir. 2001). If so, a state law claim is preempted if it asserts rights equivalent to rights under federal copyright law, which include exclusive rights to reproduce, distribute and display publicly the copyrighted work. Decisions vary on whether particular claims based on implied-in-fact contract, unjust enrichment or breach of confidence asserted rights equivalent to rights under copyright law and therefore were preempted.

PART IV

PRIVACY AND PUBLICITY

CHAPTER 15

INVASION OF PRIVACY: INTRODUCTION

Tort liability for invasion of privacy has a peculiar history. Invasion or deprivation of privacy was never recognized as a tort in English common law, but some types of invasion of privacy have been actionable in the United States since early in the twentieth century. Principal credit for this is usually given to a law review article published in 1890: "The Right to Privacy" (4 Harv. L. Rev. 193) by Samuel Warren and Louis Brandeis (later a distinguished Supreme Court justice). The primary concern of Warren and Brandeis was publication in the press of what they viewed as personal information that should not be published, including photographs. However, the first major test of whether courts would accept tort liability for invasion of privacy involved a different infringement of personal privacy: use of a person's picture in commercial advertising without consent.

In *Roberson v. Rochester Folding Box Co.*, 171 N.Y. 538, 64 N.E. 442 (1902), a young woman's picture had been used as an illustration in advertising sheets for the defendant's flour. Twenty-five thousand copies had allegedly been posted in public places, including stores and saloons. By a 4–3 majority, the New York Court of Appeals rejected the proposition that there was a right to privacy enforceable at law or equity. The decision was based upon both the absence of precedent and the belief that a right of privacy could not be limited to restraining publication of a person's likeness in advertising. It would extend to publication of a likeness in a periodical, and both written and oral commentary on a person's looks or conduct. Judge Gray wrote a strong dissent that cited the Warren and Brandeis article. He contended that "the preventive power of a court of equity" should be exercised on the basis of either analogy to established common law principle or natural justice. (The principal analogies were to the right to protection against invasion of one's person or property and to common law copyright, which provided an action to prevent publication of an unpublished writing or lecture.)

The *Roberson* decision met with public disapproval. Almost immediately, the New York legislature enacted a statute providing that:

> Any person whose name, portrait or picture is used within this state for advertising purposes or for the purposes of trade without. . .written consent. . .may maintain an equitable action. . .against the person, firm or corporation so using his name, portrait or picture, to prevent and restrain the use thereof; and may also sue and recover damages for any injuries sustained by reason of such use, and if the defendant shall have knowingly used such person's name, portrait, or picture in such manner as is forbidden or declared to be unlawful by this act, the jury, in its discretion, may award exemplary damages.

(Now in N.Y. Civil Rights Law § 51.) New York's position as the main locale of the nation's publishing and advertising industries, as well as being the principal financial center and most populous state, meant that many complaints about commercial use of a person's name or picture could be brought under the New York statute.

A few years after *Roberson*, the Supreme Court of Georgia decided to recognize a common law right of privacy. *Pavesich v. New England Life Insurance Co.*, 122 Ga. 190, 50 S.E. 68 (1905). The plaintiff's picture had been used in an insurance company's newspaper advertisement. He had not consented to this and was not one of the company's policyholders. Believing that there was a right of privacy derived from natural law and that personal liberty included a right of privacy, the court concluded that violation of the right of privacy was a tort and that it was actionable without special damages. It endorsed Judge Gray's dissent in *Roberson* and held that the plaintiff's complaint stated a cause of action. The opinion insisted that difficulty in determining the "line" between liability and non-liability was not reason to reject recognition of the right of privacy. It anticipated that the principal difficulty would be in situations where rights to freedom of speech and freedom of the press could be asserted in opposition to claims of violation of a right of privacy. But liability for using a person's likeness in advertising was thought to involve no conflict with freedom of speech or freedom of the press.

In the decades following *Pavesich*, courts in numerous states recognized tort liability for invasion of privacy in some instances, and some states enacted statutes similar to that of New York. Prosser's analysis of the cases led him to conclude that actionable invasion of privacy consisted of four distinct torts: appropriation, for the defendant's advantage, of the plaintiff's name or likeness; intrusion upon the plaintiff's seclusion or solitude, or into his private affairs; public disclosure of embarrassing private facts about the plaintiff; and publicity which places the plaintiff in a false light in the public eye. Prosser, Privacy, 48 Calif. L. Rev. 383, 389 (1960). Subsequently, the Restatement (Second) of Torts, for which Prosser served as Reporter, specified liability for these four types of invasion of privacy. Rest. 2d Torts §§ 652A–652E.

It is now well established (although not without some criticism) that there is no general tort of invasion of privacy but rather four distinct torts or categories of liability for invasion of privacy, each with different rules of liability. Some states have not accepted all four forms of liability (in New York and Virginia, the only liability is for the use of a person's name or picture made actionable by statute, and a few decisions reject liability for "false light" or publishing true "private facts"), but typically any liability for invasion of privacy is addressed in accordance with the rules of the Second Restatement. Two additional forms of liability are related to this and will also be discussed in the "Privacy and Publicity" part of this book. One is liability for infringement of the "right of publicity." This emerged from liability for commercial appropriation of a person's name or likeness. The other is liability for breach of confidence, which can provide a remedy for disclosure of sensitive personal information.

The right to privacy is limited to natural persons. An action for invasion of privacy is not maintainable by legal entities such as corporations. And there is no action for violating the privacy of a deceased person. Rest. 2d Torts § 652I. (The right of publicity is different in these respects. See pp. 282–286.)

The defendant's intent is usually not an issue in invasion of privacy cases. The privacy torts other than intrusion do not require an intent to invade the defendant's privacy. There could be liability even though the defendant had no intent to include a person's name or likeness in an advertisement without consent or to disclose sensitive private facts that were not already known. See *Flake v. Greensboro News Co.*, 212 N.C. 780, 195 S.E. 55 (1938) (plaintiff's photograph used in advertisement by mistake); *Multimedia WMAZ, Inc. v. Kubach*, 212 Ga. App. 707, 443 S.E.2d 491 (1994) (inadequate distortion of plaintiff's image during television broadcast).

There is no well-developed law of defenses to liability for invasion of privacy. Much of what has been referred to as a defense, such as "newsworthiness," actually goes to the elements of liability (in this instance, the absence of legitimate public interest in the information disclosed). It appears that the circumstances which provide an absolute privilege against liability for defamation, such as making a statement in judicial proceedings, also provide an absolute privilege against liability for invasion of privacy. The qualified privileges of defamation law may also apply. Rest. 2d Torts §§ 652F–652G. Defenses that apply to tort actions generally, such as immunity and consent, would also be valid. The Communications Decency Act, 47 U.S.C. § 230(c), bars actions against computer services that transmit or fail to remove content created by others. See *Doe v. Friendfinder Network, Inc.*, 540 F. Supp. 2d 288 (D.N.H. 2008) (fake profile and advertisements of plaintiff in sex web sites); *Doe v. America Online, Inc.*, 783 So. 2d 1010 (Fla. 2001) (computer service used to sell pornographic photographs and videotapes of minor). There is an argument that the First Amendment bars liability for publishing true facts about a person, but this has not yet been directly addressed by the Supreme Court.

CHAPTER 16

APPROPRIATION OF NAME, LIKENESS OR IDENTITY

A. APPROPRIATION AS INVASION OF PRIVACY

With the decision in *Pavesich v. New England Life Insurance Co.* and enactment of the New York statute discussed in the previous chapter, commercial appropriation of a person's name or likeness became a tort early in the twentieth century. Much of the detail on how the tort is to operate has been provided by the many reported cases in which the plaintiff sued under the New York statute. The clearest cases of liability are those in which the plaintiff's picture or name was used in a business' advertisement, as in *Pavesich* and *Roberson*, or used for a product label or business name, as in *Edison v. Edison Polyform Manufacturing Co.*, 73 N.J. Eq. 136, 67 A. 392 (Ch. 1907), and *Hirsch v. S.C. Johnson & Son, Inc.*, 90 Wis. 2d 379, 280 N.W.2d 129 (1979). There is liability for advertising use of a person's name even when the person has an actual connection to what is advertised. In *Town & Country Properties, Inc. v. Riggins*, 249 Va. 387, 457 S.E.2d 356 (1995), a real estate brokerage was held liable for advertising a house as the former home of a prominent professional football player. Reproduction in an advertisement of a news article containing the plaintiff's name or photograph can also give rise to liability. See *Canessa v. J.I. Kislak, Inc.*, 97 N.J.

Super. 327, 235 A.2d 62 (Law Div. 1967); *Flores v. Mosler Safe Co.*, 7 N.Y.2d 276, 164 N.E.2d 853 (1959).

An exception to the usual liability for advertising use of a person's name or likeness is that advertising for a book, periodical, film or broadcast may include without liability the name or picture of a person who is depicted or written about in what is advertised. See *Almeida v. Amazon.com, Inc.*, 456 F.3d 1316 (11th Cir. 2006); *Lawrence v. A.S. Abell Co.*, 299 Md. 697, 475 A.2d 448 (1984). There is, however, liability if the work being advertised actually does not involve the plaintiff at all. *Lerman v. Chuckleberry Publishing, Inc.*, 496 F. Supp. 1105 (S.D.N.Y. 1980) (cover of pornographic magazine falsely stated that magazine included photograph of plaintiff).

Most of the major informational and entertainment media are commercial in nature, and the informational or entertainment content is often near commercial advertising. To include an individual's name or likeness in what is published could be regarded as literally an appropriation of name or likeness for commercial purposes, and it often invades individual privacy. Nevertheless, inclusion of a person's name or likeness (or something else identifiably connected with an individual) in the non-advertising content of a media publication usually results in no liability for appropriation. *Jenkins v. Dell Publishing Co.*, 251 F.2d 447 (3d Cir. 1958) (magazine article); *Brooks v. American Broadcasting Companies, Inc.*, 737 F. Supp. 431 (N.D. Ohio 1990), vacated, 932 F.2d 495 (6th Cir. 1991) (television broadcast). Possibly there would be liability if the plaintiff's picture was used to illustrate an article and there was "no real relationship" between the illustration and the article. See *Finger v. Omni Publications International, Ltd.*, 77 N.Y.2d 138, 566 N.E.2d 141 (1990) (photograph of large family used to illustrate magazine report that fertilization rates might be enhanced by caffeine). But this could be considered a "false light" invasion of privacy rather than a commercial appropriation.

Some of the leading cases have involved products, such as games and trading cards, containing the names and photographs of and information about sports players or other celebrities. This has usually been treated as an actionable commercial appropriation of name, likeness or identity, or infringement of the right of publicity, even though arguably what is objected to is analogous to the informational or entertainment content of media publications rather than commercial advertising or promotion. Examples include *Palmer v. Schonhorn Enterprises, Inc.*, 96 N.J. Super. 72, 232 A.2d 458 (Ch. Div. 1967), involving a game that included short biographies and playing charts of twenty-three famous golfers, and *Rosemont Enterprises, Inc. v. Urban Systems, Inc.*, 72 Misc. 2d 788, 340 N.Y.S.2d 144 (Sup. Ct. 1973), modified, 42 A.D.2d 544, 345 N.Y.S.2d 17 (1973), in which the defendants had marketed "The Howard Hughes Game," a game for adults based on the biographical data of the famous but reclusive billionaire. Decisions vary on whether marketing photographs of the plaintiff is actionable. Liability could depend upon whether the photographs are regarded as merely products or as something related to a matter of public interest ("newsworthy"). Compare *Titan Sports, Inc. v. Comics World Corp.*, 870 F.2d 85 (2d Cir. 1989) (oversized photographs of professional wrestlers folded and stapled inside magazines), with *Paulsen v. Personality Posters, Inc.*, 59 Misc. 2d 444, 299 N.Y.S.2d 501 (Sup. Ct. 1968) (campaign-type poster of comedian who was waging mock campaign for President). In *Young v. Greneker Studios*, 175 Misc. 1027, 26 N.Y.S.2d 357 (Sup. Ct. 1941), the court sustained a complaint over the sale of mannequins with the plaintiff's likeness.

The commercial sale of names, addresses and personal details would seem to come within the tort, but plaintiffs have been unsuccessful in the few reported cases on this. See *Dwyer v. American Express Co.*, 273 Ill. App. 3d 742, 652 N.E.2d 1351 (1995) (sale to merchants of names and spending habits of credit card holders); *Remsburg v. Docusearch, Inc.*, 149 N.H. 148, 816 A.2d 1001 (2003) (sale of personal information by investigator). The principal reason given is that the name of a particular individual has little or no value, so the defendant has not appropriated for its benefit the value of the plaintiff's name or identity.

As framed by the Second Restatement, the tort is not limited to use of a person's name or likeness for marketing or other commercial purposes. It extends to other appropriations of a person's name or likeness for financial benefit, or even a non-financial benefit. There would thus be liability for impersonating the plaintiff or falsely claiming a family relationship with the plaintiff in order to obtain money, property or credit, or confidential information. Rest. 2d Torts § 652C and comments. There is some support for this in the cases. In *Schlessman v. Schlessman*, 50 Ohio App. 2d 179, 361 N.E.2d 1347 (1975), alleged forgery of the plaintiff's name to an income tax return filed by her husband was held to be an invasion of privacy. In *Steding v. Battistoni*, 3 Conn. Cir. 76, 208 A.2d 559 (1964), the plaintiff recovered damages because he was named as a plaintiff in a lawsuit without his consent. An action for invasion of privacy was also found when the plaintiff's name was included in a proposed staffing chart used in the defendant's bid for a government contract. *Moore v. Big Picture Co.*, 828 F.2d 270 (5th Cir. 1987). In *Hamilton v. Lumbermen's Mutual Casualty Co.*, 82 So. 2d 61 (La. App. 1955), an insurance company was held liable for a newspaper advertisement soliciting information about a traffic accident that appeared to come from the plaintiff but directed replies to the address and telephone number of a company employee. Under *Vanderbilt v. Mitchell*, 72 N.J. Eq. 910, 67 A. 97 (1907), there could be liability for falsely claiming to be the plaintiff's spouse or child for financial gain. The potential for liability is somewhat limited by the proposition that there is liability only if the defendant sought to obtain the value or benefit of the plaintiff's name or identity. There would not be liability for some use of the plaintiff's name, or even adoption of the same name, without appropriation of its value. Rest. 2d Torts § 652C, comments *c–d*.

B. APPROPRIATION AS INFRINGEMENT OF RIGHT OF PUBLICITY

When the defendant prominently used in its advertising the likeness or name of someone like the plaintiffs in *Roberson* and *Pavesich*, there was an invasion of personal privacy. The defendant caused an obscure private citizen to become the object of public attention, scrutiny and comment. But when the person whose likeness or name was used was already well-known to the public, there would usually be no actual impairment of privacy. The real grievance would be the unwanted association with the defendant or what the defendant was selling, the defendant's attempting to profit from use of the plaintiff's identity without sharing the profit with the plaintiff, or interference with other commercial or professional opportunities that the plaintiff might have. The interest impaired by the defendant's conduct would be primarily if not exclusively economic rather than a privacy interest. This is especially true when the plaintiff had encouraged publicity to advance or sustain the plaintiff's career.

To address this, courts in many (but not all) jurisdictions have recognized a legal claim for infringement or violation of the "right of publicity." The right of publicity is essentially a right to prevent unauthorized commercial exploitation of one's name, likeness or other elements of identity. It is an economic tort, included in the Restatement of Unfair Competition (§§ 46–49) rather than the Restatement of Torts. It protects the interests of persons whose identity has commercial value (usually but not always people with a high public profile) and limits the ability to profit from a person's fame without consent. See *Uhlaender v. Henricken*, 316 F. Supp. 1277 (D. Minn. 1970). The right of publicity tort shares some characteristics with the privacy tort of appropriation of name or likeness but differs in important respects. The right of privacy is a personal right that is not assignable and not enforceable after a person's death. The right of publicity can be assigned in whole or part and enforced by the assignee, and the prevailing position is that it attaches to deceased as well as living persons. Also, damages awarded in successful actions clearly extend to economic losses and the commercial value of what the defendant gained by wrongful use of the plaintiff's identity. See Rest. Unfair Competition § 49. An action can arise when the defendant's use of the plaintiff's identity has created a false representation that the plaintiff has created or endorsed what the defendant is selling, but such a misrepresentation is not required for liability. Rest. Unfair Competition § 46, comment *b*.

Under some statutes and judicial decisions, liability for the older tort of appropriation of name or likeness does not extend to appropriation of other indicia of identity, such as a distinct vocal style the public would recognize as the plaintiff's. See *Booth v. Colgate-Palmolive Co.*, 362 F. Supp. 343 (S.D.N.Y. 1973). But the right of publicity does. So there can be liability for commercial use of something that will evoke the plaintiff in the minds of the audience, even if it is not the plaintiff's name or picture. See *Waits v. Frito-Lay, Inc.*, 978 F.2d 1093 (9th Cir. 1992) (imitation of singer's voice in radio commercial); *Hirsch v. S.C. Johnson & Son, Inc.*, 90 Wis. 2d 379, 280 N.W.2d 129 (1979) (plaintiff's nickname used as product name); *Motschenbacher v. R.J. Reynolds Tobacco Co.*, 498 F.2d 821 (9th Cir. 1974) (racing car in television commercial having distinct markings of noted racing driver's car); *Carson v. Here's Johnny Portable Toilets, Inc.*, 698 F.2d 831 (6th Cir. 1983) (product name with phrase associated with host of much-viewed television program); *White v. Samsung Electronics America, Inc.*, 971 F.2d 1395 (9th Cir. 1992), reh'g denied (with notable dissent by Kozinski, J.), 989 F.2d 1512 (9th Cir. 1993) (television commercial that parodied plaintiff's role as host of popular television game show). Commercial use of a fictional character or persona portrayed by the plaintiff can be infringement of the plaintiff's right of publicity when the character is uniquely identified with the plaintiff, but probably not (absent other usage of the plaintiff's identity) when the plaintiff's portrayal of the character is only the most prominent, such as Bela Lugosi's portrayal of Count Dracula. See Justice Mosk's concurring opinion in *Lugosi v. Universal Pictures*, 25 Cal. 3d 813, 603 P.2d 425 (1979), and Rest. Unfair Competition § 46, comment *d*.

Whether the right of publicity does or should apply to deceased persons has been a major issue. In the *Lugosi* case, a majority of the court decided that heirs could not maintain an action for commercial exploitation of a decedent's name or likeness, at least when the decedent had not during his lifetime exploited his name or likeness in connection with a product, service or business. In a case brought by a company that had been granted the exclusive right to exploit the name and likeness of Elvis Presley, the court held that this right did not survive death. *Memphis Development Foundation v. Factors Etc., Inc.*, 616 F.2d 956 (6th Cir. 1980). The opinion acknowledged arguments in favor of a post-mortem or inheritable right of publicity, including the possible encouragement of effort and creativity in being able to provide benefits for heirs and vindication of expectations that a valuable capital asset would be created. But the court believed that both practical and philosophical considerations weighed against recognition of such a right. There would be numerous "practical problems of judicial line-drawing" in applying the right, such as how long it would last; its motivational benefits would be minimal; and giving heirs control over commercial use of their ancestor's name would not increase economic efficiency or productivity. "The memory, name and pictures of famous individuals should be regarded as a common asset to be shared, an economic opportunity available in the free market system."

Despite this, the prevailing position now is that the right of publicity does apply to deceased as well as living persons. An example is *Martin Luther King, Jr., Center for Social Change, Inc. v. American Heritage Products, Inc.*, 250 Ga. 135, 296 S.E.2d 697 (1982), an action by Dr. King's heirs over the sale of "memorial" busts in his image. Some court decisions have qualified this by requiring commercial exploitation of the right by the deceased prior to death, but sometimes exploitation in the deceased's principal career or business has been sufficient to meet this requirement (unlike *Lugosi*). See *Hicks v. Casablanca Records*, 464 F. Supp. 426 (S.D.N.Y. 1978) (Agatha Christie exploited name in connection with her literary works and plays and films based on her books). Statutes providing for a survivable right of publicity (or privacy) have been enacted in a considerable number of states. The statutes typically specify who can be a plaintiff and establish a definite (but long) limit on the right's duration. In the California statute, the limit is seventy years after the death. Cal. Civil Code § 3344.1.

In other respects, the decisions on what is and what is not an actionable violation of the right of publicity are largely in alignment with decisions on what is and what is not a tortious appropriation of name or likeness. Generally, use of a person's name or likeness (or identity) in commercial advertising, marketing, business names or product labels without consent is a violation. But it can be used without liability in advertising, marketing or labelling media works (books, periodicals, films, recordings, broadcasts and presumably Internet transmissions) in which the person is depicted or written about or has performed. See *Page v. Something Weird Video*, 960 F. Supp. 1438 (C.D. Cal. 1996) (advertising for film series; plaintiff starred in two of films); Rest. Unfair Competition § 47, comment *a*. (Liability can attach to false advertising. *Cher v. Forum International, Ltd.*, 692 F.2d 634 (9th Cir. 1982).) It can also be used in advertising the sale of something pertaining to the plaintiff that had been put on the market with the plaintiff's consent, such as a sports player trading card or a book the plaintiff had written. *Allison v. Vintage Sports Plaques*, 136 F.3d 1443 (11th Cir. 1998); Rest. Unfair Competition § 47, comment *a*.

Marketing without consent products that incorporate the names, images or biographical details of prominent persons, such as games, trading cards and T-shirts, has usually been considered a violation of the right of publicity, as in *Uhlaender v. Henricksen*, 316 F. Supp. 1277 (D. Minn. 1970) (game incorporating names and details of several hundred baseball players), and *Comedy III Productions, Inc. v. Gary Saderup, Inc.*, 25 Cal. 4th 387, 21 P.3d 797 (2001) (T-shirts and lithographs with drawing of "The Three Stooges"). There has usually been no liability for the informational and entertainment content of media (as distinct from advertising content) or original works of art (such as the drawing in *Comedy III Productions*), even though books, magazine articles and films about celebrities and artistic depictions of them can realistically be considered commercial exploitation of their fame. Courts have held that the right of publicity is not violated by a novel, film or other work of fiction that depicts a prominent person or incorporates the person's identity. *Hicks v. Casablanca Records*, 464 F. Supp. 426 (S.D.N.Y. 1978) (book and film presenting fictionalized account of Agatha Christie's mysterious disappearance in 1926); *Rogers v. Grimaldi*, 875 F.2d 994 (2d Cir. 1989) (film *Ginger and Fred*, depicting dance couple who imitated Ginger Rogers and Fred Astaire). Possibly there is an action when the defendant markets an ostensibly factual depiction of a person that contains fictionalizations not apparent to the reader or viewer. See Rest. Unfair Competition § 47, comment *c*.

Some decisions on the right of publicity do not conform to this pattern. In some cases involving non-advertising uses of a celebrity's identity, the court found violation of the right of publicity because it believed that the defendant's creation was primarily a commercial exploitation of the celebrity's fame. These include *Estate of Presley v. Russen*, 513 F. Supp. 1339 (D.N.J. 1981), involving a production that imitated the late Elvis Presley's stage shows; *Groucho Marx Productions, Inc. v. Day and Night Co. Inc.*, 523 F. Supp. 485 (S.D.N.Y. 1981), rev'd, 689 F.2d 317 (2d Cir. 1982), which arose from a Broadway play featuring performers who imitated the appearance and comedy style of the Marx Brothers; and *Doe v. McFarlane*, 207 S.W.3d 52 (Mo. App. 2006), in which the defendants' comic book character was based on a professional hockey player. *Grant v. Esquire, Inc.*, 367 F. Supp. 876 (S.D.N.Y. 1973), allowed liability if the plaintiff's picture was used "merely to attract attention" rather than in connection with a subject of public interest or legitimate comment on a public figure. It also appears that the right of publicity can be violated by an unauthorized broadcast or film of all or most of a performer's act. See *Zacchini v. Scripps-Howard Broadcasting Co.*, 433 U.S. 562 (1977), in which the plaintiff's performance at a county fair as a "human cannonball" was filmed and broadcast on a television news program over his objections.

There are also cases where sales of products such as games and trading cards did not result in liability. *Cardtoons, L.C. v. Major League Baseball Players Association*, 95 F.3d 959 (10th Cir. 1996); *C.B.C. Distribution and Marketing, Inc. v. Major League Baseball Advanced Media, L.P.*, 505 F.3d 818 (8th Cir. 2007). This is primarily because the contents were, in the courts' view, entitled to First Amendment protection. Some cases grant First Amendment protection when what is sold contains elements of the defendant's creation or expression amounting to "significant transformative elements." See *Hart v. Electronic Arts, Inc.*, 717 F.3d 141 (3d Cir. 2013) (college football video game, held over dissent to be insufficiently transformative). So far, there seems to be no First Amendment barrier against liability for truthful use of a celebrity's identity in advertisements or commercial promotions.

In some cases, defendants have contended that the plaintiff's right of publicity claim under state law is preempted by federal copyright law. Preemption is a possibility if the plaintiff's complaint involves reproduction or imitation of something that was "fixed" with the plaintiff's consent, such as a writing, photograph or recorded performance, as this is within the federal copyright statute. But preemption applies only to an assertion of "rights that are equivalent to any of the exclusive rights within the general scope of copyright." 17 U.S.C. § 301. The rights included within the right of publicity are considered distinct from copyright rights, as those do not extend to a person's name, likeness, voice or other identifying characteristics. Rest. Unfair Competition

§ 46, comment *i*. Therefore, the tort claims have usually survived preemption arguments when the claims did not conflict with the rights of a copyright holder. *E.g.*, *Brown v. Ames*, 201 F.3d 654 (5th Cir. 2000); *Downing v. Abercrombie & Fitch*, 265 F.3d 994 (9th Cir. 2001). But see *Jules Jordan Video, Inc. v. 144942 Canada Inc.*, 617 F.3d 1146 (9th Cir. 2010) (claim founded on making and selling unauthorized copies of actor's films preempted).

CHAPTER 17

INTRUSION

A. INTRODUCTION

Liability for invasion of privacy by "intrusion" or "intrusion upon seclusion" is, like liability for appropriation of name or likeness, one of the four types of privacy torts identified by Prosser. It was based on liability for various types of conduct that "intru[ded] upon the plaintiff's seclusion or solitude, or into his private affairs." Prosser, Privacy, 48 Calif. L. Rev. 383, 389 (1960). The Second Restatement's formulation of the tort, which is now authoritative in most jurisdictions, is:

> One who intentionally intrudes, physically or otherwise, upon the solitude or seclusion of another or his private affairs or concerns, is subject to liability to the other for invasion of his privacy, if the intrusion would be highly offensive to a reasonable person.

Rest. 2d Torts § 652B.

The principal example of conduct that gives rise to liability for this tort has been and remains the use of equipment to record or observe conduct in private places, or private conversations. This has included wiretapping telephone lines. *Rhodes v. Graham*, 238 Ky. 225, 37 S.W.2d 46 (1931). Installation of a listening device in the plaintiff's home or hospital room. *Roach v. Harper*, 143 W. Va. 869, 105 S.E.2d 564 (1958); *McDaniel v. Atlanta Coca-Cola Bottling Co.*, 60 Ga. App. 92, 2 S.E.2d 810 (1939). Placing a hidden camera in a bedroom. *In re Marriage of Tigges*, 758 N.W.2d 824 (Iowa 2008). And placing a camera or "see-through" panel in the bathroom of an office or store. *Koeppel v. Speirs*, 808 N.W.2d 177 (Iowa 2011); *Harkey v. Abate*, 131 Mich. App. 177, 346 N.W.2d 74 (1983). Intrusion now extends to "hacking" and other surreptitious means of gaining access to the contents of private electronic communications and files in computers. See Annot., 68 A.L.R.6th 331. Some cases require evidence that the defendant have seen or heard something private by means of the device. *E.g., Oliver v. Pacific Northwest Bell Telephone Co.*, 53 Or. App. 604, 632 P.2d 1295 (1981). But the prevailing view is that installation of a device capable of recording or observing private conduct or conversations is sufficient. *Koeppel v. Speirs*, *supra*; *Hamberger v. Eastman*, 106 N.H. 107, 206 A.2d 239 (1964).

Beyond this, liability for intrusion potentially extends to a wide variety of conduct that intrudes into places, activities or matters where privacy is expected and would be considered by many to be an egregious invasion of privacy. In many of the cases the defendant was attempting to access the plaintiff's private activities or conversations or personal information about the plaintiff. Generally it is not tortious to compile personal information. See *Tureen v. Equifax, Inc.*, 571 F.2d 411 (8th Cir. 1978); *Myrick v. Barron*, 820 So. 2d 81 (Ala. 2001). But the means of acquiring it may be, even if not a camera or electronic device. Examples include peering into the windows of a residence. *Vega v. Chicago Park District*, 958 F. Supp. 2d 943 (N.D. Ill. 2013). Opening the plaintiff's mail. *Roth v. Farner-Bocken Co.*, 667 N.W.2d 651 (S.D. 2003). Breaking into the plaintiff's confidential files. *Pearson v. Dodd*, 133 U.S. App. D.C. 279, 410 F.2d 701 (1969) (reporters not liable for receiving and publishing copies of files). Improperly accessing the plaintiff's bank or credit records. *Rodgers v. McCullough*, 296 F. Supp. 2d 895 (W.D. Tenn. 2003). And obtaining sensitive personal information about the plaintiff by misrepresentation. *Taus v. Loftus*, 40 Cal. 4th 683, 151 P.3d 1185 (2007). *Cf. Sanchez-Scott v. Alza Pharmaceuticals*, 86 Cal. App. 4th 365, 103 Cal. Rptr. 2d 410 (2001) (patient not informed that person present during breast examination was drug company salesman).

There can be liability when the defendant was not attempting to record or obtain information about something private. An action may arise from the defendant's entering the plaintiff's hotel room or hospital room. *Coombs v. J.B. Hunt Transport, Inc.*, 388 S.W.3d 456 (Ark. App. 2012); *Barber v. Time, Inc.*, 348 Mo. 1199, 159 S.W.2d 291 (1942). It may also arise from conduct that is calculated to cause great disturbance in the plaintiff's home or office, as by making many unwanted telephone calls or causing others to make calls. See *Rugg v. McCarty*, 173 Colo. 170, 476 P.2d 753 (1970) (harassing calls by creditor); *Harms v. Miami Daily News, Inc.*, 127 So. 2d 715 (Fla. App. 1961) (newspaper article telling readers to call telephone number to "hear a sexy telephone voice"). Or including the plaintiff's name and address in a sexual contact advertisement. *Vescovo v. New Way Enterprises, Ltd.*, 60 Cal. App. 3d 582, 130 Cal. Rptr. 86 (1976). There is some overlap between intrusion upon seclusion and nuisance or trespass to land. But intrusion can provide a remedy that nuisance and trespass do not, as when the plaintiff is not legally the possessor of the property where the disturbance occurred or (for trespass) when the defendant never entered the property or made a privileged entry.

Although there is usually no "intrusion upon seclusion" when the plaintiff is in a public area, there are cases in which the plaintiff has secured protection against persistent and severe disturbance while the plaintiff was attempting to conduct normal activities in public. The best-known case of this type is *Galella v. Onassis*, 353 F. Supp. 196 (S.D.N.Y. 1972), modified, 487 F.2d 986 (2d Cir. 1973), in which a "paparazzo" photographer was ordered to keep a certain distance from Jacqueline Kennedy Onassis and her children. See also *Wolfson v. Lewis*, 924 F. Supp. 1413 (E.D. Pa. 1996) (injunction against reporters attempting to obtain camera footage and "ambush" interviews for television news program); *Kramer v. Downey*, 680 S.W.2d 524 (Tex. App. 1984) (injunction and damages awarded against woman who persistently and conspicuously followed man in public after end of brief extramarital affair).

B. HIGHLY OFFENSIVE

Potential liability for intrusion is limited by the requirement that the intrusion be highly offensive to a reasonable person. Rest. 2d Torts § 652B. Whether an intrusion was highly offensive is generally considered a question to be decided by the jury or other trier of fact. *Bauer v. Ford Motor Credit Co.*, 149 F. Supp. 2d 1106 (D. Minn. 2001); *Mauri v. Smith*, 324 Or. 476, 929 P.2d 307 (1996). But courts decide as a matter of law whether an intrusion could be found to be highly offensive. *Deteresa v. American Broadcasting Companies, Inc.*, 121 F.3d 460 (9th Cir. 1997); *People for the Ethical Treatment of Animals v. Bobby Berosini, Ltd.*, 111 Nev. 615, 895 P.2d 1269 (1995). Numerous intrusion actions have failed because of a court's ruling that the intrusion was not highly offensive, as in those two cases. Examples include *Rush v. Portfolio Recovery Associates LLC*, 977 F. Supp. 2d 414 (D.N.J. 2013) (debt collection agency's numerous telephone calls to plaintiffs' home); *Wilkins v. National Broadcasting Co., Inc.*, 71 Cal. App. 4th 1066, 84 Cal. Rptr. 2d 329 (1999) (secretly videotaping plaintiffs' lunch meeting at restaurant for television program); and *Smith v. Jack Eckerd Corp.*, 101 N.C. App. 566, 400 S.E.2d 99 (1991) (physical search of plaintiff and child in store).

"Highly offensive" is not as severe a limit of liability as the "outrageous conduct" requirement of liability for infliction of severe emotional distress, as that requires a determination that the conduct has been "so outrageous in character, and so extreme in degree, as to go beyond all possible bounds of decency." Rest. 2d Torts § 46, comment *d*. In *Romero v. City of Miami*, 8 F. Supp. 3d 1321 (N.D. Okla. 2014), the court ruled that the alleged conduct of the defendants could be considered highly offensive for purposes of an intrusion claim but not extreme and outrageous for purposes of an action for infliction of emotional distress.

C. EXPECTATION OF PRIVACY

While not part of the Second Restatement's formulation of the tort, whether the plaintiff had a reasonable expectation of privacy has become increasingly important in determining liability. When the plaintiff was in or readily visible from a place open to the public, intrusion actions have failed on the ground that the plaintiff lacked a reasonable expectation of privacy in the activities observed or recorded by the defendant. *E.g.*, *Wilkins v. National Broadcasting Co., Inc.*, *supra* (plaintiffs videotaped while having lunch on restaurant patio); *Creel v. I.C.E. & Associates, Inc.*, 771 N.E.2d 1276 (Ind. App. 2002) (plaintiffs videotaped during church service open to public); *Tagouma v. Investigative Consultant Services, Inc.*, 4 A.3d 170 (Pa. Super. Ct. 2010) (plaintiff videotaped in mosque through window of building). Compare *Shulman v. Group W Productions, Inc.*, 18 Cal. 4th 200, 955 P.2d 469 (1998) (traffic accident victims had no reasonable expectation that there would not be media photography at scene, but could have had reasonable expectation of privacy in conversations with nurse and other rescue personnel, which were transmitted by microphone nurse wore for television program). It has been held that there is no reasonable expectation of privacy in the contents of a publicly accessible Internet web site, even if not intended to be publicly accessible. *Four Navy Seals v. Associated Press*, 413 F. Supp. 2d 1136 (S.D. Cal. 2005).

Actions for alleged intrusion into non-public places or activities have also failed on this ground. *E.g.*,

Danai v. Canal Square Associates, 862 A.2d 395 (D.C. 2004) (removal of letter from trash, when in office building's locked trash room); *Lewis v. Dayton Hudson Corp.*, 128 Mich. App. 165, 339 N.W.2d 857 (1983) (observation of customer in store fitting room, which had notice that area was under surveillance by store personnel); *White v. White*, 344 N.J. Super. 211, 781 A.2d 85 (Ch. Div. 2001) (wife retrieving husband's e-mail from computer used by family, which husband erroneously thought could not be read without his password); *Miller v. Blattner*, 676 F. Supp. 2d 485 (E.D. La. 2009) (disclosure of e-mails on plaintiff's work computer; employer had policy that all e-mails on company computers were property of company); *DeBlasio v. Pignoli*, 918 A.2d 822 (Pa. Cmwlth. Ct. 2007) (camera surveillance by borough mayor of occupants of police holding cells).

It appears to be the prevailing view that an action for intrusion does not arise from a defendant's recording or reporting the contents of a conversation with the plaintiff, as it should not be assumed that a conversation is not being recorded or that its contents will not be disclosed to others. See *Chaplin v. National Broadcasting Co.*, 15 F.R.D. 134 (S.D.N.Y. 1953); *Bradley v. Atlantic City Board of Education*, 736 F. Supp. 2d 891 (D.N.J. 2010); *Nader v. General Motors Corp.*, 25 N.Y.2d 560, 255 N.E.2d 765 (1970). In *Medical Laboratory Management Consultants v. American Broadcasting Companies, Inc.*, 306 F.3d 806 (9th Cir. 2002), it was held that the proprietor of a business who gave persons he did not know a tour of the premises and discussed business matters with them did not have an objectively reasonable expectation that the meeting would not be recorded with a hidden camera for a television program. Some cases do recognize a wider expectation that a conversation on personal matters or activities observed by some persons would not be recorded or reported to others, especially in a jurisdiction where recording a conversation without the consent of both parties is unlawful. *Sanders v. American Broadcasting Companies, Inc.*, 20 Cal. 4th 907, 978 P.2d 67 (1999); *Johnson v. K Mart Corp.*, 311 Ill. App. 3d 573, 723 N.E.2d 1192 (2000). *Cf. Huskey v. National Broadcasting Co., Inc.*, 632 F. Supp. 1282 (N.D. Ill. 1986) (prison inmate filmed in exercise cage by television crew).

D. PRIVILEGES

Whether the qualified privileges established in defamation law apply to liability for intrusion is a debatable point. Rest. 2d Torts § 652G states generally that the defamation law rules on "conditional" privilege apply to the "publication of any matter that is an invasion of privacy." Some cases, such as *Burris v. South Central Bell Telephone Co.*, 540 F. Supp. 905 (S.D. Miss. 1982), indicate that such a privilege is a defense to an action for intrusion. The greater number of intrusion cases do not apply a definite qualified privilege but indicate that a defendant will not be liable for conduct that would otherwise be actionable if it is a reasonable method of protecting such interests as ascertaining the validity of an insurance or disability claim, maintaining security, detecting and prosecuting unlawful conduct, or obtaining evidence for use in litigation. See *Bodrey v. Cape*, 120 Ga. App. 859, 172 S.E.2d 643 (1969); *Saldana v. Kelsey-Hayes Co.*, 178 Mich. App. 230, 443 N.W.2d 382 (1989); *N.O.C., Inc. v. Schaefer*, 197 N.J. Super. 249, 484 A.2d 729 (Law Div. 1984). In *Elmore v. Atlantic Zayne, Inc.*, 178 Ga. App. 25, 341 S.E.2d 905 (1986), a retail store successfully defended an action for observing a customer in a restroom toilet stall through a crack in the ceiling on the argument that this was reasonable to verify another customer's complaint that illegal activity was occurring there.

Froelich v. Adair, 213 Kan. 357, 516 P.2d 993 (1973), and *Leggett v. First Interstate Bank of Oregon, N.A.*, 86 Or. App. 523, 739 P.2d 1083 (1987), take the position that the privileges found in defamation law and other branches of privacy law do not apply to intrusion, in which liability is not based upon publication. Even if that is so, a defendant's object of protecting or advancing a legitimate interest may weigh against finding that the intrusion is highly offensive. In *Hernandez v. Hillsides, Inc.*, 47 Cal. 4th 272, 211 P.3d 1063 (2009), the court decided that it was not highly offensive to install hidden cameras in a two-person business office to find the person who was using a computer there at night to view pornographic web sites. See also *S.B. v. Saint James School*, 959 So. 2d 72 (Ala. 2006), in which the defendants were investigating photographs of students that were circulating at a private school.

Media personnel have no privilege to commit intrusion in order to report on a matter of public interest. *Dietemann v. Time, Inc.*, 449 F.2d 245 (9th

Cir. 1971); *Shulman v. Group W Productions, Inc.*, 18 Cal. 4th 200, 955 P.2d 469 (1998). However, an intrusion might be found not highly offensive if intended to obtain material for a news report on an important subject. (See *Shulman.*)

CHAPTER 18

DISCLOSURE OF PRIVATE FACTS

A. PUBLICATION OF PRIVATE FACTS

1. INTRODUCTION

The 1890 Warren and Brandeis article on "The Right to Privacy" was intended primarily to establish a legal remedy for invasions of privacy when the press published personal information or photographs of private individuals. Liability for this type of invasion of privacy was slow to develop, but by the time of Prosser's 1960 article there were enough cases in support for identification of "public disclosure of embarrassing private facts about the plaintiff" as one of the four privacy torts. Prosser, Privacy, 48 Calif. L. Rev. 383, 389 (1960).

§ 652D of the Second Restatement of Torts states:

> One who gives publicity to a matter concerning the private life of another is subject to liability to the other for invasion of his privacy, if the matter publicized is of a kind that
>
> (a) would be highly offensive to a reasonable person, and
>
> (b) is not of legitimate concern to the public.

This is now the generally accepted formulation of the tort. It contains four elements: (1) publicity, (2) concerning the private life of the plaintiff, (3) highly offensive to a reasonable person and (4) not of legitimate concern to the public. By implication, it is also required that the plaintiff be identifiable as the person concerned. There is "publicity. . .concerning the private life of another" only when that person is identifiable to recipients of the defendant's communication. See *Bernstein v. National Broadcasting Co.*, 129 F. Supp. 817 (D.D.C. 1955), aff'd, 98 U.S. App. D.C. 112, 232 F.2d 369 (1956); *Young v. That Was The Week That Was*, 312 F. Supp. 1337 (N.D. Ohio 1969), aff'd, 423 F.2d 265 (6th Cir. 1970) (no liability "if the plaintiff cannot be identified as the person who is the subject of the publication from the published matter itself").

2. PUBLICITY

Liability arises only when "publicity" is given to a private matter of the plaintiff. Publicity is "communicating [the matter] to the public at large, or to so many persons that the matter must be regarded as substantially certain to become one of public knowledge." Rest. 2d Torts § 652D, comment *a*. The theory of this requirement is that privacy is invaded by making a private matter public. The publicity requirement is different from the "publication" requirement of defamation liability, which is satisfied when the defendant has communicated the matter to any person other than the plaintiff.

The required publicity clearly exists when the private matter has been communicated in a mass media publication or broadcast, even if the readership or audience is fairly small. Publicity is absent when there was communication only to one individual or a small number of persons. See Rest. 2d

Torts § 652D, comment *a*. Application of the publicity requirement is less clear when a non-media defendant has communicated the private matter to more than a few persons or in a way that might be considered to have made the matter public or widely known. For example, in *Kinsey v. Macur*, 107 Cal. App. 3d 265, 165 Cal. Rptr. 608 (1980), the court decided that sending letters to (at most) twenty people was sufficient publicity. But in *Sherr v. HealthEast Care System*, 262 F. Supp. 3d 869 (D. Minn. 2017), communication to between thirty-five and forty individuals was held not to be publicity. Sending faxes to sixteen terminals located in six states that contained plaintiffs' Social Security numbers was held not to meet the publicity requirement in *Bodah v. Lakeville Motor Express, Inc.*, 663 N.W.2d 550 (Minn. 2003), rev'g 649 N.W.2d 859 (Minn. App. 2002), because the information was not substantially certain to become public. A defendant who has communicated only with one person or a few people is usually not held responsible for publicity resulting from repetition. See *Swinton Creek Nursery v. Edisto Farm Credit, ACA*, 334 S.C. 469, 514 S.E.2d 126 (1999). But it is different if the defendant knowingly provided the private fact to a journalist, who could be expected to publicize it. See *Arroyo v. Rosen*, 102 Md. App. 101, 648 A.2d 1074 (1994).

Whether posting information on a publicly available web site, or a site that can be accessed by many people, satisfies the publicity requirement has not, so far, been decided in many published cases. Some opinions have assumed, without much discussion, that to post something on the Internet is to give it publicity. *Imagine Medispa, LLC v. Transformations, Inc.*, 999 F. Supp. 2d 873 (S.D. W. Va. 2014); *Pampattiwar v. Hinson*, 326 Ga. App. 163, 756 S.E.2d 246 (2014). In *Yath v. Fairview Clinics, N.P.*, 767 N.W.2d 34 (Minn. App. 2009), however, the issue was discussed in considerable detail. The majority, referring to Rest. 2d Torts § 652D, comment *a*, concluded that a publicly accessible web page satisfied the publicity requirement because it was a communication directly to the public. The number of actual viewers was irrelevant. A concurring opinion criticized this as overbroad, treating all Internet sites alike even though some are not intended to disseminate information to a large number of people or actually viewed by a large number.

People are often more distressed and embarrassed by revelation of private facts to those they have a social or business relationship with than by revelation to a public of strangers. Recognizing this, courts in a few states, beginning with *Beaumont v. Brown*, 401 Mich. 80, 257 N.W.2d 522 (1977), have decided that there can be sufficient publicity when facts about the plaintiff are communicated to a "particular public" whose knowledge of the facts would be embarrassing to the plaintiff. The "particular public" might be fellow employees, club members, church members, neighbors or family. See also *Miller v. Motorola, Inc.*, 202 Ill. App. 3d 976, 560 N.E.2d 900 (1990). This proposition is rejected in *Bodah v. Lakeville Motor Express, Inc.*, 663 N.W.2d 550 (Minn. 2003).

3. PRIVATE MATTERS

Under the Restatement, liability attaches to publicizing a matter concerning a person's private life. Rest. 2d Torts § 652D. It therefore does not attach to publicizing a matter concerning a person's "public life." The operative distinction is between a matter that is private, in the sense that it is not known or available beyond a small number of persons, and a matter that is public, in the sense that it is known or available to members of the public generally or many of them. Public (or non-private) matters include what is in open public records and what is visible when a person is in or seen from a public place. The matter can be a fact or, if the complaint is about a photograph, the plaintiff's appearance. See Rest. 2d Torts § 652D, comment *b*.

One of the main difficulties of the private matter or "private fact" requirement has been applying it when the matter was not, before the defendant publicized it, known to many people but knowledge of it had not been tightly limited to a small number of family members and friends. This was the situation in *Multimedia WMAZ, Inc. v. Kubach*, 212 Ga. App. 707, 443 S.E.2d 491 (1994), in which a television broadcast revealed that the plaintiff had AIDS. That the plaintiff had AIDS was already known to his family, a number of friends, medical personnel and members of an AIDS support group. A majority of the court affirmed a judgment for the plaintiff. Dissenting judges would have rejected the invasion of privacy action because of the extent to which the plaintiff's condition was already known. In *Times*

Mirror Co. v. Superior Court, 198 Cal. App. 3d 1420, 244 Cal. Rptr. 556 (1988), the court decided that the plaintiff's telling "selected neighbors, friends, family members, and officials investigating the murder" that she had discovered the victim's body did not make that fact public. But in *Chisholm v. Foothill Capital Corp.*, 3 F. Supp. 2d 925 (N.D. Ill. 1998), the court decided that the plaintiff's romantic relationship with a married man was a public fact because they appeared in public as a couple and eventually cohabitated. In *Sipple v. Chronicle Publishing Co.*, 154 Cal. App. 3d 1040, 201 Cal. Rptr. 665 (1984), where the plaintiff's principal grievance was that publicizing his sexual orientation made it known to his family, the plaintiff's action failed in part because it was widely known in San Francisco and elsewhere that he was gay.

Obviously a plaintiff has no action for a publication that only reveals private facts about somebody else. But a statement about or photograph of one person may invade the privacy of another person. For example, publicizing the death of a person as a result of a murder or suicide can identify family members as the parents or spouse of a murder victim or suicide. However, invasion of privacy actions for that tend to be unsuccessful, in part because a matter of legitimate public interest is found. See Annot., 18 A.L.R.3d 873.

4. HIGHLY OFFENSIVE

A literal reading of Rest. 2d Torts § 652D suggests that the matter publicized must be highly offensive to a reasonable person; but clearly what is required is that the publicity be highly offensive. Publicizing the private matter must be something that would be highly offensive to a reasonable person. See Rest. 2d Torts § 652D, comment *c*; *Doe v. Bernabei & Wachtel, PLLC*, 116 A.3d 1262, 1267 (D.C. 2015); *Harris v. Easton Publishing Co.*, 335 Pa. Super. 141, 159–160, 483 A.2d 1377, 1386–1387 (1984). That, of course, depends largely upon what is publicized. For example, even though police surveillance of and reports on activities that are entirely lawful would be offensive to many people, there is no cause of action when what is publicized is the plaintiff's attendance at union meetings rather than something as personal and sensitive as sexual orientation, an extramarital affair, or a fatal illness. *Cf. International Union v. Garner*, 601 F. Supp. 187 (M.D. Tenn. 1985).

The "highly offensive" requirement effectively limits liability to verbal and visual revelations of the most intimate, sensitive or embarrassing personal matters. In addition to sexual matters, medical or physical conditions and nudity, publicizing the plaintiff's financial condition or transactions, being the victim of a serious crime, or misconduct (or allegation of misconduct) that is not a matter of legitimate public interest when publicized could be found highly offensive, depending on the matter revealed and the context. Courts in numerous cases have ruled that the alleged invasion of privacy was not highly offensive or could not be found highly offensive. *E.g., Grunseth v. Marriott Corp.*, 872 F. Supp. 1069 (D.D.C. 1995), aff'd, 316 U.S. App. D.C. 367, 79 F.3d 169 (1996) (plaintiff's overnight stay at hotel and charges on receipt); *Chisholm v. Foothill Capital Corp.*, 3 F. Supp. 2d 925 (N.D. Ill. 1998) (plaintiff's "public" romantic relationship with married man); *Sandler v. Calcagni*, 565 F. Supp. 2d 184 (D. Me. 2008) (plaintiff's having plastic surgery on nose); *Brown v. CVS Pharmacy, L.L.C.*, 982 F. Supp. 2d 793 (M.D. Tenn. 2013) (investigation of physician by Drug Enforcement Agency and police). When there is no definitive ruling by the trial or appellate court, the trier of fact (jury or trial judge) decides whether there was highly offensive publicity.

If a non-media defendant has given publicity to a private matter and claims there was a good reason to do so, the reason can bear on whether the publicity was highly offensive. An example is *Werner v. Kliewer*, 238 Kan. 289, 710 P.2d 1250 (1985), in which a physician disclosed a patient's psychiatric problems to the judge in the patient's divorce and child custody case. Alternatively, a qualified privilege to communicate information to protect a legitimate interest may be applied, as in a defamation case. See Rest. 2d Torts § 652G. Such a privilege was found in *Senogles v. Security Benefit Life Insurance Co.*, 217 Kan. 438, 536 P.2d 1358 (1975), in which medical information provided to a life insurance company when the plaintiff applied for life insurance was supplied to a medical information bureau in which about seven hundred life insurance companies participated. In *Young v. Jackson*, 572 So. 2d 378 (Miss. 1990), the court decided that a nuclear power station supervisor was privileged to tell workers that the plaintiff was hospitalized because of the effects of a hysterectomy, in order to allay fears that she had been injured by exposure to radiation. *Cf. Zinda v. Louisiana Pacific Corp.*, 149 Wis. 2d 913, 440 N.W.2d 548 (1989) (report in factory newsletter's "coming and goings" column that employee was terminated for falsification of employment forms).

5. NOT OF LEGITIMATE CONCERN TO PUBLIC

Under Rest. 2d Torts § 652D, a defendant can be liable for publicizing a private matter only if it is "not of legitimate concern to the public." There is no liability for publicizing a fact that itself is a matter of legitimate public concern or part of subject-matter that is of legitimate public concern. See Rest. 2d Torts § 652D, comment *d*. The operative concept of what is "of legitimate public concern" is very liberal. It includes information published "for purposes of education, amusement or enlightenment." Rest. 2d Torts § 652D, comment *j*. And typical "news" items of "genuine, even if more or less deplorable, popular appeal." Rest. 2d Torts § 652D, comment *g*. In *Jenkins v. Dell Publishing, Co.*, 251 F.2d 447 (3d Cir. 1958), the court rejected any distinction between "news for information" and "news for entertainment." Matters of legitimate public concern are often labelled as "newsworthy."

While not everything published in informational or entertainment media qualifies as a matter of legitimate public concern, or "newsworthy," so much does that there is little likelihood that an action against a conventional media publisher or journalist for publishing true information will result in a judgment for the plaintiff. One reason this is so is that liability is precluded if the fact published has some substantial relevance to or connection ("nexus") with a topic of legitimate public concern. See *Gilbert v. Medical Economics Co.*, 665 F.2d 305 (10th Cir. 1981); *Shulman v. Group W Productions, Inc.*, 18 Cal. 4th 200, 955 P.2d 469 (1998). Also, an individual's connection with a subject of legitimate public concern is usually considered "newsworthy" and thus itself a matter of legitimate public concern, even if the individual is only one example among many. Arguments that inclusion of the plaintiff's name, photograph or individual facts was not of legitimate public concern have failed.

In *Howard v. Des Moines Register and Tribune Co.*, 283 N.W.2d 289 (Iowa 1979), where a newspaper's report on deficiencies of a "county home" identified the plaintiff as one of the residents who had been involuntarily sterilized, the court said:

> [T]he disclosure contributed constructively to the impact of the article. It offered a personalized frame of reference to which the reader could relate, fostering perception and understanding. Moreover, it lent specificity and credibility to the report.
>
> In this way the disclosure served as an effective means of accomplishing the intended news function. It had positive communicative value in attracting the reader's attention to the article's subject matter and in supporting expression of the underlying theme.

> . . .[W]e do not believe the disclosure could reasonably be held to be devoid of news value.

Id., 303. See also *Gilbert v. Medical Economics Co.*, *supra* (inclusion of plaintiff's alleged medical malpractice and psychiatric and mental problems in article on inadequate "policing" of malpractice by physicians, hospitals and regulatory agencies); *Ross v. Midwest Communications, Inc.*, 870 F.2d 271 (5th Cir. 1989) (disclosure of rape victim's identity in television documentary that questioned guilt of man convicted for another rape); *Montesano v. Donrey Media Group*, 99 Nev. 644, 668 P.2d 1081 (1983) (article on police officers who died in line of duty mentioned plaintiff's involvement in hit-and-run collision in which police officer was killed twenty-three years earlier). In *Doe v. Berkeley Publishers*, 329 S.C. 412, 496 S.E.2d 636 (1998), where a newspaper had identified a jail inmate raped by another inmate, the court said it was error to separate the plaintiff's identity from the event.

In opposition to this are some decisions denying dismissal of actions for identifying plaintiffs in reportage of a newsworthy subject, as in *Baugh v. CBS, Inc.*, 828 F. Supp. 745 (N.D. Cal. 1993) (broadcast on district attorney's office's victim assistance program identified plaintiffs as victims of domestic violence), and *Y.G. v. Jewish Hospital of St. Louis*, 795 S.W.2d 488 (Mo. App. 1990) (television report on hospital's *in vitro* fertilization program identified plaintiffs as participants).

What is considered to be newsworthy, or of legitimate concern to the public, is even wider when it is connected to someone who has become a "public figure" by assuming (or seeking to attain) a prominent role in society or its institutions. "In such a case. . .the legitimate interest of the public in the individual may extend beyond those matters which are themselves made public, and. . .may include information as to matters that would otherwise be private." Rest. 2d Torts § 652D, comment *e*. In *Carafano v. Metrosplash.com, Inc.*, 207 F. Supp. 2d 1055 (C.D. Cal. 2002), aff'd, 339 F.3d 1119 (9th Cir. 2003), the court decided that public interest in the life of a popular actress included her home address in Los Angeles. What is thought to be of legitimate public interest, because of its connection to a "public figure," can extend to facts about family members and other persons associated with the public figure. See *Carlisle v. Fawcett Publications, Inc.*, 201 Cal. App. 2d 733, 20 Cal. Rptr. 405 (1962) (plaintiff's brief marriage, when a teenager, to girl who later became prominent actress, recounted eighteen years later); *Kapellas v. Kofman*, 1 Cal. 3d 20, 459 P.2d 912 (1969) (delinquency of children, in newspaper editorial opposing mother's election to city council).

Those who choose to publicize newsworthy facts about themselves can include relevant personal information about family members. See *Anonsen v. Donahue*, 857 S.W.2d 700 (Tex. App. 1993) (disclosure in television program on pregnancies resulting from rape or incest). What is newsworthy also is broader for those who have acquired public attention without seeking it—such as when a person is the victim or perpetrator of a crime; a person who is accused of a crime, or otherwise is a party or witness in a judicial proceeding; the victim of an accident or catastrophe; or someone who has performed an heroic deed or other outstanding accomplishment. See Rest. 2d Torts § 652D, comments *f, h*.

While there are many cases in which courts have decided "as a matter of law" that the matter publicized was of legitimate public concern, in the absence of such a ruling the newsworthiness or non-newsworthiness of the matter becomes an issue to be decided by the trier of fact. See *Diaz v. Oakland Tribune, Inc.*, 139 Cal. App. 3d 118, 188 Cal. Rptr. 762 (1983) (error to put burden of proof upon defendant); *Winstead v. Sweeney*, 205 Mich. App. 664, 517 N.W.2d 874 (1994).

6. CONSTITUTIONAL LAW LIMITATIONS

There is a strong argument that tort liability for publishing true information is inconsistent with freedom of speech and freedom of press under the First Amendment. See *Hall v. Post*, 323 N.C. 259, 372 S.E.2d 711 (1988). The decision of a journalist or editor that something truthful should be published, because the public would be interested in it or should know of it, would seem to be squarely within what freedom of the press protects, even if a court or jury would find the matter "non-newsworthy." The Supreme Court of the United States has deliberately declined to decide whether invasion of privacy liability for publishing true facts violates the First Amendment. Instead, in a series of decisions from *Cox Broadcasting Corp. v. Cohn*, 420 U.S. 469 (1975), to *The Florida Star v. B.J.F.*, 491 U.S. 524 (1989), the Supreme Court decided that liability was unconstitutional in the particular circumstances of the case. In *Cox Broadcasting* and *Florida Star*, the defendants had disclosed the identity of a rape victim.

The principal rule to be derived from these cases is that it would violate the First Amendment to award damages for media publication of information that is in an open public record or lawfully obtained from the government. See *Uranga v. Federated Publication, Inc.*, 138 Idaho 550, 67 P.3d 29 (2003) (publication of unsworn statement to police made forty years earlier). There were some qualifications in the Supreme Court's opinions. These included the absence of "a need to further a state interest of the highest order." But as the interest that did not prevail in *Florida Star* was the very important one of protecting the privacy of victims of sexual assaults, and a state's interest in protecting privacy could almost always be served by ensuring that sensitive information in its possession was not released, these qualifications do not operate widely.

In addition to denying liability when a broadcast or newspaper published the identity of a crime victim or details of a court case, when lawfully obtained from a government record or source, an effect of the Supreme Court's decisions is to exclude almost all potential invasion of privacy liability for reporting that a person had once been convicted, jailed, charged or arrested, no matter how minor the offense was, how long ago it occurred, and how long the plaintiff had thereafter lived as a law-abiding citizen. See *Gates v. Discovery Communications, Inc.*, 34 Cal. 4th 679, 101 P.3d 552 (2004). A defendant might otherwise be held liable on a jury's finding that publicizing the plaintiff's criminal record was highly offensive and not newsworthy. See *Briscoe v. Reader's Digest Association*, 4 Cal. 3d 529, 483 P.2d 34 (1971).

Excluding liability for publicizing true information that is "newsworthy" has been regarded as a First Amendment rule as well as a rule of tort law. Avoidance of conflict with the First Amendment is one reason for courts' generous view of what is newsworthy. See *Gilbert v. Medical Economics Co.*, 665 F.2d 305 (10th Cir. 1981). There is "considerable deference to reporters and editors, avoiding the likelihood of unconstitutional interference with the freedom of the press to report truthfully on matters of legitimate public interest. In general, it is not for a court or jury to say how a particular story is best covered." *Shulman v. Group W Productions, Inc.*, 18 Cal. 4th 200, 224–225, 955 P.2d 469, 485 (1998).

7. VIABILITY OF TORT

The viability of the tort action for publicizing a private matter is open to serious question. The prospects of success for plaintiffs are low, especially if the case reaches an appellate court. Some courts have found a triable case when the defendant has moved for dismissal or summary judgment, but affirmance of a judgment for damages is a rarity in the published decisions. Whether any liability for publicizing true information is constitutional (absent an additional basis of liability, such as breach of contract or breach of confidence) is questionable. The tort arises from a disclosure made to the "public"—not from a disclosure to those who have a family, social or business relationship with the plaintiff, which is often more damaging and distressing. It provides only an action for a monetary judgment after the plaintiff's privacy has been impaired. (As with defamation actions, injunctions against further publication are not granted, absent another ground of liability, as this would be an unconstitutional prior restraint of speech. See *Gawker Media, LLC v. Bollea*, 129 So. 3d 1196 (Fla. App. 2014).) Litigation further publicizes what the plaintiff did not want publicized.

The supreme courts of North Carolina and Oregon have rejected the action as a ground of tort liability in state law. *Hall v. Post*, 323 N.C. 259, 372 S.E.2d 711 (1988); *Anderson v. Fisher Broadcasting Companies, Inc.*, 300 Or. 452, 712 P.2d 803 (1986). The North Carolina court considered the private facts tort "constitutionally suspect." Even if it survived constitutional scrutiny, it would "add to the existing tensions between the First Amendment and the law of torts." Furthermore, it would be of little practical value because it was unlikely that juries would find a defendant liable for this tort without also finding liability for intentional infliction of emotional distress. The opinion of the Oregon Supreme Court criticized the tort on a number of grounds, including "*ad hoc*" review of newsworthiness. One reader's or viewer's "news" is another's tedium or trivia, and some editors might believe that the community should see or hear facts or ideas that the majority finds uninteresting or offensive. Because of the "publicity" requirement the print, film and broadcast media were singled out for legal restraints that would not apply to gossipmongers, letter writers or "telephone tattlers." And there appeared to be no reported case of recent years in which a plaintiff had succeeded in recovering damages.

These decisions have not been adopted, or even much noticed, by courts in other states. Without a definite ruling by the Supreme Court that the First Amendment bars liability for publicizing true information, publicizing private facts will remain one of the four categories of tort liability for invasions of privacy.

B. BREACH OF CONFIDENCE

1. LIABILITY FOR BREACH OF CONFIDENCE

In certain circumstances there can be tort liability for revelation of private information on the ground of breach of confidence. This is entirely distinct from the four types of invasion of privacy specified in the Second Restatement of Torts. Unlike the "private facts" tort, an action for breach of confidence does not require "publicity." A defendant can be liable for communicating private information to a few individuals, or only one. But liability requires a breach of confidence, and that usually is found only when the defendant was under an obligation of confidence that was violated by disclosure of the information. Many who disclose or repeat sensitive personal information are under no such obligation, so they cannot be liable. Breach of confidence thus is usually not a viable action for revelation of personal matters in mass media or gossip.

It is mainly in cases of alleged breach of confidence by health care professionals, or employees with access to confidential medical information, that courts in the United States have recognized an action for breach of confidence. See *Byrne v. Avery Center for Obstetrics and Gynecology, P.C.*, 327 Conn. 540, 175 A.3d 1 (2018); *Biddle v. Warren General Hospital*, 86 Ohio St. 3d 395, 715 N.E.2d 518 (1999). In these cases a basis for an obligation of confidence could be found in professional ethics, the expectations of patients that their medical details and private information they provided would be held in confidence, and state law recognition of a privilege against disclosure of medical information or records. See *McCormick v. England*, 328 S.C. 627, 494 S.E.2d 431 (Ct. App. 1997). A basis for finding an obligation of confidence might be found on analogous grounds in an action for breach of confidence committed by an attorney or an employee with access to confidential legal records. In *Waggenheim v. Alexander Grant & Co.*, 19 Ohio App. 3d 7, 482 N.E.2d 955 (1983), an accounting firm was held liable to a client for disclosure of confidential information. Banks have been found to be under an obligation of confidence as to customer account information, primarily on the basis that this is implied in the bank's contract with the customer. *Milohnich v. First National Bank of Miami Springs*,

224 So. 2d 759 (Fla. App. 1969); *Suburban Trust Co. v. Waller*, 44 Md. App. 335, 408 A.2d 758 (1979).

When a plaintiff's claim of breach of confidence does not involve medical information, confidences of a professional's client or bank account details, it may be difficult to attain recognition of an obligation of confidence. The plaintiff's expectation that the information would be kept confidential is not itself sufficient as a legal foundation for such an obligation. For example, in *Wynne v. Orcutt Union School District*, 17 Cal. App. 3d 1108, 95 Cal. Rptr. 458 (1971), a mother had told her son's teacher "in strict confidence" that the boy had a disease that was progressively disabling and eventually fatal. He was not yet aware of this. An action for the teacher's disclosure of this to the boy's classmates failed because the teacher was under no duty of non-disclosure. In *Evans v. Rite Aid Corp.*, 324 S.C. 269, 478 S.E.2d 846 (1996), the court held that a customer did not have an action against a pharmacy for disclosing the prescription medication the customer had obtained because the pharmacy owed no duty of confidentiality. There are, however, contrary decisions. *Fanean v. Rite Aid Corp.*, 984 A.2d 812 (Del. Super. Ct. 2009); *Anonymous v. CVS Corp.*, 188 Misc. 2d 616, 728 N.Y.S.2d 333 (Sup. Ct. 2001).

When there is an obligation of confidence, liability may extend to unintentional as well as intentional revelations of confidential information. See *Doe v. Roe*, 93 Misc. 2d 201, 400 N.Y.S.2d 668 (Sup. Ct. 1977) (psychiatrist's book, containing what patient disclosed during lengthy psychoanalysis, insufficiently disguised identity of patient); *Prince v. St. Francis-St. George Hospital, Inc.*, 20 Ohio App. 3d 4, 484 N.E.2d 265 (1985) (health insurance claim form stating plaintiff was treated for alcoholism detoxification sent to employer of plaintiff's husband).

Even though a patient may expect that confidential medical information will not be revealed without the patient's consent, the cases on breach of confidence claims against physicians typically endorse exceptions to the obligation of confidence when disclosure is considered necessary in the interests of the patient, other individuals, or even the public at large. *E.g., Horne v. Patton*, 291 Ala. 701, 287 So. 2d 824 (1973); *McCormick v. England*, 328 S.C. 627, 494 S.E.2d 431 (Ct. App. 1997). In an early case, *Simonsen v. Swenson*, 104 Neb. 224, 177 N.W. 831 (1920), the court decided that a physician was "privileged" to disclose to the proprietor of a small hotel that a guest had a contagious disease. See also *Chizmar v. Mackie*, 896 P.2d 196 (Alaska 1995) (disclosure to patient's spouse that patient had tested positive for AIDS); *Oringer v. Rotkin*, 162 A.D.2d 113, 556 N.Y.S.2d 67 (1990) (disclosure by psychologist to police and boy's family that patient made threat to boy's life during therapy session). In *Bryson v. Tillinghast*, 749 P.2d 110 (Okla. 1988), the court decided that a physician who learned that the police were looking for a suspected rapist with certain injuries was not liable for telling the police that the plaintiff had been treated for such injuries. There is no general allowance to disclose a patient's medical information to the patient's spouse, when there is no danger to the patient, the spouse or a third person that warrants the disclosure. *MacDonald v. Clinger*, 84 A.D.2d 482, 446 N.Y.S.2d 801 (1982).

2. LIABILITY OF THIRD PARTIES

Liability for breach of confidence usually requires an obligation of confidence owed by the defendant directly to the plaintiff, but there are some possibilities beyond this. One is liability for inducing a person to breach an obligation of confidence, such as a physician's obligation concerning patient medical information. This is endorsed in *Alberts v. Devine*, 395 Mass. 59, 479 N.E.2d 113 (1985), and *Morris v. Consolidation Coal Co.*, 191 W. Va. 426, 446 S.E.2d 648 (1994). A second is liability for disclosing or using confidential information the defendant acquired by wrongful means, such as breaking into files where confidential patient or client information is kept. However, in *Madden v. Creative Services, Inc.*, 84 N.Y.2d 738, 646 N.E.2d 780 (1995), where private investigators photographed documents in a law firm's office but the clients had not identified any resulting damage, the court held there was no cause of action. A third is liability for disclosing or using confidential information known to have been acquired because of someone's breach of confidence or wrongful means. As discussed in Chapter 13, this is a basis of liability under the law of trade secrets, when the confidential information has economic value as a trade secret. In the United States this has not been extended to information that the plaintiff wanted to remain confidential for non-economic reasons. In English law, liability for breach of confidence does extend to third parties who acquire such information and disclose it with knowledge of the breach of confidence or wrongful acquisition. Newspapers and other media publishers can be held liable on this basis. See *Attorney-General v. Guardian Newspapers Ltd. (No. 2)*, [1990] 1 A.C. 109 (H.L.).

3. CONSTITUTIONAL LAW LIMITATIONS

As discussed earlier (pp. 313–315), liability for communicating true information may violate the First Amendment when based on invasion of privacy; but a decision of the Supreme Court indicates that it does not violate the First Amendment when the ground of liability is the defendant's violation of an obligation of confidence, especially one arising from an agreement with the plaintiff. In *Cohen v. Cowles Media Co.*, 501 U.S. 663 (1991), the plaintiff had sued newspapers for publishing his identity as the source of a news story. He had provided the story only when promised confidentiality by the newspapers' reporters. The Supreme Court held (5–4) that liability on the basis of promissory estoppel would not violate the First Amendment. The opinion emphasized that the promissory estoppel doctrine was a law of general application that did not single out the press.

The First Amendment might, however, bar liability if the defendant is sued for disclosure of true information on the basis that it knew the information was acquired because of someone else's breach of confidence or other wrongful conduct. In *Bartnicki v.*

Vopper, 532 U.S. 514 (2001), the plaintiffs' cellular telephone conversation had been illegally intercepted and recorded. A tape of the conversation was given to a private citizen, who delivered it to a local radio station commentator. The tape was played on his program and on another station, and local newspapers published its contents. All of the parties came within statutory provisions making it unlawful to disclose the contents of a communication knowing or having reason to know the contents were obtained through illegal interception, and providing for damages. A majority of the Supreme Court held that the First Amendment precluded the application of the statutes in the circumstances of the case. Four justices concluded that the First Amendment barred liability because what the defendants disclosed was a matter of public concern and the defendants did not act unlawfully in receiving it. Two other justices decided the case on the more narrow ground that as the conversation broadcast included a threat of physical harm to others and the parties to the conversation were "limited public figures," a "matter of unusual public concern" was involved and the parties had little or no legitimate interest in maintaining the privacy of the conversation.

A judgment for damages is the usual remedy for breach of confidence, but an injunction prohibiting future disclosure is possible. Enforcement of an obligation of confidence by injunction may not violate the "no prior restraint" principle that operates in publicizing private facts and defamation cases. See *Doe v. Roe*, 93 Misc. 2d 201, 400 N.Y.S.2d 668 (Sup. Ct. 1977).

CHAPTER 19
FALSE LIGHT

A. INTRODUCTION

"Publicity that places the plaintiff in a false light in the public eye" is the final invasion of privacy tort identified by Prosser. Prosser, Privacy, 48 Calif. L. Rev. 383, 389–401 (1960). No such tort existed before Prosser identified and described it in his article and treatise on tort law. Prosser, *Handbook of the Law of Torts* 638–639 (2d ed. 1955). Prosser contended that there was such a tort in substance, citing numerous cases. In some, the basis of liability was actually another type of invasion of privacy or passing off.

The cases which came closest to suggesting liability for publicity placing the plaintiff in a false light involved the embarrassing use of a private citizen's picture to illustrate a news or magazine article on a subject the person actually was not connected with. The leading case of this nature is *Leverton v. Curtis Publishing Co.*, 192 F.2d 974 (3d Cir. 1951). A newspaper photographer had taken a dramatic photograph of a child who had nearly been hit by a car during a traffic accident. This was published in an Alabama newspaper the next day. Twenty months later the photograph was used as an illustration for a magazine article on traffic accidents, emphasizing pedestrian carelessness. (Its title was "They Ask To Be Killed.") The magazine publisher was held liable to the child for invasion of privacy. The publication of her photograph in the newspaper was a privileged invasion of privacy because her interest in being left alone was outweighed by the public interest in being informed. She was a legitimate subject of publicity for the accident in which she was involved. But use of the plaintiff's photograph to illustrate an article on pedestrian carelessness, with the implication that she had narrowly escaped death because she was careless of her own safety, was not privileged because (so far as shown in the facts) she had not been careless.

Another case of this type is *Peay v. Curtis Publishing Co.*, 78 F. Supp. 305 (D.D.C. 1948), in which a photograph of the plaintiff, a Washington, D.C., taxi driver, illustrated a magazine article depicting Washington taxi drivers as ill-mannered, contemptuous of patrons and dishonest. Although not specified in the case, presumably the plaintiff denied that she fit this description. (She also sued for libel.) The court held that the plaintiff had stated a sufficient claim for invasion of privacy. See also *Gill v. Curtis Publishing Co.*, 38 Cal. 2d 273, 239 P.2d 630 (1952) (photograph of married couple published with caption " 'love at first sight' is a bad risk"; accompanying article equated "love at first sight" with "100% sex attraction" and claimed it would be followed by divorce).

In any event, a tort of invasion of privacy by publicity placing a person in a false light was included in the Second Restatement of Torts. § 652E states:

> One who gives publicity to a matter concerning another that places the other before the public

in a false light is subject to liability to the other for invasion of his privacy, if

(a) the false light in which the other was placed would be highly offensive to a reasonable person, and

(b) the actor had knowledge of or acted in reckless disregard as to the falsity of the publicized matter and the false light in which the other would be placed.

There are thus four elements of liability: (1) publicity before the public; (2) placing the plaintiff in a false light; (3) highly offensive to the reasonable person; and (4) the defendant's knowledge of or reckless disregard for falsity of the publicized matter and the false light. A caveat to § 652E stated that no position was taken on whether there are circumstances in which there could be liability when the actor was negligent but did not know of or act with reckless disregard as to the falsity of the matter and false light. As privacy is a right pertaining only to natural persons, a legal entity such as a corporation cannot maintain an action for false light publicity. Rest. 2d Torts § 652I; *Hearts with Haiti, Inc. v. Kendrick*, 43 Media L. Rptr. 1909 (D. Me. 2015).

False light liability arises only when there is "publicity" that places the plaintiff in a false light "before the public." The publicity requirement is the same as for the tort of publicizing true private matters. (See pp. 302–304.) As stated in Rest. 2d Torts § 652D, comment *a*, publicity is communication "to the public at large, or to so many persons that the matter must be regarded as substantially certain to become one of public knowledge." Mass media publication qualifies. Communication to a small number of people does not, even if it is more than a mere handful of persons. See *Polin v. Dun & Bradstreet, Inc.*, 768 F.2d 1204 (10th Cir. 1985) (sending credit report to seventeen subscribers); *Pace v. Bristol Hospital*, 964 F. Supp. 628 (D. Conn. 1997) (communication with employees and physician at hospital where plaintiff worked). Compare *Wal-Mart Stores, Inc. v. Lee*, 348 Ark. 707, 74 S.W.3d 634 (2002) (communications to Wal-Mart supervisory personnel, police and prosecuting attorney created publicity).

B. FALSE LIGHT

The essence of false light is a portrayal of the plaintiff that is materially false. See Rest. 2d Torts § 652E, comment *b* (attribution to plaintiff of characteristics, conduct or beliefs that are false). Obviously an action for false light invasion of privacy will not succeed if the plaintiff cannot prove that the portrayal of the plaintiff was untrue. But often the defendant never contends that what the plaintiff claimed to be the portrayal was true. Instead, the issue is whether what the defendant published or communicated actually portrayed the plaintiff in the way the plaintiff claimed. Because the plaintiff must allege and then establish that there was a meaning about the plaintiff that was highly offensive, the plaintiff may allege a false meaning that was not actually taken by the people who read what the defendant had published or heard what the defendant had said.

For example, in *Martin v. Municipal Publications*, 510 F. Supp. 255 (E.D. Pa. 1981), a magazine had published a photograph of the plaintiff wearing his "mummer's" costume in the Philadelphia Mummers Parade. The caption below the photograph said, "A New Year's tribute here to all the ostriches who gave their tails to make the world free for closet transvestites from South Philly to get themselves stinking drunk." The plaintiff sued the magazine's publisher, claiming this portrayed him as a closet transvestite and drunk. The defendant plausibly denied that the magazine conveyed any such meaning, on a reasonable interpretation. The court decided this was an issue for the jury. More seriously, in *Crump v. Beckley Newspapers, Inc.*, 173 W. Va. 699, 320 S.E.2d 70 (1983), a newspaper had used a photograph of the plaintiff, a coal miner, in an article on problems faced by female miners, including discrimination and instances of severe harassment. The plaintiff claimed, and the newspaper's publisher denied, that the inclusion of her photograph in the article portrayed her as having experienced such harassment, which she had not. In this case, too, the court decided that this was an issue for the jury.

In *Cibenko v. Worth Publishers, Inc.*, 510 F. Supp. 761 (D.N.J. 1981), the decision was different. A picture in a sociology textbook showed a white policeman prodding a black man with his nightstick. The caption beneath the picture said that the social status of the offender was the most significant determinant of arrest, conviction and penalty and asked whether the officer would have acted in the same manner if the "offender" were a white male. The policeman claimed that the textbook portrayed him as racially prejudiced. The court decided that the picture and caption were not reasonably capable of conveying this meaning and dismissed the complaint.

This type of issue also appears in some cases where the plaintiff's photograph had been published in a pornographic magazine, without consent, and it was claimed this portrayed the plaintiff falsely as a person who was willing to appear in such a magazine and endorsed its contents. In *Solano v. Playgirl, Inc.*, 292 F.3d 1078 (9th Cir. 2002), where the magazine's cover implied that there was a nude picture of the plaintiff inside (he was actually shown fully dressed), the court found a triable issue of false light. In *Braun v. Flynt*, 726 F.2d 245 (5th Cir. 1984), reh'g denied, 731 F.2d 1205 (5th Cir. 1984), the plaintiff was an employee of an amusement park who performed an aquatic act with "Ralph, the Diving Pig." A publicity photograph of the plaintiff and Ralph was published in a "hard-core" pornographic magazine. The court upheld a jury's finding that the magazine created a "false impression as to [the plaintiff's] reputation, integrity or virtue" even though neither the photograph nor the accompanying caption was sexually suggestive. By contrast, in *Byrd v. Hustler Magazine, Inc.*, 433 So. 2d 593 (Fla. App. 1983), the court rejected a false light claim arising from an altered photograph of the plaintiff in a pornographic magazine because the caption made it clear that the plaintiff had not posed for the magazine and did not make an obscene gesture when the photograph was taken.

There is no false portrayal of the plaintiff if it is clear that the reference to the plaintiff is fictional rather than factual. The defendants prevailed on this ground in *Dworkin v. Hustler Magazine, Inc.*, 668 F. Supp. 1408 (C.D. Cal. 1987), aff'd, 867 F.2d 1188 (9th Cir. 1989), but not in *Peoples Bank and Trust Co. of Mountain Home v. Globe International Publishing, Inc.*, 978 F.2d 1065 (8th Cir. 1992). In that case, a supermarket tabloid had used file photographs of an elderly woman in Arkansas who delivered newspapers as illustrations for a story that a woman in Australia had to quit her work delivering news at the age of 101 because an extramarital affair with a millionaire customer left her pregnant. The tabloid's publisher contended that the story was so patently fictional that it could not be reasonably interpreted to contain actual facts about the plaintiff. The court disagreed. Even if the assertion of pregnancy could not be believed, other aspects of the story, including the extramarital affair and having to quit work delivering newspapers, could reasonably be believed. The court upheld an award of $850,000 in punitive damages.

C. HIGHLY OFFENSIVE

Under Rest. 2d Torts § 652E, for liability the false light must be highly offensive to a reasonable person. This excludes liability for many falsehoods that are embarrassing, annoying or offensive, but not highly offensive or egregious. In the reported cases plaintiffs typically allege a meaning that can be considered highly offensive, as in the examples cited in the discussion above of the false light requirement. A different example, from a significant and clever judicial opinion on false light, is to create the appearance that a hunter engaged in "the very unsportsmanlike and unethical act of shooting a goose on the ground." *Uhl v. Columbia Broadcasting System, Inc.*, 476 F. Supp. 1134 (W.D. Pa. 1979). Many meanings that are defamatory, including imputations of criminally, immorality and unprofessional conduct, can be found highly offensive. Plaintiffs often sue on the grounds of both defamation and false light. But meanings which are usually non-defamatory in themselves, such as conveying the impression that the plaintiff was a victim of a crime, or suffering from a disease, may be highly offensive. So can a false association of the plaintiff with controversial beliefs or business activities. (Cases are collected in Elder, *Privacy Torts* § 4:5 (2002).)

There are, of course, decisions that the alleged false light was not highly offensive. These include: A mistaken obituary of a person who was still alive. *Thomason v. Times-Journal, Inc.*, 190 Ga. App. 601, 379 S.E.2d 551 (1989). Identifying plaintiffs as card counters in casinos. *Doug Grant, Inc. v. Greate Bay Casino Corp.*, 3 F. Supp. 2d 518 (D.N.J. 1998), modified, 232 F.3d 173 (3d Cir. 2000). Saying that a hospital administrator was adversarial and unhelpful. *Parano v. O'Connor*, 433 Pa. Super. 570, 641 A.2d 607 (1994). Stating that a father would not agree to allow his former wife to have their children with her at her wedding unless she gave up all rights to spend Christmas with them. *Gavin v. Saltzman*, 20 Pa. D. & C. 4th 13, 22 Media L. Rptr. 1829 (C.P.

1993), aff'd, 438 Pa. Super. 701, 22 Media L. Rptr. 2447 (1994). Implying that four girls aged eight to twelve wanted to physically dominate and subdue boys at their elementary school. *Fudge v. Penthouse International, Ltd.*, 840 F.2d 1012 (1st Cir. 1988). Reporting a supposed statement by the plaintiff that her ex-husband's new wife was a home-wrecker and a witch. *Solomon v. National Enquirer Inc.*, 24 Media L. Rptr. 2269 (D. Md. 1996). And saying that a hairdresser who used a blowtorch in styling customers' hair also used it on dogs. *Morganroth v. Whitall*, 161 Mich. App. 785, 411 N.W.2d 859 (1987).

D. RECKLESS DISREGARD FOR FALSITY; NEGLIGENCE

Actions for false light invasion of privacy implicate freedom of speech and freedom of the press under the First Amendment. In a series of decisions that will be discussed in Chapter 23, the Supreme Court has held that the First Amendment requires a number of limitations on liability for defamation. These include a requirement that the defendant's knowledge of or reckless disregard for falsity be proved, by clear and convincing evidence, when the plaintiff was a public official or public figure and defamed in that capacity. That is not required when the plaintiff was not a public official or public figure, but in *Gertz v. Robert Welch, Inc.*, 418 U.S. 323 (1974), the Supreme Court held there could be no liability without fault. That is usually assumed to require proof of negligence. *Gertz* rejected the argument that proof of knowing or reckless falsehood was required when the defamatory statement was on a matter of public interest.

False light actions bear a strong resemblance to actions for defamation as they arise from communication to third parties of alleged falsehoods concerning the plaintiff. Consequently, it is generally accepted that the First Amendment limitations of defamation liability apply to false light as well. A false light action by a public official or public figure requires knowledge of or reckless disregard for falsity (the false light in which the plaintiff would be placed), and a false light action by a private figure requires at least negligence in this regard. However, the Supreme Court has applied a requirement of knowing or reckless falsehood, not negligence, in two false light cases involving private figures. In *Time, Inc. v. Hill*, 385 U.S. 374 (1967), the court held that for "false reports of matters of public interest," the First Amendment required for liability the defendant's knowledge of or reckless disregard for falsity. In *Cantrell v. Forest City Publishing Co.*, 419 U.S. 245 (1974), decided after *Gertz*, the court applied the standard of knowing or reckless falsity in upholding a judgment for the plaintiffs in their false light action.

The uncertainty about what First Amendment rules actually apply in false light actions was addressed in the Second Restatement of Torts by making the defendant's knowledge of or reckless disregard for the falsity of the publicized matter, and the false light, a "black letter" requirement of false light liability in § 652E, but with a "caveat" leaving open the possibility that a negligence standard might apply to false light actions by private figures under *Gertz v. Robert Welch, Inc.* See Rest. 2d Torts § 652E, comment *d*. In the absence of Supreme Court guidance, state courts and lower federal courts have divided on the standard of fault to be applied.

Some courts have decided or assumed that *Time, Inc. v. Hill* continues to provide the First Amendment rule for all false light cases. *E.g.*, *Dodrill v. Arkansas Democrat Co.*, 265 Ark. 628, 590 S.W.2d 840 (1979); *McCall v. Courier-Journal and Louisville Times Co.*, 623 S.W.2d 882 (Ky. 1981). A number have retained knowledge or reckless disregard of falsity as a state law requirement because it is in Rest. 2d Torts § 652E and because it is thought to be a desirable limit on false light liability. These include *Meyerkord v. Zipatoni Co.*, 276 S.W.3d 319 (Mo. App. 2008); *Welling v. Weinfield,* 113 Ohio St. 3d 464, 866 N.E.2d 1051 (2007); and *Colbert v. World Publishing Co.*, 747 P.2d 286 (Okla. 1987). In other cases, the court has concluded that *Gertz v. Robert Welch, Inc.*, applies to false light cases and negligence should be the standard of liability when the plaintiff is not a public figure or official. *Wood v. Hustler Magazine, Inc.*, 736 F.2d 1084 (5th Cir. 1984); *Russell v. Thomson Newspapers, Inc.*, 842 P.2d 896 (Utah 1992); *Crump v. Beckley Newspapers, Inc.*, 173 W. Va. 699, 320 S.E.2d 70 (1983). If the false light publicity did not pertain to a matter of public interest, *Time, Inc. v. Hill* can be distinguished and liability based on negligence allowed. See *West v. Media General Convergence, Inc.*, 53 S.W.3d 640 (Tenn. 2001).

E. ACCEPTANCE OR REJECTION

The false light tort, as described in Rest. 2d Torts § 652E, has been accepted as part of tort law in most states. But it has been rejected by the supreme courts of Colorado, Florida, Minnesota, North Carolina and Texas. Arguments for and against the tort are expressed in the opinions delivered in these cases, including dissents, and in cases where the state supreme court decided not to reject the tort.

A major argument for rejection of the false light tort is that it allows an action for harmful false communications about an individual and thus largely duplicates the field occupied by defamation law, but without the protections afforded by defamation law's requirement that the publication convey a defamatory meaning and other rules that limit liability. These include the special damage requirement for some defamation, privileges, short statutes of limitations, procedural requirements, and various state laws that apply to defamation, including retraction statutes. False light claims have been made with, or instead of, claims of defamation in order to avoid those rules, with mixed success. *E.g.*, *Fellows v. National Enquirer, Inc.*, 42 Cal. 3d 234, 721 P.2d 97 (1986) (special damage requirement); *Colbert v. World Publishing, Co.*, 747 P.2d 286 (Okla. 1987) (statute of limitations). A majority of the court in *Cain v. Hearst Corp.*, 878 S.W.2d 577 (Tex. 1994), was persuaded to reject the false light tort because of the overlap with other torts—not only defamation but also other privacy torts and infliction of emotional distress—and the chilling effect on speech and press publication that possible false light liability would have. See also *Jews for Jesus, Inc. v. Rapp*, 997 So. 2d 1098 (Fla. 2008); *Renwick v. News and Observer Publishing Co.*, 310 N.C. 312, 312 S.E.2d 405 (1984).

It could be added that under older cases such as *Leverton v. Curtis Publishing Co.* (pp. 325–326, *supra*), privacy was the interest protected. The defendant was liable because the defendant made the plaintiff an object of public attention without justification. The lack of justification (or "privilege") was because the plaintiff was not actually connected with the subject-matter of the publication that presumably would be of interest to the public. But under Rest. 2d Torts § 652E, false light liability resembles defamation. In both, liability depends upon the truth of what is communicated, the primary harm is injury to reputation, and there is no requirement that the plaintiff's privacy be impaired. A public figure who was too well-known to have really suffered loss of privacy can bring a false light action, as in *Douglass v. Hustler Magazine, Inc.*, 769 F.2d 1128 (7th Cir. 1985).

The principal arguments for acceptance of the tort are that the interests protected by defamation liability and invasion of privacy liability are different—defamation liability protects interests in reputation; liability for invasion of privacy protects persons' interests in being left alone and sensitivities about what other people do or can learn about them—and false light liability addresses needs that are not met by liability for defamation or one of the other privacy torts. There is a need to have a remedy for serious but non-defamatory falsehoods given publicity. Concerns about the unpredictability of being held liable for false light, and the effects on freedom of speech and freedom of the press, do not warrant complete rejection of the tort: liability is adequately limited by the requirements of publicity, offensiveness and knowledge of or reckless disregard for falsity. See *Godbehere v. Phoenix Newspapers, Inc.*, 162 Ariz. 335, 783 P.2d 781 (1989); *West v. Media General Convergence, Inc.*, 53 S.W.3d 640 (Tenn. 2001); *Cain v. Hearst Corp.,* 878 S.W.2d 577, 584–589 (Tex. 1994) (Hightower, J., dissenting). The opinion in *Welling v. Weinfield*, 113 Ohio St. 3d 464, 866 N.E.2d 1051 (2007), contended that legal protection was necessary because "thanks to the accessibility of the Internet," barriers to generating publicity are slight, ethical standards regarding the "acceptability of certain discourse" have been lowered, and the ability to do harm has increased.

PART V

DEFAMATION

CHAPTER 20

DEFAMATION: INTRODUCTION

Defamation law provides a remedy for injury to reputation. A plaintiff potentially has an action for defamation when the defendant has communicated something that injured or had a likelihood of injuring the reputation of the plaintiff. For centuries defamation has been one of the most actively litigated areas of tort law. It has deep roots in English common law. The historical development of defamation in England explains much of the shape of the law today, including the existence of two defamation torts—libel and slander—rather than one. English cases remain important sources of precedent in the United States. But defamation law in the United States has also been shaped by uniquely American developments, especially the creation by Supreme Court decisions of constitutional law doctrines that limit defamation liability. New methods of communication, from the first appearance of the printing press to the Internet, have contributed to the development of defamation law. The telegraph, telephone, camera photography, motion pictures, radio, television and computers all created issues for courts to decide, and some still do.

Defamation has a strong claim to being the most complex area of tort law. In combination the requirements for stating and proving a *prima facie* case, defenses, relevant statutory provisions and constitutional doctrines can make defamation a daunting subject. Studying and understanding defamation law is less difficult when it is appropriately divided into its component parts and sub-parts.

The three major divisions of defamation law are (1) the elements of the *prima facie* case: what must be alleged and established by the plaintiff in order for the defendant to be held liable; (2) the common law defenses to liability: truth, absolute privileges and qualified privileges; and (3) the constitutional law doctrines, established by the Supreme Court under its interpretations of the First Amendment, that limit liability for defamation. Remedial issues, especially assessment of damages, may either be considered within one of the three divisions or separately. The elements of the *prima facie* case that apply to all defamation actions are (a) communication to a person other than the plaintiff (b) of something that conveys a defamatory meaning (a meaning harmful to reputation) (c) that is understood to refer to the plaintiff. (In texts, including this one, the first of those elements is usually the last to be discussed.) This makes sense because without these three elements the plaintiff's reputation could not be harmed. Additional requirements may apply. Some arise from distinctions between libel and slander. State defamation law is fairly consistent on most main points concerning the elements of liability and defenses, but there is considerable variation in procedural matters and assessment of damages, including what evidence is admissible and the effect of retractions.

Until the Supreme Court's decision in *New York Times Co. v. Sullivan*, 376 U.S. 254 (1964), constitutional law did not limit tort liability for defamation. Now it does. It is usually the plaintiff whose pleadings and evidence must meet the requirements of the constitutional law of defamation. For the most part, the constitutional doctrines operate separately from the common law rules of liability and defenses; they do not provide substitutes for the common law rules. (The major exception to this concerns the burden of proof on whether the defamation was true or false.) In many of the reported cases of recent times, the dispositive issue is one of constitutional law rather than common law. Defendants often win a case on a constitutional law point when they would have been held liable under the common law rules.

Under the common law, there can be liability for defamation without any fault on the defendant's part. Liability depends upon the meaning of the communication to those who see or hear it, not what the defendant intended. A defendant can be liable without any intent to defame the plaintiff, or anyone else; to convey the meaning that was taken by those who saw or heard what was communicated; to communicate a meaning that was false; or even to refer to the plaintiff. Whether there was negligence in these respects is also irrelevant to the plaintiff's cause of action, although it has some role in qualified privileges. The one qualification to this concerns the requirement of "publication." The defendant is not liable unless the defendant intended to communicate with a person other than the plaintiff or had reason to anticipate that someone other than the plaintiff would see or hear what the defendant wrote or said. In contrast, fault or its absence plays a very important role in the constitutional law doctrines that limit defamation liability. Under *Gertz v. Robert Welch, Inc.*, 418 U.S. 323 (1974), the First Amendment bars liability without fault in most but maybe not all defamation cases. Under *New York Times Co. v. Sullivan* and cases that followed it, the First Amendment bars liability to a plaintiff defamed in the capacity of "public official" or "public figure" unless it is proved that the defendant acted with knowledge of falsehood or reckless disregard for truth or falsity.

At present, the main legal rules in each of the three divisions are stable. The issues for judicial decision tend to be how to apply or elaborate the rules rather than what the basic rule actually is. The Supreme Court has shown little inclination in the last three decades to change the constitutional law doctrines that its decisions have established. However, it could do this at any time.

Who may be defamed. Any human being can have a cause of action for defamation, but one of the requirements of a defamation action is that the defamed party be alive at the time the defamatory matter was published. There is no cause of action for defamation of a deceased person. Someone who defames a deceased person is not liable to the deceased's estate or family members. However, when defamation of a deceased person also carries a defamatory meaning about someone still living, that person has an action. Rest. 2d Torts § 560 and comment *a*. Under provisions of state survival statutes, even when the defamed person was alive at the time of the defamatory publication, a defamation action may not survive the death of the defamed person or the person who communicated the defamatory matter.

Defamation actions can be brought by corporations, partnerships, associations, and other entities that can sue or be sued. See Rest. 2d Torts §§ 561–562. They are thought to have a reputation that can be damaged by defamation. Defamatory meanings alleged in an action brought by a business or non-profit entity usually are imputations of fraud or deceit, other dishonesty, reprehensible conduct in its operations, or adverse reflections on its solvency or creditworthiness. A typical problem in an action by a business is whether the defendant's statement had a meaning that was defamatory or was a non-defamatory criticism of the plaintiff's business methods, products or services. See *National Refining Co. v. Benzo Gas Motor Fuel Co.*, 20 F.2d 763 (8th Cir. 1927); Annot., 104 A.L.R.5th 523. Another problem is whether defamation of employees or officers of a business entity, especially a principal officer or partner, also defames the entity. *E.g.*, *Neiman-Marcus Co. v. Lait*, 107 F. Supp. 96 (S.D.N.Y. 1952) (corporation could be defamed and damaged by report that it employs "seriously undesirable personnel"); *Cohn v. Am-Law*, 5 Media L. Rptr. 2367 (N.Y. Sup. Ct. 1980) (libel of lawyer in professional capacity also libel of firm).

A defamation action cannot be maintained by a government, or a government department or agency. *City of Chicago v. Tribune Co.*, 307 Ill. 595, 139 N.Y. 86 (1923); *Derbyshire County Council v. Times Newspapers Ltd.*, [1993] A.C. 534 (H.L.). See Annot., 45 A.L.R.3d 1315. This rule is based primarily on protection of the right of citizens to criticize governmental bodies without fear of liability. The rule has been extended to agencies and entities owned by governments that conduct commercial activities. *College Savings Bank v. Florida Prepaid Postsecondary Education Expense Board*, 919 F. Supp. 756 (D.N.J. 1996).

CHAPTER 21
DEFAMATORY COMMUNICATION

A. DEFAMATORY CONTENT

1. DEFAMATORY MEANINGS

The essence of defamation is a communication whose meaning is harmful to the reputation of another. A statement or other communication is defamatory when its content is harmful to reputation, or would cause a person to be shunned. If it is only harmful in some other way, it is not defamatory. For example, if the defendant erroneously reported that the plaintiff had died, causing the plaintiff to lose customers or clients, there would be no defamation action. See *Decker v. Princeton Packet, Inc.*, 116 N.J. 418, 561 A.2d 1122 (1989). The remedy, if any, would be for injurious falsehood. If the statement was offensive or distressing to the plaintiff but not harmful to reputation, the remedy, if any, would be for infliction of emotional distress or invasion of privacy.

The truth or falsity of a statement, or the meaning it conveys, is irrelevant to whether it is defamatory. To say that the plaintiff is an embezzler or serial adulterer is defamatory regardless of whether it is true or false. However, as there is no defamation liability when the defamatory meaning is true, defamation is sometimes described as an action for false statements harmful to reputation. Plaintiffs in defamation cases are typically expected to include in their pleadings an allegation that the defamatory meaning was false.

Anything that conveys a meaning harmful to reputation can be defamatory. It can consist of words, pictures, physical conduct or some combination of them. Defamatory matter need not even be intended to convey information to another person. Statements of opinion, as well as statements of fact, can be defamatory. However, for reasons discussed later (see pp. 419–421, 441–442), there may not actually be liability if the statement of opinion does not contain or imply a factual assertion that is not true. Many defamatory meanings arise from what is implied in a communication, as distinct from direct statements.

An often-repeated definition of defamation is that of Baron Parke in *Parmiter v. Coupland*, (1840) 6 M. & W. 105, 151 Eng. Rep. 340 (Ex.): a "publication. . .which is calculated to injure the reputation of another, by exposing him to hatred, contempt, or ridicule." Recognizing that this definition is too narrow, courts have expanded upon it in various ways—for example, a "statement that tends to expose a person to public contempt, hatred, ridicule, aversion or disgrace." *Thomas H. v. Paul B.*, 18 N.Y.3d 580, 584, 965 N.E.2d 939, 942 (2012). Prosser defined defamation as "that which tends to injure 'reputation' in the popular sense; to diminish the esteem, respect, goodwill or confidence in which the plaintiff is held, or to excite adverse, derogatory or unpleasant feelings or opinions against him." Prosser & Keeton, *The Law of Torts* 773 (5th ed.

1984). The prevailing concept today is that stated in Rest. 2d Torts § 559: "A communication is defamatory if it tends so to harm the reputation of another as to lower him in the estimation of the community or to deter third persons from associating or dealing with him."

This includes statements that imply no deficiency in the plaintiff's personal morality or integrity but could cause people to avoid association with the plaintiff. The principal example is an imputation of mental illness or impairment, but it is also applicable to imputations that the plaintiff has a serious and contagious disease. See Rest. 2d Torts § 559, comment *c*. Another example, although now out of date, is the imputation that the plaintiff was illegitimate (born outside marriage). See Annot., 53 A.L.R. 548. A publication that would cause great ridicule of the plaintiff has been held to be defamatory, even when it contained no negative implication about the plaintiff's conduct or character, because the ridicule affected the plaintiff's reputation. He would forever be associated with it in the minds of others. *Burton v. Crowell Publishing Co.*, 82 F.2d 154 (2d Cir. 1936). This falls within the definition of defamation in *Parmiter v. Coupland*.

Communications which convey that the plaintiff is lacking in "creditworthiness"—the plaintiff cannot or may not be able to repay debts—are generally not defamatory when the plaintiff does not conduct a business. However, they generally are defamatory when the plaintiff does conduct a business, as imputations of this kind have such a tendency to damage parties engaged in business. See Annot., 99 A.L.R.2d 700; Annot., 49 A.L.R.3d 163.

Many of the meanings found to be defamatory do involve imputations of criminal conduct, misconduct in or unfitness for the occupation or business the plaintiff engages in, or the position the plaintiff holds (or aspires to hold), or want of integrity or morality. It is not necessary for there to be a definite allegation of the plaintiff's guilt or want of good character in order for a communication to be defamatory. A publication that places the plaintiff under suspicion of misconduct or bad character is defamatory, as this is harmful to reputation. It is thus defamatory to state that a person is under investigation or a suspect. See *Lewis v. Daily Telegraph Ltd.*, [1964] A.C. 234 (H.L.). Or that the plaintiff has been arrested. See Annot., 93 A.L.R.3d 625. Similarly, a publication that creates suspicion of misconduct but is ambiguous about the plaintiff's guilt is defamatory, as in *Lawrence v. Bauer Publishing & Printing Ltd.*, 89 N.J. 451, 446 A.2d 469 (1982).

Stating or implying that there was some deficiency in a person's conduct or character is not necessarily defamation. There have been many cases in which it was debatable whether a certain meaning was defamatory or not. Examples include: The father of a celebrity actor has revealed the actor's "love secrets" to a magazine for publication. *Selleck v. Globe International, Inc.*, 166 Cal. App. 3d 1123, 212 Cal. Rptr. 838 (1985) ("susceptible of a defamatory meaning"). A reporter is "heartily detested" by most of his fellow journalists. *Murphy v. LaMarsh*, [1971]

2 W.W.R. 196, (1970) 18 D.L.R.3d 208 (B.C.C.A.) (judgment of liability affirmed). The plaintiff has been fired, or terminated from employment. *Denny v. Mertz*, 84 Wis. 2d 654, 267 N.W.2d 304 (1978) (jury issue of defamatory meaning); *Nichols v. Item Publishers, Inc.*, 309 N.Y. 596, 132 N.E.2d 860 (1956) (removal from office not defamatory). A dentist has been sued for alleged "unskillful and negligent" dental work that caused injury and disease. *Twiggar v. Ossining Printing & Publishing Co.*, 161 App. Div. 718, 146 N.Y.S. 529 (1914) (not libellous "per se" without implication of general unskillfulness or general ignorance). Whether a certain type of meaning is defamatory is primarily an issue of law to be decided by the court. But when the meaning is one that may be considered defamatory, in the circumstances of the case, it is likely that the trier of fact (usually but not always a jury) will make a decision on whether it was defamatory.

The primary role of the trier of fact is to decide what meaning was conveyed to those who saw or heard what was communicated by the defendant. For example, if the defendant said that a doctor "took advantage" of patients, was this understood to mean financial impropriety, sexual impropriety or neither? (The context in which the defendant's statement was made would bear on this.) Did the return of a check marked "account closed" put the plaintiff under suspicion of fraud? If the defendant said that the plaintiff often went to the Tenderloin, did this convey the implication that he went to the brothels there? If the defendant said that the plaintiff was injured in a bank robbery, was this understood to mean that the plaintiff was the robber or someone present during the robbery? If the defendant said that the plaintiff's son was a "bastard," was this understood to mean the plaintiff gave birth to a child "out of wedlock" or understood as a term of abuse aimed at the son? (Abusive language with no factual content is generally treated as non-defamatory.) The court decides whether the defendant's communication could reasonably have been understood to have a meaning alleged by the plaintiff. If so, the trier of fact decides whether the communication actually was so understood. See *Belli v. Orlando Daily Newspapers, Inc.*, 389 F.2d 579 (5th Cir. 1967); *Denny v. Mertz*, 84 Wis. 2d 654, 267 N.W.2d 304 (1978); Rest. 2d Torts § 614, comment *b*. Under Rest. 2d Torts § 563, the meaning of a communication is what a recipient would reasonably or correctly understand to be the meaning intended.

Rest. 2d Torts § 559 states that a communication is defamatory if it "tends so to harm the reputation of another as to lower him in the estimation of the community." The relevant "community" is society at large. If the communication would "lower" the plaintiff in the estimation of a small community with distinct beliefs, but not in the estimation of many in the larger community, the defendant is not liable, even though the impact on the plaintiff's reputation in the small community is the plaintiff's primary concern. See Rest. 2d Torts § 559, comment *e*. In *Weiner v. Time & Life, Inc.*, 133 Misc. 2d 622, 507 N.Y.S.2d 784 (Sup. Ct. 1986), the plaintiff alleged that a report in a national magazine had damaged his reputation by causing friends, associates and acquaintances to believe he had violated Orthodox Jewish law. The court dismissed the action. "Community" for purposes of defamation was not the small "highly Orthodox" Jewish community with which the plaintiff associated.

There is greater difficulty when society at large is divided on whether certain types of conduct or character traits are discreditable or cause to avoid association with a person. The division may result from wider social acceptance of what once generally was not accepted, or the opposite. A statement imputing "unchastity" is a classic type of defamation (see pp. 374–375), but many people today do not believe it is immoral for an unmarried person to have sexual intercourse. Some still do. When necessary, courts are likely to apply the statement of Justice Holmes in *Peck v. Tribune Co.*, 214 U.S. 185, 190 (1909): if the communication "would hurt the plaintiff in the estimation of an important and respectable part of the community, liability is not a question of a majority vote." The question in the case, which arose when there was a strong movement in the United States to establish Prohibition, was whether it was libellous to include the plaintiff's picture in an advertisement for whisky, with an endorsement of the product.

A controversial issue today is whether imputations that the plaintiff is homosexual or has engaged in homosexual conduct should continue to be treated as defamatory, as before. See Annot., 7 A.L.R.6th 135. There has been much change in public opinion, and in laws on same-sex conduct and relationships, but an allegation or implication of homosexuality can still be quite damaging. In *Albright v. Morton*, 321 F. Supp. 2d 130 (D. Mass. 2004), aff'd *sub nom. Amrak Productions, Inc. v. Morton*, 410 F.3d 69 (1st Cir. 2005), the court held that it was not defamatory to state or imply that the plaintiff was homosexual. The court believed that "in this day and age" identifying a person as homosexual would not discredit him in any "considerable and respectable class of the community," and that to find this defamatory would validate the view that homosexuals were immoral and legitimate prejudice against them. See also *Yonaty v. Mincolla*, 97 A.D.3d 141, 945 N.Y.S.2d 774 (2012), holding that describing the plaintiff as gay or bisexual was not slander per se.

When the complaint is the attribution to the plaintiff of political views or views on social issues that many in the community strongly oppose, courts have usually decided there is no defamation. *E.g.*, *Washburn v. Wright*, 261 Cal. App. 2d 789, 68 Cal. Rptr. 224 (1968) ("extremist" and membership in John Birch Society); *Chicago, Rock Island & Pacific Railway Co. v. Medley*, 55 Okla. 145, 155 P. 211 (1916) ("labor agitator"); *Rawlins v. McKee*, 327 S.W.2d 633 (Tex. Civ. App. 1959) ("radical" "leftwinger" "backed and financed by. . .labor bosses"). Allegations that the plaintiff was a Communist or supporter of Communism, at a time when the Soviet Union was an adversary of the United States, were, however, regarded as defamatory. *E.g.*, *Utah State Farm Bureau Federation v. National Farmers Union Service Corp.* 198 F.2d 20 (10th Cir. 1952); *Herrmann v. Newark*

Morning Ledger Co., 48 N.J. Super. 420, 138 A.2d 61 (App. Div. 1958), on reh'g, 49 N.J. Super. 551, 140 A.2d 529 (App. Div. 1958). Defamation actions based on general allegations or insinuations that the plaintiff is a racist are likely to be rejected, but an allegation of specific racist conduct that can be proved false is a valid basis for a defamation action. *E.g.*, *Schrottman v. Barnicle*, 386 Mass. 627, 437 N.E.2d 205 (1982) (use of racial epithet); *Roots v. Montana Human Rights Network*, 275 Mont. 408, 913 P.2d 638 (1996) ("Ku Klux Klan organizer"); *Herlihy v. Metropolitan Museum of Art*, 214 A.D.2d 250, 633 N.Y.S.2d 106 (1995) (anti-Semitic remarks). See generally Annot., 62 A.L.R.4th 314.

The "community" standard, and the proposition that defamation is what would discredit a person in the estimation of "right-thinking persons," have operated to deny defamation actions for statements conveying the meaning that the plaintiff gave information to the police or other law enforcement authorities. Although this might harm the plaintiff's reputation among those with whom the plaintiff associated, and many people disapprove of informers, the meaning was not one that would in the courts' view harm the plaintiff's reputation among "right-thinking" or "respectable" persons. *Clawson v. St. Louis Post-Dispatch, L.L.C.*, 906 A.2d 308 (D.C. 2006) (plaintiff, a journalist and private investigator, said to be "FBI informer"); *Rose v. Borenstein*, 119 N.Y.S.2d 288 (N.Y. City Ct. 1953) (diamond broker and cutter accused of informing customs authorities that defendants were in illegal possession of diamonds, causing loss of employment); *Michtavi v.*

New York Daily News, 587 F.3d 551 (2d Cir. 2009) (newspaper reports that inmate serving sentence for narcotics offenses planned to cooperate with prosecutors and testify against organized crime figure). But see *Westby v. Madison Newspapers, Inc.*, 81 Wis. 2d 1, 259 N.W.2d 691 (1977) (report that plaintiffs spied on their political-activist neighbors as paid informants could be found defamatory).

2. DEFAMATION WITH EXTRINSIC FACTS

In many defamation cases, an alleged defamatory meaning about the plaintiff arises from the combination of what is contained in the communication by the defendant and facts known by persons who saw or heard the contents of the communication. These facts are known as "extrinsic facts," as they are outside what the defendant communicated. There are two categories of relevant extrinsic facts. The first consists of facts that give a defamatory meaning to the communication. The second consists of facts that would cause people to understand it to refer to the plaintiff. An example involving both would be a libel action over a report in a Greenville newspaper about a fire with many fatalities at 567 Hay Street. The president of Greenville Manufacturing Industries claims he was defamed because the newspaper report said the landlord of the building was the president of the city's largest employer, which he is, so the report was understood as pertaining to him, and because it is known to some readers that 567 Hay Street was occupied by a brothel. The report would be understood by those readers as conveying that the plaintiff was the proprietor, or at least the landlord, of a house of prostitution. It could also be claimed that he was defamed by the implication that he was indifferent to the safety of the occupants of the building, but that does not depend upon the extrinsic fact of what the building was used for.

The plaintiff must plead and prove these details. Traditionally, the pleading of the extrinsic facts that allegedly gave rise to a defamatory meaning is called the "inducement"; the pleading of the extrinsic facts that allegedly caused the defendant's communication to be understood as referring to the plaintiff is called the "colloquium"; and the alleged defamatory meaning conveyed is called the "innuendo." See Rest. 2d Torts § 563, comment *f*. Today, "innuendo" is frequently used to refer to a defamatory meaning implied in a communication, including one that does not depend on extrinsic facts.

The classic example of a publication that had no indication of a defamatory meaning "on its face," but was defamatory by reason of extrinsic facts, is a newspaper announcement that Mrs. Morrison had given birth to twins, at a time when she had been married for less than two months. *Morrison v. Ritchie & Co.*, (1902) 4 F. 645 (Scot. Ct. Sess.). A less dated variation of this would be such an announcement with the extrinsic fact that Mr. Morrison was separated from Mrs. Morrison at the time a child could have been conceived, giving rise to the innuendo that she had committed adultery. In a prominent English case, a newspaper had published a photograph with the caption "Mr. M. Corrigan, the race horse owner, and Miss ___ [the report of the case omits the name], whose engagement has been announced." Corrigan was married to another woman at the time. She sued the newspaper's publisher for libel, claiming that to those who knew her, the caption created the innuendo that she was an immoral woman who cohabitated with Corrigan without being married to him. The Court of Appeal upheld a judgment in her favor, rejecting the argument that the defendants could not be liable without knowledge of the extrinsic facts that created the defamatory inference about the plaintiff. *Cassidy v. Daily Mirror Newspapers, Ltd.*, [1929] 2 K.B. 331 (C.A.). In an analogous American case, the plaintiff sued her former husband because his application for a marriage license stated the marriage would be his first, implying (to those who knew of the plaintiff) that the plaintiff had not been his wife and that she lived with him as his mistress. *Smith v. Smith*, 236 N.Y. 581, 142 N.E. 292 (1923).

In such cases, the court decides whether the contents of what was communicated by the defendant could reasonably have been understood by those aware of the extrinsic facts to have the defamatory meaning(s) alleged by the plaintiff. If the court's decision on this is "yes," the trier of fact decides whether the communication was so understood. The parties may be permitted to present testimony by those who saw or heard the communication as to the meaning they placed upon it. This is not allowed in some jurisdictions. Defendants can now claim the protection of the constitutional law rule of no liability without fault (see pp. 430–432) when they had no reason to know that what they published had a defamatory connotation.

Although there is no defamation liability when the meaning of the communication would damage the plaintiff's reputation with only a small proportion of the population (see pp. 352–353), a defendant can be liable when only a few people had knowledge of the extrinsic facts that caused a communication to have a defamatory meaning about the plaintiff. See *Bindrim v. Mitchell*, 92 Cal. App. 3d 61, 155 Cal. Rptr. 29 (1979). There also can be liability when only a few people possess the expert knowledge needed to take a defamatory meaning from what was published, as when a book or article (or portions of it) is erroneously attributed to a professional author and it contains major errors that only experts in the same field would notice, causing them to believe that the named author is incompetent. See *Ben-Oliel v. Press Publishing Co.*, 251 N.Y. 250, 167 N.E. 432 (1929).

B. REFERENCE TO PLAINTIFF

1. DEFAMATION'S APPLICATION TO PLAINTIFF

A statement with a defamatory meaning cannot harm a person's reputation unless the statement is understood to refer or pertain to that person. Accordingly, it is a requirement of liability that the defamatory communication be "of and concerning" the plaintiff. The communication must reasonably have been understood to refer to the plaintiff. It is sufficient if any recipient of the communication reasonably so understood it. However, if most recipients did not, this can shed doubt on whether it was reasonable for anyone to understand the communication as defaming the plaintiff. See Rest. 2d Torts § 564, comment *b*. As discussed in the previous section, the understanding that the communication pertains to the plaintiff can arise from recipients' knowledge of extrinsic facts (information outside what is stated or implied within the communication). The court decides whether the communication could reasonably have been understood to refer to the plaintiff in its defamatory meaning. If so, the trier of fact decides whether the communication actually was so understood. See *Coats v. News Corp.*, 355 Mo. 778, 197 S.W.2d 958 (1946); Rest. 2d Torts § 614, comment *b*.

Decisions on these questions usually depend upon the particular facts of the case unless "group defamation" is involved. (That is discussed below.) There are some fact patterns that appear in a considerable number of cases. One is that the defendant's statement carries a defamatory meaning about a person who is described in a certain way and both the plaintiff and another person fit that description. For example, in *Helmicks v. Stevlingson*, 212 Wis. 314, 250 N.W. 402 (1933), the defendant had said that a bank was "loaned to death by [a] former cashier." The plaintiff had been the cashier when the bank closed, but there were other former cashiers. The court held 4–3 that the defendant's demurrer should have been sustained because the statement did not sufficiently identify the plaintiff as the person referred to. In another recurring fact pattern, the defamatory statement refers to a named individual, but there is more than one person with the same name in the area where the statement is published. With this the tendency is to allow the defamation action to proceed, so the defendant can be liable to a person other than the individual the defendant intended to refer to. *E.g., Washington Post Co. v. Kennedy*, 55 App. D.C. 162, 3 F.2d 207 (1925).

In other cases, the content of the communication and extrinsic facts make it reasonable to understand the communication as referring to the plaintiff alone, but other persons fit the reference. For example, in *Davis v. Macon Telegraph Publishing Co.*, 93 Ga. App. 633, 92 S.E.2d 619 (1956), a newspaper had reported the arrest of "Wayman Davis. . .and his brother." The plaintiff was the only one of Wayman Davis' brothers who lived or ever had lived in the county where the newspaper was published and the purported arrest occurred. However, there were three other brothers. They resided out of state and were there at the time. The court allowed the action to proceed. A different fact pattern is presented when the plaintiff claims to have been defamed because the plaintiff's photograph was used to illustrate a news or magazine article, or an advertisement, which did not mention or refer to the plaintiff. In some, the plaintiff's photograph was mistakenly or misleadingly used to illustrate a report about a crime or criminal, but the text correctly identified the criminal. In at least the latter type of case, the plaintiff has usually been held to have a defamation action against the publisher. *E.g., Petransky v. Repository Printing Co.*, 51 Ohio App. 306, 200 N.E.

647 (1935); *James v. Fort Worth Telegram Co.*, 117 S.W. 1028 (Tex. Civ. App. 1909). *Cf. Peck v. Tribune Co.*, 214 U.S. 185 (1909) (plaintiff's picture in advertisement for whisky).

A more general problem presented by some cases is whether a communication could be found to have made any defamatory reference to the plaintiff when any adverse reflection on the plaintiff is, at most, a debatable inference from what was communicated and extrinsic facts. For example, in *Cassidy v. Daily Mirror Newspaper, Ltd.* (discussed above at pp. 357–358), was the report of Mr. Corrigan's engagement to Miss ___ capable, on a reasonable interpretation, of defaming Mrs. Corrigan? (The court decided it was.) Does a statement about a teenager's criminal activity and use of heroin defame his parents? (The court in *Beresky v. Teschner*, 64 Ill. App. 3d 848, 381 N.E.2d 979 (1978), decided that this could not be understood to refer to the parents.) Does a news report that a man is confined in a county jail without legal authority defame the county sheriff, who had some responsibility for the jail? (In *Boone v. Herald News Co.*, 27 Tex. Civ. App. 546, 66 S.W. 313 (1901), the jury decided it did not.)

In *New York Times Co. v. Sullivan*, 376 U.S. 254 (1964), the doubtful interpretation of the *New York Times* advertisement that prevailed in the Alabama state courts—it was defamation of the plaintiff because the advertisement criticized actions of the police in Montgomery and the plaintiff was the city commissioner responsible for supervision of the police department—undoubtedly was a factor in the

Supreme Court's decision to grant certiorari and consider the *Times'* First Amendment arguments. The court held it to be a violation of the First Amendment to impose liability to a government official for an otherwise impersonal criticism of government operations on the premise that the public was aware that an agency was under the official's direction and control and might criticize the official for deficiencies in the agency's performance.

2. GROUP DEFAMATION

So-called "group defamation" is treated distinctly from other cases in which there is an issue about applying the requirement that the defamatory statement refer to the plaintiff (or be "of and concerning" the plaintiff). A group defamation case is one in which the defamatory statement refers to all members of a group of persons. For example, "All of the jurors in the case accepted bribes." Or to some members of a group without identification of the individuals the defamatory allegation applies to. For example, "Some of the jurors in the case took bribes," or "one juror was bribed to prevent a conviction."

Whether a member of the group referred to can maintain a defamation action depends upon whether the court will rule that the statement can be understood to refer to the plaintiff individually. Rest. 2d Torts § 564A. That in turn depends upon the size of the group and the proportion of the whole group the defamatory allegation applies to (all, most, some, few, or one). A defamation action might be allowed when the statement means that one of three persons committed a theft, but not when it means that some person in a group of twenty committed a theft. *Blaser v. Krattiger*, 99 Or. 392, 195 P. 359 (1921). *Cf. Arcand v. Evening Call Publishing Co.*, 567 F.2d 1163 (1st Cir. 1977) (allegation of misconduct by one member of twenty-one member police department). Under the Restatement and a number of cases, an important consideration is whether the statement attached "a high degree of suspicion" to each member of the group. Rest. 2d Torts § 564A, comment *c*. In some cases, courts have rejected actions when only some members of the group (not all) were accused. *E.g.*, *Bull v. Collins*, 54 S.W.2d 870 (Tex. Civ. App. 1932). But that is not the prevailing view today.

The best-known group defamation case is *Neiman-Marcus v. Lait*, 13 F.R.D. 311 (S.D.N.Y. 1952). The book *U.S.A. Confidential* alleged that some models and an unspecified number of the saleswomen of the Neiman-Marcus store in Dallas were "call girls" and that most of the male sales staff were homosexuals. At the time there were nine models, twenty-five salesmen and 382 saleswomen. The court held that the plaintiff salesmen could maintain an action, as suspicion attached to all of them, but the saleswomen constituted too large a group for the public to interpret the book's statement as a reference to any individual. The defendants apparently conceded that the models could sue. In *Fawcett Publications, Inc. v. Morris*, 377 P.2d 42 (Okla. 1962), the court upheld a large award of damages to a member of a football team with sixty to seventy members when a magazine had reported that members of the team were given an illegal drug. The court preferred the criterion of the "intensity of the suspicion cast upon the plaintiff" to a flat rule barring actions when the group is "large." Nevertheless, it is unlikely that an action can succeed when there is defamation of a group much larger than the twenty-five salesmen in *Neiman-Marcus v. Lait.*

Because of the size of the groups involved, and the implausibility of understanding the statements to apply to each person in the group, there is no individual or class action for defamatory criticism of a professional or occupational group. *Thomas v. Jacksonville Television, Inc.*, 699 So. 2d 800 (Fla. App. 1997) (Florida commercial net fishermen); *McCullough v. Cities Service Co.*, 676 P.2d 833 (Okla. 1984) (doctors of osteopathy). Or for defamatory disparagement of an ethnic or religious group. *Puerto Rican Legal Defense Fund v. Grace*, 9 Media L. Rptr. 1514 (N.Y. Sup. Ct. 1983) (Puerto Ricans living in New York); *Khalid Abdullah Tariq Al Mansour Faissal Fahd Al Talal v. Fanning*, 506 F. Supp. 186 (N.D. Cal. 1980) (Moslems).

3. FICTION, SATIRE, DOCUDRAMAS

A written or dramatic work, presented to the public as a work of fiction with characters that are fictional (or deceased), usually cannot be grounds for a defamation action. But sometimes it can, when a character in the work can be identified with the plaintiff and it is reasonable to interpret the work as a factual defamatory portrayal of the plaintiff's conduct or character. This may be reasonable because of the work's plot and the description of the character. Possibly also because of the character's name. Explicit identification of the work as fictional (*e.g.*, as a novel), or a disclaimer that it is not intended as a portrayal of any actual person, bears on whether it is reasonable to interpret the work as a factual portrayal of the plaintiff, but it is not conclusive. See Rest. 2d Torts § 564, comment *d*.

An example is *Corrigan v. Bobbs-Merrill Co.*, 228 N.Y. 58, 126 N.E. 260 (1920). The defendant published a sensational novel, one of whose chapters brought the hero into New York City's Jefferson Market Court and the courtroom of an unsavory magistrate named Cornigan. The plaintiff was a magistrate named Corrigan who sat in the Jefferson Market Court. While finding errors requiring a new trial, the court generally sustained the plaintiff's libel action. The opinion noted the literary tradition of fictional works depicting as imaginary events "drawn or distorted from real life." The most prominent case of recent decades is *Bindrim v. Mitchell*, 92 Cal. App. 3d 61, 155 Cal. Rptr. 29 (1979). The court held, over a strong dissent, that the author and publisher of a novel could be liable because of the portrayal of a character who, like the plaintiff, was a practitioner of "nude marathon therapy." In a number of important respects the novel's character differed from the plaintiff, but the narrative of the novel paralleled an actual nude therapy session conducted by the plaintiff and some witnesses identified the character with the plaintiff.

It is insufficient for liability that readers or viewers of a story recognize that a character in it is based on the plaintiff. There must be something in the content of the story that would cause a reasonable reader or viewer to understand the character as a factual portrayal of the plaintiff's conduct. (This is accepted in the majority opinion in *Bindrim v. Mitchell*.) The Restatement formulation is that it must be reasonable for the readers or audience of the work "to understand that a particular character is intended to portray [the plaintiff]." Rest. 2d Torts § 564, comment *d*.

This usually, but not inevitably, will protect against liability for a satire of the plaintiff or satire that uses the plaintiff's name. The typical, or at least reasonable, reader or viewer will understand from the contents of the work or where it is published (as in a comedy magazine or comedy television show) that it is not intended as a factual portrayal of the plaintiff. See *Frank v. National Broadcasting Co., Inc.*, 119 A.D.2d 252, 506 N.Y.S.2d 869 (1986); *New Times, Inc. v. Isaacks*, 146 S.W.3d 144 (Tex. 2004). In a notable case, the defendants avoided liability (barely) on the ground that the plot of the magazine story the plaintiff complained of was such a fantasy that it could not reasonably be understood as describing actual facts about her. *Pring v. Penthouse International, Ltd.*, 695 F.2d 438 (10th Cir. 1982).

In contrast, when the work is a "docudrama," it is understood as a portrayal of actual persons. It contains true facts about them, but also invented dialogue and plot segments. It may be reasonable for viewers to believe the invented elements are factual, when there is little to identify to viewers the portions of the docudrama that are not historic fact. However, in *Partington v. Bugliosi*, 56 F.3d 1147, 1155 (9th Cir. 1995), the court said that viewers "would be sufficiently familiar with this genre to avoid assuming that all statements within them represent assertions of verifiable fact. . . .[M]ost of them are aware by now that parts of such programs are more fiction than fact."

C. LIBEL AND SLANDER

1. INTRODUCTION

The existence of two defamation torts—libel and slander—is a product of English legal history. They have different origins. Briefly stated, slander, in the sense of making a false accusation against another, was an offense under ecclesiastical law. It could be oral or written. Church courts did not award damages. Beginning in the sixteenth century, common law courts began to entertain actions seeking damages for slander. These were brought as actions on the case. Actions on the case arose from legally wrongful conduct that caused specified damage. Courts recognized some exceptions to the requirement that damage be specifically alleged and proved, so there were categories of slander actionable "per se."

Libel originated as a crime. For some time, libel prosecutions were conducted in the Court of Star Chamber, which was principally concerned with written material of a seditious (political) nature. Truth was not a defense. The court could order a defamer to pay damages. This encouraged defamed persons to seek redress in the Star Chamber. Proof of actual damage was not required. With the abolition of the Court of Star Chamber, the common law courts acquired jurisdiction over criminal and civil libel proceedings. They continued to apply the different rules of liability for libel and slander, but with the distinction that written defamation gave rise to a libel action and oral defamation gave rise to a slander action. Truth became a defense to both. See Rest. 2d Torts § 568, comment *b*; Lovell, The "Reception" of Defamation By the Common Law, 15 Vand. L. Rev. 1051 (1962).

For the most part, libel and slander now have common rules of liability. In many contexts it is accurate to refer to liability for defamation without specifying libel or slander. The principal importance of the distinction between libel and slander is that a slander action requires the plaintiff to plead and prove special damage, unless the alleged slander is "slander per se"; a libel action does not require this (under the common law, damage is presumed), unless the "libel per quod" doctrine operates. (This is discussed later.)

2. WHETHER DEFAMATION IS LIBEL OR SLANDER

A defamation action can potentially arise from any human creation or conduct that conveys a defamatory meaning about a person, whether intended or not. In most actions for defamation, it is clear whether the action should be for libel or slander. Written or pictorial defamation is libel. Oral communication is usually slander, but there may be a libel action when defamatory written material is read aloud or an oral communication is intended to be and is reduced to writing. See Rest. 2d Torts § 568, comments *d–f*. Also, as discussed below, a broadcast or recording may be treated as libel even though the defamatory content is in the sound.

Defamatory gestures and sign language (formal and informal) are regarded as slander, as these are transitory communications similar to the spoken word. See Rest. 2d Torts § 568, comment *d*. Other conduct conveying a defamatory meaning might be classified as either slander or libel. A person may be defamed by conduct that is not intended to communicate anything, if it is witnessed by someone other than the plaintiff—for example, putting the plaintiff in handcuffs or a ward for the insane. A dishonored check might imply a credit risk or dishonesty. When police or security personnel lead a person out of a retail store, bystanders are likely to think that the person had attempted a theft or fraud. See Annot., 46 A.L.R.4th 403.

New methods of communication emerging in the nineteenth and twentieth century required decisions on whether the cause of action for defamatory content was libel or slander. For motion pictures it was libel, even if the defamation was in the sound. Film was similar to writing in that it was permanently recorded and had a visual component. See Annot., 99 A.L.R. 878. Probably other defamation involving sound recordings is libel also. There is more division about the classification of radio and television broadcasts. A live radio broadcast is a purely oral communication, and the number of people who hear or read a defamatory communication is usually irrelevant to whether it is libel or slander. (A defamatory oral statement to a large crowd is slander. A defamatory letter sent to one person is libel.) So a radio broadcast could be classified as slander. However, the prevailing view is that the action for a defamatory statement in a radio or television broadcast is libel. *E.g.*, *Matherson v. Marchello*, 100 A.D.2d 233, 473 N.Y.S.2d 998 (1984). This is the position of Rest. 2d Torts § 568A. Under some state statutes, it is slander. Whether defamatory oral communication transmitted through the Internet would be treated as a broadcast, even if it did not did reach a large audience, is an open question.

3. PER SE CATEGORIES

An action for slander requires the plaintiff to plead and prove "special damage" unless the defamatory meaning of what was communicated by the defendant fits into one of four categories of "slander per se." Collectively the "per se" slanders may be viewed as types of slander especially likely to cause harm to reputation, but that is not the rationale for their existence. They are the results of the evolution of slander centuries ago. Slander that is not slander per se is traditionally labelled "slander per quod." In common law pleading, "per quod" introduced specifications of damage.

Imputations of crime. The oldest category of slander per se consists of statements imputing the commission of a crime. The crime does not have to be identified in precise or legally correct terms. But general imputations of criminality or involvement in criminal activity, such as an imputation that the plaintiff has been involved in organized crime, are not slander per se. *Privitera v. Town of Phelps*, 79 A.D.2d 1, 435 N.Y.S.2d 402 (1981).

Courts have developed rules to limit this category of slander per se to imputations of more serious crimes or imputations that are likely to be injurious to reputation. These rules vary from state to state, but the operative limits tend to be the level of the crime in the state's criminal law, the punishment for the crime, or whether it is a crime of "moral turpitude." The Restatement rule is that an imputation of crime is slander per se if the offense imputed would, if committed in the place of publication, be punished by imprisonment or "regarded by public opinion as involving moral turpitude." Rest. 2d Torts § 571.

Imputations of loathsome disease. There are numerous diseases that might cause a person to be excluded from society, if it is believed that the person has the disease. But this category of slander per se has been limited to a small number of diseases identified several centuries ago: venereal diseases, leprosy and "the plague." Rest. 2d Torts § 572 leaves open the possibility of extension to imputations of some other "loathsome and communicable disease." The court in a recent case held (with obvious reluctance to use the term "loathsome") that an imputation of HIV infection is a per se slander because it can cause societal disapproval and shunning. *Nolan v. State*, 158 A.D.3d 186, 69 N.Y.S.3d 277 (2018). The imputation must be having the disease at present, not in the past. Diseases that result in death or recovery within a short time are not included. Rest. 2d Torts § 572, comments *c–d*.

Imputations concerning a person's business, trade, profession or office. An imputation of misconduct in or unfitness for the plaintiff's business, trade, profession or office is an important category of slander per se. It includes general disparagement of a person's fitness to practice a profession or trade, such as statements that a physician is incompetent or a "quack," as well as allegations of specific misconduct. It also includes imputations of insolvency, or potential insolvency, that apply to the plaintiff's business. See Rest. 2d Torts § 573, comment *e*.

The slanderous words must be spoken "in relation to" (or "with reference to") the plaintiff's business, trade, profession or office, or at least impute conduct or character incompatible with it. It is not sufficient to allege that the plaintiff was or would be harmed in the plaintiff's business or profession. *Liberman v. Gelstein*, 80 N.Y.2d 429, 605 N.E.2d 344 (1992). For example, in *Harris v. Hirsh*, 228 A.D.2d 206, 643 N.Y.S.2d 556 (1996), a supervisor's statement that a train crew dispatcher took drugs was not slander per se because it was not "specifically related" to the plaintiff's status as a crew dispatcher. A statement meaning that the plaintiff is a drunkard is not slander per se unless it is understood to mean that the plaintiff is intoxicated while working. Compare *Weidberg v. La Guardia*, 170 Misc. 374, 10 N.Y.S.2d 445 (Sup. Ct. 1939) (mayor calling lawyer "a bum in a gin mill"), with *Swan v. Thompson*, 124 Cal. 193, 56 P. 878 (1899) (master mariner said to be in habit of getting drunk). A statement that a clergyman has committed adultery might be slander per se, on the basis of moral unfitness for the office, but not a statement that a physician has committed adultery. See *Jones v. Jones*, [1916] 2 A.C. 481 (H.L.); Rest. 2d Torts § 573, comments *c*, *e*.

Imputation of unchastity or other sexual misconduct. Imputations of unchastity became a category of slander per se in the nineteenth century. Strictly speaking, unchastity is to have sexual intercourse outside marriage, but other sexual conduct has been included. See *Minyard Food Stores, Inc. v. Goodman*, 50 S.W.3d 131 (Tex. App. 2001), rev'd, 80 S.W.3d 573 (Tex. 2002). This imputation was a per se slander only for females, as unchastity was thought to be a social disgrace for a woman but not for a man. The Restatement, acknowledging but not endorsing the rule that it is slander per se to impute unchastity to a woman, describes the category as slander "that imputes serious sexual misconduct." Rest. 2d Torts § 574.

In view of the greatly altered societal attitudes about extramarital sex and present strength of gender equality as a legal policy, it is doubtful that either the gender differentiation or the proposition that an imputation of consensual sexual conduct outside marriage is generally slander per se is valid law today. In some cases it has been held that an imputation of male homosexuality is a per se slander. *E.g.*, *Nazeri v. Missouri Valley College*, 860 S.W.2d 303 (Mo. 1993). Altered societal attitudes and legal changes concerning homosexual conduct may now lead courts to rule that this is not slander per se, as in *Yonaty v. Mincolla*, 97 A.D.3d 141, 945 N.Y.S.2d 774 (2012).

4. LIBEL PER QUOD

When libel and slander became distinct torts in English law, it became clear that all libel was actionable without pleading and proving special damage. But in the United States, libel cases in many jurisdictions required that special damage be pleaded and proved in certain circumstances. This became known as the "libel per quod" doctrine.

The principal libel per quod rule was that statements that were defamatory only by reference to extrinsic facts required special damage for liability. Some courts also developed a rule that statements which were not necessarily defamatory—they might be construed in a non-defamatory sense—required special damage. There was division on whether a statement that would otherwise be libel per quod was to be classified as libel per se (libel actionable without special damage) when the defamatory meaning fit one of the four slander per se categories.

The libel per quod doctrine denied redress to some people who were libelled, but it had the advantage of protecting from liability defendants who were unaware that their statements would have a defamatory connotation. That advantage has been eroded by the Supreme Court's prohibition of liability without fault in *Gertz v. Robert Welch, Inc.*, 418 U.S. 323 (1974) (at least when the statement involved a "matter of public concern"). See Rest. 2d Torts § 569, comment *b*.

The Restatement position is that all libel is actionable without special damage. Rest. 2d Torts § 569. Some courts have abandoned their previous adherence to the libel per quod doctrine, but it remains valid in a considerable number of states. See Sack, *Defamation* § 2:8.3 (5th ed. 2017).

5. SPECIAL DAMAGE, PRESUMED DAMAGE, ACTUAL DAMAGE

When libel or slander is actionable "per se," no pleading and proof of special damage or actual damage is required. Harm to the plaintiff's reputation is presumed, and damages can be awarded without evidence showing any specific harm. Damages can also be awarded for any actual harm indicated by the evidence, including financial loss and emotional distress. See Rest. 2d Torts § 621.

When libel or slander is actionable "per quod," special damage must be pleaded and proved. The definition of special damage is narrow. It must be a loss caused by harm to reputation attributable to the defendant's defamatory communication. And it must be loss of a "pecuniary" or economic nature. Damage to reputation as such, or an adverse change in the attitude of other people toward the plaintiff, is not special damage. Neither is the plaintiff's emotional suffering or illness because of worry about the defamation. See Rest. 2d Torts § 575, comments *b–c*; *Tacket v. Delco Remy Division of General Motors Corp.*, 937 F.2d 1201 (7th Cir. 1991).

Loss of employment and loss of trade are classic examples of special damage. However, courts traditionally have been strict in requirements of pleading and proof. An action may fail because the plaintiff has not identified specific economic losses and shown how they were caused by the defendant's defamatory falsehood. In this respect, defamation actionable with special damage resembles injurious falsehood. See *Erick Bowman Remedy Co. v. Jensen Salsbery Laboratories*, 17 F.2d 255 (8th Cir. 1926).

Special damage is a liability requirement, not a limitation on what is recoverable when there is liability. When special damage is proved, damages for other consequences of defamation can be recovered. These include damages for injury to reputation generally and emotional distress. Rest. 2d Torts § 575, comment *a*, § 621, comment *a*. (In the Restatement, special damage is called "special harm.")

Some courts have narrowed the distinction between "per se" and "per quod" defamation by requiring in all cases proof of some actual harm to reputation, or at least actual harm to some type. See Annot., 36 A.L.R.4th 807. Under current constitutional doctrine only damages for "actual injury," not presumed and punitive damages, may be awarded when the defamatory statement involved a matter of public concern and the defendant did not have knowledge of or reckless disregard for its falsity. *Gertz v. Robert Welch, Inc.*, 418 U.S. 323 (1974), as interpreted in *Dun & Bradstreet, Inc. v. Greenmoss Builders, Inc.*, 472 U.S. 749 (1985).

There is considerable variation in state law on how damages are to be assessed in a defamation case and what evidence is admissible for purposes of the assessment. This is primarily due to variations in state case law, but also to some extent statutory enactments. A majority of states have adopted statutes concerning retraction. A retraction of a defamatory statement does not prevent liability, but under the statutes the defendant's timely retraction or the plaintiff's failure to properly demand a retraction can limit the damages that are awarded. Most of the statutes protect only traditional print and broadcast media, or only newspapers and periodicals, rather than defamation defendants generally. See Sack, *Defamation* § 11:2 (5th ed. 2017).

D. PUBLICATION

1. PUBLICATION REQUIREMENT

Publication is a basic requirement of liability for defamation. In defamation law, publication means communication by the defendant to a person other than the plaintiff (the person who is defamed). It does not mean printing or mass communication. There is no publication if no one other than the defendant or the plaintiff sees or hears the defamatory matter.

The rationale of the publication requirement is that a person's reputation can be damaged by defamation only if it is communicated to a third party. See Rest. 2d Torts § 577, comment *b*.

The publication requirement is usually satisfied in libel and slander cases by the defendant's intentional communication of the defamatory matter to someone other than the plaintiff. If the defamatory matter was seen or heard by a third person, but the defendant intended to communicate only with the plaintiff or to no one (as when the statement defaming the plaintiff was placed in the defendant's files), the parties are likely to contest whether publication occurred. Putting aside cases in which the plaintiff caused the defamatory matter to be communicated to the third person, whether publication is found usually has depended on whether or not the defendant anticipated or reasonably should have anticipated the likelihood of a third person reading or hearing the defamatory communication. See Annot., 92 A.L.R.2d 219. If the defendant mailed to the plaintiff a letter with defamatory content, publication would be found if the defendant had reason to anticipate the letter being opened and read by someone else, perhaps because it was sent to the plaintiff's business office, but not if the defendant reasonably assumed the letter would be read only by the plaintiff, as is typical when a letter in a sealed envelope is addressed to the plaintiff at the plaintiff's home address. Compare *Rumney v. Worthley*, 186 Mass. 144, 71 N.E. 316 (1904), with *Weidman v. Ketcham*, 278 N.Y. 129, 15 N.E.2d 426 (1938). If the defendant had a conversation with the plaintiff in person or over the telephone, publication may be found if the defendant had reason to anticipate the conversation being overheard, but not if this was unlikely. Compare *McNichol v. Grandy*, [1931] S.C.R. 696, [1932] 1 D.L.R. 225, with *Smith v. Jones*, 335 So. 2d 896 (Miss. 1976).

The Restatement applies a negligence standard to cases of unintentional publication. Rest. 2d Torts § 577. A defendant can be liable if the defendant created an unreasonable risk that the defamatory matter would be communicated to a third person. Rest. 2d Torts § 577, comment *k*. In *Morrow v. II Morrow, Inc.*, 139 Or. App. 212, 911 P.2d 964 (1996), the defendants avoided liability for a defamatory file memo that the author had deleted from his computer, without realizing it had been saved on a network, because negligence could not be found. Negligence might be found if the defendant mistakenly communicated with a third person when intending to communicate with the plaintiff. Rest. 2d Torts § 577, comment *l*.

Publication by plaintiff. When a defendant has communicated defamatory matter to the plaintiff and the plaintiff then repeats it or shows it to a third person, the defendant is usually not responsible for publication to the third person. A recognized exception is when the defendant sends a document to the plaintiff with knowledge that the plaintiff will need to show it to a third person because the plaintiff cannot read it. There thus is publication when the defendant sent a defamatory document to the plaintiff with knowledge that the plaintiff is illiterate or blind, or will need to have the document translated. See Rest. 2d Torts § 577, ills. 10–11.

A debatable extension of this is to find publication by the defendant when the defendant had reason to know the plaintiff would need to show or repeat the defamation to a third person for some other reason. In a case where the defendant sent a fourteen-year-old boy a letter accusing him of a break-in and theft, the court held that the defendant was subject to liability because he must have foreseen that the boy would necessarily show the letter to a family member because of the fear it would cause. *Hedgpeth v. Coleman*, 183 N.C. 309, 111 S.E. 517 (1922). Defendants have been held liable in some other instances of "compelled self-publication" by plaintiffs. These include cases of former employees of the defendant who allegedly were compelled, when seeking new employment, to repeat the defendant's defamatory explanation of why the employee was discharged. A number of state supreme courts have, however, rejected such claims, in part for policy reasons. Liability would discourage employers from communicating to employees the reasons for termination of employment, or honest communication about an employee's performance, while encouraging former employees to repeat the defamation, or even to create a tort action. *E.g.*, *Exxon Mobil Corp. v. Rincones*, 520 S.W.3d 572 (Tex. 2017). See Annot., 62 A.L.R.4th 616.

When defamatory meaning is not understood. It is apparently accepted, on the basis of a few relevant cases, that there is no publication if the only third person who heard or saw the defamatory words did not understand the language in which the words were spoken or written. *Economopoulos v. A.G. Pollard Co.*, 218 Mass. 294, 105 N.E. 896 (1914); Rest. 2d Torts § 577, comment *d*. It has also been held that there was no publication when the words were spoken in the presence of children who were too young to understand the defamatory expression. *Sullivan v. Sullivan*, 48 Ill. App. 435 (1892). Or to a person who could understand the defamatory meaning but did not know to whom it referred. *Weidman v. Ketcham*, 278 N.Y. 129, 15 N.E.2d 426 (1938). This is questionable. The plaintiff's reputation could be damaged by repetition of the words to someone who did understand their defamatory significance.

Repetition. Someone else's repetition of the defendant's defamatory communication is not another publication by the defendant, unless it is directed or intended by the defendant. The defendant can, however, be held liable for harm caused by repetition on the ground that this is harm resulting from the defendant's earlier publication of the defamatory matter. Formerly a defendant was responsible only for the defendant's own publication and that of the defendant's agents, but the modern tendency is to extend liability to harm caused by repetition that was reasonably to be expected. That harm may fulfill the special damage requirement in cases where liability requires pleading and proof of special damage. See Rest. 2d Torts § 576. The standard of repetition "reasonably to be expected" may be applied strictly, as in *Geraci v. Probst*, 15

N.Y.3d 336, 938 N.E.2d 917 (2010), or liberally to include repetition that is reasonably foreseeable, as in *Tunca v. Painter*, 965 N.E.2d 1237 (Ill. App. 2012).

2. RESPONSIBILITY FOR PUBLICATION

A communications carrier or Internet service that only provides the means for transmission of messages is not a publisher. It is thus not liable for the transmission or delivery of defamatory messages in its system. *Anderson v. New York Telephone Co.*, 35 N.Y.2d 746, 320 N.E.2d 647 (1974) (telephone); *Lunney v. Prodigy Services Co.*, 94 N.Y.2d 242, 723 N.E.2d 539 (1999) (Internet). Otherwise, anyone who actively participates in the communication of defamatory content is considered to have published it (if it reaches a party other than the plaintiff and defendant) and is potentially liable. This includes distributors such as libraries, sellers of print and visual media, broadcasters, printers, and carriers that physically deliver material with defamatory content. (As discussed below, some have a degree of protection from liability as "secondary publishers" or "secondary distributors.") See Rest. 2d Torts § 581. Anyone who repeats the defamatory statement of someone else is also a publisher. Rest. 2d Torts § 578.

Developments in computer technology and usage have generated new questions about responsibility for defamatory communications. Most of the questions have no definitive answers to date. For example, does an Internet service provider's creation of a "news group" or "chat room" or "electronic bulletin board" make it the publisher of messages posted there? (The court in *Lunney v. Prodigy Services Co.*, *supra*, held that the provider was not a publisher on the facts of the case.) Is a defendant responsible for publication if it can remove material from view on the Internet, but does not do so after being notified that it is defamatory? Is it a publisher if it screens content or removes some content? Does a search engine publish the contents of what it directs the user to? Does the creator of a web page with hyperlinks to an article publish the defamation in the article? (No, according to the court in *Life Designs Ranch, Inc. v. Sommer*, 191 Wash. App. 320, 364 P.3d 129 (2015).)

A federal statute enacted in 1996 preempts some of these questions. Communications Decency Act, 47 U.S.C. § 230. The statute was intended to protect providers of computer services and other "interactive" media from being treated as publishers, and thus subject to liability, on account of efforts to block or remove "objectionable" online material. It also was intended to promote development of interactive media and the Internet by limiting the potential for liability. 47 U.S.C. § 230(b). The statute specifies that "No provider or user of an interactive computer service shall be treated as the publisher or speaker of any information provided by another information content provider." 47 U.S.C. § 230(c). This legislation has been interpreted to immunize computer service providers from tort liability for transmitting or failing to remove or screen material posted by a third party, even when the provider had been notified of the presence of the material and its defamatory nature. See *Zeran v. America Online,*

Inc., 129 F.3d 327 (4th Cir. 1997); *Blumenthal v. Drudge*, 992 F. Supp. 44 (D.D.C. 1998). The immunity potentially extends to anyone who maintains a web site in which others can post comments or other material. See *Collins v. Purdue University*, 703 F. Supp. 2d 862 (N.D. Ill. 2010). In that respect the Communications Decency Act promotes freedom of speech rather than censorship.

Responsibility for defamation on premises. A person in control of premises (building or land) may be held responsible for publication of defamation that someone else has posted on or in the premises. There is no liability merely because the defamation was posted. Liability arises from the continued presence of the defamation after its presence is known to the defendant and the defendant could have removed it. See Rest. 2d Torts § 577, comment *p*. The main rationales of the relevant cases are that the proprietor of the premises is responsible for republication of a libel when the proprietor knowingly allows it to remain after a reasonable opportunity to remove it. *Hellar v. Bianco*, 111 Cal. App. 2d 424, 244 P.2d 757 (1952). Or that it can be found that the proprietor has ratified or adopted the posted item's content if it has not been removed. *Tacket v. General Motors Corp.*, 836 F.2d 1042 (7th Cir. 1987). In *Scott v. Hull*, 22 Ohio App. 2d 141, 259 N.E.2d 160 (1970), the court decided that liability required some positive act by the defendant. Failure to remove defamatory graffiti, even after a demand for its removal, was not actionable.

Secondary publishers (secondary distributors). "Secondary publishers," or "secondary distributors," are those who deliver or distribute defamatory material produced by others. Typical secondary publishers are carriers, libraries and vendors of books, newspapers, magazines, films and art. It is usually impractical for such businesses to examine what they stock or distribute for defamatory content. Liability, or the risk of liability, could deter them from operating. The common law developed a doctrine that protected secondary publishers from responsibility for communication of defamation under certain conditions. The Restatement rule is that "one who only delivers or transmits defamatory matter published by a third person is subject to liability if. . .he knows or has reason of its defamatory character." Rest. 2d Torts § 581(1). A secondary publisher who distributes or transmits defamatory material, but does not know or have reason to know of its defamatory character, is not liable.

The Restatement does not specify who has the burden of proof on whether the defendant had "reason to know of its defamatory character" or define what that is. However, the Restatement's comments indicate that reason to know of an item's defamatory character might be found in the defendant's knowledge that an author, publisher, newspaper or magazine had a history of publishing "scandalous" items. Rest. 2d Torts § 581, comments *d–e*. According to *Dworkin v. Hustler Magazine, Inc.*, 611 F. Supp. 781 (D. Wyo. 1985), "scandalous" is to be read as "defamatory." Distributors have no general duty to examine items for defamatory content before making them available, to avoid liability.

Printers and those who repeat or republish defamatory matter created by others are not secondary publishers, so they do not have this protection from liability. The law is divided on whether a station that carries a broadcast coming from a network or another station is a secondary publisher. Under the Restatement, radio and television broadcasting is primary publication, not secondary. Rest. 2d Torts § 581(2). Both primary and secondary publishers are now protected to some extent by the constitutional doctrine of no liability without fault. (See pp. 430–432.)

Single and multiple publication. Under English common law, each communication of defamatory material is a publication that gives rise to a separate cause of action. In *Duke of Brunswick and Luneberg v. Harmer*, (1849) 14 Q.B. 185, 117 Eng. Rep. 75, the defendant's recent sale of a copy of a newspaper he had published seventeen years earlier was a publication that allowed the plaintiff to bring a libel action. It was not barred by the six-year statute of limitations.

In most American states, the "multiple publication rule" has, by judicial decision or statute, been replaced by the "single publication rule." Under the single publication rule, there is only one cause of action against a defendant for any single edition of a book, newspaper or journal. There is also one cause of action for a single exhibition of a film or broadcast, or when the same communication is heard by two or more persons. See *Shirley v. Bozanich*, 31 Cal. 4th 1230, 80 P.3d 676 (2003). The rule is set forth in Rest. 2d Torts § 577A.

The principal effects of the single publication rule are to prevent a multiplicity of lawsuits against a defendant for the same defamatory material and to have the statute of limitations run from the defendant's original publication of the defamatory item, not from the latest communication or delivery of a copy. As a separate action can be brought for each edition of a work, the plaintiff may contend that the defendant published different editions because of some changes in content, or differences in format such as hardcover and paperback editions of books, or theatre and DVD editions of films. See Annot., 41 A.L.R.4th 541. There are now cases on application of the single publication rule to Internet publication. There is a new publication for statute of limitations purposes when there are modifications or additions to a web site that are related to the substance of the defamatory material, but not when the modifications or additions are unrelated to the defamation or do not alter its substance. See *Petro-Lubricant Testing Laboratories, Inc. v. Adelman*, 233 N.J. 236, 184 A.3d 457 (2018); *Woodhull v. Meinel*, 145 N.M. 533, 202 P.3d 126 (Ct. App. 2008).

Despite the wide adoption of the single publication rule, the trend is not to apply the rule to non-media publication. With non-media publication, the single publication rule is not needed to prevent numerous lawsuits about the same defamatory item. If the statute of limitations began to run when the defamation was first communicated to a third person, the limitation period could expire before the plaintiff learned of the defamation. See *Hukic v. Aurora Loan Services*, 588 F.3d 420 (7th Cir. 2009); *Musto v. Bell South Telecommunications Corp.*, 748 So. 2d 296 (Fla. App. 1999).

CHAPTER 22
COMMON LAW DEFENSES

A. TRUTH

In principle, there is liability only for publication of defamation that is false, not for publication of defamation that is true. Plaintiffs in defamation cases are typically expected to allege the falsehood of what the defendant communicated. However, the law of defamation has not required the plaintiff to prove falsity as an element of the plaintiff's cause of action. Truth has been a defense to be pleaded and proved by the defendant. Defendants have often chosen not to defend a defamation action on grounds of truth.

The defense of truth is traditionally called "justification." When proved, truth is a complete defense to liability. Apart from precedent, the main rationale for the truth defense in the common law is that a person whose conduct or character actually was what it was represented to be in the defendant's statement should not have an action. See *M'Pherson v. Daniels*, (1829) 10 B. & C. 263, 272, 109 Eng. Rep. 448, 451 (K.B.) (Littledale, J.).

Today the main rationales to bar liability for true but defamatory publications are freedom of expression and the value of true information to the public. The First Amendment guarantees of freedom of speech and freedom of the press probably exclude liability for the true defamation, even when published to cause harm to the plaintiff. The Supreme Court has held that when the defendant's statement was on a matter of public concern, the First Amendment requires the plaintiff to bear the burden of proving falsity. *Philadelphia Newspapers, Inc. v. Hepps*, 475 U.S. 767 (1986). This reallocates the burden of proof in many but not all defamation cases. It could also operate to exclude liability for statements that are true for First Amendment purposes even if not sufficiently true to prevent liability under the common law. (See pp. 438–441.)

What must be true. Although often stated in different terms, the basic common law principle is that to defeat a defamation action, the defamatory imputation or imputations (meanings) conveyed by what the defendant published must be true. Small discrepancies between the defendant's statement and what is found to be the truth do not defeat a truth defense if the substance of the defamatory meaning, or "sting" of the defamation, is true. But "A plea of truth as justification must be as broad as the alleged libel and must establish the truth of the precise charge therein made." *Crane v. New York World Telegram Corp.*, 308 N.Y. 470, 475, 126 N.E.2d 753, 757 (1955). A statement or illustration may contain a false defamatory meaning because of what can be inferred from it.

What must be proved true (or false, if the plaintiff has the burden of proof) depends upon what the plaintiff alleges to be the meaning(s) of the allegedly defamatory communication and which meaning(s) the trier of fact finds were actually conveyed. If the meaning conveyed is a specific act of misconduct, truth is the plaintiff's commission of that act, or an act that is substantially the same. If the meaning is a more general pattern of bad conduct, proof of a single instance of misconduct does not show truth. See *Wakley v. Cooke*, (1849) 4 Exch. 511, 154 Eng. Rep. 1316 ("libellous journalist" not justified by an instance of libel). Some statements, such as that the plaintiff is a "thief," might be interpreted to mean either one who has committed an act of misconduct or one who commits such acts repeatedly. It also might be interpreted to mean either being presently a thief or being a thief at some time, past or present. The trier of fact is to decide what meaning the statement conveyed and then whether it is true. See *Hughes v. Hughes*, 122 Cal. App. 4th 931, 19 Cal. Rptr. 3d 247 (2004).

The literal truth of a statement does not entitle the defendant to judgment if the statement communicated a defamatory meaning pertaining to the plaintiff that is not true. See *Duncan v. Record Publishing Co.*, 145 S.C. 196, 143 S.E. 31 (1927). A true statement may carry with it a false imputation because it is ambiguous, such as a statement that the plaintiff had worked in a house of prostitution. See *Crellin v. Thomas*, 122 Utah 122, 247 P.2d 264 (1952). A literally true statement may convey a false defamatory meaning because of what is omitted. For example, a statement about the plaintiff and another person might suggest an extramarital affair by omission of additional facts, as in *Memphis Publishing Co. v. Nichols*, 569 S.W.2d 412 (Tenn. 1978). The juxtaposition of two correct statements might be defamatory, as alleged in *Church of Scientology v. Flynn*, 744 F.2d 694 (9th Cir. 1984).

The defendant told an audience that his airplane was forced to make an emergency landing because of water in the fuel tanks shortly after he rejected a settlement offer from the plaintiff. This, of course, created the suspicion that the plaintiff was responsible for the water in the fuel tanks. A defamatory statement that is true about the person it is intended to refer to can convey a false defamatory meaning when it is reasonably understood to refer to someone else, as when both have the same name. *E.g.*, *Gasperini v. Manginelli*, 196 Misc. 547, 92 N.Y.S.2d 575 (Sup. Ct. 1949).

It is standard law that such statements as "It has been reported that. . .," "It is rumored that. . .," "He told me that. . .," and "X accused Y of. . .," cannot be "justified" by proof that there was such a report, rumor, statement or accusation. The substance of what was reported, rumored, stated or charged must be shown to be true. See *Stern v. Piper*, [1997] Q.B. 123 (C.A.); Rest. 2d Torts § 581A, comment *e*. Otherwise, people could be harmed by the spread of defamatory reports and gossip, with no redress, as long as the speaker did not endorse the truth of what was being repeated. But when the defendant has reported that the plaintiff is under investigation for something or a suspect, some cases have found truth in the report being correct concerning the existence of the investigation or the plaintiff's status as a suspect, even if the plaintiff was innocent. See *Global Relief Foundation, Inc. v. New York Times Co.*, 390 F.3d 973 (7th Cir. 2004); *Jewell v. NYP Holdings, Inc.*, 23 F. Supp. 2d 348 (S.D.N.Y. 1998).

Opinions in many cases have found truth when the defamatory publication was "true in substance" or "substantially true." This has allowed defendants in some of the cases to prevail when there was more than a minor difference in detail between the defendant's statements and what was shown to be true (such as the location of the plaintiff's misconduct or the amount the plaintiff stole). "Substantial truth" is sometimes explained to mean that the substance, gist or sting of the defamatory meaning is true. Or that the defendant's statement would have the same effect on the mind of the reader or listener (for the plaintiff's reputation) as what was proved to be true. See *Masson v. New Yorker Magazine, Inc.*, 501 U.S. 496, 516–517 (1991); *McKee v. Laurion*, 825 N.W.2d 725, 730 (Minn. 2013).

There are some cases in which courts found "substantial truth" when there was a considerable difference between the defendant's statement and what was shown to be the true and the difference must have been one that would affect the plaintiff's reputation in a different way. For example, in *Nanji v. National Geographic Society*, 403 F. Supp. 2d 425 (D. Md. 2005), *National Geographic* magazine had reported that the plaintiff was sentenced for raping a girl. He actually had not been convicted of rape or sexual assault, but evidence of this was a basis for conviction on other charges.

B. ABSOLUTE PRIVILEGES

Defamation law has a set of absolute privileges. When applicable they operate as a complete bar to liability, regardless of whether the defendant lacked reasonable grounds for the defamatory statement or published it with improper motives. The primary absolute privileges are related to the functions of government. There are distinct privileges corresponding to the three branches: legislative, executive and judicial. Additional absolute privileges or bars to liability operate outside governmental proceedings.

1. LEGISLATIVE AND EXECUTIVE PRIVILEGE

Legislative privilege. Statements made in the proceedings and official publications of the national and state legislatures, including committees, are absolutely privileged under common law, state constitutions and the federal constitution (the "Speech and Debate Clause" of Article I, section 6). As the constitutional privilege is somewhat broader than the common law privilege, it is constitutional law that is controlling in most cases.

Anything said by a legislator on the floor of the chamber or within a committee hearing is clearly privileged. What has been contentious in some cases is the extent to which the privilege attaches to a legislator's activities other than participation in the formal meetings of the legislature and its committees, especially communications with constituents and officials of the executive branch. In *Hutchison v. Proxmire*, 443 U.S. 111 (1979), the Supreme Court held that the Speech and Debate Clause did not protect a senator's newsletters, press releases, statements in interviews and telephone calls, even though they republished statements made on the floor of the Senate. Another issue is the application of absolute privilege to members of legislative staffs. Under *Gravel v. United States*, 408 U.S. 606 (1972), a legislator's assistant, acting on behalf of the legislator, has the privilege the legislator, acting personally, would have. See also Rest. 2d Torts § 590.

Members of local legislatures do not enjoy such pervasive protection from defamation liability. State law is divided on whether absolute or qualified privilege applies to members of local legislative bodies. Remarks made during a meeting that are not relevant to its official business may not be privileged. See Annot., 40 A.L.R.2d 941. The Restatement endorses an absolute privilege. Rest. 2d Torts § 590, comment *c*.

Executive privilege. Privilege attaches to the communications of officials in the executive branch of government that are made in the course of their official duties. The law is divided on which executive officials have an absolute privilege and what connection with the official's official duties a communication must have in order for it to be privileged.

In *Barr v. Matteo*, 360 U.S. 564 (1959), the Supreme Court decided that absolute privilege for federal officials extended into the lower ranks of the bureaucracy. It also decided that the privilege applied when "the action. . .taken was within the outer perimeter of [defendant's] line of duty." This is the law for state officials in a few states, but not in most. Most states limit absolute privilege to higher-ranking officials of government departments, agencies and diplomatic missions, and of the government as a whole. Other officials have a qualified privilege. State law also tends to require a greater connection between the communication and the official's duties than "within the outer perimeter of [the] line of duty."

Decisions are divided as to whether privilege applies to statements made in an official's communications with members of the public or the press that concern the official's duties but are not official acts. It may depend on whether the official is of higher or lower rank and whether such an official is expected to give information to the press or public. Compare *Schlinkert v. Henderson*, 331 Mich. 284, 49 N.W.2d 180 (1951) (member of state liquor control commission privileged to release to press letter to civil service commission concerning proposed reorganization), with *Carradine v. State*, 511 N.W.2d 733 (Minn. 1994) (state trooper had absolute privilege for statements in arrest report but not statements to press about arrest). Statutory immunities that protect government employees from tort liability generally, for acts within the scope of their employment, may apply.

2. JUDICIAL PROCEEDINGS

The absolute privilege for statements in judicial proceedings plays a very important, although often unstated, role in litigation. The absolute privilege allows witnesses, attorneys and judges to speak and write freely with little risk that they will be sued for defamation. The privilege tends to be applied widely in order to avoid the chilling effects that fear of being sued would have.

Statements in judicial proceedings. Absolute privilege applies to oral and written statements made within judicial proceedings by the participants: judges, magistrates, counsel, parties, witnesses and jurors. See Rest. 2d Torts §§ 585–589. It extends to statements made before a case reaches open court, as in pleadings, affidavits, depositions, briefs and pre-trial conferences. It extends, as well, to official reports of judicial proceedings and possibly also authoritative non-official reports.

For statements by attorneys, and often for statements of judges and other participants, American courts have attached a requirement that the statement have some "connection" or "relationship" or "relevance" to the judicial proceeding at hand. In practice this requirement is very loose. Due allowance is made for latitude in arguments to the court, and witnesses are not denied protection when they misconceive the issues in the case or the questions put to them. The few statements found "unconnected" and thus not entitled to absolute privilege are mainly personal criticisms that could not reasonably be thought to have pertinence to the substance or conduct of the proceeding. See *Sussman v. Damian*, 355 So. 2d 809 (Fla. App. 1977).

The judge's privilege is for statements made in a judicial capacity. A judge loses the protection of absolute privilege if it is found that the statement was made in a non-judicial capacity. This occurred when a state supreme court judge issued a press release explaining her recusal in a case. *Yoder v. Workman*, 224 F. Supp. 2d 1077 (S.D. W. Va. 2002). Although not a defamation case, *Forrester v. White*, 484 U.S. 219 (1988), indicates that a judge would not be acting in a judicial capacity if the judge defamed an employee in an employment evaluation or discharge.

Statements in "quasi-judicial" proceedings. Absolute privilege usually applies to proceedings in governmental agencies or tribunals that are not strictly judicial but resemble judicial proceedings. See Annot., 45 A.L.R.2d 1296. It can also apply to non-governmental bodies that perform "quasi-judicial" functions that otherwise might be performed by a court or government agency, including grievance and disciplinary proceedings of professional societies—especially state bar associations. See Annot., 77 A.L.R.2d 493; Annot., 9 A.L.R.4th 807. Another application is to statements in arbitration proceedings established by contract, as in *Yeung v. Maric*, 224 Ariz. 499, 232 P.3d 1281 (Ct. App. 2010).

Statements made in connection with pending or contemplated litigation. Many defamatory statements are made in connection with pending or contemplated litigation but not formally introduced in it. These are usually statements in communications between an attorney, or agent of an attorney, and potential witnesses, consultants, clients and other attorneys (including attorneys for opposing clients). These statements, unlike those made within judicial proceedings, are not controlled or supervised by a judicial officer. Nevertheless, the trend of modern case law is to apply absolute privilege, as the statements are connected to judicial proceedings and denying absolute privilege could hinder frank communication. *E.g.*, *Hawkins v. Harris*, 141 N.J. 207, 661 A.2d 284 (1995). See Annot., 36 A.L.R.3d 1328; 23 A.L.R.4th 932. The privilege has been extended to an attorney's communications with potential clients to solicit their participation in litigation. *Simpson Strong-Tie Co., Inc. v. Stewart, Estes & Donnell*, 232 S.W.3d 18 (Tenn. 2007). The privilege usually has not been extended to statements about pending or contemplated litigation made to the media. See *Jacobs v. Adelson*, 130 Nev. 408, 325 P.3d 1282 (2014).

3. OTHER LIABILITY BARS

No-publication doctrines. As discussed earlier (pp. 378–380), "publication" is a requirement of defamation liability. At one time there was considerable support for the proposition that there is no publication when an employee or agent of a business communicates with another employee or agent of the same business. This in effect creates an absolute privilege for internal communications of a corporation or other business entity. The trend of the more recent decisions, in jurisdictions where the question has not been settled by prior cases, is that there is publication and no absolute privilege. If there is publication, qualified privilege will usually apply to intra-corporate communications made in the interests of the business. See *Hagebak v. Stone*, 133 N.M. 75, 61 P.3d 201 (Ct. App. 2002); *Wallulis v. Dymowski*, 323 Or. 337, 918 P.2d 755 (1996).

There are also some cases finding no publication when the communication is from one spouse to the other, including *Springer v. Swift*, 59 S.D. 208, 238 N.W. 171 (1931). The more modern view is that publication occurs but that spousal communication should be protected by absolute privilege. Rest. 2d Torts § 592.

Publication required or authorized by law. There is authority that an absolute privilege applies to publications required by law—for example, a notice or document that an official or private party is legally required to publish. See Rest. 2d Torts § 592A. In *Weber v. Cueto*, 209 Ill. App. 3d 936, 568 N.E.2d 513 (1991), this was applied to a lawyer required by attorney disciplinary rules to report suspected misconduct by another lawyer. It appears that when a person is privileged to publish a statement, a party that provides appropriate means of publication shares the privilege, but the provider's privilege may be qualified even if the author's privilege is absolute. See Rest. 2d Torts § 612.

Consent. The plaintiff's consent is a complete defense to liability for defamation, as it is in other torts. It is sometimes included in lists of absolute privileges. See Rest. 2d Torts §§ 583–584. For example, in *Lee v. Paulsen*, 273 Or. 103, 539 P.2d 1079 (1975), the court held there was absolute privilege by reason of the plaintiff's consent when, at a public hearing, a teacher's attorney asked that the reason for the teacher's dismissal be stated.

Consent can be a difficult issue to resolve when the defamatory statement is in a communication that the plaintiff had agreed to in advance without seeing its contents, such as a letter of recommendation, reference, credit report, report of test results or report of an investigation. Probably the best generalization is that agreeing to this type of communication in advance is not in itself sufficient for a finding of consent, but consent would be found if the plaintiff had reason to anticipate the type of defamatory statement that was made or if the defendant could reasonably believe the plaintiff consented to the defamatory statement. See Rest. 2d Torts § 583, comment *d*. Compare *Gengler v. Phelps*, 92 N.M. 465, 589 P.2d 1056 (Ct. App. 1978) (consent when plaintiff applied for new employment on form that included consent to inquire of present employer, which had given plaintiff notice of termination); and *Christiansen v. Marvin*, 273 Or. 97, 539 P.2d 1082 (1975) (consent when teacher requested statement of reasons her contract was not renewed and had reason to know statement would be defamatory); with *Nelson v. Whitten*, 272 F. 135 (E.D.N.Y. 1921) (request for reference letter not consent to defamation).

C. QUALIFIED PRIVILEGES (CONDITIONAL PRIVILEGES)

The common law developed a set of "qualified" or "conditional" privileges that were bars to defamation liability. The principal qualified privileges are privileges to make statements in the interests of the maker or recipient of the communication, or a third party; the privilege to make statements in the public interest; the privilege to publish reports of public proceedings; the privilege to publish "fair comment"; and the privilege of officials of government who do not have absolute privilege. These privileges have made it possible to act to protect private or public interests or inform the public without the deterrent of the usual liability for libel or slander if someone was defamed in error. But the protection from liability is not absolute.

Qualified privilege is usually distinguished from absolute privilege on the ground that qualified privilege does not bar liability when it is established that the statement was made with malice, whereas absolute privilege applies irrespective of malice. As discussed below (pp. 412–415), there are actually a number of grounds other than malice that will cause a claim of qualified privilege to fail.

1. PRIVILEGES FOR PROTECTION OF INTERESTS

The privileges for protection of an interest are often attributed to the statement in *Toogood v. Spyring*, (1834) 1 C. M. & R. 181, 193, 149 Eng. 1044, 1049–1050 (Ex.), that there is a qualified defense, depending upon the absence of actual malice, when a defamatory communication "is fairly made by a person in the discharge of some public or private duty, whether legal or moral, or in the conduct of his own affairs, in matters where his interest is concerned." The Restatement states that:

> Occasions making a publication conditionally privileged afford a protection based upon a public policy that recognizes that it is essential that true information be given whenever it is reasonably necessary for the protection of one's own interests, the interests of third persons or certain interests of the public. In order that the information may be freely given, it is necessary to afford protection against liability for misinformation given in an appropriate effort to protect or advance the interest in question. . . .[These privileges] give protection from liability only when exercised for the purpose for which they are given and with reasonable care that no more harm shall be done to the interests of others than is necessary to accomplish the end for which the privilege is given.

Rest. 2d Torts, Scope Note preceding § 593.

The privileges are frequently grouped into the categories of (1) protection of an interest of the maker of the defamatory statement, (2) protection of an interest of another person, (3) protection or furtherance of a common interest, and (4) protection of the public interest. The Restatement places protection of the interest of a family member (of either the maker or recipient) in a separate category. Rest. 2d Torts §§ 594–598. These privileges operate primarily in cases of non-media publication of defamatory statements. Decisions on whether a defendant's statement was privileged (or communicated on a "privileged occasion") are very numerous and usually dependent on the facts of the case. It can be difficult to derive definite legal rules from these decisions. Potentially there are no limits to these privileges other than the generalities of *Toogood v. Spyring* and the Restatement overview.

Protection of interest of maker of defamatory statement (interest of publisher). The Restatement formulation of this privilege is that it applies when the person who publishes (communicates) the statement reasonably believes that there is information which affects a sufficiently important interest of the publisher and that the recipient's knowledge of the defamatory matter will be of service in the lawful protection of the interest. Rest. 2d Torts § 594. Any lawful interest can be protected. The privilege operates primarily to protect property and economic interests—for example, to prevent or resolve misappropriation of property or to enforce a monetary claim. Existing business interests can be protected, although not by defaming a competitor in order to acquire more trade. Physical safety and family relationships can also be protected by the privilege. See Rest. 2d Torts § 594, comments *f–j*. Evaluations of an employee's job performance are usually included in the privilege. *E.g., Bals v. Verduzco*, 600 N.E.2d 1353 (Ind. 1992); *McCone v.*

New England Telephone & Telegraph Co., 393 Mass. 231, 471 N.E.2d 47 (1984).

Application of the privilege may be questioned when the defendant can claim to derive some benefit from publishing information but no specific protection of an interest by the recipient of the information—for example, communication to customers or other employees of the grounds for discharge of an employee or representative. The decisions are divided. See *Browne v. Prudden-Winslow Co.*, 195 App. Div. 419, 186 N.Y.S. 350 (1921) (company privileged to notify customers of salesman's dismissal on grounds of dishonesty and injury to business); *Shannon v. Taylor AMC/Jeep, Inc.*, 168 Mich. App. 415, 425 N.W.2d 165 (1988) (vehicle dealer not privileged to tell customers that parts manager fired for dealing in stolen parts); *Richmond v. Southwire Co.*, 980 F.2d 518 (8th Cir. 1992) (small-town employer privileged in statement to local newspapers that employees terminated after investigation into possession and use of drugs on company property); *Worley v. Oregon Physicians Service*, 69 Or. App. 241, 686 P.2d 404 (1984) (employer privileged to explain to employees reasons for plaintiff's discharge, which implied theft, in interests of security and employee morale); *Haddad v. Sears, Roebuck and Co.*, 526 F.2d 83 (6th Cir. 1975) (store manager not privileged to tell employees who worked under service manager and sought explanation for his discharge the reasons for it). Some authority finds no privilege when the recipient of the communication has no interest or duty in the matter. See *M. Rosenberg & Sons, Inc. v. Craft*, 182 Va. 512, 29 S.E.2d 375 (1944).

Protection of reputation. Defamatory statements published to protect the reputation of the publisher are a subset of statements published to protect the interest of the publisher. They are sometimes treated separately because statements published to the general public can be within the privilege, if in response to something that was widely publicized, and because, when the defendant responded to criticism by the plaintiff, a strong attack on the plaintiff's credibility may be within the privilege. *E.g.*, *Chaffin v. Lynch*, 83 Va. 106, 1 S.E. 803 (1887) (defendant referring to plaintiff's "known character as a liar"); *Mencher v. Chesley*, 193 Misc. 829, 85 N.Y.S.2d 431 (Sup. Ct. 1948) (defendant responding to his dismissal by plaintiff from government position with statement charging plaintiff with official malfeasance and being a Communist). Generally traducing an accuser's character is not within the privilege. See Annot., 41 A.L.R.3d 1083.

Protection of interest of another person. Protection of the interest of the recipient of the defamatory statement, or a third person, is a ground for qualified privilege. Under *Toogood v. Spyring*, the privilege applies when the statement "is fairly made by a person in the discharge of some public or private duty, whether legal or moral." (See pp. 404–405.) The duty can be no more than a socially accepted standard of good conduct. According to the Restatement, the privilege is applicable when the recipient of the statement is a person "to whom publication is. . .within the generally accepted standards of decent conduct." The Restatement requires that the maker of the statement reasonably believe the information affects a sufficiently important legitimate interest of the recipient or third person. Rest. 2d Torts § 595(1).

Whether a statement, or the "occasion" in which it was published, is privileged depends to a large extent on the existence and nature of economic, family and social relationships between the parties involved (the parties to the communication and the parties whose interests may be affected). Whether the statement was requested or volunteered also plays a significant role. The value of the interest to be protected obviously is of great weight. See Rest. 2d Torts § 595, comments *d–j*. Presumably the interest of highest value is personal safety, followed by protection of property. But the most typical illustration of this privilege is a reference furnished to someone who will decide whether to employ or extend credit to the plaintiff or select the plaintiff for some position. A statement regarded as unwarranted meddling will be denied privilege, usually on the ground that the defendant was under no duty to make it. *Burton v. Mattson*, 50 Utah 133, 166 P. 979 (1917), is a classic example.

Common interest. The common interest privilege overlaps the privileges to protect the interests of the publisher of the defamatory statement and to protect the interests of other persons. However, it is distinct in allowing privilege on the basis of the recipients' interests in being informed, rather than on the basis that action to protect the interests might result from the communication. See Rest. 2d Torts § 596. There is also greater allowance for methods of communication that might reach some persons who do not have the interest, such as an organizational newsletter, when they are an efficient means of communicating with those who do have the interest.

The common interest advanced is usually that of members of an organization, institution or business enterprise to which both the originator of the communication and the intended recipients belong. Thus, employees and investors of a business and members of churches, labor unions, professional associations, non-profit institutions and community associations are privileged to communicate with one another on matters that touch their interests as employees, investors or members. A common interest is also found for co-owners of property and members of a family. The Restatement extends the privilege to information that recipients are "entitled to learn" by reason of the common interest. Rest. 2d Torts § 596, comments *c–e*. It seems to be sufficient that it is important for recipients to learn of the information. See *Zinda v. Louisiana Pacific Corp.*, 149 Wis. 2d 913, 440 N.W.2d 548 (1989), in which a factory newsletter listed by name reasons for employee terminations.

In some cases involving publication in mass media, defendants have claimed qualified privilege on the basis of the general public's interest in being informed or the media's common interest with the public in the provision of information. Courts have usually decided that qualified privilege does not apply. *Brown v. Kelly Broadcasting Co.*, 48 Cal. 3d 406, 771 P.2d 406 (1989); *Rouch v. Enquirer & News of Battle Creek*, 427 Mich. 157, 398 N.W.2d 245 (1986); *Bingham v. Gaynor*, 203 N.Y. 27, 96 N.E. 84 (1911).

Public interest. The privilege to make statements in the "public interest" is much narrower than the term implies. It primarily applies to statements made to government officials and agencies about matters within their official responsibilities. This includes complaints made to a government official about the alleged actions of another official. It also includes communications to law enforcement officials, such as police and prosecuting attorneys, concerning alleged or suspected unlawful activity, and communications to agencies responsible for the licensing or discipline of occupational groups about misconduct by a person within the agency's jurisdiction. See Rest. 2d Torts § 598, comment *e*; Eldredge, *The Law of Defamation* 492–502 (1978).

A communication concerning a government agency's relations with private citizens, such as recipients of government contracts or businesses regulated by the government, also comes within the privilege. See *A & B-Abell Elevator Co., Inc. v. Columbus/Central Ohio Building & Construction Trades Council*, 73 Ohio St. 3d 1, 651 N.E.2d 1283 (1995). Because of the public interest in the prevention of crime, the privilege can extend to communication with someone who is not a government official but may act to prevent criminal activity or apprehend a suspected criminal. See Rest. 2d Torts § 598, comment *f*. This would include private security personnel. See *Pate v. Service Merchandise Co., Inc.*, 959 S.W.2d 569 (Tenn. App. 1997).

Informal complaints to law enforcement agencies, prosecuting attorneys, magistrates, administrative tribunals and professional discipline bodies have sometimes been held to be absolutely, not conditionally, privileged as the initial step in judicial or quasi-judicial proceeding. See *Ledvina v. Cerasani,* 213 Ariz. 596, 146 P.3d 70 (Ct. App. 2006); *5-State Helicopters, Inc. v. Cox*, 146 S.W.3d 254 (Tex. App. 2004). *Contra, Fridovich v. Fridovich*, 598 So. 2d 65 (Fla. 1992); *Caldor, Inc. v. Bowden*, 330 Md. 632, 625 A.2d 959 (1993). A complaint made to a professional body, such as a medical society or bar association, might be accorded the same privilege as a complaint to a professional licensing or disciplinary body established by the state. See Annot., 9 A.L.R.4th 807.

2. QUALIFICATIONS ("ABUSES") OF QUALIFIED PRIVILEGE

When a statement is published in circumstances of qualified privilege, the publisher will not be liable unless one of the qualifications upon the privilege applies. There are several grounds for loss of the protection of qualified privilege. When applicable, the defendant will be liable for the defamatory statement unless another defense is established. In these circumstances, it is typically said that the privilege was "forfeited" or "exceeded" or "abused." Relevant factual questions are decided by the trier of fact.

Lack of belief in or grounds for statement. Qualified privilege does not protect a defamatory statement published without a good faith belief that it is true. A defendant is subject to liability if it is proved that the statement was published with knowledge of its falsity or reckless disregard of whether it was true or false.

Whether qualified privilege is "abused" by publishing a defamatory statement without reasonable ground to believe it is true is the subject of considerable division of authority. The decision in *Gertz v. Robert Welch, Inc.*, 418 U.S. 323 (1974), that there was to be no liability without fault in defamation cases has caused reconsideration of this question. It is not clear that this rule applies to every defamation case. It might not apply when the defamation involved no matter of public concern. (See pp. 431–432.) But if there can be no liability without fault, a qualified privilege conditioned on reasonable grounds for the defamatory statement would be redundant. For this reason the Second Restatement and some judicial decisions have moved from lack of reasonable grounds to knowledge of or reckless disregard for falsity as the requirement for abuse of qualified privilege. Rest. 2d Torts § 600. See Rest. 2d Torts, Special Note preceding § 593. It is possible that a state may adopt knowledge of or reckless disregard for falsity as abuse for some privileges, such as public interest and statements of lower-ranking public officials, while retaining lack of reasonable grounds for other privileges, such as furtherance of a private interest.

Wrong purpose. Qualified privileges based upon protection of an interest require that the defendant act for the purpose of protecting that interest. There is an abuse of the privilege if protection of the interest was not the primary purpose, or at least a substantial purpose, of the defendant's publication of the defamatory statement. Rest. 2d Torts § 603. This includes defamatory statements made because of malice in the sense of spite, ill will or a desire to cause harm. See Rest. 2d Torts § 603, comment *a*. It also includes reports of alleged misconduct that ostensibly were within the public interest or private interest privileges but were shown to have been made to advantage the defendant at the plaintiff's expense. See *Fridovich v. Fridovich*, 598 So. 2d 65 (Fla. 1992); *Over v. Schiffling*, 102 Ind. 191, 26 N.E. 91 (1885).

Excessive publication. Qualified privilege does not protect publication of a defamatory statement to more persons than are reasonably believed necessary for protection of the interest involved. Usually there is an abuse of the privilege if the defendant has knowingly used a means of communication that conveys the defamatory statement to persons whose knowledge of it will not protect or advance the interest. However, if this was reasonable because it was not practical to limit communication to persons owed a duty or possessing an interest in receiving the statement, there would be no abuse. Excessive publication would usually be found when the defendant made an accusation of misconduct where it could be overheard, absent exigent circumstances. See Rest. 2d Torts § 604 and comments.

Unprivileged content. It is an abuse of qualified privilege to include in a defamatory statement matter unrelated to the purpose for which the privilege is given. See Rest. 2d Torts § 605 (abuse if defendant did not reasonably believe matter to be necessary to accomplish purpose for which privilege given). This is most clearly seen where the privilege protects a specific interest and information contained in the statement is irrelevant to the interest, as when a credit report contains information that does not bear on the subject's creditworthiness, an employment reference contains details of the subject's personal life irrelevant to the subject's suitability for employment, or a report to law enforcement personnel about a person's suspected unlawful activity includes matters not connected to the suspect's guilt or apprehension.

Malice. Qualified privilege is typically described as a privilege that does not extend to defamatory statements actuated by malice, so malice is a standard ground for finding abuse of qualified privilege. Many cases address whether there was sufficient evidence of malice. But courts vary considerably in their usage of the term in connection with qualified privilege. The principal definition or concept of malice in tort law is spite, ill will or desire to cause harm. But a number of courts have included improper purpose, and some have used malice to signify any state of mind, including knowledge or reckless disregard of falsity, that makes publication an abuse of qualified privilege. See Sack, *Defamation* §§ 9:3.1–9:3.3 (5th ed. 2017).

The Restatement omits malice from the "black letter" rules on abuse of qualified privilege and gives defamatory publication made solely from spite or ill will as an example of publication that is not intended to serve the interest protected by privilege. Rest. 2d Torts § 603, comment *a*. For purposes of the constitutional law of defamation, the Supreme Court has defined "actual malice" as knowledge or reckless disregard of falsity. This definition has caused a few courts to abandon prior definitions of the malice that defeats common law privilege and substitute knowing falsehood or reckless disregard. See *Marchesi v. Franchino*, 283 Md. 131, 387 A.2d 1129 (1978); *Barreca v. Nickolas*, 683 N.W.2d 111 (Iowa 2004). *Contra*, *Great Coastal Express, Inc. v. Ellington*, 230 Va. 142, 334 S.E.2d 846 (1985).

3. REPORTS OF PUBLIC PROCEEDINGS

The privilege for reports of public proceedings goes by several different names, including "reporter's privilege," the privilege of "fair report," and the "record libel" privilege. It is essentially a privilege to publish accurate reports of the contents of official (governmental) acts and proceedings without being liable to a person defamed in the report. It applies to reports of judicial proceedings, including evidence introduced in the case. The privilege is primarily of value to the news media, but it extends to anyone who reports on or describes official acts and proceedings. See Rest. 2d Torts § 611 and comments.

The fundamental requirement of the privilege is that the report be substantially accurate or correct—accurate as an account of the proceedings, not as a description of the plaintiff's conduct or character. Application of the substantial accuracy requirement may resemble application of the "substantial truth" criterion when it is claimed that the defamation is true (see p. 395). The report also must be "fair" in the sense that it is not decidedly one-sided or so selective in what it states as to be misleading. With that qualification, the reporter is free to select the portions of the proceedings to be reported. Defamatory additions by the reporter, even if related to the proceedings, are outside the privilege. See Rest. 2d Torts § 611, comment *f*.

In many situations it is clear that the report published by the defendant is within the privilege. However, there are a number of issues about the extent of the privilege on which precedent is either too divided or too sparse to produce a settled rule. See Sack, *Defamation* § 7:3.5[B] (5th ed. 2017). Probably the most important of these is, in general, whether the privilege extends beyond reports of the official acts of government to reports of public officials' statements about governmental acts or affairs—for example, press statements of government officials or statements of law enforcement personnel about arrests and investigations. It appears that the wider view of the privilege is now the prevailing position.

E.g., *Short v. News-Journal Co.*, 58 Del. 592, 212 A.2d 718 (1965) (statement of IRS district office); *Whiteside v. Russellville Newspapers, Inc.*, 295 S.W.3d 798 (Ark. 2009) (information from police).

Other issues include whether the privilege applies to reports of proceedings and records that are not open to the public or available to the public; whether the privilege to report the contents of judicial proceedings extends to pleadings, affidavits and other papers filed in the case but not yet acted upon by the court; whether the privilege applies to reports of the proceedings of a foreign government; and whether the privilege has any application to reports of meetings that are public, in the sense of being open to the public, but not governmental. Rest. 2d Torts § 611 and a few cases extend the privilege to reports of a meeting that is open to the public and deals with a matter of public concern. This is debatable, as the privilege is premised to a large extent on the importance of the public being informed of and able to supervise the actions of government. See *Lee v. Dong-A Ilbo*, 849 F.2d 876 (4th Cir. 1988).

Under the common law, the privilege to publish reports of public proceedings is a qualified privilege. It is not abused by excessive publication—the report can be made to anyone—but it is abused by publication actuated by malice (ill will, spite or purpose to cause injury). See Rest. Torts § 611. Publication of statements in the proceedings known to be false might also be treated as an abuse. Under the Second Restatement, neither is an abuse of the privilege. Rest. 2d Torts § 611. This in effect makes the privilege absolute, although conditioned upon accuracy and "fairness." Some courts have adopted this position. *Moreno v. Crookston Times Printing Co.*, 610 N.W.2d 321 (Minn. 2000); *Salzano v. North Jersey Media Group Inc.*, 201 N.J. 500, 993 A.2d 778 (2010). *Contra, Thomas v. Telegraph Publishing Co.*, 155 N.H. 314, 929 A.2d 993 (2007).

4. FAIR COMMENT

Another common law privilege of some importance is "fair comment," or "fair comment on a matter of public interest." That phrase incorporates three of the requirements of the fair comment privilege: the defamation must be comment rather than fact; it must be fair; and it must be on a matter of public interest. Additional requirements are that the facts on which the comment is based must be identified in the defendant's statement or generally known by those to whom it is published, and those facts must either be true or privileged matter, such as an accurate report of judicial or other governmental proceedings. See *A.S. Abell Co. v. Kirby*, 227 Md. 267, 176 A.2d 340 (1961). The main advantage of the privilege for defendants is that comment within the privilege does not have to be proved true to the satisfaction of a court or jury.

While easy to state in general terms, the requirements of the privilege have been difficult to apply in many cases, especially the requirement that the defamatory matter be comment rather than fact. The core concept of comment, for purposes of the privilege, appears to be something that is an observation upon or criticism of or conclusion from facts and is recognizable as opinion by the recipient of the statement. If the defendant set out a fact and then made an observation on it, the latter is likely to be interpreted as comment. If the defendant made a statement without referring to the facts on which it is based, it is likely to be taken as implying facts and therefore factual. Imputations of corrupt or dishonorable motives are also likely to be treated as factual. See *A.S. Abell Co. v. Kirby*, *supra*; *Mashburn v. Collin*, 355 So. 2d 879 (La. 1977).

The requirement that the comment be "fair" cannot be taken literally. Harsh, extreme and prejudiced comments have been within the privilege. *E.g.*, *Cherry v. Des Moines Leader*, 114 Iowa 298, 86 N.W. 323 (1901). The requirement is likely to be interpreted to mean either that the statement be one that a fair person, however prejudiced or obstinate, could honestly hold on the facts stated. See *Merivale v. Carson*, (1887) 20 Q.B.D. 275 (C.A.). Or that the statement express the maker's honest opinion. See *Dowling v. Livingstone*, 108 Mich. 321, 66 N.W. 225 (1896); Rest. Torts § 606(1)(b). As fair comment is a qualified privilege, the defendant will lose its protection if it was made because of malice, or at least a purpose to cause harm. See Rest. Torts § 606(1)(c).

Many matters of public concern or interest fit the requirement that the comment be on a matter of public interest. See Rest. Torts § 606, comment *a*. Comment on private conduct that has no substantial connection with a matter of public interest would be outside the privilege.

Fair comment has receded in importance because of the constitutional law discussed in the next chapter. Defamation actions that formerly would have been defended on the ground of fair comment now tend to be defended on constitutional law grounds. It is unlikely that the fair comment privilege would provide more protection from liability than current constitutional law.

CHAPTER 23

CONSTITUTIONAL LAW

A. INTRODUCTION

With the exception of the right to trial by jury, constitutional law did not affect liability for defamation until *New York Times Co. v. Sullivan*, 376 U.S. 254 (1964). In that case, the Supreme Court decided for the first time that the First Amendment's guarantees of freedom of speech and freedom of the press, as applied to the states by the Fourteenth Amendment, required a limitation of liability for defamatory statements. In subsequent cases, the Supreme Court has held that additional limitations were required. The result is a complex body of constitutional rules that limit liability for defamation, substantively or procedurally. Most are to be applied in addition to, not in substitution for, the common law rules of defamation. In many cases, however, the court rules for the defendant on constitutional law grounds without deciding how the common law is to apply to the case.

The Supreme Court's opinions must be examined in order to know the reasoning for the decisions and the context in which the decisions were made. In this chapter it is only possible to identify the rules established by the Supreme Court's decisions and the primary points on how they are applied. The Supreme Court's opinions provide some guidance on how the rules are to be applied, but for the most part this has been left to other courts. The relevant case law from state courts and lower federal courts is now very large. The main rules have remained the same for several decades, but substantial change or addition by a Supreme Court decision is always a possibility.

The Supreme Court's decisions have been premised to a large degree on the reasoning that it is necessary to limit liability for false defamatory statements in order to avoid the "chilling effect" of potential liability on speech that is not or may not be false. These decisions have produced a freedom from the risk of defamation liability that was unknown before *New York Times Co. v. Sullivan* and does not exist outside the United States. It has transformed American journalism and had a great impact on American politics.

The disparity between American law and the law of other nations, including those whose defamation law is based on English common law, has become more important with the availability of world-wide communication through the Internet. One outgrowth of this is the enactment in 2010 of federal legislation that blocks enforcement in the United States of foreign defamation judgments when the defendant would not have been liable under domestic state defamation law and First Amendment rules. 28 U.S.C. §§ 4101 *et seq.*

The main rules established by the Supreme Court's decisions are:

- There is liability for defamation of a public official only when it is proved that the defendant published the statement with knowledge of its falsity or with reckless disregard for whether it was true or false (a state of mind described as "actual malice"). *New York Times Co. v. Sullivan*, 376 U.S. 254 (1964).

- There is liability for defamation of a public figure (defamed in that capacity) only when it is proved that the defendant published the statement with knowledge of its falsity or with reckless disregard for whether it was true or false. *Curtis Publishing Co. v. Butts*, 388 U.S. 130 (1967).

- For private figures (persons who are not public officials or public figures), the limitations are that there is to be no liability without fault and damages are to be limited to compensation for actual injury (no punitive or presumed damages) unless knowledge or reckless disregard of falsity is proved. *Gertz v. Robert Welch, Inc.*, 418 U.S. 323 (1974). However, the limitation of damages does not apply when the defamatory statement did not involve a matter of public concern. *Dun & Bradstreet, Inc. v. Greenmoss Builders, Inc.*, 472 U.S. 749 (1985).

- The plaintiff must bear the burden of proving the statement's falsity, when the statement was on a matter of public concern. *Philadelphia Newspapers, Inc. v. Hepps*, 475 U.S. 767 (1986).

- For defamation liability, when the statement was on a matter of public concern, the statement must be one that on a reasonable interpretation contained "actual facts" about the plaintiff that are provably false. There is no liability for expressions that could not reasonably be interpreted as stating provably false facts. *Milkovich v. Lorain Journal Co.*, 497 U.S. 1 (1990).

There are also some subsidiary rules. These include: When "actual malice," *i.e.*, knowledge or reckless disregard of falsity, must be proved, courts are required to determine whether there is clear and convincing evidence of it. See *Anderson v. Liberty Lobby, Inc.*, 477 U.S. 242 (1986). Actual malice can be found when a defendant, knowing what the plaintiff had said, published as quotations statements that differed materially in meaning from the plaintiff's actual words. *Masson v. New Yorker Magazine, Inc.*, 501 U.S. 496 (1991). Defendants can be liable on the basis of vicarious liability. *Cantrell v. Forest City Publishing Co.*, 419 U.S. 245, 253–254 (1974). A public official or public figure cannot avoid the actual malice requirement by suing for infliction of emotional distress instead of defamation. *Hustler Magazine, Inc. v. Falwell*, 485 U.S. 46 (1988). Defamation liability is not to arise from criticism of government operations because of a public official's responsibility for those operations. *New York Times Co. v. Sullivan*, *supra*; *Rosenblatt v. Baer*, 383 U.S. 75 (1966). In addition, under *Near v. Minnesota ex rel. Olson*, 283 U.S. 697 (1931), there can be no "prior restraint" of defamatory speech. This rules out at least preliminary injunctions as a remedy for defamation.

As the First Amendment specifies freedom of the press and the Supreme Court cases establishing limitations of defamation liability all involved media publication, it can be argued that at least some of the limitations do not apply to non-media publication. The Supreme Court has not explicitly decided this question. Its decision in *Philadelphia Newspapers, Inc. v. Hepps*, was limited to media defendants. But in the *Dun & Bradstreet* case, the plurality opinion pointedly declined to endorse a distinction between media and non-media defendants, which was the basis of the lower court's decision, and the distinction was rejected by the justices who did not join that opinion. Consequently, the law at present is that the First Amendment limitations on defamation liability do apply to non-media as well as media defendants. See *Maethner v. Someplace Safe, Inc.*, 929 N.W.2d 868 (Minn. 2019). However, to the extent that there is less protection from liability for statements that are not on matters of public concern, this primarily affects non-media publication. In an era in which almost anyone can easily communicate to a large audience through the Internet, a distinction between media and non-media publication would be difficult to maintain. See *Obsidian Finance Group, LLC v. Cox*, 740 F.3d 1284 (9th Cir. 2014).

States are free to provide greater protection from liability than the Supreme Court's decisions require. Some limit awards of damages more strictly—for example by prohibiting punitive damages. *E.g.*, *Stone v. Essex County Newspapers, Inc.*, 367 Mass. 849, 330 N.E.2d 161 (1975). Several states require knowledge or reckless disregard of falsity when the plaintiff was not a public figure or public official but the defamatory statement was on a matter of public concern or public interest. *Walker v. Colorado Springs Sun, Inc.*, 188 Colo. 86, 538 P.2d 450 (1975); *Senna v. Florimont*, 196 N.J. 469, 958 A.2d 427 (2008). A few states, including New York, have unique rules. In addition, many states have adopted so-called "anti-SLAPP" statutes that provide for early dismissal or striking out of defamation actions in which defendants will not be held liable because of constitutional protection of freedom of speech. See Sack, *Defamation* § 16:2.3 (5th ed. 2017).

B. THE "ACTUAL MALICE" REQUIREMENT

"Actual malice" has been used in *New York Times Co. v. Sullivan* and later cases to mean knowledge of falsity or reckless disregard for truth or falsity. It does not mean or include malice in its usual meaning in tort law, which is a motivation of ill will, spite, or desire to cause harm. Consequently, a defendant cannot be liable to a public official or public figure on proof that the defendant published the defamatory statement because of ill will toward the plaintiff or a desire to cause harm. The Supreme Court has equated reckless disregard for truth with "high degree of awareness of. . .probable falsity." *Garrison v. Louisiana*, 379 U.S. 64, 74 (1964). And with "entertain[ing] serious doubts as to the truth of [the] publication." *St. Amant v. Thompson*, 390 U.S. 727, 731 (1968). Actual malice might also be found when the defendant deliberately decided not to acquire knowledge of facts that might confirm the falsity of what the defendant was going to publish ("purposeful avoidance of the truth"). *Harte-Hanks Communications, Inc. v. Connaughton*, 491 U.S. 657, 692–693 (1989).

Generally, the failure to verify information received from other persons before publishing it is not reckless disregard. See *Gertz v. Robert Welch, Inc.*, 418 U.S. 323, 332 (1974). In the *New York Times* case, the newspaper's failure to check the accuracy of what it published against news stories in its files was held not to be reckless disregard. The improbability of the defamatory statement being true may be some evidence of knowledge or reckless disregard of falsity, but it is not sufficient on its own. See *Revell v. Hoffman*, 309 F.3d 1228 (10th Cir. 2002).

Application of the actual malice requirement to publication of fiction and satire is uncertain. As Presiding Justice Files said when dissenting in *Bindrim v. Mitchell*, 92 Cal. App. 3d 61, 88, 155 Cal. Rptr. 29, 45 (1979), "when the publication purports to be fiction, it is absurd to infer malice because the fiction is false." One possibility is the test of whether the defendant knew of or had reckless disregard for the probability that the publication would be interpreted to state false facts about the plaintiff. See *New Times, Inc. v. Isaacks*, 146 S.W.3d 144 (Tex. 2004).

The requirement that knowledge or reckless disregard of falsity be proved has made it almost impossible for public officials to win a defamation case in most circumstances. A final judgment for a public figure plaintiff is not as rare. There have been prominent cases of "tabloid" publishers being held liable to a public figure, as in *Burnett v. National Enquirer, Inc.*, 144 Cal. App. 3d 991, 193 Cal. Rptr. 206 (1983). But usually there is insufficient evidence to clearly prove that the defendant knew what it published was false or seriously doubted its truth.

C. THE "FAULT" REQUIREMENT

The Supreme Court's opinion in *Gertz v. Robert Welch, Inc.*, 418 U.S. 323 (1974), forbids liability without fault in defamation cases. The court did not define fault, but it is generally thought that the Supreme Court established negligence as the threshold requirement of liability. (It was so interpreted in the dissenting opinions.) The court undoubtedly had in mind failure to exercise sufficient care to ensure that what was published was accurate. Negligence might also be found in publishing a statement that could be interpreted to have a meaning that the defendant did not intend. See *New England Tractor-Trailer Training of Connecticut, Inc. v. Globe Newspaper Co.*, 395 Mass. 471, 480 N.E.2d 1005 (1985). The plaintiff has the burden of proving the defendant's fault. *Philadelphia Newspapers, Inc. v. Hepps*, 475 U.S. 767 (1986). The *Gertz* opinion suggests that the defendant is not to be found at fault when the content of a factual misstatement would not "warn a reasonably prudent editor or broadcaster of its defamatory potential." 418 U.S. 323, 348.

One of the general issues is whether a claim of journalistic negligence should be treated as a claim of professional negligence, with expert testimony admissible and possibly even required to provide evidence on the professional standard of care, or whether it is to be treated as a claim of "ordinary" negligence. The latter view prevails, although industry practice is relevant. See Annot., 37 A.L.R.4th 987. Another issue is whether a defendant can be found negligent for publishing, without verification, the contents of a news report provided by "wire services" such as Associated Press. The usual decision is that negligence cannot be found; there is no duty to independently verify news reports from reputable wire services. *E.g.*, *Appleby v. Daily Hampshire Gazette*, 395 Mass. 32, 478 N.E.2d 721 (1985); *Howe v. Detroit Free Press, Inc.*, 219 Mich. App. 150, 555 N.W.2d 738 (1996), aff'd, 457 Mich. 871, 586 N.W.2d 85 (1998). It is unlikely to be negligent to report as news, without independent verification, information that a public official has provided about routine government action such as arrests. See *Benson v. Griffin Television, Inc.*, 593 P.2d 511 (Okla. App. 1979). Beyond this, if a plaintiff can prove that the defendant published something that was defamatory and materially false, there often will be a substantial argument that this would have been prevented by sufficient care.

The limitations of liability adopted in *Gertz v. Robert Welch, Inc.*, appeared to apply to all defamation cases. But the court decided in *Dun & Bradstreet, Inc. v. Greenmoss Builders, Inc.*, 472 U.S. 749 (1985), that the *Gertz* rule that damages were to be compensation for actual injury, unless "actual malice" was proved, did not apply when the defamatory statement did not involve a matter of public concern. This immediately raised the question of whether the other *Gertz* rule, that of no liability without fault, was also not to apply when the defamatory statement did not involve a matter of public concern. Justice White's concurring opinion believed this was implied in the principal opinion, and some lower courts have agreed. See *Snead v. Redland Aggregates Ltd.*, 998 F.2d 1325 (5th Cir. 1993). But there does not seem to be any major resurgence of liability without fault in state defamation law. The fault requirement is explicitly retained in a number of cases, including *New England Tractor-Trailer Training of Connecticut, Inc. v. Globe Newspaper Co., supra.*

D. PUBLIC OFFICIALS

New York Times Co. v. Sullivan, 376 U.S. 254 (1964), established the rule that a public official could not recover damages for defamation without proof that the defamatory statement was made with "actual malice," defined as knowledge of the statement's falsity or reckless disregard for whether it was false. The plaintiff in the case was an elected official, but the rule clearly applies to many appointed officials as well. It also applies to candidates for elective office. *Monitor Patriot Co. v. Roy*, 401 U.S. 265 (1971). The Supreme Court's opinion in *Rosenblatt v. Baer*, 383 U.S. 75 (1966), stated that "the 'public official' designation applies at the very least to those among the hierarchy of government employees who have, or appear to the public to have, substantial responsibility for or control over the conduct of government affairs." It also stated that the *New York Times* rule applies when "a position in government has such apparent importance that the public has an independent interest in the qualifications and performance of the person who holds it, beyond the general public interest in the qualifications and performance of all government employees." 383 U.S. 75, 85, 86.

While clearly implying that there are some government employees who are not "public officials" for purposes of a defamation claim, the *Rosenblatt v. Baer* concept of public official is expansive, and it has been applied in an expansive way in the lower federal courts and state courts. It seems that anyone in a supervisory or decisionmaking position will be classified as a public official if the defamation is connected to the plaintiff's role in that position. In addition to applying the *Rosenblatt v. Baer* criteria, courts have emphasized whether the plaintiff's position was one of power over and visibility to members of the public. For this reason, lower-ranking law enforcement officers have been held to be public officials in most although not all instances. So have employees of social services agencies who have authority in child welfare cases. See Annot., 44 A.L.R.5th 193.

The largest division in the case law concerns whether public school teachers without a supervisory position are to be classified as public officials. A teacher has considerable discretion and power over the lives of students. The public is interested in and scrutinizes the conduct of the teachers. However, they are not involved in the administration of laws and directives that individuals and businesses must comply with. And in modern school systems, classroom teachers' freedom to decide what and how to teach and how to interact with students is limited by control from "above." There is also division in the case law on whether a person or business performing services under contracts with governmental agencies is a public official, although that is more dependent upon the facts of the case.

Under *Rosenblatt v. Baer*, the "actual malice" requirement applies to defamatory statements about former public officials, when related to their conduct in office, unless "a person is so far removed from a former position of authority that comment on the manner in which he performed his responsibilities no longer has the interest necessary to justify the *New York Times* rule." 383 U.S. 75, 87 n. 14. It has been assumed in some cases that holders of public office in foreign countries are to be treated as public officials. But this is questioned in *Lopez v. Univision Communications, Inc.*, 45 F. Supp. 2d 348 (S.D.N.Y. 1999).

A plaintiff is unlikely to avoid the knowing or reckless falsehood requirement by arguing that the defamation did not pertain the plaintiff's position as a public official. Anything that might touch upon the official's fitness for office, including a charge of some criminal conduct in the distant past, is within the

New York Times rule. *Monitor Patriot Co. v. Roy*, 401 U.S. 265 (1971).

E. PUBLIC FIGURES

In the companion cases of *Curtis Publishing Co. v. Butts* and *Associated Press v. Walker*, 388 U.S. 130 (1967), the Supreme Court decided that proof of "actual malice," *i.e.*, knowledge of or reckless disregard for falsity, was required in defamation actions brought by a "public figure." In many cases since then it has been clear that the plaintiff was, when defamed, a public figure and that the defamation was connected to what made the plaintiff a public figure. But in many other cases this has been vigorously contested. There is now a very large and difficult-to-digest body of case law on public figure status. See Annot., 19 A.L.R.5th 1. There are some Supreme Court opinions that provide guidance—most importantly *Gertz v. Robert Welch, Inc.*, 418 U.S. 323 (1974); *Time, Inc. v. Firestone*, 424 U.S. 448 (1976); and *Wolston v. Reader's Digest Association, Inc.*, 443 U.S. 157 (1979)—but for the most part the law has been developed in the lower federal courts and state courts. Some have laid down their own set of criteria for determination of whether a plaintiff was public figure.

There are a few things that are clear. One is that a person becomes a public figure by engaging in activities that draw to the person the attention of the public, or a portion of the public. Second, a person can become a public figure by voluntarily becoming involved in a public controversy. (In *Associated Press v. Walker*, Walker was a public figure because he had assumed a prominent role in controversy over federal government action to enforce desegregation in the South. In *Gertz v. Robert Welch, Inc.*, the plaintiff was held not to be a public figure by virtue of his representation of a client in a controversial case, as he had not "thrust himself" into the controversy or sought public attention in order to influence the outcome of the controversy.) Third, one does not become a public figure solely by becoming involved in an event or subject of public interest that has been publicized. Fourth, whether the person was sufficiently prominent to have access to the media or other "channels of effective communication" for rebuttal of the defamation is of some weight. Fifth, there are two categories of public figure. One consists of persons of great prominence and influence who are considered public figures for all purposes. The other consists of persons who have gained prominence or attention in connection with a limited range of issues or subject-matter. These are known as "limited purpose public figures."

The concept of limited purpose public figure holds out the possibility that a person who is known to the public in connection with some issues or activities will avoid the actual malice requirement on the ground that the defamation was unrelated to those issues or activities. But its main effect has been to produce decisions that the plaintiff was a limited purpose public figure because the plaintiff had acquired some public recognition connected to issues or activities that the defamation pertained to. Plaintiffs have been held to be limited purpose public figures because they engaged in activity that predictably could embroil them in a public controversy. *E.g.*, *Clyburn v. New World Communications, Inc.*, 284 U.S. App. D.C. 212, 903 F.2d 29 (1990). Local prominence makes one a public figure for purposes of a locally disseminated publication. See *Greenbelt Corporation Publishing Association, Inc. v. Bresler*, 398 U.S. 6 (1970).

Because the Supreme Court's opinions have emphasized whether or not the plaintiff had "thrust" himself or herself into a public controversy, lower courts have stated the plaintiff's injection into a controversy, prior to the defamation, as a requirement of limited purpose public figure status. *E.g., Fitzgerald v. Penthouse International, Ltd.*, 691 F.2d 666 (4th Cir. 1982); *Thomas M. Cooley Law School v. Kurzon Strauss, LLP*, 759 F.3d 522 (6th Cir. 2014). There are decisions that a plaintiff who was well-known locally was not a public figure because the plaintiff had not been involved in a public controversy. *E.g.*, *Wayment v. Clear Channel Broadcasting, Inc.*, 116 P.3d 271 (Utah 2005) (local television reporter); *Blue Ridge Bank v. Veribanc, Inc.*, 866 F.2d 681 (4th Cir. 1989) (bank). This is questionable. In *Curtis Publishing Co. v. Butts*, the plaintiff was considered a public figure because of his prominent position as athletic director and former head football coach at the University of Georgia, not because of any controversy he had been involved in. It is possible for a person to become an "involuntary public figure" through involvement in a controversy, but this is considered a rarity. See Annot., 17 A.L.R.7th Art. 1.

Former public figures. Whether a "former public figure" must prove knowing or reckless falsehood in a defamation action is an unsettled question. A former public figure is someone who was a private person at the time the defamatory statement was published but was a public figure at some time in the past.

In *Wolston v. Reader's Association, Inc.*, 443 U.S. 157, 169–172 (1979), Justices Blackmun and Marshall concluded that public figure status could end over time and had in that case. But the decision in most relevant cases is that a person continues to be a public figure indefinitely for purposes of statements that concern the person's past role as a public figure. This permits the publication of histories with defamatory material about former public figures who are still alive, without a large risk of litigation and liability. The leading case is *Street v. National Broadcasting Co.*, 645 F.2d 1227 (6th Cir. 1981).

F. TRUTH AND FALSITY

Burden of proof. Under the common law of defamation, the falsity of the defendant's statement, or the meaning it conveys, is not something a plaintiff must prove. Truth is a defense for the defendant to plead and prove, if the defendant wishes to do so. (See p. 391.) In *Philadelphia Newspapers, Inc. v. Hepps*, 475 U.S. 767 (1986), the Supreme Court held that the First Amendment required that the plaintiff have the burden of proving falsity in order to recover damages for defamation in speech on a matter of public concern. The court concluded that the common law rule had to give way because of its "chilling" effect on speech on matters of public concern and the possibility of liability for speech that was actually true.

The decision was limited to media defendants. However, as explained earlier at p. 427, the First Amendment rules on defamation liability apply to both media and non-media publication. Although not required to do so by *Hepps*, some states have decided to place the burden of proving falsity on the plaintiff when the defamatory statement was not on a matter of public concern. *Voyles v. Sandia Mortgage Corp.*, 196 Ill. 2d 288, 751 N.E.2d 1126 (2001); *Benson v. Northwest Airlines, Inc.*, 561 N.W.2d 530 (Minn. App. 1997).

Protection of true statements. The opinion of the court in *Philadelphia Newspaper, Inc. v. Hepps*, discussed the truth or falsity of "speech" in general terms. It was not specific on what had to be proved false. In view of the strong protection of true speech in *Hepps* and other cases, it is arguable that the First Amendment protects true statements from defamation liability, even if they contain defamatory connotations that are not true. This has not been explicitly addressed by the Supreme Court. The constitutional issue seems to have been avoided in other courts by decisions that the defamatory publication was "true" because its statements were accurate—for example, *Global Relief Foundation, Inc. v. New York Times Co.*, 390 F.3d 973 (7th Cir. 2004), in which the defendants reported that the plaintiff was being investigated for financial support of terrorist activities. It has been decided in some cases that a public official or public figure cannot maintain an action based on a false defamatory insinuation arising from an accurate statement. *Pietrafeso v. D.P.I., Inc.*, 757 P.2d 1113 (Colo. App. 1988); *Mihalik v. Duprey*, 11 Mass. App. Ct. 602, 417 N.E.2d 1238 (1981). *Contra, Turner v. KTRK Television, Inc.*, 38 S.W.3d 103 (Tex. 2000).

Neutral reportage. The "neutral reportage doctrine" originated in *Edwards v. National Audubon Society, Inc.*, 556 F.2d 113 (2d Cir. 1977). The Supreme Court has not addressed it. The essence of the neutral reportage doctrine is that the First Amendment protects from liability accurate news reports of accusations that are newsworthy in themselves, even though the reporter doubts the truth of the accusations. The report must be neutral in the sense that it does not endorse the truth of the accusations.

A number of courts have rejected the doctrine. One reason is that it appears to conflict with the Supreme Court's allowance of defamation liability to public officials and public figures when the defendant entertained serious doubts about the truth of what it published. See *Norton v. Glenn*, 580 Pa. 212, 860 A.2d 48 (2004). Among courts that have accepted the doctrine, there is disagreement about its applicability or limitations. *Edwards v. National Audubon Society, Inc.*, applied the doctrine to reportage of charges made by a "responsible, prominent organization" against a public figure.

Some courts have held that the doctrine does not apply to reports of accusations about private figures. *Khawar v. Globe International, Inc.*, 19 Cal. 4th 254, 965 P.2d 696 (1998); *Owens v. CBS Inc.*, 173 Ill. App. 3d 977, 527 N.E.2d 1296 (1988). *Contra, April v. Reflector-Herald, Inc.*, 46 Ohio App. 3d 95, 546 N.E.2d 466 (1988). Others have held that the doctrine is limited to reportage of charges by a "responsible" prominent person or organization. *Fogus v. Capital Cities Media, Inc.*, 111 Ill. App. 3d 1060, 444 N.E.2d 1100 (1982). *Contra, Barry v. Time, Inc.*, 584 F. Supp. 1110 (N.D. Cal. 1984). Another possible limit, endorsed in *Barry*, is that the reported accusation be made by a party to an existing controversy.

Statements that are opinion, conjecture or not provably false. The Supreme Court's opinion in *Gertz v. Robert Welch, Inc.*, included the statement "Under the First Amendment there is no such thing as a false idea. However pernicious an opinion may seem, we depend for its correction not on the conscience of judges and juries but on the competition of other ideas. But there is no constitutional value in false statements of fact." 418 U.S. 323, 339–340. In the years following *Gertz*, numerous courts interpreted this passage to mean that there could be no defamation liability for statements of opinion, although that was not an issue in the *Gertz* case.

In *Milkovich v. Lorain Journal Co.*, 497 U.S. 1 (1990), the Supreme Court held that there is no First Amendment rule preventing defamation liability for statements categorized as opinion. However, it decided that for statements on a matter of public concern, there could not be liability unless the statement could reasonably be interpreted as stating "actual facts" about the plaintiff and contained a factual connotation that was provably false. Statements which implied an assertion of fact that could be proved false could be the basis of defamation liability even though they were phrased as opinion. If the plaintiff was a public official or public figure, the plaintiff would have to prove that the defendant made the statement with knowledge or reckless disregard of its false factual implications. A private figure would have to show the defendant's fault concerning the false connotations of the statement.

Since then, there have been numerous cases in state courts and lower federal courts with decisions on what can be called a "*Milkovich* issue." Many statements of opinion clearly are not provably false, but it often can be debatable whether a statement of opinion, evaluation or conjecture implied factual assertions that can be proved false. It may not be clear that the defendant was speculating about facts and not implying knowledge that a defamatory inference about the plaintiff is correct. Even if it was clear, *Milkovich* may allow liability when the defendant's speculation is probably false. But the *Milkovich* opinion includes "rhetorical hyperbole" among the statements that are not to be interpreted as stating "actual facts." The decisions in the cases on applying *Milkovich* do not fit an overall pattern, but often the defendant has prevailed. See Sack, *Defamation* § 4:2.4 (5th ed. 2017).

G. MATTERS OF PUBLIC CONCERN

In *Rosenbloom v. Metromedia, Inc.*, 403 U.S. 29 (1971), the plurality opinion held that the First Amendment required a private figure to prove the defendant's knowledge or reckless disregard of falsity when suing for a defamatory statement on a matter of public or general interest. This was rejected by the majority in *Gertz v. Robert Welch, Inc.*, 418 U.S. 323 (1974), in part because it was thought undesirable to have judges deciding on an *ad hoc* basis whether a publication addressed issues of public or general interest. The level of First Amendment protection was to depend on whether the plaintiff was a public official, public figure or neither. Nevertheless, the Supreme Court decided in *Dun & Bradstreet, Inc. v. Greenmoss Builders, Inc.*, 472 U.S. 749 (1985), that the *Gertz* case's limitation of damages did not apply "when the defamatory statements do not involve matters of public concern." Plaintiffs could be awarded presumed and punitive damages without proof that the defendant published the defamation with knowledge of or reckless disregard for its falsity.

This in effect requires courts to decide whether or not the defamatory publication involved a matter of public concern, when the plaintiff seeks presumed or punitive damages, unless knowledge or reckless disregard for falsity has been proved. As the Supreme Court's decision in *Philadelphia Newspapers, Inc. v. Hepps*, 475 U.S. 767 (1986), was limited to "speech" on a matter of public concern, courts might also need to decide whether the defamation of the plaintiff involved a matter of public concern for purposes of allocating the burden of proof on truth or falsity.

In *Snyder v. Phelps*, 562 U.S. 443 (2011), the Supreme Court, after observing that "the boundaries of the public concern test are not well defined," said, "Speech deals with matters of public concern when it can 'be fairly considered as relating to any matter of political, social, or other concern to the community,' or when it 'is a subject of legitimate news interest; that is, a subject of general interest and of value and concern to the public.' " The "content, form, and context" of the speech, "as revealed by the whole record," was to be examined. 562 U.S. 443, 452–453.

There is not a large volume of visible case law in which the court has decided, against the contentions of the defendant, that the defamatory statement did not involve a matter of public concern. Decisions applying the *Rosenbloom v. Metromedia, Inc.*, rule for statements on a matter of public or general interest might be applied by analogy. It appears that defamatory reports in mass media (print and broadcast) are generally assumed or held to be on a matter of public concern, whereas defamatory statements addressed to only one or a few people may well be found not to involve a matter of public concern.

These can include such statements as a complaint about the handling of a business transaction, a criticism of an employee's job performance, or an accusation of misconduct that does not have public repercussions. See *Williams v. Continental Airlines, Inc.*, 943 P.2d 10 (Colo. App. 1996); *Saunders v. Van*

Pelt, 497 A.2d 1121 (Me. 1985); *Cooper v. Portland General Electric Corp.*, 110 Or. App. 581, 824 P.2d 1152 (1992). In the *Dun & Bradstreet* case, a 5–4 majority decided that the defendant's erroneous report that a construction contractor had filed for bankruptcy did not involve a matter of public concern—primarily because it was a credit report that was provided for profit and made available only to five subscribers. The contents of an Internet web site might not be on a matter of public concern even if intended to inform or influence the general public. See *W.J.A. v. D.A.*, 210 N.J. 229, 43 A.3d 1148 (2012).

Damages recoverable. Under *Gertz v. Robert Welch, Inc.*, as interpreted in *Dun & Bradstreet, Inc. v. Greenmoss Builders, Inc.*, presumed damages and punitive damages can be awarded when the defamatory statement did not involve a matter of public concern or when it is proved that the defendant had knowledge of or reckless disregard for its falsity. Otherwise, damages are limited to "compensation for actual injury." As explained in the *Gertz* case, this goes beyond compensation for "out-of-pocket" loss and injury to the plaintiff's reputation. It includes compensation for mental suffering and humiliation. But the award of damages must be supported by evidence in the case, unlike what is permitted when damage is presumed from publication of the defamatory statement. State law limits on presumed and punitive damages also apply.

H. INJUNCTIONS

It has long been the rule in the United States (but not England and other common law jurisdictions) that courts do not grant injunctions in defamation actions. Courts do not issue orders which prohibit the communication or repetition of defamatory statements or other defamatory material. See Annot., 47 A.L.R.2d 715. In part this is based on the right to jury trial and the First Amendment doctrine that there is to be no prior restraint of speech. See *Near v. Minnesota ex rel. Olson*, 283 U.S. 697 (1931). Courts also do not order retraction of defamatory statements found to be false. See *Kramer v. Thompson*, 947 F.2d 666 (3d Cir. 1991). As discussed in Chapter 11, plaintiff's seeking injunctions may sue for injurious falsehood instead of defamation. (See pp. 179–181.)

The right to have a defamation case tried by a jury and the "no prior restraint" rule do not necessarily bar the issuance of an injunction after a final determination in the court that a defamatory statement is false. Some courts have approved the issuance of "narrowly tailored" injunctions against repetition of statements found at a trial to be defamatory and false. See *Balboa Island Village Inn, Inc. v. Lemen*, 40 Cal. 4th 1141, 156 P.3d 339 (2007); *Hill v. Petrotech Resources Corp.*, 325 S.W.3d 302 (Ky. 2010). In *Kinney v. Barnes*, 443 S.W.3d 87 (Tex. 2014), the court rejected the issuance of injunctions against repetition of defamation. It reasoned that such injunctions were an unconstitutional prior restraint of speech, even if granted after a trial, and that any effective injunction would "chill" protected speech. However, it permitted injunctions that would require removal from web sites of content that had been "adjudicated defamatory."

PART VI

LEGAL PROCESS

CHAPTER 24

MALICIOUS PROSECUTION

A. INTRODUCTION

There are three tort actions for wrongful initiation or use of legal process. One, known as "malicious prosecution," is for the wrongful initiation or continuation of criminal proceedings. The second is an analogous tort for the wrongful initiation or continuation of civil proceedings, which goes by a variety of names. The third tort, for the wrongful use of either criminal or civil process, is "abuse of process." They are covered in detail in Rest. 2d Torts §§ 653–682 and Rest. 3d Torts—Economic Harm §§ 21–26.

The tort of malicious prosecution has well-established elements of liability. To be liable, the defendant must have initiated or continued a criminal prosecution against the plaintiff, with malice and without probable cause, and the prosecution must have terminated in favor of the plaintiff. In principle, actual damage is also an element of liability, but damage is readily found in the emotional distress and injury to reputation that a wrongful prosecution causes, as well as in legal expenses and economic losses caused by the prosecution. In most malicious prosecution cases, liability depends upon the application of the liability rules to the facts rather than resolution of questions of law; but there are some important legal questions on which authority is divided—for example, what qualifies as a termination in favor of the plaintiff.

The requirements of liability and the immunities of prosecutors and police officers deny the tort action to most people who have been prosecuted but not convicted of a criminal offense. This is usually defended on the ground that the interests of society require that parties assisting in the enforcement of the criminal law be protected from the risk of lawsuits and liability if a prosecution does not result in conviction. See Rest. 2d Torts Introductory Note preceding § 653. Malicious prosecution is generally not a viable cause of action for people who are exonerated after years of imprisonment for a crime they did not commit. Compensation for wrongful conviction and imprisonment may be available under a federal or state statute.

B. INITIATION OF CRIMINAL PROCEEDING

An action for malicious prosecution arises from a criminal proceeding against the plaintiff. There is no requirement concerning the seriousness of the crime or the potential penalty. The crime can be a petty offense with a small fine as the penalty. A criminal proceeding commences, for purposes of a malicious prosecution action, when a judicial official or tribunal issues an arrest warrant or a summons requiring a person to appear in court or respond to criminal charges, when a grand jury issues an indictment, or when a prosecutor files an information. (It is not commenced by the filing of a complaint or affidavit.) Rest. 2d Torts § 654 and comments; Rest. 3d Torts—Economic Harm § 21, comment *b*. Under the Restatements, criminal proceedings are also initiated by a valid warrantless arrest, but this is doubtful. *Van Audenhove v. Perry*, 11 Cal. App. 5th 915, 217 Cal. Rptr. 3d 843 (2017), holds that there is no malicious prosecution action when a warrantless arrest did not result in charges against the plaintiff. When a warrantless arrest is unlawful, there can be an action for false imprisonment.

C. RESPONSIBILITY OF DEFENDANT

A defendant is subject to liability for malicious prosecution if the defendant initiated the criminal proceeding, procured its initiation, actively continued the proceeding, or caused its continuation. Rest. 2d Torts §§ 653, 655; Rest. 3d Torts—Economic Harm § 21, comments *c*, *e*. In the United States, most of not all of any criminal prosecution is conducted by a public prosecutor. Public prosecutors acting in an official capacity have an absolute privilege against liability for the initiation or continuance of criminal proceedings. Rest. 2d Torts § 656; Rest. 3d Torts—Economic Harm § 21, comment *f*; *Knapper v. Connick*, 681 So. 2d 944 (La. 1996). The only possible action for malicious prosecution is against someone else who can be held responsible for the initiation or continuance of the criminal proceedings. A person who has honestly provided information to the police, prosecutor or court and left to the public prosecutor decisions about the initiation or continuance of a criminal proceeding is usually not considered responsible in the sense required for liability. See Rest. 2d Torts § 653, comments *d*, *g*; Rest. 3d Torts—Economic Harm § 21, comments *c–d*.

Responsibility for initiation or procurement of prosecution. In general, a private party or law enforcement official is considered responsible for initiating or procuring a prosecution commenced by a public prosecutor or another public official in two situations. One is when the prosecution was commenced because the defendant urged or pressured the prosecutor or other official to act. The other is when the defendant caused the prosecution by providing information that the defendant knew to be false or misleading, or at least did not honestly believe to be true. The rationale is that in these situations the prosecution was not the product of an independent judgement by the public prosecutor or official. A defendant might be held responsible for a prosecution by supplying a third party with information known to be false or urging a third party to demand prosecution. See Rest. 2d Torts § 653, comments *d–g*; Rest. 3d Torts—Economic Harm § 21, comment *c*.

Responsibility for continuance of prosecution. A defendant can be found responsible for continuance of a prosecution by urging its continuance, or causing its continuance by providing (out of court) information known to be false or not genuinely believed to be true. See Rest. 3d Torts—Economic Harm § 21, comment *e*. There might also be responsibility if the defendant withheld from the public prosecutor information indicating the plaintiff's innocence of the charge after earlier initiating or procuring the prosecution in good faith. *Id.*; *Banks v. Nordstrom, Inc.*, 57 Wash. App. 251, 787 P.2d 953 (1990). Persons who support a prosecution by providing testimony as witnesses are generally not responsible for continuance of the prosecution, even when the testimony is knowingly false, as witnesses are not in control of a prosecution and they have absolute immunity from tort liability (absolute privilege) as to their testimony. See Rest. 3d Torts—Economic Harm § 21, comment *d*. On occasion, a defendant's perjured testimony together with other conduct has been a basis for holding the defendant responsible for continuance of a prosecution. See *Fusario v. Cavallaro*, 108 Conn. 40, 142 A. 391 (1928).

D. FAVORABLE TERMINATION

There is a potential action for malicious prosecution only when the criminal proceedings terminated in favor of the accused person. Rest. 2d Torts § 658; Rest. 3d Torts—Economic Harm § 21(d). This bars a malicious prosecution action while the criminal proceedings are pending and when prosecution ended with an unreversed conviction. The conviction cannot be impeached by allegations that it was obtained by fraud or perjury. Rest. 2d Torts § 658, comment *c*. See Annot., 69 A.L.R. 1062.

Acquittal of the accused is not required. Any type of action by a judge, magistrate, public prosecutor or grand jury that terminates the criminal proceedings without a conviction can potentially be considered a termination in favor of the accused, even if new charges based on the same alleged misconduct would not be barred on grounds of double jeopardy. This includes refusal of a grand jury to indict and formal abandonment of a prosecution by the public prosecutor (as by entry of a *nolle prosequi*). Rest. 2d Torts § 659; Rest. 3d Torts—Economic Harm § 23, comment *c*. However, termination of criminal proceedings without a conviction has been held not to qualify as a favorable termination, for purposes of malicious prosecution liability, in a number of circumstances.

Termination of criminal proceedings without a conviction does not qualify as a favorable termination when it resulted from an agreement or compromise with the accused person, or an "act of mercy" by the prosecutor that the accused person accepted. Termination because the accused has prevented a successful prosecution by misconduct, such as interference with witnesses or evidence, or by leaving the jurisdiction, also does not qualify as a favorable termination. Rest. 2d Torts §§ 660–661; Rest. 3d Torts—Economic Harm § 23, comment *d*.

Under some decisions, dismissal or acquittal of a criminal charge is not a favorable termination when the defendant has been convicted on a charge arising from substantially the same set of facts. *Kossler v. Crisanti*, 564 F.3d 181 (3d Cir. 2009); *Neff v. Neff*, 247 P.3d 380 (Utah 2011). Under other decisions, an acquittal is a favorable termination even when the accused was convicted on related charges. *Janetka v. Dabe*, 892 F.2d 187 (2d Cir. 1989); *Cuthrell v. Zayre of Virginia, Inc.*, 214 Va. 427, 201 S.E.2d 779 (1974).

There is a major division of authority on whether the circumstances of the termination must imply that the plaintiff was not guilty of the criminal charge.

This has been required in a number of cases. Dismissal of a charge when the stated or apparent reason was that the available evidence was insufficient for conviction would qualify as a favorable termination, but not dismissal for lack of jurisdiction, time limitations or procedural reasons. See *Bearden v. BellSouth Telecommunications, Inc.*, 29 So. 3d 761 (Miss. 2010). Another line of authority requires only that the termination not be inconsistent with innocence. Thus a dismissal on a ground unrelated to guilt or innocence, such as absence of jurisdiction, elapse of time, double jeopardy or procedural requirements would qualify as a favorable termination. See *Smith-Hunter v. Harvey*, 95 N.Y.2d 191, 734 N.E.2d 750 (2000); Rest. 3d Torts—Economic Harm § 23, comments, *a*, *c*. There is also division of authority on whether discharge of the accused by writ of habeas corpus is a favorable termination. See Annot., 30 A.L.R.2d 1128.

Actual guilt defense. Even though a malicious prosecution cannot succeed unless the criminal proceedings terminated in favor of the plaintiff, the defendant can successfully defend the action by proof that the plaintiff was in fact guilty. *Ware v. United States*, 971 F. Supp. 1442 (M.D. Fla. 1997); *Threefoot v. Nuckols*, 68 Miss. 116, 8 So. 335 (1890). As the malicious prosecution action is a civil claim, the standard of proof on this is the balance of probabilities, not proof beyond reasonable doubt. Allowing the defendant to raise the issue of the plaintiff's guilt after the plaintiff was acquitted in the criminal case is not regarded as inconsistent with or a collateral attack on the judgment in the criminal proceedings, as acquittal signifies only that the accused's guilt had not been proved beyond a reasonable doubt. See Rest. 2d Torts § 657 and comments; Rest. 3d Torts—Economic Harm § 21, comment *g*.

E. PROBABLE CAUSE

Liability for malicious prosecution requires proof that the defendant initiated or continued the criminal proceedings without probable cause. Although want of probable cause is a critical element of a malicious prosecution action, the authorities are not consistent on what constitutes probable cause. It is clear that probable cause incorporates a reasonableness standard applied to what is believed by the defendant when initiating or continuing the prosecution, but it has been defined or described in a number of different ways. A widely accepted definition of probable cause is an actual and reasonable belief that the accused is guilty of the offense. *E.g.*, *Nassar v. Concordia Rod and Gun Club, Inc.*, 682 So. 2d 1035 (Miss. 1996); *O'Connor v. Tice*, 281 Va. 1, 704 S.E.2d 572 (2011). This is in substance the position of Rest. 2d Torts § 662 and Rest. 3d Torts—Economic Harm § 22. In *White v. State ex rel. Montana State Fund*, 371 Mont. 1, 11–12, 305 P.3d 795, 804 (2013), the definition is "reasonable grounds for suspicion, supported by circumstances reasonably strong in themselves to warrant a reasonably prudent and cautious [person] to believe that the accused is guilty of the offense charged."

There is some authority for finding probable cause when the facts would make it reasonable to believe that the accused probably was guilty. See *Fabiano v. City of Palos Hills*, 336 Ill. App. 3d 635, 642, 784 N.E.2d 258, 266 (2002) (probable cause is "a state of facts that would lead a person of ordinary care and prudence to believe or to entertain an honest and sound suspicion that the accused committed the offense charged"). In a small minority of jurisdictions, probable cause depends solely on whether the facts would make it reasonable to believe that the accused was guilty, without also requiring that the defendant actually believe in the defendant's guilt. See *Roberts v. Federal Express Corp.*, 842 S.W.2d 246 (Tenn. 1992).

Whatever the definition, whether the defendant had probable cause to initiate or (if responsible for the proceedings' continuance) continue the criminal proceedings has often been a hotly-contested issue in malicious prosecution litigation, including numerous cases in which the plaintiff was arrested for theft after walking out of a store with goods that had not been paid for. *E.g., Gustafson v. Payless Drug Stores Northwest, Inc.*, 269 Or. 354, 525 P.2d 118 (1974); *Richey v. Brookshire Grocery Co.*, 952 S.W.2d 515 (Tex. 1997). Or charged with passing a bad check after writing a check that "bounced." *E.g., Blackford v. Wal-Mart Stores, Inc.*, 912 F. Supp. 537 (S.D. Ga. 1996); *Dunn v. Alabama Oil & Gas Co.*, 42 Tenn. App. 108, 299 S.W.2d 25 (1956).

In most jurisdictions, it is the court rather than the jury that decides whether the defendant had probable cause. The jury's role is limited to deciding relevant factual questions, including what information the defendant possessed when initiating or procuring the prosecution of the plaintiff. In some jurisdictions, when the evidence would permit but not compel a finding that the defendant lacked probable cause, the decision is made by the jury. The prevailing rule is sometimes attributed to judicial concerns that juries would too readily decide there was a want of probable cause because of the plaintiff's innocence. See Annot., 87 A.L.R.2d 183.

A defendant can have probable cause if mistaken about the relevant facts, when the mistake is reasonable. See Rest. 2d Torts § 662, comments *e–h*, *j*; Rest. 3d Torts—Economic Harm § 22, comment *b*. There is less allowance for mistakes about the relevant law, including the mistaken belief that the plaintiff's conduct constituted a crime. Authority on this ranges from the position that there is no probable cause when a mistake about the law causes prosecution for a crime the accused did not commit to the position that a reasonable mistake about the law is to be treated like a reasonable mistake about the facts. However, when an attorney advised that there was probable cause for a criminal proceeding, the recipient of the advice is often deemed to have probable cause for that reason, and it is usually not reasonable for a lay person to initiate a criminal proceeding without being informed of the relevant law. So jurisdictional variations in how mistakes of law are treated may not affect the outcome. See Rest. 2d Torts § 662, comment *i*; Rest. 3d Torts—Economic Harm § 22, comment *c*.

There is a specific rule that a defendant in a malicious prosecution case is considered to have probable cause if the defendant made a full disclosure of relevant information the defendant was aware of to a public prosecutor, or private attorney, and acted on the attorney's advice in bringing or continuing the criminal proceedings against the plaintiff. See Annot., 10 A.L.R.2d 1215; Rest. 2d Torts § 666; Rest. 3d Torts—Economic Harm § 22, comment *d*. The weight of authority is that reliance upon the advice of other persons who might be thought to know the law, such as lay magistrates, court clerks and police officers, does not provide probable cause. See Annot., 48 A.L.R.4th 250.

There are also specific rules under which the decision of a magistrate to commit or bind the accused for further proceedings, indictment of the accused by a grand jury or conviction of the accused in a trial creates a presumption of probable cause, even though the proceedings later terminated in favor of the accused. The presumption can be rebutted by evidence that the decision was the product of fraud, perjury, suppression of evidence or other corruption, but not by a showing that the decision was wrong. See Annot., 68 A.L.R.2d 1168 (magistrate's decision); Annot., 28 A.L.R.3d 748 (grand jury indictment); Annot., 86 A.L.R.2d 1090 (conviction); Rest. 3d Torts—Economic Harm § 22, comment *e*.

F. MALICE (IMPROPER PURPOSE)

The term "malicious prosecution" implies that malice is an element of liability, and so it is. But malice in the law of malicious prosecution has come to mean improper purpose, prosecuting a person for a purpose other than "bringing to justice" someone believed to have committed a criminal offense. The malice element of liability is acting primarily for a purpose other than bringing an offender to justice when initiating, procuring or continuing a criminal proceeding. Rest. 2d Torts § 668; Rest. 3d Torts—Economic Harm § 21(c).

Malice in the common law sense of acting out of hostility, spite or a desire to cause harm is not itself the malice element of liability for malicious prosecution. But if this was the primary reason for the defendant's procuring the criminal proceedings against the plaintiff, the defendant acted primarily for a purpose other than bringing an offender to justice and can be held liable. There is also improper purpose when the defendant acted primarily for private gain, such as inducing the plaintiff to pay money or hand over property, even when the defendant was legally entitled to payment or the property. When there was both a desire to see the plaintiff prosecuted and to obtain payment or property, it can be difficult to ascertain whether the private object was the primary purpose. Improper purpose can also be found when the defendant did not actually believe that the accused was guilty. Without believing that the accused was guilty, or at least probably guilty, the defendant could not have initiated or continued prosecution primarily for the purpose of "bringing an offender to justice." See Rest. 2d Torts 668, comments *d–g*; Rest. 3d Torts—Economic Harm § 21, comment *h*.

If the defendant's primary purpose in having the plaintiff prosecuted was to obtain evidence of guilt or deter persons from committing a crime, the defendant acted primarily for a purpose other than prosecuting someone believed to be guilty and therefore can be liable for malicious prosecution, even though in a sense the defendant was acting to enforce the criminal law. See *Glover v. Fleming*, 36 Md. App. 381, 373 A.2d 981 (1977) (complaint filed because "we wanted to find out who the guilty party was"); *Hammond v. Rowley*, 86 Conn. 6, 84 A. 94 (1912) (plaintiff charged with unlawfully taking oysters from oyster grounds in order to deter entries onto leased oyster beds).

Evidence of the defendant's purpose can be circumstantial. *E.g.*, *South Arkansas Petroleum Co. v. Schiesser*, 343 Ark. 492, 36 S.W.3d 317 (2001) (motivation of ill will could be inferred from failure to provide exculpatory information to police and county prosecutor); *Royal Oil Co., Inc. v. Wells*, 500 So. 2d 439 (Miss. 1986) (false charge of embezzlement from cash register may have been motivated by hostility on account of plaintiff's interracial marriage). Improper purpose can usually be inferred from lack of probable cause. Consequently, evidence leading to a finding that the defendant lacked probable cause can serve as evidence allowing a finding that the defendant had an improper purpose in bringing or continuing criminal proceedings against the plaintiff. See Rest. 2d Torts § 669; Rest. 3d Torts—Economic Harm § 21, comment *h*. Absence of probable cause is not inferred from a finding of improper purpose. Rest. 2d Torts § 669A; Rest. 3d Torts—Economic Harm § 22, comment *h*.

CHAPTER 25

WRONGFUL CIVIL PROCEEDINGS (MALICIOUS PROSECUTION OF CIVIL PROCEEDINGS)

A. INTRODUCTION

Most jurisdictions now recognize a tort action for the wrongful initiation or continuation of civil proceedings that is analogous to the action for wrongful initiation or continuation of criminal proceedings." The civil proceedings tort has a number of different names, including "wrongful civil proceedings," "malicious prosecution of civil proceedings," "wrongful use of civil proceedings" and "malicious use of process." (It should not be confused with the distinct tort of abuse of process.)

The elements of liability are the elements of liability for malicious criminal prosecution with adaptations for application to civil proceedings. To be liable, the defendant must have initiated or continued a civil proceeding, with malice and without probable cause; the proceeding must have terminated in favor of the plaintiff; and damage to the plaintiff must have resulted from the proceeding. In many but not a majority of jurisdictions, the proceeding must have resulted in "special damage" or "special injury." Because of these requirements, most people who have been sued but not held liable cannot win an action for malicious prosecution.

The tort has been extended to procurement or continuance of administrative proceedings in a government agency or tribunal. This applies primarily to disciplinary proceedings and proceedings which could lead to a fine or revocation of a license or permit. See Rest. 2d Torts § 680; Rest. 3d Torts—Economic Harm § 24, comment *h*; *Stolz v. Wong Communications Limited Partnership*, 25 Cal. App. 4th 1811, 31 Cal. Rptr. 2d 229 (1994) (distinguishing adjudication of competing applications for license from administrative proceedings against a party).

There can be a malicious prosecution action for initiating or proceeding with a baseless counterclaim, as a counterclaim is an action seeking judicial relief. The orthodox view is that there is no malicious prosecution action for making or continuing a baseless defense. See Annot., 65 A.L.R.3d 901; Rest. 3d Torts—Economic Harm § 24, comment *c*; *Young v. Allstate Insurance Co.*, 119 Haw. 403, 198 P.3d 666 (2008). However, in *Aranson v. Schroeder*, 140 N.H. 359, 671 A.2d 1023 (1995), the court created a cause of action for malicious defense, with requirements parallel to those of the action for malicious prosecution of civil proceedings.

B. RESPONSIBILITY OF DEFENDANT

As in the action for malicious prosecution of a criminal proceeding, a defendant is subject to liability for malicious prosecution of a civil proceeding if the defendant initiated the proceeding, procured its initiation, actively continued the proceeding or caused its continuation. This can readily be established when the defendant was the plaintiff in the civil proceeding or an attorney who commenced or litigated the proceeding for the plaintiff. A third party might be liable for procuring or causing the continuation of the proceeding. When the prior proceeding was an administrative proceeding in a governmental agency or tribunal, in which the defendant was not the moving party, the basis on which a defendant could be held responsible would be analogous to the basis on which a defendant could be held responsible for procuring or continuing a criminal proceeding. See Rest. 2d Torts § 674 and comments; Rest. 3d Torts—Economic Harm § 24, comment *c*.

C. FAVORABLE TERMINATION

The prior proceeding must have terminated in favor of the plaintiff in the tort action. There is no cause of action if the termination was not favorable, or if the prior proceeding has not terminated. This bars counterclaims alleging that the main action was brought without probable cause and for an improper purpose. Favorable termination is not required when the plaintiff had no opportunity to be heard in the prior proceeding, as when the proceeding was *ex parte*. (Attachment of property is a typical example.) Related claims in the prior proceeding may be considered together for purposes of ascertaining whether success on one was actually a favorable termination. See Rest. 2d Torts § 674, comments *j–k*; Rest. 3d Torts—Economic Harm § 24, comment *e*.

There is division of authority on whether the termination of the prior proceedings must in some sense be on the merits of the claim rather than for such reasons as lack of jurisdiction, statute of limitations, *res judicata* or procedural requirements. See Annot., 30 A.L.R.4th 572. *Lackner v. LaCroix*, 25 Cal. 3d 747, 602 P.2d 393 (1979), and *Palmer Development Corp. v. Gordon*, 723 A.2d 881 (Me. 1999), are among the decisions requiring that the termination relate to the merits of the claim. *Contra*, *Hammond Lead Products, Inc. v. American Cyanamid Co.*, 570 F.2d 668 (7th Cir. 1977); *Cult Awareness Network v. Church of Scientology International*, 177 Ill. 2d 267, 685 N.E.2d 1347 (1997). Voluntary dismissal of a claim may be examined to ascertain whether it implied that the claim was not sufficient to succeed on the merits. Generally, dismissal as part of a compromise or settlement does not qualify as a favorable termination, but it might be established that a particular claim was dropped because it lacked merit. See Rest. 3d Torts—Economic Harm § 24, comment *e*.

Proof (on the balance of probabilities) that the plaintiff was actually guilty of the offense is a defense to an action for malicious prosecution of criminal proceedings (see pp. 457–458), but there is no analogous defense to an action for malicious prosecution of civil proceedings. The defendant cannot raise as a defense that the plaintiff actually was liable and relitigate the claim advanced in the earlier case. Termination of the prior proceeding in favor of the plaintiff in the malicious prosecution action is conclusive. See Rest. 2d Torts § 674, comment *e*; Rest. 3d Torts—Economic Harm § 24, comment *e*.

D. PROBABLE CAUSE

Want of probable cause is a critical element of liability. Probable cause to initiate or continue a civil proceeding is necessarily very different from probable cause to initiate or continue a criminal proceeding. Criminal prosecution is not justifiable unless it is reasonably believed that the accused is likely to be guilty. Civil proceedings are usually justifiable when it is reasonably believed that there is some chance that a court will rule in favor of the claim and the action is not brought for an improper purpose. It is legitimate to make a claim that depends on an argument for modification of existing law that has a small chance of success. It is expected that much of the detailed evidentiary support for a civil action will be developed in investigation and discovery after an action is commenced. See Rest. 3d Torts—Economic Harm § 25, comment *a*.

Recognizing this, probable cause for a civil proceeding tends to be defined in substance as a reasonable belief that a claim may be held valid. This involves judgements about both the relevant law and the prospects of proving the necessary facts. See Rest. 2d Torts § 675 and comments. Rest. 3d Torts—Economic Harm § 25 provides:

> Probable cause to initiate a civil claim exists if the facts and circumstances would cause a reasonably prudent person to believe:

(a) that the facts on which the claim is based can be established to the satisfaction of the trier of fact; and

(b) that there is a reasonable chance the claim will be held valid under applicable law, or that the claim is based on a good-faith argument for the extension, modification, or reversal of existing law.

Probable cause is primarily an objective standard. There is some controversy about whether it is also subjective in requiring an actual belief in the factual and legal basis of the action brought. This is required in Rest. 2d Torts § 675 but not Rest. 3d Torts—Economic Harm § 25, following *Sheldon Appel Co. v. Albert & Oliker*, 47 Cal. 3d 863, 765 P.2d 498 (1989). Even if probable cause does not theoretically have a subjective component, what a person actually knows bears on whether the person has probable cause to initiate or continue an action, and a person who knows the factual assertions in a claim are untrue does not have probable cause. See Rest. 3d Torts—Economic Harm § 25, comment *b*.

When an attorney is sued for initiating or continuing a civil proceeding on behalf of a client, the probable cause determination might depend upon whether the court has adopted the position that probable cause exists if, on the objective standard of a reasonable attorney, the claim made was legally tenable, as in the *Sheldon Appel* case. It has been held that an attorney has probable cause when the claim was legally tenable based on what the client told the attorney, without regard to whether the attorney made a reasonable investigation into the facts. *Lucero v. Stewart*, 892 F.2d 52 (9th Cir. 1989). An opposing view is that facts the attorney could have learned by a diligent effort prior to filing the action are to be considered. See *Nelson v. Miller*, 227 Kan. 271, 607 P.2d 438 (1980). The client in the proceeding has probable cause if the client acted on the advice of counsel in bringing or continuing the proceeding, provided the client made a full disclosure of relevant facts and had no reason to doubt the lawyer's impartiality or competence. Rest. 3d Torts—Economic Harm § 25, comment *e*.

Following the rule established for claims of malicious prosecution in criminal proceedings, in most jurisdictions it is the court rather than the jury that decides whether the defendant had probable cause to initiate or continue civil proceedings. The jury decides any relevant factual issues, including what was known or believed by the defendant. See Annot., 87 A.L.R.2d 183. If the plaintiff in the earlier action won in the trial court but the judgment was reversed or vacated, there will be a presumption that there was probable cause for the action. This is subject to rebuttal when it can be shown that the trial court judgment was obtained by fraud, perjury or other improper means, or that the judgment was void. See Annot., 58 A.L.R.2d 1422.

E. MALICE (IMPROPER PURPOSE)

The malice element in this tort is actually improper purpose, as in malicious prosecution of criminal proceedings. A defendant is subject to liability if it is found that the defendant had initiated, procured or continued the civil proceedings with an improper purpose. Improper purpose in this context is usually defined as a primary purpose other than securing the proper adjudication of the lawsuit. Rest. 2d Torts § 676; Rest. 3d Torts—Economic Harm § 24(c).

Proper purpose for a civil claim is quite different from, and much more expansive than, proper purpose for a criminal proceeding. It is perfectly proper to initiate a civil claim to secure a private advantage, such as obtaining money or control of property, as long as it is the remedy authorized by law if the claim is upheld. Improper purpose is most clearly established when it is proved that the defendant initiated or continued the civil claim to gain some other advantage. Most commonly this is to thwart a business or property transaction, or to cause delay in order to postpone the time when the defendant must make payment or cease use of property. For example, in *Johnson v. Mount Ogden Enterprises, Inc.*, 23 Utah 2d 169, 460 P.2d 333 (1969), the defendant had obtained a temporary injunction restraining the plaintiffs from cutting off a supply of water to the defendant. A few days later the defendant elected to dismiss the case. It was found that the defendant had brought suit solely for the purpose of using the plaintiffs' water without right until another water system could be installed. Improper purpose can also be found when the primary reason for the suit was spite, hostility, harassment or causing embarrassment. See Rest. 2d Torts § 676, comment *c*; Rest. 3d Torts—Economic Harm § 24, comment *d*.

Whether there was actually an improper purpose is less clear when the plaintiff contends that the defendant commenced or continued the earlier proceeding in order to obtain an "undeserved" or "unmerited" settlement. A purpose to obtain a settlement can be improper when the settlement is not related to the merits of the legal claim that is made or when it is known that the claim has no merit. See Rest. 2d Torts § 676, comment *c*; Rest. 3d Torts—Economic Harm § 24, comment *d*. A lawyer's object of receiving a contingency fee payment from a settlement or judgment is generally not an improper purpose. Rest. 2d Torts § 674, comment *d*; *Miskew v. Hess*, 21 Kan. App. 2d 927, 910 P.2d 223 (1996). But this is apparently subject to the qualification that it would be an improper purpose when the anticipated settlement is based on a claim known to have no merit or unrelated to the merits of the claim brought. See *Korn v. Epstein*, 727 A.2d 1130 (Pa. Super. Ct. 1999).

Improper purpose is inferred when it is found that the defendant knew the claim had no merit. It is also can be inferred when it is found that the defendant did not have probable cause. The absence of probable cause provides an evidentiary basis for a finding of improper purpose. However, it may not be enough to warrant a finding that the defendant had an improper purpose. This would ordinarily be the case when the defendant is a lawyer who initiated or conducted litigation for a client. See Rest. 3d Torts—Economic Harm § 24, comments *d*, *f*.

F. SPECIAL INJURY (SPECIAL DAMAGE)

An additional requirement, in force in many but not a majority of states, is "special injury" or "special damage." It originated as a rationale for allowing a malicious prosecution action when the earlier case was not a criminal matter, but it has long operated to bar malicious prosecution claims for the commencement or continuation of many civil actions, including most where the remedy sought was a money judgment.

Courts are not entirely consistent on what qualifies as special injury. It may be found in either the type of proceeding brought or the result of the proceeding. In a number of cases it is said there must have been an arrest of the plaintiff, seizure of property, or injury which would not necessarily result from a like cause of action. *E.g.*, *Schwartz v. Schwartz*, 366 Ill. 247, 250, 8 N.E.2d 668, 670 (1937); *One Thousand Fleet Limited Partnership v. Guerriero*, 346 Md. 29, 37, 694 A.2d 952, 956 (1997). The opinion in *O'Toole v. Franklin*, 279 Or. 513, 516, 569 P.2d 561, 563 (1977), states that the requirement is satisfied when the proceeding involved immediate interference with the person, property, income or credit of the plaintiff. *Myhre v. Hessey*, 242 Wis. 638, 644–645, 9 N.W.2d 106, 109 (1943), lists as instances in which a malicious prosecution action can be brought suits in which property is attached or a person is arrested, bankruptcy proceedings, equity cases in which the plaintiff was excluded from possession of property, proceedings to have a person declared insane and placed under guardianship, and juvenile court proceedings. The emphasis on injury that would not necessarily result from actions of the type brought has led to a decision that the interference with property in an attachment or foreclosure proceeding is not special injury. *Petrich v. McDonald*, 44 Wash. 2d 211, 266 P.2d 1047 (1954).

Courts in a number of states have rejected arguments for abolition of the special injury requirement, or liberalizing it to treat injury to professional reputation or increased malpractice insurance costs as special injury when the plaintiff had been sued for professional negligence. *E.g.*, *Berlin v. Nathan*, 64 Ill. App. 3d 940, 381 N.E.2d 1367 (1978); *O'Toole v. Franklin*, *supra*. Their reasons include concerns that without the special injury requirement, there would be a multitude of "countersuits" by former defendants and honest claims would be deterred by the prospect of such suits. See *Friedman v. Dozorc*, 412 Mich. 1, 312 N.W.2d 585 (1981).

CHAPTER 26

ABUSE OF PROCESS

The essence of abuse of process is use of legal process, criminal or civil, primarily to accomplish a purpose or object for which it is not intended, causing harm to the plaintiff. Rest. 2d Torts § 682; Rest. 3d Torts—Economic Harm § 26. Liability is based on the defendant's use of the process and the purpose for which it was used. Abuse of process was first recognized as a tort in *Grainger v. Hill*, (1838) 3 Bing. N.C. 212, 132 Eng. Rep. 769 (C.P.). The defendants were creditors of the plaintiff, a ship's master. They had the plaintiff arrested and held until he handed over the ship's register to the defendants. As in *Grainger v. Hill*, an abuse of process action provides a remedy for misuse of legal process that is not provided by an action for malicious prosecution because of its requirements of want of probable cause, favorable termination, and (in many jurisdictions) special injury.

A frequently expressed concept of abuse of process is use of process to obtain a "collateral advantage" or "collateral objective"—something that is not legitimately obtained by the process itself. *E.g.*, *Board of Education of Farmingdale Union Free School District v. Farmingdale Classroom Teachers Association, Inc.*, 38 N.Y.2d 397, 343 N.E.2d 278 (1975); *Layton v. Chase*, 82 S.D. 270, 144 N.W.2d 561 (1966). Examples include excessive attachment (attachment of property worth much more than the moving party's claim) to coerce payment of a debt. *Nevada Credit Rating Bureau v. Williams*, 88 Nev.

601, 503 P.2d 9 (1972). A suit used to deter the defendant from making further complaints against the plaintiff. *Rogan v. Rungee*, 165 Conn. App. 209, 140 A.3d 979 (2016). Bringing litigation concerning a vacant lot to prevent its sale and development. *Vittands v. Sudduth*, 49 Mass. App. Ct. 401, 730 N.E.2d 325 (2000). Use of a trademark infringement action to drive out a competitor. *United Tactical Systems, LLC v. Real Action Paintball, Inc.*, 143 F. Supp. 3d 982 (N.D. Cal. 2015). Use of litigation against an art authenticator to force him to recant his opinion that a work of art was not that of a famous painter. *Seltzer v. Morton*, 336 Mont. 225, 154 P.3d 561 (2007). And having a person committed to a mental institution to thwart his efforts to have a police officer discharged from his position. *Sarvold v. Dodson*, 237 N.W.2d 447 (Iowa 1976).

Active use of criminal process to induce the person arrested or prosecuted to repay a debt, pay for damage or loss, discontinue a claim or vacate property is ground for an abuse of process action. See *Flynn v. Songer*, 399 S.W.2d 491 (Ky. 1966); *White v. Apsley Rubber Co.*, 181 Mass. 339, 63 N.E. 885 (1902); *Ritterbusch v. Holt*, 789 S.W.2d 491 (Mo. 1990); Annot., 27 A.L.R.3d 1202. Abuse of process may be claimed when the alleged victim of a criminal offense offered to have the charges dropped if the accused paid for damage or loss. But this could be considered an act of leniency that is not abuse of process. See the majority and dissenting opinions in *Ellis v. Wellons*, 224 N.C. 269, 29 S.E.2d 884 (1944).

A court may find no abuse of process when the process was used to obtain its legitimate object, but allegedly with an improper underlying purpose. An example is *Hauser v. Bartow*, 273 N.Y. 370, 7 N.E.2d 268 (1937), in which the defendant had sought court appointment as (in substance) conservator of the plaintiff's property, claiming he was mentally incompetent, allegedly with the motive of financial benefit to herself rather than protection of the plaintiff's interests. Another is *Willis v. Parker*, 814 So. 2d 857 (Ala. 2001), in which a landlord had brought an eviction action against a tenant in order to evict the tenant, allegedly with the purpose of driving the tenant out of business. When a civil claim is brought or continued, the object of obtaining a favorable settlement of that claim is not collateral and does not support an action for abuse of process. See *Detenbeck v. Koester*, 886 S.W.2d 477 (Tex. App. 1994); Rest. 3d Torts—Economic Harm § 26, comment *e*. But abuse might be found if the process is used to induce settlement or discontinuance of other claims between the parties. See *Spellens v. Spellens*, 49 Cal. 3d 210, 317 P.2d 613 (1957).

For liability there must be an act or combination of acts constituting use of the process. There is not a clear difference between use of process for an improper purpose and initiating process with an improper purpose, for which the remedy (if any) is an action for malicious prosecution. Some courts require proof of an act by the defendant after the process was issued, as in *C. C. & J., Inc. v. Hagood*, 711 So. 2d 947 (Ala. 1998), and *Bell ex rel. Snyder v. Icard,*

Merrill, Cullis, Timm, Furen and Ginsburg, P.A., 986 S.W.2d 550 (Tenn. 1999).

As favorable termination of the process is not required, the defendant in a civil action can bring a counterclaim alleging that the plaintiff's use of the main action was an abuse of process. An abuse of process action is almost always brought by a party against whom the process was directed, but occasionally the action is brought by someone else. The leading example is *Board of Education of Farmingdale Union Free School District v. Farmingdale Classroom Teachers Association*, 38 N.Y.2d 397, 343 N.E.2d 278 (1975), in which a board of education alleged it was the target when an attorney for a teachers association issued subpoenas to eighty-seven teachers, requiring the board to employ substitutes. Courts in a number of cases have decided that an abuse of process action does not arise from use of process in administrative proceedings. See *Moore v. Western Forge Corp.*, 192 P.3d 427 (Colo. App. 2007); *Gordon v. Community First State Bank*, 255 Neb. 637, 587 N.W.2d 343 (1998). *Contra*, *Hillside Associates v. Stravato*, 642 A.2d 664 (R.I. 1994).

It may be an advantage that abuse of process is not a precisely delineated tort. It can be extended when needed to provide a remedy for improper use of judicial process that does not come within the stringent requirements of an action for malicious prosecution. See *Ellis v. Wellons*, 224 N.C. 269, 275, 29 S.E.2d 884, 887 (1944) (Stacy, C.J., dissenting). It cannot, however, provide a remedy for harm caused by a threat to institute legal proceedings. That can only be found, if at all, in some other tort, such as interference with prospective advantage.

INDEX

References are to Pages
